7/25

The Point of View of the Universe

The Point of View of the Universe

Sidgwick and Contemporary Ethics

Katarzyna de Lazari-Radek
and Peter Singer

OXFORD
UNIVERSITY PRESS

Great Clarendon Street, Oxford, OX2 6DP,
United Kingdom

Oxford University Press is a department of the University of Oxford.
It furthers the University's objective of excellence in research, scholarship,
and education by publishing worldwide. Oxford is a registered trade mark of
Oxford University Press in the UK and in certain other countries

First Edition published in 2014

Impression: 1

Published in the United States of America by Oxford University Press
198 Madison Avenue, New York, NY 10016, United States of America

British Library Cataloguing in Publication Data
Data available

Library of Congress Control Number: 2013954154

ISBN 978-0-19-960369-5

Printed and bound by
CPI Group (UK) Ltd, Croydon, CR0 4YY

To the next generation:
Jan, Izzy, Zofia, Coco, Amalia, and Rafael

Preface

If you think of classical utilitarianism at all, you probably think of Jeremy Bentham or John Stuart Mill. We believe that you should think of Henry Sidgwick. Bentham, of course, was the founder of English utilitarianism, and Mill's *Utilitarianism* is still the most widely read of the nineteenth-century texts. But Sidgwick's *The Methods of Ethics* far surpasses, in philosophical depth, any of the ethical writings of Bentham or Mill. Regrettably, Sidgwick's masterpiece is still not widely known. This, however, is slowly changing, and we hope to accelerate the pace of that change.

Admittedly, no one would recommend *The Methods of Ethics* as lively reading. Alfred N. Whitehead is said to have found it so 'stodgy' that it put him off reading another book on ethics.[1] On the other hand, C. D. Broad wrote in 1930 that 'Sidgwick's *Methods of Ethics* seems to me to be on the whole the best treatise on moral theory that has ever been written'.[2] J. J. C. Smart used very similar language, in 1956, when he described *The Methods* as 'the best book ever written on ethics'.[3] Derek Parfit has added his support to the 'best ever' view, adding by way of explanation: 'There are some books that are greater achievements, such as Plato's *Republic* and Aristotle's *Ethics*. But Sidgwick's book contains the largest number of true and important claims.'[4]

Even Sidgwick's opponents acknowledge his significance. G. E. M. Anscombe was so adamantly opposed to Sidgwick's views that she suggests that those who think like him show 'a corrupt mind'. Nevertheless, she describes modern English moral philosophy as an epoch marked by a change Sidgwick brought about, so much so that,

---

[1] Roy Harrod wrote: 'I remember Alfred Whitehead telling me that he had read *The Methods of Ethics* as a young man and found it so stodgy that he had been deterred from ever reading any books on ethics since.' Harrod, *The Life of John Maynard Keynes*, 76, quoted in Williams, 'The Point of View of the Universe', 184.

[2] Broad, *Five Types of Ethical Theory*, 143.

[3] Smart, 'Extreme and Restricted Utilitarianism', 344–54.

[4] Parfit, *On What Matters*, p. xxxiii.

in her view, 'the differences between the well-known English writers on moral philosophy from Sidgwick to the present day are of little importance'. It was Sidgwick, she writes, who began the modern era in which the dominant—and, she thought, deplorable—view in moral philosophy is that 'the right action' is the action that produces the best possible consequences.[5] John Rawls saw utilitarianism as the most serious rival to his own theory of justice, and Sidgwick as its greatest exponent.

We are in full agreement with Broad, Smart, and Parfit. The reason why *The Methods* is not as widely read as Mill's *Utilitarianism* is quite simple—it is a demanding book to read. German philosophy has a reputation for being difficult, but English utilitarianism always seemed rather easy to understand. Mill has a lively, conversational style. Sidgwick, in contrast, as C. D. Broad wrote,

seldom allowed that strong sense of humour, which is said to have made him a delightful conversationalist, to relieve the uniform dull dignity of his writing. He incessantly refines, qualifies, raises objections, answers them, and then finds further objections to the answers. Each of these objections, rebuttals, rejoinders, and surrejoinders is in itself admirable, and does infinite credit to the acuteness and candour of the author. But the reader is apt to become impatient; to lose the thread of the argument: and to rise from his desk finding that he has read a great deal with constant admiration and now remembers little or nothing. The result is that Sidgwick probably has far less influence at present than he ought to have...

In writing this book, one of our aims has been to enable you to appreciate Sidgwick's thought without having to face the difficulties of reading all 500 pages of *The Methods*. Thereby we hope to restore *The Methods*, or at least its key chapters, to its rightful place as the book to which the reader seeking to understand utilitarianism at its best should turn, and to gain for Sidgwick the recognition that is due to one of the greatest of ethical thinkers. To advance this goal, we begin each chapter of this book with a section in which we seek to present Sidgwick's ideas on the topic of that chapter in as clear and straightforward a manner as possible. Because our aim in these sections is to enable you to grasp what Sidgwick wrote, usually in a much more complex way, in his original text, we reserve our assessment of

---

[5] Anscombe, 'Modern Moral Philosophy', 1–19.

Sidgwick's arguments for the subsequent sections of each chapter. We do not cover all the topics that Sidgwick does, but we have chosen those that seem to us most interesting and important.

Our second and more significant aim is to defend utilitarianism. Sidgwick himself denied that he wrote *The Methods* for this purpose, and in one important respect, he failed to do it. We have attempted to develop his ideas in a way that overcomes some of the problems he faced, and shows how, consistently with his approach, objections to utilitarianism made since his time can also be met. Thus in each chapter the remaining sections are focused on the contemporary debate over the issues presented in the exposition of Sidgwick's ideas in the first part of the chapter. You will see that these issues are not in any way peculiar to Sidgwick. They include the most fundamental problems of ethics. But on many of these issues, Sidgwick provided penetrating and plausible answers. In reading *The Methods* we repeatedly find Sidgwick making points that are still at the centre of current philosophical discussions. On one important aspect of his overall position, however, for reasons we explain in Chapter 7, we part company with him. This allows us to provide a more complete justification of utilitarianism than he himself was able to achieve.

This book is not a study of the history of ideas. We treat Sidgwick as if he were a contemporary philosopher, to be listened to, but also to be argued with. We start with some biographical details mainly to provide you with some understanding of the kind of person Sidgwick was, rather than to provide clues to the interpretation of his philosophy. This is, we think, how Sidgwick would have preferred to be treated: to be assessed by the cogency of his reasoning, and not as a philosopher living in a particular time and place. This cannot, of course, be an absolute rule. Like every other philosopher, he *was* a philosopher living in a particular time and place, and sometimes it helps to notice this. As Bart Schultz has pointed out, Sidgwick, like many others of his era, thought that there are 'inferior' and 'superior' races' as well as 'civilized' and 'uncivilized' peoples. In his *Principles of Political Economy* and *Elements of Politics* he justified British colonialism and the expansion of European culture, which he considered superior to those over which the imperial powers ruled.[6] In holding such beliefs, Sidgwick was no worse—but also no better—than most of his contemporaries, but today it takes some goodwill to read such statements as an expression of his ongoing desire to make the world a better place. We have to remember that in many ways the world seemed different to him than it seems to us.

We will also make no attempt to present Sidgwick's philosophy as a whole. We concentrate on issues discussed in *The Methods* and, with a few relatively minor exceptions, do not follow his thoughts in his other writings. We do this for three reasons. First, although *The Methods* is not as widely read as we would wish, it is by far the best-known of Sidgwick's works. Second, five editions of *The Methods* were published during Sidgwick's lifetime, and at the time of his death, he was working on revisions for the sixth edition. *The Methods* is therefore the work that best presents his most carefully considered views. Third, and not coincidentally, *The Methods* discusses the most fundamental and important problems of ethics.

We begin, in Chapter 1, by asking the most basic questions: What is ethics? What are its methods? And what is the task of the philosopher investigating ethics? Sidgwick defines a method of ethics as a rational procedure for deciding what we ought to do. He groups these rational procedures into three different types: egoism, intuitionism, and utilitarianism, thus limiting the possible rivals to utilitarianism to two; one of which, egoism, many ethical thinkers find repellent. We consider whether he has, by this move, preempted some viable ethical theories from getting a proper hearing in his work.

Because a method of ethics is a rational procedure for deciding what we ought to do, we will, in Chapter 2, ask what rationality amounts to, when it comes to practical reasoning, and what reasons for actions we can have. Philosophical accounts of reasons for action can be divided according to whether the reasons provided are subjective or objective. We argue that normative reasons for actions are objective.

---

[6] See Schultz, *Henry Sidgwick: Eye of the Universe*, 272–3, and the same author's 'Mill and Sidgwick, Imperialism and Racism'.

One very important step in Sidgwick's progression towards the best rational procedure for deciding what we ought to do is his careful examination of the morality of common sense, from which he concludes that this view does not constitute a philosophically precise method of ethics. In Chapter 3 we will ask whether Sidgwick was justified in rejecting common sense morality. Sidgwick grounds his own theory, not on our common sense moral judgments, but on our intuitive knowledge of the truth of some self-evident axioms. For this reason, his approach raises an important question of methodology that we discuss in Chapter 4. Contemporary ethics often assumes that normative ethical theories can only be justified by reaching what Rawls called a 'reflective equilibrium' between theory and considered moral judgments. Sidgwick, by contrast, seeks a self-evident foundation on which to build a normative theory. We investigate whether Sidgwickian 'foundationalism' is a viable alternative to reflective equilibrium.

What are these axioms that Sidgwick thought are self-evident? They are: an axiom of justice ('whatever action any of us judges to be right for himself, he implicitly judges to be right for all similar persons in similar circumstances'), an axiom of prudence ('a smaller present good is not to be preferred to a greater future good'), and an axiom of benevolence ('each one is morally bound to regard the good of any other individual as much as his own, except in so far as he judges it to be less, when impartially viewed, or less certainly knowable or attainable by him'). In Chapter 5 we comment on these axioms in the light of the work of more recent thinkers such as R. M. Hare and John Mackie on universalizability, Bernard Williams, Michael Slote, and Larry Temkin on time preference, and finally Williams again as well as Rawls on utilitarianism and maximization.

Although Sidgwick thought that utilitarianism could be grounded on self-evident axioms, he was troubled by the fact that the axiom of benevolence is in conflict with a different principle that seemed to him difficult to deny, namely that, for every individual, 'his own happiness is an end which it is irrational for him to sacrifice to any other'. This principle, Sidgwick saw, led to egoism, and so practical reason seems to endorse both egoism and utilitarianism. Sidgwick held that this 'dualism of practical reason' showed that reason cannot, after all, be a complete guide to what we ought to do. Moreover, if we always have sufficient reason to do what is in our own interests—so that acting in our own interests would always be rational, but not rationally required—then that seems to sharply diminish the importance of an ethical theory like utilitarianism, based as it is on the idea of acting with impartial concern for others. Sidgwick's inability to overcome the dualism meant that he was unable to conclude that utilitarianism is the only rationally defensible way of deciding what we ought to do. Egoism survives as an unattractive, but still possible, alternative.

In Chapter 6 we look more closely at this issue, which Sidgwick called 'the profoundest problem of ethics'. We consider the ways in which David Gauthier, David Brink, and Derek Parfit have sought to overcome or reduce the scope of the problem. We find their proposals unsatisfactory, and in Chapter 7 we offer our own solution to it.

If we can overcome the dualism of practical reason we are left with the axiom of universal benevolence that tells us to maximize the good, impartially. The final step Sidgwick would then need to take would be to argue that this good is happiness, for then he would have reached his goal of finding a rational procedure that can tell us what we ought to do. In Chapter 8 we divide theories of the good into internalist and externalist theories, and explore the most plausible versions of desire-based theories, which are internalist, and of perfectionist accounts, which are externalist. Then in Chapter 9 we investigate the nature of happiness and pleasure and consider Sidgwick's version of hedonism, which combines elements of both internalism and externalism.

We usually think of morality as stating its obligations in terms of principles and rules. There is, however, a problem with the principle of benevolence. It seems that in the real world, a principle that tells us always to maximize the good may, for various reasons, be counterproductive. It might, for example, be too difficult for moral agents to calculate all the consequences of their actions, so that they tend to bring about worse consequences than they would if they acted on simpler rules. As this example shows, we can distinguish the question of what is the correct criterion for deciding whether an act ought to be done (which may be that it leads to the best consequences) from the question of what is the best decision procedure for people to follow (which may be to obey a set of not-too-complicated rules). This distinction—and the possibility that sometimes an act may be right only if it does not set a bad example that will lead others astray—leads Sidgwick to suggest that it can sometimes be right to do in secret what would be wrong if done openly. We discuss this issue in Chapter 10, and in Chapter 11, the related question of how demanding morality can be.

Our final chapter is devoted to three topics that may seem quite distinct. First, should we take into account only the happiness of human beings, or of all those capable of experiencing pleasure and pain? Second, in dividing resources between those whose happiness we should take into account, should we favour an egalitarian distribution, or one that gives priority to those who are worse off, or should we simply aim at increasing happiness as much as possible, irrespective of how it is distributed? Finally, we investigate a question first raised by Sidgwick, but more recently developed in far greater depth by Parfit: should we, in maximizing happiness, be concerned only about those who already exist, or who will exist independently of what we do, or should we also be concerned about merely possible beings, whose very existence depends on the choices we make?

In this book we make the strongest case we can for the views that Sidgwick defended. Thus, with regard to the basis of ethics, we argue that ethical judgments can be true or false, and that these normative truths do not describe any natural facts about the world. With regard to what we ought to do, we push as far as we can to defend classical hedonistic utilitarianism. We recognize that there remain many points at which one could object to this view, but it has the great merit of being clear and straightforward. Whether or not classical utilitarianism is ultimately judged to be correct, there will be much to be learnt from a discussion of its strengths as well as its weaknesses.

Acknowledgements

We begin by thanking the following people, who took time to read all or part of our early drafts of this book, and whose comments and suggestions helped us greatly to improve the final version: Richard Chappell, Simon Cotton, Roger Crisp, Jonathan Dancy, Angus Deaton, Joshua Greene, Chris Heathwood, Brad Hooker, Thomas Hurka, Dale Jamieson, Adam Lerner, Mariko Nakano-Okuno, Derek Parfit, Theron Pummer, Jerry Schneewind, Bart Schultz (to whom we also owe our title), Jeff Sebo, Mark Silberg, Walter Sinnott-Armstrong, Anthony Skelton, Lawrence Torcello, Alex Voorhoeve, and anonymous reviewers for *Ethics* and for Oxford University Press. We are especially grateful to Peter Momtchiloff, our editor at OUP, for his good advice and encouragement.

We would like to thank the Polish National Science Center (NCN) for financially supporting this project.

Three chapters of this book draw on material we previously published in journals: chapter 7 on 'The Objectivity of Ethics and the Unity of Practical Reason', *Ethics*, 123/1 (2012), 9–31; chapter 10 on 'Secrecy in Consequentialism: A Defence of Esoteric Morality', *Ratio*, 23 (2010), 34–58; and chapter 11 on 'How much more demanding is utilitarianism than common sense morality?' *Revue Internationale de Philosophie*, 2013/4 (n. 266), pp. 427–438. We thank these journals for the opportunity to try out our arguments in their pages.

Our families have given us constant support. We are very grateful for their understanding of the importance of the project to us.

Finally, we want to express our appreciation to each other for the past three years in which we have worked together on this book, often initially defending different views but in the end always ready to listen to each other and find common ground. Philosophy is a constant dialogue and having this dialogue together over the issues we cover in the following pages was much more fruitful than musing in our separate heads would have been.

From Katarzyna de Lazari-Radek: I would like to express my special gratitude to Jerry Schneewind, Bart Schultz, Roger Crisp, and Samuel Scheffler for assistance that goes back to the earliest days of my study of Sidgwick, when I was just a graduate student starting to think about my Ph.D. on the moral philosophy of Henry Sidgwick. I first heard of Sidgwick from my supervisor, Professor Andrzej Kaniowski, but I did not then know much about him, nor did I have anything except *The Methods of Ethics* on my bookshelf. No Polish library possessed a single book on Sidgwick, and they had very few on utilitarianism either. At that time I could not afford to buy foreign books, and the resources that are available on the internet today did not exist. In an English encyclopedia of philosophy, however, I found a sentence saying that the best book written on Sidgwick was *Sidgwick's Ethics and Victorian Moral Philosophy* by J. Schneewind. Desperate as I was, I decided to write to him and ask for whatever advice he might be willing to give on how to start, what to read and how to get a copy of his book. I found his e-mail address and sent off my message. In half an hour I had a response from Professor Schneewind telling me that his book (his own copy) was on the way to me. He offered his help with my research needs and wrote that he had written to Bart Schultz and Roger Crisp to help me as well. In two weeks I had enough material to start my Ph.D. Samuel Scheffler helped me in the same way. I will always think of this as one of the kindest things that has happened to me. It also showed me something about the spirit of academia that I would like to pass on to future generations.

Katarzyna de Lazari-Radek,
Institute of Philosophy,
Faculty of History and Philosophy,
University of Lodz

Peter Singer
University Center for Human Values,
Princeton University
&
School of Historical and Philosophical Studies,
University of Melbourne

Contents

Contents

A Biographical Prologue

For philosophy and history alike have taught...
to seek not what is 'safe,' but what is true.[1]

1. Beginnings

 Henry Sidgwick was born on 31 May 1838 in Skipton, Yorkshire, the fourth child of the Reverend William Sidgwick, a grammar school headmaster, and Mary Croft. He was only 3 years old when his father died. In 1852 Sidgwick was sent to Rugby school, one of the best in England. This was the result of the encouragement of Edward White Benson, a cousin of Sidgwick's father, who was later to become both the husband of Sidgwick's sister Mary and the archbishop of Canterbury. Sidgwick remembers Benson's influence throughout his years at Rugby and also on the choice of Trinity College, Cambridge, where he started studying in 1855. At the time, he later wrote, he 'had no other ideal except to be a scholar as like [Benson] as possible'.[2] He remained in various posts at Trinity College and the University of Cambridge for the next 45 years.

 From the beginning, Sidgwick was an outstanding student. In his second term at Cambridge he obtained the Bell Scholarship. A year later he was awarded the Craven Scholarship for classical studies—'far the greatest of University prizes'—which was worth £75 a year, and for which all the best scholars at all year levels competed. Sidgwick communicated the good news to Benson:

I was astounded by the appearance of the University Marshal in my rooms to communicate to me the exhilarating intelligence which I hope you received as soon

---

[1] A. Sidgwick, E. Sidgwick, *A Memoir*, 62.
[2] A. Sidgwick, E. Sidgwick, *A Memoir*, 11.

as electricity could convey it. My first idea, although I had been thinking about the Craven lately a good deal, was a vague fancy that I was about to be hauled up for some offence committed against the statutes of the University. Soon, however, the benign and at the same time meaning smile of that remarkable personage conveyed a misty idea of some news divinely good. It was not, however, till the oracular words, 'You are elected to the Craven Scholarship' had passed his lips that I realised the tremendous fact. I then gave a wild shriek, leapt up into the air, and threw up my arms above my head.... The worthy marshal, however, who is, I suppose, accustomed to all the various manifestations of ecstasy, remained imperturbable; seemed loftily amused by my inquiring when I should call on the Vice-Chancellor, ... and condescended to agree to come next morning to receive his sovereign, as I had no money about me.[3]

With the Craven there came another award which turned out to be more important than the money—an invitation to join the Apostles. Sidgwick's interest in philosophy developed as a result of the Saturday evening discussions with this select group of the brightest students at Cambridge. He later wrote that his election to the Apostles had 'more effect on my intellectual life than any one thing that happened to me afterwards'.[4] What did he find so special about the Apostles? Here is his answer:

I can only describe it as the spirit of the pursuit of truth with absolute devotion and unreserve by a group of intimate friends, who were perfectly frank with each other, and indulged in any amount of humorous sarcasm and playful banter, and yet each respects the other, and when he discourses tries to learn from him and see what he sees. Absolute candour was the only duty that the tradition of the society enforced. No consistency was demanded with opinions previously held—truth as we saw it then and there was what we had to embrace and maintain, and there were no propositions so well established that an Apostle had not the right to deny or question, if he did so sincerely and not from mere love of paradox. The gravest subjects were continually debated, but gravity of treatment, as I have said, was not imposed, though sincerity was.[5]

The idea of complete sincerity in the pursuit of truth became a crucial element in Sidgwick's life, both as a philosopher and as a human being, although as we shall see, in his view sincerity did not imply that one ought to be transparent about everything.

[3]   A. Sidgwick, E. Sidgwick, A Memoir, 17.
[4]   A. Sidgwick, E. Sidgwick, A Memoir, 34.
[5]   A. Sidgwick, E. Sidgwick, A Memoir, 34–35.

2. Belief and Reason

In 1859, after four years of studies, Sidgwick was appointed a Fellow and Lecturer in Classics at Trinity College. Though he had become interested in moral issues, no possibility of teaching ethics was then given to him—the so-called 'Moral Sciences' were taught only by professors. He began his philosophical studies with the work of John Stuart Mill, but soon formed the view that philosophy was not likely to answer his most important questions about 'the nature of man and his relation to God and the universe'. Sidgwick had been brought up in a religious family and at first the existence of God and the truth of Christianity were no doubt as obvious to him as anything else. However, his studies and his scrupulous nature and persistent desire to learn the truth inevitably led him to reassess his beliefs. There were too many questions to which he could not find satisfying answers, and what once seemed obvious now began to appear without a firm basis. Victorian England at this time, with the discoveries of Lyell, Darwin, and Huxley, was the scene of many debates in which reason was opposed to religious belief. In this conflict, from the beginning of his academic career, Sidgwick's choice was clear. In 1861 he wrote in his journal: 'In no "spiritual pride" but with a perhaps mistaken trust in the reason that I find in me I wish to show forth in my own life the supremacy of reason.'[6]

At first Sidgwick hoped that scientific studies of language, culture, and history would help him find a reasonable justification for religious teachings. This was consistent with the spirit of the Cambridge Apostles:

What was fixed and unalterable and accepted by us all was the necessity and duty of examining the evidence for historical Christianity with strict scientific impartiality; placing ourselves as far as possible outside traditional sentiments and opinions, and endeavouring to weigh the pros and cons on all theological questions as a duly instructed rational being from another planet—or let us say from China—would naturally weigh them.[7]

---

[6] Schneewind, *Sidgwick's Ethics*, 25, citing a manuscript from Sidgwick's papers at Trinity College, Cambridge.

[7] A. Sidgwick, E. Sidgwick, *A Memoir*, 40.

Accordingly, Sidgwick devoted three years to learning Arabic and Hebrew; but then he started to wonder if he might be wasting his time:

I began...to think that the comparative historical study which I had planned would not really give any important aid in answering the great questions raised by the orthodox Christianity from which my view of the Universe had been derived. Was Jesus incarnate God, miraculously brought into the world as a man? Were his utterances of divine authority? Did he actually rise from the grave with a human body glorified, and therewith ascend into heaven? Or if the answers to these questions could not strictly be affirmative in the ordinary sense of the term, what element of truth, vital for mankind, could be disengaged from the husk of legend, or symbolised by the legend, supposing the truth itself capable of being established by human reasoning?[8]

The inability of historical studies to answer these questions led Sidgwick back to philosophy and when in 1867 he was offered a lectureship in Moral Sciences, he accepted it, 'determined to throw myself into the work of making, if possible, a philosophical school in Cambridge'.[9]

Sidgwick's inability to believe in the Church and its teachings led him to a decision that threatened his career as a philosopher, even though it was the result of his commitment to the search for the truth. When Sidgwick started teaching at Cambridge, every Fellow had to subscribe to the Thirty-Nine Articles of the Anglican Church. Some of the Fellows took this as a technical requirement—they had to say that they accepted the Articles, but they did not have to do so sincerely. Not Sidgwick. Already at the end of 1860 in a letter to his friend Oscar Browning he wrote:

I think I could juggle myself into signing the Articles as well as any one else: but I really feel that it may at least be the duty of some—if so *emou ge* [for me, anyway]—to avoid the best-motived perjury.[10]

How deeply troubling the problem was for him is apparent from the fact that the first letter Sidgwick wrote to Mill, in 1867, was not about philosophy but about this issue. After apologizing for writing a long letter, which was coming from 'a perfect stranger', Sidgwick raised the

---

[8]   A. Sidgwick, E. Sidgwick, *A Memoir*, 37.
[9]   A. Sidgwick, E. Sidgwick, *A Memoir*, 38.
[10] A. Sidgwick, E. Sidgwick, *Memoir*, 62.

question of religious tests, and referred to discussions about where 'the line between expedient conformity and inexpedient hypocrisy is to be drawn'. Mill did not offer Sidgwick any practical advice, but suggested that Sidgwick turn his attention to the larger question of what, on utilitarian grounds, ought to be the exceptions to the rule that we should tell the truth.[11]

Finally, in spring 1869, Sidgwick acted. He wrote to his mother:

> Many thanks for your letter. It reached me at a critical point of my career. I have just resigned my Assistant Tutorship and informed the Authorities that I intend to resign my Fellowship very shortly. It is not impossible that they may appoint me lecturer in spite of this, though I hardly expect it. I will tell you when anything is decided. Meanwhile it is a secret. You may be glad to hear that the Master expressed himself very kindly about me in communicating my resignation to the College. In fact every one is very kind, and if I am not reappointed it will not be from want of goodwill, but from a conviction that the interests of the College do not allow it. Whatever happens I am happy and know that I have done what was right. In fact, though I had some struggle before doing it, it now appears not the least bit of a sacrifice, but simply the natural and inevitable thing to do.[12]

Trinity College did appoint Sidgwick to a lectureship, a position that did not require subscribing to the Articles, and he was able to continue his academic career. Thus his resignation did him no harm, and because as a lecturer, rather than a Fellow, he was no longer a member of the governing body of the College, it may have contributed to the completion of his greatest work. After *The Methods of Ethics* was published he wrote to Browning: 'I often think that if I had not resigned my Fellowship I should never have written my book.'[13]

It was also at this time that Sidgwick began his efforts to enhance educational possibilities for women at Cambridge. Women could not, at the time, become students of the university, but in 1870, Sidgwick organized, with others, 'Lectures for Ladies' and the following year, took the bold step of renting a house in which the ladies attending the lectures could live. This led to the founding of Newnham Hall, which today is Newnham College.

---

[11] Sidgwick to Mill, 28 July 1867; Mill to Sidgwick, 3 Aug. 1867 and 26 Nov. 1867.
[12] A. Sidgwick, E. Sidgwick, *A Memoir*, 196–7.
[13] A. Sidgwick, E. Sidgwick, *A Memoir*, 321.

Sidgwick's resignation influenced the attitudes of others and con-tributed to the movement against the requirement that Fellows of Cambridge, Oxford, and the University of Durham must accept the Church of England's central doctrines. That reform was achieved in 1871 when religious tests were abolished by an Act of Parliament. Sidgwick was then able to return to his previous post. In 1883 he was appointed to the Knightbridge Professorship of Moral Philosophy, the most prestigious position that a moral philosopher could hold at the university.

3. Towards *The Methods of Ethics*

The Preface to the sixth edition of *The Methods of Ethics* includes an autobiographical sketch of Sidgwick's philosophical development. The utilitarianism of Mill, he writes, brought him

relief from the apparently external and arbitrary pressure of moral rules which I had been educated to obey, and which presented themselves to me as to some extent doubtful and confused; and sometimes, even when clear, as merely dog-matic, unreasoned, incoherent. (*ME* p. xvii)[14]

Comparing Mill's utilitarianism and Whilliam Whewell's intuition-ism, Sidgwick found the intuitionists 'hopelessly loose...in their definitions and axioms'. At first Sidgwick was attracted both by Mill's psychological hedonism (every man seeks his own happiness) and his ethical hedonism (every man should seek the general happiness); but he came to see the combination of the two as incoherent. We must choose one or the other; but on what grounds can we do so? Mill had acknowledged that sometimes one can best serve the happiness of others by an 'absolute sacrifice' of one's own happiness. The hero, Mill wrote, could prize the happiness of others more than his own happi-ness.[15] But Sidgwick knew that, whether or not he could be a moral hero, he 'was not the kind of moral hero who does this without rea-son; from *blind* habit'. He didn't even wish to be that kind of hero, because that kind of hero was certainly not a philosopher. Sidgwick's

[14] References in the text to *ME* followed by a page number are to Henry Sidgwick, *The Methods of Ethics*, 7th edn (London: Macmillan, 1907).

[15] Mill, *Utilitarianism*, ch. 2, §19.

allegiance was to reason ahead of universal happiness; before sacrificing his own happiness for the good of the whole, he needed a reason for so doing.

The search for a justification for such a sacrifice led Sidgwick to part company with Mill and 'recognize the need of a fundamental ethical intuition' on which the utilitarian position could be based. Sidgwick read Kant again, but concluded that Kant could not give him the answer he was looking for—a demonstration that self-interest is subordinate to duty. He believed that a rational egoist could accept both the Kantian principle and the Hobbesian principle of self-preservation and say:

I quite admit that when the painful necessity comes for another man to choose between his own happiness and the general happiness, he must as a reasonable being prefer his own, *i.e.* it is right for him to do this on my principle. No doubt, as I probably do not sympathise with him in particular any more than with other persons, I as a disengaged spectator should like him to sacrifice himself to the general good: but I do not expect him to do it, any more than I should do it myself in his place. (*ME* pp. xix–xx)

Neither of his 'masters', Kant and Mill, could convince Sidgwick that self-interest is any less 'undeniably reasonable' than self-sacrifice. He turned to the work of Joseph Butler, an 18th-century philosopher and theologian who became bishop of Durham and had an influence on David Hume and Adam Smith, as well as on Sidgwick. Butler argued that 'Reasonable Self-love' is 'one of the two chief or superior principles in the nature of man'.[16] Butler referred to the 'Dualism of the Governing Faculty', an expression that Sidgwick changed into his own well-known 'Dualism of Practical Reason'. Reading the earlier intuitionists Henry More and Samuel Clarke, he found the axiom he needed for justifying utilitarianism: 'That a rational agent is bound to aim at Universal Happiness.' Sidgwick was a utilitarian again, though 'on an Intuitional basis'. In this way he could unite the two seemingly opposed moral theories, intuitionism and utilitarianism; but he did not, as we will see, find a way out of the conflict between self-interest and utilitarianism.

---

[16] Sidgwick is here referring to Joseph Butler, *Fifteen Sermons Preached at Rolls Chapel*, sermon 11, first publ. in 1726.

In 1874, when Sidgwick was finishing the first edition of *The Methods of Ethics*, he wrote to a friend: 'The book solves nothing, but may clear up the ideas of one or two people a little.'[17] The modesty is typical of the man and of his conception of his role as a philosopher. He did not believe that he would be able to present the final truths of ethics.

In the remaining 26 years of his life, though Sidgwick wrote many other books, he continued to rewrite *The Methods*: a second edition was published in 1877, a third in 1884, a fourth in 1890, a fifth in 1893, and a posthumous sixth edition, based in part on revisions he had prepared, in 1901, with a seventh edition (correcting a few minor errors from the sixth) in 1907. This seventh edition is now the standard text of *The Methods*.

4. Marriage

In 1876, at the age of 38, Sidgwick married Eleanor Mildred Balfour, who was then 31 and came from a distinguished and politically influential family. Her father, who had died when she was a child, had been a Member of Parliament, and her mother could trace her ancestry back to Sir Robert Cecil, a leading statesman under both Elizabeth I and James I. The family lived in a mansion of eighty rooms on an estate of 10,000 acres.[18] Sidgwick first got to know Eleanor's brother, Arthur Balfour, who was his student at Cambridge. Arthur later followed his father into Parliament, and subsequently became leader of the Conservative Party and Prime Minister. Eleanor had been educated at home, but she moved to Cambridge in 1875 to live in Newnham Hall and study mathematics, for which she had a particular talent. Sidgwick was, as we have seen, the key figure in the founding of Newnham Hall, but he and Eleanor bonded also because of their mutual interest in research into psychic phenomena. Sidgwick had formed a group to explore, by scientific methods, such questions as whether there is survival after the death of the body

---

[17]   A. Sidgwick, E. Sidgwick, *A Memoir*, 284.
[18]   Schultz, *Henry Sidgwick: Eye of the Universe*, 295, based on J. Oppenheim, 'A Mother's Role'.

and, as one member of the group put it, 'Is the universe friendly?'[19] Eleanor, Arthur, and another brother, as well as her sister's husband, Lord Rayleigh (who subsequently received the Nobel Prize for Physics), were members of that group, initially known as 'the Sidgwick group' and later as the Society for Psychical Research. Sidgwick and other members of the group attended séances, but were always disappointed in the results, which often suggested fraud.

The marriage was a meeting of minds. Sidgwick wrote to his mother that while Eleanor 'is not exactly perfect' what was positive in her was 'quite quite good...I cannot imagine her doing anything wrong'. William James thought that they were 'the incarnation of pure intellect—a very odd appearing couple'.[20] Odd or not, Eleanor undoubtedly had a fine intellect—she is the co-author, with Rayleigh, of three papers on electricity published by the Royal Society. Henry and Eleanor had no children, and E. M. Young, in his biography of Arthur Balfour, states that Sidgwick was impotent.[21] He may have been more romantically attracted to men than to women. In his papers, under the heading 'My Friends', are some jottings in which he mentions two unnamed friends and about each writes 'I love him'. There is also a line that reads: 'Some are women to me, and to some I am a woman.'[22] One of Sidgwick's friends was the poet and literary critic John Addington Symonds, who wrote *A Problem in Greek Ethics,* a eulogy of homosexuality in ancient Greece published, at the time, in a limited privately distributed edition. After Symonds's death in 1893, Sidgwick worked with Symonds's literary executor to remove references to Symonds's homosexuality from what was to be published of his literary remains. This was, after all, the period of the trial and imprisonment of Oscar Wilde, and on this issue—in contrast to the issue of requiring College Fellows to subscribe to the Thirty-Nine Articles—Sidgwick evidently thought that the time for reforming public morality was not ripe.

[19] Schultz, *Henry Sidgwick: Eye of the Universe,* 287.
[20] Schultz, *Henry Sidgwick: Eye of the Universe,* 299.
[21] Schultz, *Henry Sidgwick: Eye of the Universe,* 779. Note to p. 414.
[22] Schultz, *Henry Sidgwick: Eye of the Universe,* 415.

5. Later Life and Death

After publishing *The Methods* Sidgwick wrote *Outlines of the History of Ethics for English Readers*, which appeared first as a long article in the *Encyclopaedia Britannica* in 1878 and then was published as a book in 1886. His interests in economics and politics resulted in *The Principles of Political Economy* (1883), *The Scope and Method of Economic Science* (1885), and *The Elements of Politics* (1891). He was the author of many articles, essays, and reviews in the leading periodicals of his time, and was particularly interested in making ethics more practical and relevant to the moral issues of his time. Towards the end of his life he collected some of his writings on applied ethics in a volume called *Practical Ethics* (1898).

Sidgwick's writing suffers from what is one of his greatest virtues as a philosopher—his ability to see all sides of a question, which often led him to qualify his statements and digress to deal with objections. Those who heard him speak, however, often had a very different impression from that left by his writings. John Neville Keynes, a Cambridge economist, colleague of Sidgwick, and the father of the more famous John Maynard Keynes, wrote:

It was extraordinary how illuminating he would be, whatever turn the conversation might take: on one topic after another he had something interesting to say, and what he said was always to the point and suggestive. He had an excellent memory, and there seemed to be no limit to the range of his knowledge. He was a capital storyteller: his supply of apposite stories—they were always pertinent to the previous conversation, never brought in merely for their own sake—seemed inexhaustible. And all his talk was touched by a subtle, delicate humour that added to its charm.[23]

Leslie Stephen recalled that Sidgwick had a stammer, but used it to good effect: 'His hearers watched and waited for the coming thought which then exploded the more effectually.' Sidgwick was also good at bringing other people into the conversation: 'He would wait with slightly parted lips for an answer to some inquiry, showing a keen interest which encouraged your expectation that you were about to say a good thing, and sometimes, let us hope, helped to realise the expectation.'[24]

---

[23] J. N. Keynes, 'Obituary', 591, cited in A. Sidgwick, E. Sidgwick, *A Memoir*, 316.

[24] A. Sidgwick, E. Sidgwick, *A Memoir*, 315.

These conversational skills no doubt became even more valuable in 1880, when Eleanor was appointed Vice-Principal of Newnham and the Sidgwicks lived, during term, in rooms in the college. Sidgwick played his part in college life, and his role became more significant still when Eleanor became Principal in 1891. Under Eleanor's direction—and in part because of her donation of £30,000, a very significant sum in those days—the college thrived and expanded. Portraits of both Eleanor and Henry still hang in the Newnham College dining hall.

Early in May 1900, shortly before his 62nd birthday, Sidgwick was diagnosed with cancer and told that he did not have long to live. Later that month he travelled to Oxford, for he had promised to give a lecture to the Philosophical Society there. He took the opportunity to tell his brother Arthur of his impending death. Arthur later recalled that Sidgwick had said that knowing what was to come had led him to ask himself whether he had 'done his work and lived his life as he had meant'. His verdict was that he had, in the main, done his work to the best of his power, 'whatever the worth of it'.[25]

Sidgwick was operated on at the end of May and then taken to the Rayleigh estate, in Terling, Essex, to await the end. After a short remission, his condition deteriorated and he died on 28 August 1900. He was buried in the church cemetery in Terling, Essex, after a ceremony that used the Church of England funeral service. Sidgwick had given no explicit directions about his funeral, but in May he had said to Eleanor, with regard to the Church of England service, that 'not to use it was what seemed to him most in harmony with his views and actions in life' and if it were not used, he would like to have the following words said over his grave: 'Let us commend to the love of God with silent prayer the soul of a sinful man who partly tried to do his duty. It is by his wish that I say over his grave these words and no more.'[26]

---

[25] Schultz, *Henry Sidgwick: Eye of the Universe*, 715. The original source is a letter from Arthur Sidgwick.
[26] A. Sidgwick, E. Sidgwick, *A Memoir*, 599.

6. Sidgwick's Reputation

The first edition of *The Methods* was widely reviewed and discussed.[27] Most reviews were positive, although there were exceptions, including a very critical essay by F. H. Bradley. Just 12 years after the publication of the first edition, Hastings Rashdall wrote that:

> *The Methods of Ethics* has long been recognized as a philosophical classic. It is one of those books of which it is safe to prophesy that no advance in philosophic doctrine will ever render them obsolete. It is not merely a piece of acute and subtle philosophical criticism but a work of art with a unity and beauty of its own as much as a Dialogue of Plato or of Berkeley.[28]

John Neville Keynes, too, writing after Sidgwick's death, described *The Methods* as 'so striking and original in character and of such fundamental importance as fairly to entitle the work to be regarded as epoch-making'.[29]

Sidgwick's high reputation began to be challenged early in the 20th century. To members of the Bloomsbury group, strongly influenced by G. E. Moore, he was seen as a relic of the Victorian era, a period that they viewed with scorn. Among this group was John Maynard Keynes, who after reading Sidgwick's memoir remarked in a letter to a friend that Sidgwick 'never did anything but wonder whether Christianity was true and prove it wasn't and hope that it was'.[30] Like other young members of the Bloomsbury group, John Maynard Keynes was under the spell of G. E. Moore, and had come to believe that Moore's *Principia Ethica* was so extraordinary a work that its 'wonder and originality' could not possibly be exaggerated.

---

[27] The first reviews appeared in *Mind* in 1876: Alexander Bain, 'Mr. Sidgwick's Methods of Ethics', 178–97, and Henry Calderwood, 'Mr. Sidgwick and Intuitionism', 197–206. In 1877 F. H. Bradley wrote an extensive critical text titled 'Mr. Sidgwick's Hedonism: An Examination of the Main Argument of the Methods of Ethics'. It was initially published privately and later included in his *Collected Essays*. In the same year F. Y. Edgeworth published a short book on *The Methods* titled: *New and Old Methods of Ethics*.

[28] Rashdall, 'Professor Sidgwick's Utilitarianism', 200; we owe this reference to M. G. Singer, 'The Many Methods of Sidgwick's Ethics', 422–3.

[29] Keynes, 'Obituary', 587.

[30] From a letter of J. M. Keynes to B. Swithinbank, 27 Mar. 1906 (Keynes Papers, King's College, Cambridge), from B. Schultz, *Henry Sidgwick: Eye of the Universe*, 4.

(Most philosophers today regard *Principia Ethica* as considerably less wonderful and original than *The Methods,* on which it draws heavily.) Moore's influence on the younger Keynes was so strong that he wrote to a friend 'I even begin to agree with Moore about Sidgwick—that he was a wicked edifactious person.'[31] ('Edifactious' does not appear in the *Oxford English Dictionary* and we will leave it to the reader to guess what Keynes may have meant by it.)

Sidgwick's insistence that there are moral truths we can know by intuition was accepted by G. E. Moore and W. D. Ross, the most influential British moral philosophers of the first half of the 20th century; though as we shall see, they differed from him over what these moral truths are. To that extent Sidgwick's approach to ethics, if not the content of his views, remained influential until the Second World War. Already during the 1930s, however, the rise of logical positivism meant that the new generation of philosophers consigned both Ross and Sidgwick to the outer darkness where, according to the tenets of logical positivism, those who utter unverifiable, and therefore meaningless, non-tautologous propositions belong.[32] After the war this approach to philosophy prevailed. It was succeeded by the view that the role of philosophy was to show that substantive philosophical problems could be resolved—or perhaps better, dissolved—by analyzing the way we use ordinary language. This style of doing philosophy left no room for substantive moral argument. Hence for two decades most English-speaking philosophers had little regard for normative ethical theory. That began to change in the 1960s when students demanded that their courses should be relevant to the world in which they lived, and to the issues that concerned them, like racial equality and the war in Vietnam. In the ensuing revival of normative and practical ethics, Sidgwick began to be read and appreciated once again. By the beginning of the 21st century, it was not unusual for *The Methods* to be ranked among the best books on ethics ever written.

---

[31] From a letter quoted in R. F. Harrod, *The Life of John Maynard Keynes,* 114.

[32] John Deigh has argued that the decline of interest in Sidgwick's ethics was due to the epistemology on which it was based falling out of favour with analytic philosophers; see his 'Sidgwick's Epistemology', 435–46. Skelton argues against some of Deigh's claims in 'On Sidgwick's Demise: A Reply to Professor Deigh', 70–7, and Deigh replies in 'Some Further Thoughts on Sidgwick's Epistemology', 78–89.

1

What is Ethics?

1. Sidgwick's Approach to Ethics

Sidgwick's masterpiece is called *The Methods of Ethics*; but what is a 'method of ethics'? The term is unusual in ethics, and Sidgwick may have taken it from John Stuart Mill's *System of Logic,* a work that he admired, and which discussed methods of scientific investigation. Science has its methods, and uses them to obtain knowledge. Can ethics be put on the same footing by developing and refining its methods?[1] In the very first sentence of book I, Sidgwick defines a 'Method of Ethics' as 'any rational procedure by which we determine what individual human beings "ought"—or what it is "right" for them—to do, or to seek to realize by voluntary action'. In the next sentence he explains that he uses the word 'individual' deliberately, to differentiate ethics from politics, which he sees as concerned with the proper constitution and public conduct of governed societies.

Ethics is a study of what we ought to do, not of what is the case. Hence it is to be distinguished from those areas of sociology or psychology that study morality as a social practice, or examine the psychological factors that lead us to make the ethical judgments we make or the extent to which they influence our behaviour. This doesn't mean that there is no connection between ethics and the descriptive sciences. We cannot decide what ought to be, or know how to bring it about, without knowledge of how things are. Moreover

[1] Schneewind, *Sidgwick's Ethics,* 194.

Sidgwick believes that, if we are trying to find out what we ought to do, a good place to begin is with the answers that our fellow humans have given to this question, and this too requires knowledge of facts. Nevertheless, Sidgwick is clear that determining what *is* is essentially different from determining what is *right* and which judgments about right and wrong are true.

How then should we go about deciding what we ought to do? Most people, Sidgwick observes, draw on a variety of different principles, applying them in shifting, confused, and even inconsistent combinations. The task of philosophers is to examine these principles, ensure that they are internally consistent, or if not revise them so that they are consistent. The different ways of deciding what we ought to do need to be consolidated into a small number of 'methods of ethics' and then we must see if these methods conflict because it is, Sidgwick tells us, 'a fundamental postulate of Ethics, that so far as two methods conflict, one or other of them must be modified or rejected' (*ME* 6).

So what are these methods and what are these different practical principles that 'the common sense of mankind is prima facie prepared to accept as ultimate'? We need to set aside, first, ends that depend on some further goal. A doctor may tell a patient that he ought to exercise, but this advice presupposes that the patient wants to be healthy. If he prefers a life without exertion to good health, the 'ought' has no further hold on him. A method of ethics must be about ends that are not optional in this way (*ME* 7).

The man who prefers an indolent life does not take his own good health as an end, but presumably that is because he thinks that he will be happier if he does not exercise, and he wants happiness for its own sake. Most people would agree, Sidgwick says, that to act in your own interests, and thus to seek your own happiness, is 'a manifest obligation'. (Sidgwick is here quoting Butler.) We may baulk at the idea of describing the pursuit of our own happiness as an obligation, perhaps because people are all too ready to do it anyway, but we are likely to agree that people ought to care for their own happiness, and that there would be something odd—perhaps even irrational—in being totally unconcerned about it. Thus Sidgwick has arrived at the first candidate for the status of an ultimate principle: the principle that we ought to be concerned for our own happiness. The method based on this principle is the method of egoism.

Although most people would agree that one's own happiness is an ultimate end, common moral opinion also takes many other rules as fundamental, for example rules requiring us to act honestly and justly. Generally speaking, Sidgwick says, these rules are regarded as binding, irrespective of the consequences of obeying them. They present themselves to us intuitively, as directly or self-evidently true, and their validity is, or appears to be, categorical; that is, independent of any other principles or ultimate ends. Hence the approach to ethics based on these rules constitutes another method of ethics, which Sidgwick calls the method of intuitionism. In obeying these rules, we achieve the goal of our own moral perfection or excellence (ME 8).

Egoists would, of course, reject the idea that it can be right to follow a rule for the rule's sake, irrespective of its consequences. In their view, it would be right to follow a rule only if doing so will improve the prospects of achieving one's own happiness. But there is also another possible basis for rejecting the idea of following rules regardless of the consequences. We might take the ultimate end to be, not our own happiness, but everyone's happiness. This is the utilitarian view. Utilitarians hold that rules are to be followed only to the extent that obeying them will help to bring about the general happiness; aiming at the general happiness is the one categorical duty, and all other duties are applications of it.

We have therefore arrived at three distinct 'methods of ethics' which Sidgwick will proceed to examine in detail—not so much to prove them valid or invalid, but rather to give, as he says, a 'critical exposition' of each method (ME 78). In the history of ethical thought, all three of these methods of reasoning—egoism, intuitionism, and utilitarianism—have been implicit in many of the approaches taken, but Sidgwick's focus is not on the history of these schools of thought, nor on the specific ethical theories that have resulted from their use. Instead he wants to examine them as occupants of some kind of logical space, or as he puts it: 'as alternatives between which—as far as they cannot be reconciled—the human mind seems to me necessarily forced to choose, when it attempts to frame a complete synthesis

of practical maxims and to act in a perfectly consistent manner'
(*ME* 12).

Why just these three methods, and not others? Sidgwick does discuss three other possible ultimate reasons for action: that we should
do what God wills, that we should seek self-realization, and that we
should live in accordance with our nature. With regard to the view
that we should act in accordance with God's will, he makes the wry
comment that 'There is indeed a difficulty in understanding how
God's Will can fail to be realized, whether we do right or wrong...'
He then mentions a more practical difficulty with taking God's will as
a reason for acting: to do so we would need to know what God's will
is. If it is claimed that we can know this only by revelation, then obviously to know what we ought to do we must go beyond the scope of
ethics. If on the other hand it is claimed that we can know the divine
will by the use of our reason, then we are going to engage in the same
process of thought that Sidgwick is already planning, and the appeal
to God's will does not offer any special criterion of what is right.

The suggestion that we seek self-realization could, Sidgwick notes,
be understood as a form of the method of egoism, since self-realization
is arguably what best promotes our own interests. Alternatively, it
could be seen as a form of the principle that we should live in accordance with our own nature. This latter principle, Sidgwick points out,
only makes sense on the assumption that nature shows some form of
design, and hence that by looking at human nature, we can discover
the kind of life we were designed to live. For if the natural world is
aimless, how can it determine what we ought to do? Advocates of this
view also fail to specify what they mean by 'natural'. Is every human
impulse natural? If not, how are we to determine which impulses are
natural and which are not? Not, surely, by rejecting the less common
ones as unnatural, nor by discovering which occurred earlier in our
development, for, as Sidgwick writes, there is no ground for assuming
that 'Nature abhors the exceptional, or prefers the earlier in time to
the later'; and he adds that, if we look at the history of our species, we
find that some of our most admirable impulses, like philanthropy, or
love of knowledge, are both rarer and appeared later than other, less
admirable impulses (*ME* 81–2). Once such confusions are exposed,

however, attempts to derive what ought to be by appealing to what our nature is stand revealed as palpable failures.

2. The Scope of Ethics

The most striking aspect of Sidgwick's definition of a method of ethics is its breadth. For Sidgwick ethics is concerned with what it is rational and reasonable to do, and *any* rational procedure by which we determine what individual human beings ought to do will count as a method of ethics. There are no constraints on the upshot of rationality. If there are overriding reasons to act in accordance with an ultimate principle, then that principle is, for Sidgwick, an ethical principle—and conversely, if something truly is an ultimate ethical principle, it cannot be irrational to act on it. This definition enables him to classify egoism as a method of ethics.

Sidgwick's understanding of 'ethics' is wider than 'morality' as employed by many philosophers today. R. M. Hare, one of the most significant figures in 20th-century British moral philosophy, argued that if I make a moral judgment, I must be prepared to universalize it—and that means that I must be willing to apply the judgment irrespective of who gains or loses from it.[2] The fact that I will be happier if I embezzle millions of dollars from my employer does not show that this is what I ought to do, because when we make moral judgments, the fact that *I* am the one who gains is not relevant. I would have to apply the same judgment even if I were the employer, and someone else were the embezzler, or if I were neither of these but the employees who had to take wage cuts, or the consumers who had to pay higher prices, to make up for the losses—and of course I would not want to do that. Thus universalizability rules out 'first person egoism'— that is, the form of egoism that makes an ineliminable reference to the speaker's interests. 'Third person egoism'—represented by the principle 'Everyone ought to do what is in his or her own interests'— is universalizable, because it contains no first person pronouns or proper names. But if I accept third person egoism, I must accept that

---

[2]   Hare, *Freedom and Reason*, ch. 3, and *Moral Thinking*, ch. 6.

the thief who steals my wallet is doing what he ought to do—as long as he has correctly judged that the theft is in his interest.

Since universalizability is, for Hare, a matter of how we use moral language, the first person egoist cannot, on Hare's view, make genuine moral judgments. The first person egoist can, however, consistently be an amoralist, declining to make any moral judgments at all. Whether any form of egoism is a rational position to hold is a separate question that would require more substantive argument. We will consider David Gauthier's defence of rational egoism in Chapter 6, when we discuss Sidgwick's problem of the dualism of practical reason; for our present purposes, it is sufficient to note that this question cannot be answered by a definition of 'morality' or an account of how we use moral language.

John Rawls regards egoism as consistent, and therefore not irrational, but 'incompatible with what we intuitively regard as the moral point of view'.[3] For Rawls, egoism is not an alternative conception of what it is right to do, but 'a challenge to any such conception'. Derek Parfit agrees. He refers to the way Sidgwick uses 'ought' as the 'decisive-reason' sense, according to which 'what we ought to do' means 'what we have decisive reasons to do'. He thinks, however, that there is a distinct 'moral ought' that is worth preserving. In this distinct sense, it would be misleading to use 'ought' to mean 'what we have decisive reasons to do'. He points out that: 'We often believe that we have decisive reasons to act in some way, though we do not believe that we ought morally to act in this way.'[4] In a note in which he discusses some of Sidgwick's mistakes, he writes: 'He should have distinguished more clearly between the concept of what we ought morally to do, and of what we have most reason to do.'[5]

Hare, Rawls, and Parfit are no doubt right about how moral language is commonly used. Sidgwick himself is not oblivious to this usage, for he occasionally acknowledges that it is common to distinguish prudential judgments from moral judgments (for example, *ME* 25). He uses 'ethics' in a wider sense, however, and we think it is to

---

[3] Rawls, *A Theory of Justice*, 117.
[4] Parfit, *On What Matters*, Volume One 166.
[5] Parfit, *On What Matters*, Volume One, 453, note to p. xl.

Sidgwick's credit that he did not seek to make a merely terminological point about the nature of ethics. Since one of the aims of this book is to expound Sidgwick's position, we will follow Sidgwick's terminology. This means using 'ought' in the wide sense—what Parfit calls the 'decisive-reason' sense—so that to say that people ought to do something is to say that they have decisive reasons to do it.

Nothing substantive depends on the usage we adopt. If we had adopted the narrower usage, we could still have asked what it is rational for an individual to do, and the egoist's answer would have remained a possible answer to that question, alongside the method of intuitionism and the method of utilitarianism. We might then have called egoism a 'method of rational choice' rather than a 'method of ethics' and the contest for the best 'method of ethics' in this narrow sense of the term would then have been—at least as far as Sidgwick's chosen 'methods' are concerned—between intuitionism and utilitarianism. As we shall argue in Chapter 6, however, the victory for 'ethics' would prove hollow if egoism turns out to be superior as a method of rational choice.[6]

If Sidgwick did not distinguish clearly between 'ethics' and 'morality', nor between what we have most reason to do and what morality requires us to do, he may have assumed that when we say that an act is morally wrong, we imply that we have decisive reasons not to do it. Many people regard it as strange to contemplate that reason and morality could come apart—that is, that the morally right thing to do might be something quite different from what we have most reason to do. Internalists about the relationship between reason and morality, or moral rationalists as they are sometimes called, hold that if something is morally wrong, then we have a reason not to do it (strong moral rationalists say that we have an overriding reason not to do it). Externalists about the relationship between reason and morality hold that the reasons for doing what is right lie outside morality—for instance, in feelings of empathy or compassion for others, or perhaps

---

[6] Sidgwick's approach now seems quite contemporary. Scanlon observes at the outset of *Being Realistic about Reasons* that, although English-language moral philosophy in the second half of the 20th century tended to focus on the meanings of moral judgments, today the pendulum has swung back towards a focus on what we have most reason to do.

in the desire to be rewarded in heaven, or to maintain one's reputation as an ethical person. Strong moral rationalism gains support from the oddity of recommending one course of conduct as morally right, while at the same time saying that it would be rational to do something else. Does not such a view undermine morality altogether? This troubling possibility is one ground for preferring the wider usage, in which what we ought to do is what it is rational to do. Then the question does not even arise; but as we have said, nothing really hangs on the terminological issue, because we still have to discuss, for example, whether it is rational to show concern for others, rather than only for oneself. We shall return to these issues in Chapters 6 and 7.

3. The Aim of Ethics

What is the point of doing moral philosophy? Are moral philosophers like some kind of secular preacher, who, appealing to reason rather than to divine revelation, tells you what you ought to do? We recognize expertise in physics, medicine, mathematics, and history, but many people find the idea that philosophers are, or can be, 'moral experts' disturbing or even offensive. We can easily accept that we do not know much about how computers work, so when our computers cease to work properly, we seek expert assistance. But what is it that moral philosophers know that other people do not? And how can that help us decide what we ought to do? On moral issues, we tend to believe, people should think for themselves.

Sidgwick believes that moral philosophy, when done well, enables us to get clearer and better answers to the central question: 'What ought I to do?' This is possible because 'the unphilosophic man is apt to hold different principles at once, and to apply different methods in more or less confused combination' (ME 6). Consistently with that view, Sidgwick sees the aim of the study of ethics as 'to systematise and free from error the apparent cognitions that most men have of the rightness or reasonableness of conduct' and to find 'valid ultimate reasons for acting or abstaining' (ME 77–8). The aim of the moral philosopher is not merely to 'define and formulate the common moral opinions of mankind', but 'to tell men what they ought to think, rather than what they do think: he is expected to transcend Common Sense in his premises, and is allowed a certain divergence from Common Sense in his conclusions' (*ME* 373).

Sidgwick believes that moral judgments are about something real, and we can get them right or we can get them wrong. Careful reflection on the nature and ground of our judgments, of the sort that he himself undertakes in *The Methods of Ethics,* will reduce the likelihood of error. So those who spend some of their time thinking and reflecting about ethics are more likely to give a true answer to the question 'What ought I to do?' than those who do not do this. That makes moral philosophers moral experts, at least relative to the unreflective others, even if Sidgwick was too modest to claim that title for himself.

4. Why Only These Methods of Ethics?

As we have seen, Sidgwick chooses only three methods—egoism, intuitionism, and utilitarianism—for detailed examination. Terence Irwin has challenged Sidgwick's justification for selecting just these methods. He points out that when Sidgwick defends his choice of methods, he says that he is interested in methods 'which are logically connected with the different ultimate reasons widely accepted' and goes on to say that 'such reasons were supplied by the notions of Happiness and Excellence or Perfection... regarded as ultimate ends, and Duty as prescribed by unconditional rules' (*ME* 78). In the case of happiness, because we can aim at it either for ourselves or universally, Sidgwick presents two methods—egoistic hedonism and universalist hedonism. One could expect, Irwin writes, that he would do the same with perfectionism, and present egoistic perfectionism and universalist perfectionism.[7] Moreover, a distinct reason for action is given by the idea that moral principles are unconditionally binding, without any further reference to any ends that they promote. That should make five methods, the first four what we now call now teleological, and the last a deontological one. Sidgwick reduces this

---

[7] See Irwin, *Development of Ethics,* 449.

to three by absorbing the goal of excellence or perfection, whether aimed at for oneself or universally, into the deontological method of perfectionism.[8]

Irwin believes that Sidgwick has no satisfactory reason for this move. First, Irwin sees no ground for dividing the goal of happiness into egoistic and universalist variants while not treating the goal of perfection in the same way, and second he sees no reason for treating teleological perfectionism and deontological intuitionism as the same method.[9]

Sidgwick has anticipated this criticism. In the first chapter of *The Methods*, he refers to the fact that the goal of happiness can be pursued either for oneself or for everyone. He then turns to the goal of excellence or perfection, and comments: 'At first sight, indeed, the same alternatives present themselves.' There is, however, a difference. We are all familiar with circumstances in which we face a choice between our own happiness and the happiness of others. Similarly, we can imagine circumstances in which we face a choice between our own perfection or excellence, and the excellence or perfection of others. (Perhaps we would have to betray our friends in order to prevent many others falling under a corrupting influence.) In the case of happiness, many thinkers urge that I should be prepared to give up my own happiness for the sake of the happiness of others, but when it comes to excellence or perfection, Sidgwick notes, 'no moralist who takes Excellence as an ultimate end has ever approved of such sacrifice' and 'no one has ever directed an individual to promote the virtue of others except in so far as this promotion is compatible with, or rather involved in, the complete realisation of Virtue in himself' (*ME* 10–11). In other words, universal perfectionism as a teleological method of ethics that parallels universal hedonism by trying to maximize what it takes to be of ultimate value is a friendless non-starter.[10]

---

[8] Irwin, *Development of Ethics*, 449.

[9] Irwin, *Development of Ethics*, 452.

[10] Anthony Skelton has pointed out to us that Hastings Rashdall, in *The Theory of Good and Evil* (a work he dedicated 'to the memory of my teachers, Thomas Hill Green and Henry

That might still leave us with four methods, rather than three; but Sidgwick also offers a reason for holding that perfectionism is not an independent method. Instead, he argues, it has to be grounded on the deontological approach that is central to his method of intuitionism:

And since Virtue is commonly conceived as the most valuable element of human Excellence...any method which takes Perfection or Excellence of human nature as ultimate End will *prima facie* coincide to a great extent with that based on what I called the Intuitional view: and I have accordingly decided to treat it as a special form of this latter. (*ME* 11)

This passage is followed by a footnote in which Sidgwick explains that later in his book he will argue that Perfectionism cannot be an Ultimate End. We shall discuss that argument in Chapter 8; here Sidgwick is limiting himself to explaining why, although the goal

---

Sidgwick'), came close to approving of the sacrifice of one's own virtue for the greater good of others. Rashdall writes:

> in considering one's own moral good, there may be cases in which it may be right, just in order to do one's duty, to adopt a course of action which may be likely on the whole to have an injurious effect on one's own character, in that sense of character in which a man is made better or worse by influences not under the immediate control of his own will. It may sometimes be right for a man to adopt a profession which in the long run may have a lowering effect upon his ideals and upon his conduct, in preference to one which would be likely to have a more elevating influence; or in innumerable other ways to face temptations which he does not know that he will always be able to resist rather than to purchase his own moral purity at the cost of other people's well-being. (*The Theory of Good and Evil*, ii. 46–7)

Skelton points out that, for Rashdall, well-being includes virtue (*The Theory of Good and Evil*, 37) and therefore this implies that Rashdall thinks it right to sacrifice one's own virtue to increase the virtue of others. On the other hand, after the passage quoted, Rashdall immediately goes on to counter such an implication by writing:

> But still, this admission does not involve any abandonment of our previous contention—that it can never be right for a man to do an immediately wrong act for the sake of any other advantage to himself or others. By choosing the greater good, he has done his duty (even in choosing a course which may in the long run react in some ways unfavourably upon his own character), and by doing his duty he has chosen the greatest good for himself. He would have become a worse man by taking the opposite course. Paradox as it may seem, he would have become a less moral man on the whole by attaching too high a value to his own Morality.

So it seems that, for Rashdall, it is not possible to sacrifice one's virtue by doing what is right, for that would not be a sacrifice of one's own virtue.

of happiness leads to two distinct methods, the goal of perfectionism does not, and indeed does not even constitute an independent
method.

Sidgwick returns to this question in his subsequent justification of
his selection of the three methods in the chapter on 'Ethical Principles
and Methods' where he admits that 'almost any method may be connected with almost any ultimate reason by means of some—often
plausible—assumption' and that this makes it difficult to classify ethical systems, as their affinities with each other may vary depending
on whether one is comparing the ultimate ends, or the method. He
says that, in deciding how to classify ethical systems, he will take the
distinctness of the methods as paramount. Since the view that perfection is the ultimate end takes right conduct to be determined by
axioms of duty that we know intuitively, it falls under the method of
intuitionism (*ME* 83–4).

Sidgwick's explanation of why he lumps together perfectionism and
common sense morality under the umbrella of the method of intuitionism may not satisfy everyone. Even those who think Sidgwick
should have treated perfectionism as a separate method, however,
must admit that Sidgwick does take the arguments in favour of perfectionism into account, when he considers whether perfectionism is
an ultimate end.

Now that we have understood why Sidgwick chooses the three
methods of egoism, intuitionism, and utilitarianism, we will consider
whether he is on firm ground in rejecting possible methods of ethics based on God's will, self-realization, and acting according to our
nature.

Sidgwick mentions that 'many religious persons' regard the fact
that God wills us to do something as the highest reason for doing
it. That statement remains true today, and makes this point worth
a fuller discussion. We share Sidgwick's difficulty in understanding
how we *could* do something that is contrary to the will of an omnisci-
ent, omnipotent creator, who must have been able to foresee, when he
created the universe, every action of every human being, and presumably has the ability to change each and every one of our actions, if he
wishes to do so. The usual story that theists tell here is that God gave

us free will, because that is so great a good that it outweighs all the bad things that humans have used their free will to do. We find this dubious on both metaphysical and ethical grounds. Metaphysically, this idea will not work unless free will is understood as agents making uncaused choices, for if our choices can have causes and still be free, God could have arranged the causes so that we freely choose to do only what he wants us to do. But we find the idea of uncaused choices mysterious, and even if we could understand it, we cannot see how we could be responsible for choices that are not caused by anything at all. Ethically this argument is dubious because it implies that the value of free will is so great that it outweighs all the atrocities that humans have committed, including the slaughters of all the wars that have ever occurred, plus the Nazi holocaust, Stalin's crimes, the killing fields of Cambodia, and so on and on, for tens of thousands of years. And then to that we must add up all the individual acts of cruelty committed on a daily basis, and we should not forget the vast amount of suffering that humans inflict on untold billions of animals. We find it hard to accept that having free will is *so* good that it can outweigh all that.

If, however, this difficulty can be overcome, the view that our knowledge of God's will gives us a rational procedure for finding out what we ought to do must still face a dilemma.

How do we know what God's will is? Has God revealed his will to us in a sacred text, or do we have to use our reason to discover what he wants us to do? If God has revealed his will to us, then discovering what we ought to do involves interpreting the sacred text, or perhaps judging between different claimants to be the one to whom God revealed his will. Either way, as Sidgwick points out, it becomes a religious activity, rather than a philosophical one, and hence 'beyond the range of our study'. This would imply that we should abandon philosophical ethics, but Sidgwick seems not to take this possibility very seriously, for he goes on to write another 430 pages of almost entirely secular ethics. This is consistent with accepting the other horn of his dilemma for the theistic moralist: that we have to use our reason to discover what God wills. On that interpretation, of course, Sidgwick's effort to discover what we have most reason to do could also be seen as an effort to discover what God wills us to do. (Sidgwick could not accept the beliefs of the Church of England, but the words he asked to have said at his funeral service suggest that he was a theist of some sort.) God makes a reappearance in the concluding chapter of *The Methods of Ethics*, not as a source of knowledge of what we ought to do, but as a possible source of a self-interested motivation for doing it, and hence of harmonizing egoism and utilitarianism. We will say more about this in Chapter 6.

Like the idea of doing what God wills, the idea of living according to nature still has followers, both in the popular sense of, say, objecting to same-sex marriage as 'unnatural' and in the more philosophical sense of natural law theory. John Stuart Mill wrote an essay opposing the appeal to nature in moral arguments, saying that the many confusing associations of the word 'nature' make it one of 'the most copious sources of false taste, false philosophy, false morality, and even bad law'.[11] Mill pointed out that by 'nature' we may mean everything that exists, or everything that exists *apart* from human beings and untouched by human agency. In the former sense, everything we do is natural, including building freeways, curing disease, making pink candy canes, and creating embryos in laboratories. In the latter sense, a virgin forest may be natural, but it is not possible for us, as human agents, to do what is natural.

Sidgwick's objection is different. He clearly has natural law theory in mind when he writes that those who use 'natural' in a way that has some positive ethical overtones usually suppose that by observing human nature we can discover how humans were designed to live. If nature is aimless, however, we have no reason to derive 'what ought to be' from 'what is'. Despite renewed attempts to defend natural law since Sidgwick wrote these words, we have seen none that show how it is possible to derive values from natural facts about the world. The 'new natural law' of theorists like Germain Grisez and John Finnis avoids this objection only by assuming that our reason can show us that there are some self-evident goods, such as life, health, knowledge,

---

[11] Mill, *On Nature*, 7.

friendship, and marriage. It thus becomes a form of intuitionism, rather than a distinct method of ethics.[12]

The third of the possible methods that Sidgwick rejects is self-realization, which today is more likely to be explored in self-help books and other works of popular psychology than in the writings of moral philosophers. The idea that we should pursue self-realization because it will make us happier is, as Sidgwick points out, a factual claim that, if true, makes the pursuit of self-realization part of the method of egoism. If, on the other hand, the idea is that we ought to realize ourselves because it is in our nature to do so, we are back to deducing values from facts about nature.

Sidgwick was right, then, to reject the three possible methods of ethics that he considers but does not accept. Perhaps, though, there are others with stronger claims that he does not even discuss? Let's take, for example, the normative views that Derek Parfit discusses in *On What Matters*, a book that in some ways can be seen as a contemporary equivalent of *The Methods of Ethics*. Like Sidgwick, Parfit focuses on three broad normative theories: Kantianism, consequentialism, and contractualism. Of these three, consequentialism is Sidgwick's utilitarianism, though in a form that leaves it open what the ultimate good is. What about Kantianism and contractualism? Sidgwick was familiar with them. Why did he not consider either of them to be a method of ethics?

Sidgwick does not include contractualism as a method of ethics because, as he tells us in the opening sentence of *The Methods of Ethics*, by a method of ethics he means any rational procedure that enables us to say what 'individual human beings' ought to do, and he then adds that he uses the word 'individual' to distinguish the study of ethics from that of politics, 'which seeks to determine the proper constitution and the right public conduct of governed societies'. It seems likely, therefore, that Sidgwick regarded contractualism as belonging to politics rather than ethics, since the leading social contract theorists, like Hobbes and Locke, were concerned, first and foremost, to set out the grounds of the obligation of the governed to obey the government.

[12] See Finnis, *Natural Law and Natural Rights*, and Germain Grisez, *The Way of the Lord Jesus*.

Contractualism today is more readily seen as an ethical theory, rather than a political one, but it still seeks to determine the right *public* standard for conduct and an answer to questions like 'In living together, what standards of right and wrong should we all accept?' or in Thomas Scanlon's version 'What standards cannot be reasonably rejected by anyone?' These are important and interesting questions, but they are not Sidgwick's 'What ought I to do?' Sidgwick of course had no way of considering the versions of contractualism later put forward by Rawls and Scanlon, but we doubt that they would have persuaded him to regard contractualism as an independent method of ethics. For one thing, Sidgwick was interested in the whole of ethics, and not only, as Rawls was, those parts of it concerned with just institutions, or as Scanlon is, with what we *owe* to each other. Moreover, as we shall explain more fully in Chapter 10, he would have denied that the answer to 'What ought I to do?' has to refer to a *public* standard, or has to be justifiable *to others* in a way that goes beyond them being simply justifiable.

As far as Kantianism goes, Sidgwick includes Kant among 'intuitional moralists' (*ME* 366), although without explaining in what respect he is an intuitionist. Sidgwick discusses Kant's ethics more fully in his *Outlines of the History of Ethics,* saying there that the English moral philosopher whom he most closely resembles is Richard Price, a contemporary of Kant, who certainly was an intuitionist. The points on which Sidgwick sees Kant and Price as in agreement include the idea that we ought to do what is right for its own sake, not for the consequences we thereby bring about; that an action is not good unless done from a good motive; that no natural inclination can provide a good motive, but rather that we should act because we see that doing so is our duty; and that this 'seeing' something as our duty comes from our reason. Sidgwick also notes, however, that Kant is more philosophically consistent than Price in recognizing that the criterion of rightness must, on such a view, depend on some formal properties of the action, rather than on the material facts, which would inevitably be related to the motive or consequences of the action.[13]

---

[13] Sidgwick, *Outlines of the History of Ethics,* 271–2.

In his posthumously published autobiographical note Sidgwick writes that, after initially agreeing with Mill that Kant's ethics is a 'grotesque failure', he later reread Kant and 'was impressed with the truth and importance of its fundamental principle—*Act from a principle or maxim that you can will to be a universal law*', which he says put the 'golden rule' of the gospel 'into a form that commended itself to my reason' (*ME* p. xvii). This recognition was apparently not sufficient, however, for Sidgwick to consider that Kant had a unique method of ethics distinct from the method of intuitionism because Sidgwick could not accept its metaphysical basis; that is, Kant's attempt to base morality on freedom. Sidgwick thought that this attempt relied on a 'fundamental confusion' between the kind of freedom that involves our reason triumphing over our inclination, and thus is achieved only when we do what is right, and the more common sense of freedom, in which we can also choose to do wrong, and which is implied by the idea that if we do choose what is wrong, we deserve blame or punishment (*ME* p. xvii). If Kant's famous principle of universal law cannot depend on material facts, however, nor on the concept of freedom, what can it be based on? Only, Sidgwick believed, on something that we grasp intuitively, and so Kant must be an intuitionist.

Sidgwick considers Kant's principle to be important, in that he thinks that no action based on a maxim that one cannot will to be a universal law could be ethical; but he does not think that the reverse holds. He argues that people who act conscientiously may hold opposing views, and each of them may be able to will that the maxim of their action should be a universal law. But since they disagree, they cannot both be right. Hence the categorical imperative cannot be the sole criterion of moral rightness, as Kant thought it was. That, Sidgwick thinks, is 'an error analogous to that of supposing that Formal Logic supplies a complete criterion of truth' (*ME* 209–10). Kantians will no doubt claim that Sidgwick has failed to understand Kant correctly, but exactly what the correct interpretation of Kant's categorical imperative is remains controversial. Since we have no desire to venture into the thickets of Kant interpretation, we will not offer an opinion on whether Kant's ethics offers a distinct and defensible method of ethics. Parfit argues that it is only defensible in a form that converges with both rule consequentialism and Scanlon's form of contractualism. If we accept this argument, the question is not whether Kant's theory can be interpreted or modified in a manner that makes it more defensible than Sidgwick believes it to be, but whether such an interpretation leaves it sufficiently distinct from other methods of ethics, including those that Sidgwick discusses.[14]

Sidgwick would no doubt classify most other plausible candidates for methods of ethics as variants of the method of intuitionism. So, for example, in considering whether 'living in accordance with nature' provides a basis for a method of ethics, Sidgwick mentions the idea of natural rights, and says that this conception faces the problem of establishing some reason, beyond mere custom, that is a plausible moral principle. This problem can only be solved, he says, by appealing to some ultimate good, such as happiness or perfection, or by appealing to some other principle, which will be known by intuition. In either case, natural rights will become an element in a different method, not a distinct method of its own (*ME* 82–3). We agree that derivations of rights tend to be based either on some form of rule consequentialism, or on intuition. How else can we decide what rights people have, and when, if ever, they may be overridden? As R. M. Hare put, 'rights are the stamping ground of intuitionists'.[15] The same could be true of virtue ethics, since virtues figure prominently in Sidgwick's discussion of intuitionism, but Sidgwick has another objection to virtue ethics, which we will consider in Chapter 8, when we discuss his view on ultimate value.

We conclude that Sidgwick does not reject plausible 'methods of ethics' in order to make it easier for him to reach his desired conclusion. Yes, he could have classified perfectionism differently, and then had four methods rather than three, and perhaps if he were writing today he could include forms of Kantianism or contractualism as distinct methods. But methods are not the same as ethical theories, and so we should not expect Sidgwick to discuss all the well-known philosophical traditions. Sidgwick tells us in the first paragraph of the

---

[14] Parfit, *On What Matters*, Volume One, chs. 8–10.
[15] Hare, 'Abortion and the Golden Rule', 203.

preface to the first edition of *The Methods* that 'it does not deal, except by way of illustration, with the history of ethical thought' (*ME* p. vii). More importantly, the fact that he does not regard every distinctive ethical theory as a method of ethics does not mean that these theories do not get considered. As we will see in the following chapters, all of the major metaethical and normative ethical theories do get discussed at some point in *The Methods*.

2

Reason and Action

1. Sidgwick on Practical Reason and the Nature of Ethical Judgments

When Sidgwick explains what a method of ethics is, he speaks of it as a 'rational procedure'. Can ethics really be based on reason? In this chapter we discuss the nature of practical reason and what we have reasons for doing. We begin, as usual, by setting out Sidgwick's position. This will lead to some of the central philosophical questions about ethics. Are moral judgments objective or subjective? What role can reason play in our decisions about what we ought to do?

Chapter 3 of book I of *The Methods of Ethics* is headed 'Ethical Judgments'. Sidgwick begins by noting that we commonly believe that 'wrong conduct is essentially irrational and can be shown to be so by argument'. We know, he acknowledges, that it is not reason alone that influences people to act ethically, but appeals to reason are nevertheless, he claims, 'an essential part of all moral persuasion' (*ME* 23). On the other hand, he continues, many people agree with Hume's view that 'Reason is, and ought only to be the slave of the passions, and can never pretend to any other office than to serve and obey them.' On Hume's view, the underlying motive for every action must always be some non-rational 'passion' or as we would now call it, desire. Reason is subordinate to desire, and it is a mistake to think that there can ever be any conflict between the two of them.

Sidgwick therefore sets out the issue between his own position and Hume's. He begins by pointing out that we have all had the experience of a conflict between our non-rational or irrational desires and our reason. We may have an appetite for some indulgence that we know to be imprudent (perhaps Sidgwick is here thinking of eating more than is good for us) or we may be angry and therefore desire to do something that we know to be unjust or unkind (here Sidgwick may have in mind a desire to strike out in some way at a person with whom we are angry, although we know it would be wrong to do so).[1] When these things happen, Hume would agree that our reason plays *some* role: we use it to work out the means to our ends ('Where can I get more of that delicious cake?' 'How can I get revenge on that brute?') and also to work out what will happen if we do the action we are con-templating ('It will be bad for my health to be so overweight' or 'My friends will shun me if they discover I am so vengeful'). The question is whether this is *all* that our reason can do in such situations. Is the situation, in fact, not so much a conflict between desire and reason, but a conflict among desires, with reason limited to the role of bring-ing to our mind facts relevant to our various desires (*ME* 23–5)?

Sidgwick argues that reason plays more than this limited role. He begins his argument indirectly, by considering what account of moral judgments can be given by those who think that deciding what we ought to do is, at bottom, a matter of choosing one set of non-rational desires over a different set of non-rational desires. The first possibility he considers is that the term 'right' applies only to means, and not to ends. This would be consistent with retaining a link between 'right' and 'in accordance with reason' for, on the view we are considering, reason can be used to judge whether a means is suitable for achieving a given end, but it cannot judge the end itself. Sidgwick no doubt has in mind Hume's instrumentalist view of reason, which is still com-monly taken for granted in contemporary economics. Against this view, Sidgwick points out that we regard some actions, for example those we call just, as 'right' irrespective of the ends that they bring about, and we also regard the choice of some ends—such as the com-mon good of society, or general happiness—as 'right'. So the proposal

---

[1] The examples are ours rather than Sidgwick's.

that 'right' applies only to the means to an end does not account for the moral judgments we make (*ME* 26).

Next Sidgwick examines the possibility that the term 'right' does not refer to any kind of judgment of reason, but instead is a description or expression of present or future feelings. As Sidgwick puts it, on this view the sentence 'Truthspeaking is right' means no more than 'the idea of truthspeaking excites in my mind a feeling of approbation or satisfaction'. What Sidgwick has to say about this view is applicable, not only to Hume and his followers, but to all those who defend some form of ethical subjectivism, including views that were fully developed only after Sidgwick's time, such as emotivism and expressivism. Sidgwick accepts that the feeling of approbation which we may call 'moral sentiment' may accompany moral judgments, but considers it absurd to maintain that a statement about the existence of this feeling is *all* we are saying when we say 'Truth ought to be spoken'. After all, if one person says 'Truth ought to be spoken' and another says 'Truth ought not to be spoken' these propositions contradict each other; but it is perfectly possible that the two people who utter those two different sentences have different feelings of approbation. So true coexisting facts—the facts about what these two people approve—result in two contradictory propositions, and that is impossible (*ME* 26–7).

To this argument against subjectivist theories of ethics, Sidgwick anticipates the objection that even if, when we make moral judgments, we think we are stating propositions that can be true or false, and can contradict each other, all that we have any ground for saying, or all that the reasonable person can, on reflection, affirm, is the subjective fact of the feeling of approval or disapproval.[2] Sidgwick agrees that we utter many statements that because of a certain form seem to be about something objective but really express only our subjective feelings—his examples are statements like 'The air is sweet' or 'The food is disagreeable'. If such statements are challenged we will probably be content to fall back on affirming that we feel these things to be so. But this is not the case with moral approbation, Sidgwick argues,

---

[2] Sidgwick here anticipates the sceptical view that John Mackie was later to put forward, generally known as the 'error theory'. See Mackie, *Ethics: Inventing Right and Wrong*.

because then we have the conviction 'that the conduct approved is "really" right—*i.e.* that it cannot, without error, be disapproved by any other mind'[3] (*ME* 27).

This point shows only that we do not think of our moral judgments as simply expressing our feelings; but we still do not know that this conviction is well founded. Sidgwick points out that when we change our minds about things on which we have well-formed moral habits, our previous feelings may persist despite the change in our judgment. If, for instance, we are in the habit of telling the truth, but then come to believe that in some peculiar circumstances we ought not to tell the truth, we may still feel repugnance when we do not tell the truth; but this feeling of repugnance is compatible with, and quite different from, our judgment that we are doing what is right. To what, then, does that judgment refer? Some of the moral philosophers who regard ethical judgments as based on feelings hold that these judgments do not refer to our own individual feelings, but to the feelings of others in our society, or perhaps of all humanity.[4] But if we come to a new moral conviction that differs not only from our own previous conviction, but from the convictions of everyone else in our society, or even in the entire world, the fact of this difference will not necessarily prevent us continuing to hold firm to the new conviction.

Up to this point Sidgwick has tried to prove that our moral judgments are not statements about feelings of approbation or aversion. Next he dismisses the view that the meaning of a moral judgment is bound up with the existence of sanctions that may punish or reward people in accordance with whether they do what is right. Sidgwick considers this mistaken because when we say that a man is morally bound to do something, we do not mean merely that he will be subject to sanctions—whether legal or social—if he does not do it (*ME*

---

[3] Like most philosophers until very recently, Sidgwick was here relying on his own observations. There is now some research that seeks to discover whether ordinary people do in fact have the conviction that, if two people reach conflicting moral judgments, one of them must be in error. See e.g. Sarkissian *et al.*, 'Folk Moral Relativism', 482–505.

[4] Sidgwick may have had Adam Smith in mind, for Smith defends such a view in his *Theory of the Moral Sentiments*, part III, ch. 1.

29). There are many things that we think people ought to do, although we know that if they do not do it, they will not face any serious penalties; and sometimes, when we think that the conventionally accepted morality of our society is wrong, we may strongly believe that something is the right thing to do, even though we know that we will suffer social sanctions for doing it.

After this Sidgwick considers the possibility that the meaning of 'I ought to do this' does require that there will be a penalty if I do not do it, but the penalty is divinely, rather than socially, ordained, so that the statement means 'God will punish me if I do not'. Sidgwick rejects this, first because some people do not believe in the existence of divine punishment and yet still have moral convictions, and secondly because if we accept this understanding of the moral terms, then we can hardly say that it is *right* or *just* for God to punish sinners and reward the righteous, because this would be saying nothing more than that God *will* punish and reward these people (*ME* 31).

What, then, does Sidgwick think the moral terms *do* mean? Sidgwick's answer is that 'the notion which these terms have in common is too elementary to admit of any formal definition'. It cannot be resolved into any simpler constituent parts. All we can do, he thinks, is try to make it clearer by saying how it relates to other notions in our moral thought, and distinguishing it from different notions with which it is liable to be confused (*ME* 32).

The judgment that 'X ought to be done', when taken in 'the stricter ethical sense' is for Sidgwick a 'dictate' or 'precept' of reason. By that he means, first, that a moral judgment is 'a possible object of knowledge' and this means that all rational beings would come to the same view, if they judge truly (*ME* 33). Secondly, knowing the truth of a moral judgment provides an impulse or motive to action in 'rational beings as such'. Sidgwick does not offer an explicit account of what a 'rational being as such' would be like, but we do get clues to what he has in mind when he goes on to contrast such beings with human beings, in whom he says that knowledge of the truth of a moral judgment is only one motive among others, and not always, and perhaps not usually, a predominant one. He then adds that the very idea that a moral judgment is an 'imperative' suggests some kind of conflict between reason and non-rational impulses, and the same is true of terms like 'ought', 'duty', and 'moral obligation', which therefore 'cannot be applied to the actions of rational beings to whom we cannot attribute impulses conflicting with reason', although we can say that what such beings do is right (*ME* 34–5). From this we can conclude that when Sidgwick refers to 'rational beings as such' he has in mind beings lacking any impulses conflicting with reason. This is consistent with the fact that the only other passages in *The Methods* in which he uses this phrase are in book III, in a special note on the argument by which Kant seeks to establish the duty of promoting the happiness of others. Sidgwick scrutinizes Kant's claim that 'all rational beings as such are ends to each' and therefore 'humanity exists as an end in itself' (*ME* 390).[5] Sidgwick does not consider Kant's argument cogent, but he does appear to accept as conceivable Kant's idea of rational beings as such, and Kant's assumption that such beings would differ from human beings in not being subject to non-rational impulses, which includes 'empirical desires and aversions'. Thus rational beings as such would only have desires and impulses that were given to them by reason. Presumably they would lack the desires and aversions that human beings, with a non-rational side to their nature, happen to have, but which other rational beings, with a different empirical nature, might not have.

For now, however, let us return to human beings, for whom moral judgments are a kind of 'unconditional or categorical imperative'. Sidgwick observes that some people may simply deny that they can find in their consciousness any such imperative. If they lack completely any notion of moral obligation, Sidgwick says that he doesn't know how to impart it to them (*ME* 35). But he thinks that many of those who say that they lack this notion may really mean only that they lack the notion of an obligation that should be fulfilled for its own sake, rather than because of its consequences. These people would not reject the idea that there are some universal ends (like general happiness) at which it is ultimately reasonable to aim, and if they

---

[5] Sidgwick is here quoting, in his own translation, from Kant's *Groundwork of the Metaphysic of Morals*.

would accept this idea, then Sidgwick would say to them that to recognize an end as ultimately reasonable already involves recognizing that there is an obligation to do what will bring about that end.

Moreover, even egoists who do not recognize universal ends, but do recognize their own interest as something at which it is ultimately reasonable to aim, still accept that there is a 'dictate of reason'. For on this view, when the end of pursuing one's own interest conflicts with one's irrational desires, reason directs that we pursue our interests. Hence the idea of what we 'ought' to do has a place in an egoistic view as much as in any ordinary moral system (*ME* 35–6).

What, though, if the sceptic about practical reason goes further still, and denies that reason prescribes *any* end at all? The sceptic might, for example, take the view that the agent's own greatest good is not something that he 'ought to' do, or has any kind of obligation to aim at, but rather is merely the ultimate end he most desires (*ME* 36). Sidgwick argues that, even on that view, the notion of 'ought' remains. There will still be hypothetical imperatives that prescribe the fittest means to any end at which we are aiming. Imagine that a doctor tells you that if you wish to be healthy, you ought to rise early. This is not the same as saying that early rising is an indispensable condition of being healthy. The word 'ought' says something more than a description of the physiological facts. It implies that, if you were to adopt the end of preserving your health, and refuse to take the means that are necessary to achieving this end, even when you can do so at no cost to anyone, including yourself, you would be unreasonable (*ME* 37). This is what the doctor's suggestion that, if health is your end, you ought to rise early, adds to the mere factual statement that if you do not rise early you will not be healthy. To do without the basic notion that something ought to be done is much more difficult than we might at first imagine. Hence sweeping scepticism about the use of the moral 'ought' is not an easy way of resisting Sidgwick's idea that ethical judgments present themselves to us as dictates of reason.

As we have just seen, in the chapter on 'Ethical Judgments' Sidgwick argued that our knowledge of the truth of a moral judgment can provide a motive for action in human beings, although it may be only one motive among others. This view seems directly contrary to Hume's view that only desires can move us to action, and so requires further explanation and defence. In the following chapter, on 'Pleasure and Desire', Sidgwick returns to the topic of reason as a motivating force, this time discussing what he calls 'the emotional characteristics of the impulse that prompts us to obey the dictates of Reason' (*ME* 39). The reference to an impulse with some emotional aspects now looks closer to Hume's view, especially given that Sidgwick tells us that in *The Methods* '"Desire" is primarily regarded as a felt impulse or stimulus to actions tending to the realisation of what is desired'[6] (*ME* 43 n. 8). Does this mean that Sidgwick thinks there is some emotionally laden impulse that everyone experiences when they grasp the truth of a moral judgment? He acknowledges that these 'emotional characteristics' can be different in different people and even for the same person they can vary at different times, and he gives some examples: for someone who supports rational egoism 'the ruling impulse' can be '"calm" or "cool" self-love'. For a utilitarian it can be 'to do what is judged to be reasonable as such', which is commonly blended with 'sympathy and philanthropic enthusiasm'. Some take reason to be a source of truth external to themselves, and for them there may be a 'sentiment of Reverence for Authority' which could be seen impersonally, or as reverence for a supreme being. This conception of reason as an external authority can be seen as something that is 'irresistibly forced on the reflective mind' and thus as opposed to our own will; alternatively, however, we can identify our self with reason, in which case accepting the authority of reason becomes a form of self-respect, and we can even be moved by the impulse of freedom, if we see our sensual impulses as liable to enslave our rational self. A different kind of impulse towards doing what is right is aspiration or admiration of the moral beauty of virtue, and there are other possible 'phases of emotion' too. What all these impulses have in common with each other is the characteristic of being 'inseparable from an apparent cognition—implicit or explicit, direct or indirect—of *rightness* in the conduct to which they prompt'. There will be

---

[6] For further discussion see Shaver, 'Sidgwick on Moral Motivation'. We owe several of the quotes in this chapter to Shaver's fine scholarly essay.

differences in 'the efficacy of these different emotions' but their 'primary practical effect does not appear to vary so long as the cognition of rightness remains unchanged' (*ME* 40).

Sidgwick returns to this idea in the final chapter of *The Methods* when he is discussing the extent to which feelings of sympathy can motivate us to act in accordance with utilitarianism. In the course of this discussion he distinguishes sympathy from what he calls 'strictly moral feelings'. As an example of a strictly moral feeling, he gives the 'sense of the ignobility of Egoism' which he views as 'the normal emotional concomitant or expression of the moral intuition that the Good of the whole is reasonably to be preferred to the Good of a part' (*ME* 500). As we shall see in Chapter 5, this intuition is one he takes to be self-evident, and therefore a 'dictate of reason'. So Sidgwick is saying that there are some feelings that are the 'normal emotional concomitant or expression' of a self-evident moral truth that we grasp by our reason. At the same time, he acknowledges that the exact proportions of these strictly moral feelings, and of other feelings such as sympathy, will vary between individuals and at different times in the life of a single individual. The contrast with Hume has now reappeared, for it seems that, according to Sidgwick, our belief that something is right can lead us to act. Granted, it leads us to act by giving rise to an impulse or feeling, but nevertheless for Sidgwick motivation can start with a cognition—that is, with grasping the truth of a moral judgment. Ethics, Sidgwick tells us, is primarily concerned with these cognitions and its object is to try to systematize them and free them from error.

2. The Debate over Objectivity in Ethics

The twentieth century saw a surge of interest in meta-ethics, or more specifically, in questions about what it is to make a moral judgment and whether moral judgments can be true or false. Much of the work done in ethics during the first half of the century was a response to the argument against the 'naturalistic fallacy' presented by G. E. Moore in *Principia Ethica*. Moore, a student of Sidgwick's, argued that many philosophers before him, including John Stuart Mill, had committed the fallacy by attempting to define words such as 'good' in terms of natural qualities like 'pleasant' or 'desired'. This was not a new point— Sidgwick had already insisted that moral notions are of a different character from notions describing empirical qualities like 'pleasant' or 'desired'. Sidgwick, unlike Moore, did not claim any novelty for this insight, which goes back to earlier English philosophers like Ralph Cudworth, Samuel Clarke, Richard Price, and Thomas Reid.[7]

Moore held that the way to avoid the naturalistic fallacy is to accept that the term 'good' is like 'yellow' in referring to a simple, indefinable quality. W. D. Ross, the leading British moral philosopher of the 1920s and 1930s, agreed with Sidgwick and Moore that the basic moral concepts are indefinable, although as we shall see in the next chapter, he disagreed sharply with Sidgwick and Moore on normative questions. In 1936 Alfred Ayer, then only 26, published *Language, Truth and Logic*, a manifesto for logical positivism, in which he agreed with Sidgwick and Moore that the basic moral notions are 'unanalyzable', but for completely different reasons. Ayer claimed that the reason why ethical notions are unanalyzable is that they are 'pseudo-concepts'. Moral judgments that use those concepts cannot be true or false. Instead they are used to express our positive or negative attitudes or emotions towards the subject of the judgment. This approach, which became known as 'emotivism', gave rise to a whole new theory, or family of theories, about the meaning of ethical terms. Because emotivists held that moral judgments do not state anything that can be known, emotivism is one of a family of theories known as 'noncognitivism'.

Many philosophers thought that emotivism was unsatisfactory because it fails to explain the role that reason plays in discussion about moral issues. R. M. Hare attempted to overcome this weakness by developing a different noncognitivist view, according to which moral judgments are prescriptions. On this view, moral judgments do not state facts. They belong to the same general type of sentence as imperatives, but differ from ordinary imperatives because to make

---

[7] For the history of the precursors to Moore's naturalistic fallacy argument, see Prior, *Logic and the Basis of Ethics*.

a judgment that one 'ought' to do something is to prescribe that it be done universally. To reach the conclusion that we can prescribe an action universally, we need to use our reason to ascertain whether we are able to accept that prescription in all situations, real or hypothetical, that are similar in their universal features to the situation in which I find myself. Hence reason enters into the discussion, at least to this extent. More recently, Allan Gibbard and Simon Blackburn have developed another form of noncognitivism known as expressivism. All these noncognitivist theories deny that ethical judgments state any kind of belief, or assert anything that can properly be judged to be true or false, at least in a strong sense of true and false. Gibbard and Blackburn think that there is a 'minimalist' sense of truth in which moral judgments can be true or false; this is not, however, the sense of 'true' that most people have in mind when they say that it is true that more people live in China than in the United States. In general, noncognitivists hold that we make moral judgments in order to express our feelings or attitudes, or to prescribe certain actions, and to encourage others to take the same attitude or do those actions.

Sidgwick is strongly opposed to this whole approach. Moral utterances state beliefs, he holds, and are uttered to present the truth about our obligations and our reasons for actions. Sidgwick is therefore a cognitivist and an objectivist. The latter term is more specific because it is possible to be a cognitivist and a subjectivist, holding that moral judgments state beliefs about something that can be true or false, but denying that moral judgments present some truth that holds for everyone, independently of their attitudes or those of their culture or community. For a cognitivist subjectivist, whether the judgment 'helping the poor is good' is true or false depends on the attitude of the person making the judgment. Cultural relativists are also cognitivists, for they hold that the truth conveyed by 'stealing is bad' is that the society or culture to which the speaker belongs disapproves of stealing. Therefore for the following discussion we will focus on the more significant distinction between subjectivists and objectivists, rather than on that between cognitivists and noncognitivists. We will argue, along Sidgwickian lines, that subjectivism has such implausible implications that we should reject it in favour of objectivism.

In the following section, we focus on what we see as the core of the dispute between subjectivism and objectivism: whether there can be objective reasons for action. We see this as more fundamental than disputes about whether some form of noncognitivism gives a better account of the meaning of the moral terms than cognitivism. If we answer this latter question negatively, rejecting noncognitivism, we would still need to ask whether any naturalistic cognitivist account of the meaning of the moral terms can overcome the familiar objections to naturalism. If they cannot, then Sidgwick's non-naturalist cognitivism is vindicated. This would, however, be a lengthy discussion that would take us far from Sidgwick's understanding of ethics as concerned with reasoning about what we ought to do. Although Sidgwick does, as we have seen, pay some attention to the accounts that were put forward by philosophers before him of the meanings of statements like 'I ought to do this', he was always much more concerned with how we can reason about what we ought to do.[8]

3. Why Subjectivism is Implausible

An objectivist believes that we should base our judgments about what we ought to do on normative reasons for action rather than on the desires we have when we decide what to do. In a given situation we may have several conflicting reasons, each of which would give us sufficient grounds to act in a certain way. Sometimes one of these reasons will be of greater importance and will outweigh all the others; it will then be a decisive reason, one that leaves us with only one rational action. We can have reasons to act that we do not know about: I may have a reason not to sail my yacht out into the ocean, as there is a storm coming, but I do not know this fact about the weather. An objectivist also believes that we can have reasons to act even if our inclinations are, on balance, strongly opposed to acting on that reason. We may say that we have a reason to help a drunken man find shelter on a winter night so cold that without shelter he would die,

---

[8] For a forceful defence of non-naturalist cognitivism, see Parfit, *On What Matters*, Volume Two, Part Six.

even if the revulsion we feel at the idea of approaching him overpowers any desire we have to save his life.

Subjectivists deny that reasons can be objective. When they talk about our reasons for action, they mean only reasons that are conditional on us having certain desires and wants. Reason might then tell us how best to satisfy those desires. Sidgwick rejects this view, using as his example 'a man who declines to take the right means to attain his own happiness, on no other ground than that he does not care about happiness'. Sidgwick comments that most of us would regard this as irrational (*ME* 7). Subjectivists would, presumably, deny that this is irrational. Derek Parfit offers a more specific example of the kind of thing that Sidgwick describes: the case of a person with 'Future Tuesday Indifference'.[9] This person cares about his pleasures and pains in just the same way as we do, with one important exception—he doesn't care about them if they happen on any future Tuesday. If given a choice between slight pain or agony, he always prefers the slight pain, unless the agony will occur on a future Tuesday. So, he will choose slight pain on Sunday rather than agony on Monday, but since he is indifferent to what happens to him on future Tuesdays, he will choose agony on Tuesday rather than slight pain on Monday. His strange thinking is not based on any false beliefs. He knows that the pain he will experience will be his, and he understands very well the difference between slight pain and agony. He thinks:

I know that some future event would cause me to have some period of agony. Even after ideal deliberation, I have no desire to avoid this agony. Nor do I have any other desire or aim whose fulfillment would be prevented either by this agony, or by my having no desire to avoid this agony.[10]

A subjectivist would have to admit that there is nothing irrational about the person with Future Tuesday Indifference. He simply differs from us in what he desires. But that seems implausible. As Parfit puts it: 'That some ordeal would be much more painful is a strong reason

---

[9] Parfit, *Reasons and Persons*, 124, and *On What Matters*, Volume One, 56.

[10] Parfit, *On What Matters*, Volume One, 74. Parfit builds upon an example and an argument given by Thomas Nagel. Nagel described a person who is going to travel to Rome and realizes that in future he will regret that he doesn't know any Italian, though he has no desire to learn it now. See Nagel, *The Possibility of Altruism*, 58–9.

not to prefer it. That this ordeal would be on a future Tuesday is no reason to prefer it.'

We agree that the person with Future Tuesday Indifference is behaving irrationally. It is just crazy to be indifferent to agony when it happens on a future Tuesday, while dreading it as much as we all do on any other day. If today is Monday, and the person with Future Tuesday Indifference has, in order to avoid the momentary pain of a straightforward injection in his arm, just chosen to suffer eight hours of agony tomorrow, then tomorrow—a *present* Tuesday, not a *future* Tuesday—he will not be indifferent to the agony he is feeling, and he will bitterly regret the decision he made today. Moreover he will know that it was his choice that led to his present agony. Granted, we all make mistakes, but most of us learn from them. The man with Future Tuesday Indifference never does. If next Monday he is faced with the same choice, he will make the same decision, and will again bitterly regret it the next day.

People with Future Tuesday Indifference may not exist, but we all sometimes behave a little like the person with Future Tuesday Indifference. We may postpone going to the dentist, for instance, even though we are well aware that the postponement will mean more pain in future, overall, than we would experience if we go to the dentist now. Our acting in this way seems clearly irrational but, if it is the best means to satisfying our present desires, a subjectivist cannot say that it is irrational.

It is important to notice that we are talking here of *future* agony. If I am now experiencing a sensation that I have no desire to stop, then what I am feeling could not be agony. This is true by definition, for agony is a severe form of pain and pain differs from other states of mind at least partly in that it is a state of mind that, considered for its own sake, gives rise to a desire that it should end. (We discuss how best to understand pain and pleasure in Chapter 9.) But it is compatible with this definition of agony that I have no present desire to avoid a future experience of agony.

A subjectivist might try to argue that the fact that I can predict that in future I will regret the choice that leads to my experiencing agony (whereas I will not in future reject the choice that leads to my experiencing slight momentary pain) gives me now a desire-based reason to choose differently. But for a subjectivist, my predictions about my future feelings cannot give me a present reason unless I have a present desire to avoid that future regret. Future feelings and desires do not exist now. Therefore unless I have some present desire about them, subjectivists cannot claim that my future feelings can give me a reason to act in a certain way now. Subjectivists believe that desires give me reasons. In the absence of a relevant present desire, however, the reason would have to precede, and give rise to, the desire. To hold that my future desires give me present reasons would be to import a concept of prudential rationality—indeed, as we shall see in Chapter 5, a version of the axiom of prudence that Sidgwick believes to be a self-evident objective principle of reason—into subjectivism. That would be the kind of account of reasons for action that an objectivist might give and a subjectivist cannot accept.

Finally, a subjectivist might attempt to argue that Future Tuesday Indifference is irrational because the names of the days of the week are arbitrary—we might have chosen a calendar based on a 10-day week, as the French revolutionaries did—and even a subjectivist can rule out desires that are based on purely arbitrary features.[11] This claim is dubious, because a subjectivist must accept desires as they are, and people do have desires based on arbitrary features. For example, a Polish nationalist might desire to defend the present boundaries of Poland, even though this desire is to defend a territory that was defined in arbitrary ways at the end of the Second World War. But even if we allow the subjectivist to regard desires as irrational when they are based on something as arbitrary as the days of the week, we can restate Future Tuesday Indifference as, say, Future Full Moon Indifference, and it is no less irrational to be indifferent to agony that occurs around the time of some future full moon than it is to be indifferent to agony that occurs on a future Tuesday.[12]

---

[11] See Smith, 'Desires, Values, Reasons, and the Dualism of Practical Reason', 120.

[12] We owe this point to Richard Chappell, 'Natural Arbitrariness'.

4.   Why Morality is Not like Football

Many people believe that certain moral judgments are true independently of anyone's attitudes, including their own. We believe, for
example, that a child's death is normally something bad. We think that
we have reasons to prevent a child's death even if we have no desire to
save the child, and no other kind of favourable attitude towards saving the child, and do not particularly feel like preventing the child's
death. As Parfit puts it: 'Subjective theories imply that we have no
object-given reasons to want ourselves or others to live happy lives,
and no such reasons to have any other good aim.'[13] Subjectivists would
accept this because on the view they hold there are no object-given
reasons for anything. But they would deny that it follows from this
that we have no reasons to do anything, or that, as Parfit puts it, 'nothing matters'. Instead, they would argue, we can have reasons based
on our desires—both self-interested desires and altruistic or compassionate ones—for wanting ourselves and others to live happy lives,
and for various other good aims. Parfit argues, however, that subjectivists cannot sustain this line of argument, because for them to think
that we have such subjective reasons for wanting these things, they
would need to argue that our desires and attitudes give us reasons
for wanting them. But for subjectivists, either all our desires and attitudes give us reasons for acting, or none of them do—they cannot set
criteria for deciding, independently of the desires themselves, which
desires give us reasons for acting. That would lead to some form of
objectivism. To hold that all my desires give me reasons for acting, we
would have to accept that my desire to cause myself to be in agony, for
its own sake, gives me a reason for action, as does my desire to count
the number of blades of grass in my lawn. Since people have no reason to cause themselves agony for its own sake, nor to count blades
of grass in lawns, we should reject this view, and reject the idea that
desires, in themselves, give us reasons for action.[14]

---

[13]   Parfit, *On What Matters*, Volume One, 106.
[14]   Parfit, *On What Matters*, Volume One, 81–91, 101–7; the example of counting blades of
grass comes from Rawls, *A Theory of Justice*, 379.

A subjectivist can claim that, although there is nothing that matters impartially, or on its own, this doesn't show that nothing matters to me or to you. But a subjectivist's statement that something matters to someone can only describe the psychological fact that the person does care about something. To this Parfit says: 'We all know that people care about certain things. We hoped that philosophers, or other wise people, would tell us more than that.'[15]

Simon Blackburn is an expressivist, and therefore a subjectivist, in the sense in which we have been using the term, but he thinks that it makes sense not only to make moral judgments like 'kicking babies for fun is wrong' but also to say that this moral judgment is true, and that anyone who thinks otherwise is mistaken.[16] To accept Blackburn's view, however, brings us close to some kind of mental schizophrenia. If I utter the sentence 'It is wrong that people are starving to death in Somalia and we are doing nothing to help them' and at the same time think that in saying this I am just expressing my attitude, rather than stating anything that is true, then there is no way in which my judgment can express the idea that what I am saying is important independently of my present attitude toward it. I can of course *say* that the situation I have described is wrong, and would be wrong even if I were to change my mind about it, but in doing so I am still only expressing my present attitude. Someone who knows me well might say to me:

You want people to help victims of famine and you want Brazil to win the next World Cup. You seem to be just as passionate about football as you are about help for the starving—maybe more so. But your present desires give me no reason to support Brazil, and no reason to help the famine victims.

What can I say, on the subjectivist view, to persuade my friend that there is a difference in my attitude to these two things? Most of us would try to give reasons why it is wrong not to help to alleviate a famine, and these reasons might refer to, for example, the preventable suffering of the victims. On the other hand we would acknowledge that one's choice to support a football team may be arbitrary.

---

[15] Parfit, *On What Matters*, Volume One, 107.
[16] See e.g. Blackburn, *Ruling Passions*, 317–18, and more generally, 304–20.

Perhaps we would explain it—by saying, for instance, that we had a close friend from Brazil, with whom we used to watch the games. But this is an explanation more than it is a reason, and it is certainly not a reason for others to support Brazil. Since expressivists do not believe that we can ground our moral judgments in reasons, they cannot rely upon this difference to distinguish their attitudes to the great moral issues of our day from their attitudes to football games. Nor is it easy to see how else they can draw that distinction. Yet there is surely a sense in which, although millions of people may care passionately about who wins a football game, the outcomes of sporting contests do not *really* matter. (We are here putting aside secondary consequences of the outcomes of sporting contests, such as the happiness or misery of the supporters of the teams, which may really matter.) Hence if expressivists cannot explain how our attitudes to moral issues are significantly different from, and matter more than, our allegiances to sporting teams, it seems that expressivists cannot defend the claim that moral issues *really* matter.

5. Can Objective Moral Truths Motivate?

For Hume when I say that X ought to be done, my judgment results from a particular kind of 'passion' or feeling about doing X. This feeling is also the basis of my motivation to do X. It moves me, in the appropriate circumstances, to do X. Sidgwick takes a different view. He regards the judgment 'X ought to be done' as essentially a 'dictate' or 'precept' of reason. The judgment, in other words, states that there is a normative reason for doing X and Sidgwick thinks that it can motivate us. Early in *The Methods* he writes that 'we are moved to action not by moral judgment alone, but also by desires and inclinations that operate independently of moral judgment', which implies that moral judgment alone can move us, to some extent, without other desires and inclinations; and he repeats this idea when he says that the judgment 'X ought to be done' is 'only one motive among others which are liable to conflict with it, and it is not always—perhaps not usually—a predominant motive' (*ME* 5, 34). We are here talking of 'motivation to act' in a sense that does not imply that we do act in accordance with the motivation. Rather, we mean that whatever is motivating me to do X inclines me towards doing X, but whether it is sufficient to lead me to do X will depend on the circumstances, and especially on the strength of the conflicting motivations I have. The normative motivation for doing X may also be supported by other motives for doing what is right: 'we do not conceive', Sidgwick writes, 'that it is by reason alone that men are influenced to act rightly'[17] (*ME* 23).

If objective reasons can motivate us, can they do that directly, without the intervention of a desire or feeling? Or is it, as at least some of Sidgwick's comments suggest, that objective reason can only motivate us by producing in us an emotion or desire that is the 'normal concomitant or expression' of our appreciating the objective reasons that we have to act in a particular way? Kant thought that objective reason can act directly on our will. The categorical imperative, he claimed, is rationally binding on all moral agents, irrespective of what desires or passions they may have.[18] Thomas Nagel, in *The Possibility of Altruism*, also holds that objective reasons can motivate us directly. He argues that the assumption that all motivation 'has desire at its source' is either obviously false or trivially true. To make this point he distinguishes motivated and unmotivated desires. If I am hungry, my desire to eat is unmotivated—I just have it. On the other hand, if I notice that there is no food at home, and so form the desire to find a grocery store, my desire is motivated by my knowledge of the lack of food in my home. (Forming this desire does not imply that I am now hungry.) The claim that all motivation is based on unmotivated desire is obviously false, as the example shows. If motivated desires are included, however, then the ascription of a desire to every intentional act adds nothing to the explanation of the intentional act, and the claim that all motivation is based on desire becomes one about the way we use the words 'motivation'

---

[17] For experimental confirmation of this commonplace observation, including laboratory manipulation of the degree to which altruistic motivation determines the action chosen, see Fehr and Fischbacher, 'The Nature of Human Altruism', 785–91.

[18] Kant argues for this claim in his *Groundwork of the Metaphysics of Morals*.

and 'desire' and hence a tautology.[19] For instance, suppose I believe that I ought to do what I can to reduce suffering, and so I give to a charity that protects children from malaria. Clearly, I am motivated to reduce suffering. Perhaps I have had a strong emotional response to images of children suffering from malaria and this makes me give to the charity. That would be an unmotivated desire, like hunger. Perhaps, though, I have no such emotional response, and instead my desire to give is wholly motivated by my belief that I ought to do what I can to reduce suffering. Saying that I am giving because I *desire* to reduce suffering does not enable us to distinguish between these two very different possibilities. In fact it adds no further information to the statement that I was motivated to give by my belief that I ought to reduce suffering.

This argument shows that insisting that all motivation must be based on desire does not get us very far. Nevertheless, the idea that normative reasons, unaided by desires, can motivate us remains somewhat mysterious. Those who defend this view of the motivating power of objective normative judgments need to explain how people can accept a moral judgment as true, but not care at all about that truth and not be motivated to refrain from acting contrary to that judgment.[20] In contrast, many philosophers regard it as a major advantage of a noncognitivist theory of ethics that it provides a necessary connection between making a moral judgment and being motivated to act on it. If my moral judgment already expresses my positive emotion or attitude towards doing X, there is no problem in explaining why I am motivated to do X. If we think that moral motivation is *internal* to a moral judgment—in other words, if we think that the judgment 'I ought to do X' implies 'I have some motivation to do X'—then objectivists have a problem. They must explain how the existence of an objective truth could give rise to motivation in everyone who comes to believe it, even though the emotions and attitudes that human beings have vary with their individual nature and

[19] Nagel, *The Possibility of Altruism*, 27–30.
[20] Mackie makes this point in *Ethics: Inventing Right and Wrong*, 38–42.

circumstances. Objectivity in ethics seems to be at odds with the idea that motivation is internal to morality.[21]

Sidgwick says two different things that we can draw upon in order to solve this problem, and in the remainder of this chapter we will develop his comments and assess his position. In order to understand the significance of Sidgwick's claims, however, we first need to draw a distinction between normative reasons and motivating reasons.

Consider first a situation in which you have a reason to do something, but do not know this, because you lack the relevant information. You want to visit your friend in the city, and you believe that the train is the best way to get there, so you go to the station. But the train drivers are on strike today. If you knew this, you would go to the bus stop, for when the trains are not operating, the bus is the best way to get to the city. An objectivist about reason might say that, in the absence of a belief that the trains are on strike, the reason you have to go to the bus stop does not motivate you but you have a reason to go there all the same. Hume would have put this in a different way, but his theory has no deep difficulty in explaining this sense of not being motivated by a reason for action, because he accepts that reason can show us which means are conducive to satisfying our desires. So if you have the relevant information, reason can tell you that going to the bus stop is the best way of satisfying your desire to visit your friend. In that sense, Hume could say that, when you are ignorant about the train strike, you have a reason to go to the bus stop, because it would motivate you, if you were fully informed.

Now let us imagine a different case, in which you do not lack any relevant information. Suppose that you feel a twinge in your tooth and you know from previous experience that this is likely to develop into an agonizing toothache. For some people this would become a motivating reason, because they would now have a desire to avoid the future toothache, but you don't care about things that are more than a day or two in the future. What you now desire is not to experience the mild discomfort that, if you go to the dentist, you will experience this

---

[21] This (together with Hume's theory of motivation) makes up the moral problem discussed by Smith in *The Moral Problem*.

afternoon. The fact that this is the only relevant desire you have now, however, does not mean that you have no reason to go to the dentist. On the contrary, you do have a reason for going to the dentist—if you do not go to the dentist today you will experience much more pain in future than you would experience if you go. To be more precise, you have a normative reason for going to the dentist but given your present set of desires, this is not for you a motivating reason to go.

What account would Hume give of this situation? He draws a distinction between calm and violent passions, and he can say that your more violent passion to avoid going to the dentist this afternoon has overridden your calmer passion to experience less pain overall. But in the example we described, there was no calm passion to experience less pain overall. And even if there were such a calm passion, Hume cannot say of someone that it was irrational of her to allow the violent passion to override the calm passion, for to do that he would need to say that the weaker passion overrode the stronger, and he has no way of reaching such a judgment of the relative strengths of the passions, at the time you made your choice, independently of the action that resulted. Hume himself states that it is not contrary to reason 'to prefer even my own acknowledg'd lesser good to my greater, and have a more ardent affection for the former than for the latter'.[22] The problem is not how to give an account of such choices, by explaining what desires moved the person to make the choice, but to find a basis for critical assessment of the choice that was made. For the Humean, it seems, there is none.

In the example we have just given, only your own interests are at stake, but the same problem arises, perhaps even more acutely, when other reasons are involved. Suppose that you can save the life of a child, with no more than minor inconvenience to yourself. This gives you a normative reason to save the life of the child. Perhaps you do not know that it is so easy for you to save the life of the child, and if you did know this, it would be in accordance with your desires to do so. Then the follower of Hume will agree that there is a sense in which you have a reason to save the life of the child, just as in our first

---

[22] Hume, *A Treatise of Human Nature*, 2.3.3.6.

example, you had a reason to go to the bus stop. But perhaps you have this information, and simply do not desire to save the life of the child. Then the Humean cannot say that you have a reason to save the life of the child. Sidgwick, on the other hand, can say that you have a normative reason to save the child. He must then face the further question: how is this normative reason connected with your motivation to save the child?

A normative reason could motivate directly, without giving rise to any desire except in the trivial sense of a desire motivated by appreciation of the normative reason; or it could motivate by giving rise to a desire that is distinct from the normative reason itself. Sidgwick suggests the first possibility when he says that a moral judgment is a 'dictate of reason' that gives rise to an impulse or motive to action, for although he first says that it does this in rational beings as such, he implies that it is also to some extent motivating in humans when he says that in us it is 'only one motive among others which are liable to conflict with it' and is not necessarily or perhaps not usually a predominant motive (*ME* 34). He suggests the second possibility when he describes emotions or impulses that are inseparable from, or the normal concomitant of, or an expression of, the judgment that an act is right.

Nagel's argument, in *The Possibility of Altruism*, succeeds in showing that direct normative motivation is *possible*. It cannot be rejected simply by repeating the dogma that all motivation is based on desire. On the other hand, it seems impossible to prove that normative reasons actually do motivate human beings directly. We can never exclude the possibility that a person who appears to be directly motivated by a normative reason is not in fact motivated by something else.

What of the idea that accepting a moral judgment has some kind of normal concomitant desire that motivates us to act in accordance with it? This offers an explanation of normative motivation that makes it more readily understandable. There is, however, an obvious objection to this view. How can we know that everyone who accepts the truth of a moral judgment is going to experience a particular emotion or feeling or impulse to do what the judgment tells us is the right thing to do? Or to put it another way: why should we believe that grasping a normative reason will invariably lead to the corresponding motivating reason? In fact, don't we know very well that there are some human beings who are of normal intelligence, and seem able to understand moral judgments, but are completely lacking in motivation to do what they judge to be right?[23] The most glaring examples of this are those we call 'psychopaths' or 'sociopaths' (although the official psychiatric term that most closely corresponds to the popular term is 'anti-social personality disorder').

6. Does Normative Reason Motivate?

i. The Psychopath as Counter-Example

Psychopaths typically are callous, impulsive, manipulative, and anti-social. Criminals with psychopathic tendencies are, after release from prison, more than three times as likely to commit violent crimes as non-psychopathic criminals.[24] Yet psychopaths appear to differ from the rest of us emotionally, rather than in terms of reasoning capacities. On IQ tests, many psychopaths show normal intelligence.[25] If they are asked to make moral judgments about particular situations, they make judgments with which most of us would agree. This applies even to their own actions, which they may be quite ready to judge as wrong, although they will often make excuses for their crimes, or treat them as if they were peccadilloes. Recent research has shown—contrary to an earlier study—that they are able to discriminate between acts that are morally wrong and acts that merely breach a social convention.[26] The ways in which psychopaths are different from normal people become evident when they are shown videos of strangers in pain. Normal people begin to sweat, and their blood pressure rises; these symptoms are not present, or are present to a much lower degree, in psychopaths. Similarly, showing normal people frightening faces causes activity in the brain areas associated

---

[23] Nichols invokes psychopaths as an argument against the idea that morality is based on reason in his 'How Psychopaths Threaten Moral Rationalism'.

[24] Rice and Harris, 'Psychopathy and Violent Recidivism'.

[25] Blair *et al.*, *The Psychopath*, 23–4.

[26] Borg and Sinnott-Armstrong, 'Do Psychopaths Make Moral Judgments?'

with emotion and motivation. Again, psychopaths show markedly less activity. When psychopaths hurt someone—or think of hurting someone—they do not feel about it as others do. It seems not to be significant to them.[27]

Does the existence of psychopaths pose a difficulty for Sidgwick's view that grasping the truth of a moral judgment has a 'normal emotional concomitant or expression' that motivates one to do as the judgment prescribes? Sidgwick did not, of course, say that such motivation is always successful; on the contrary, he suggested that perhaps it is usually not the predominant motive. But this reply is inadequate for the case of psychopaths because it doesn't seem that the emotions really exist at all in them, or not to any noticeable extent. On the other hand Sidgwick's inclusion of the word 'normal' in the phrase we are discussing does offer a way of dealing with psychopaths, for they are not normal. If Sidgwick's position holds true for 99 per cent of the population, that is all he needs.[28] Still, it would be helpful to understand how it is that people who appear to know what is right and wrong can also seem entirely unmoved by this knowledge.

R. D. Hare, in a study of psychopathy entitled *Without Conscience*, offers several examples of the difficulty of making sense of what psychopaths say and do. One psychopath, interviewed in prison, says: 'My mother is a great person, but I worry about her. She works too hard. I really care for that woman, and I'm going to make it easier for her.' When asked about the money he stole from his mother, however, this person replied: 'I've still got some of it stashed away and when I get out it's party time!'[29] There is, obviously, a practical contradiction between what this person says about caring for his mother, and about his future plans, but the psychopath doesn't even notice this. In the same book Hare describes another person who, on his way to a party, decided to buy some beer and realized that he had left his wallet at home. Instead of walking back the six or seven blocks to

---

[27] Blair *et al.*, *The Psychopath*, 51–62.

[28] The estimate that psychopaths are approximately 1% of the population comes from C. S. Neumann and R. D. Hare, 'Psychopathic Traits in a Large Community Sample', 897–8.

[29] R. D. Hare, *Without Conscience*, 138, quoted by Kennett and Fine, 'Internalism and the Evidence from Psychopathy and Acquired Sociopathy', 177.

get his wallet, he robbed the nearest gas station, using a heavy piece of wood to attack and seriously injure the attendant.[30] Obviously, he lacked any emotional concern for the well-being of the attendant, but apart from that, his reluctance to walk back home for his wallet led, quite predictably, to his arrest and incarceration. That seems evidence of a failure of reasoning, on top of the emotional deficit. The title of the work in which the term 'psychopath' first appeared—Harvey Cleckley's *The Mask of Sanity*—suggests that psychopaths merely appear to be sane. Among Cleckley's distinguishing characteristics of psychopathy are 'lack of insight into the impact of their behavior' and 'failure to plan ahead'. 'Lack of realistic long-term goals' is an item on *Hare's Psychopathy Checklist—Revised*, a widely used diagnostic tool.[31] On the basis of such evidence, Heidi Maibom has argued that psychopaths are not rational beings, even when their IQ is normal.[32]

This picture of psychopathy might enable a defender of the view that objective reason can be motivating for normal people to turn the tables on Hume and his followers. The psychopath, lacking concern for anyone's interests or projects, including his own, is like the person with Future Tuesday Indifference. If you want the beer *now* and you don't want to walk back home to get it, then you rob the gas station. The fact that you are likely to spend the next few years in prison doesn't count with you at the time you commit the crime, because at that moment you don't care about that. Predictably you will, in future, desire not to be incarcerated, but if this desire does not motivate you at the time you commit the crime, a Humean cannot say that the psychopath was acting irrationally. As we saw when discussing Future Tuesday Indifference, for a Humean to attempt to argue that someone (in this case, the psychopath) is acting contrary to reason, because his present desire is inconsistent with his future desires (in this case, not to be in prison), is to acknowledge that there are constraints on what it is rational for you to do that are independent of your present desires, and once this is accepted, the pure desire-based

[30]   R. D. Hare, *Without Conscience*, 58–9.

[31]   Cited in Baron-Cohen, *The Science of Evil*, 68; see R. D. Hare, *PCL-R: Hare's Psychopathy Checklist*.

[32]   Maibom, 'Moral Unreason' and 'The Mad, the Bad, and the Psychopath'.

position has been abandoned. To judge the psychopath's attack on the attendant as irrational, it has to be accepted that reason—in particular, the requirement to give weight to desires one will have in future—has a role to play in action that goes beyond the merely instrumental role of enabling us to get what we presently want. This opens a door through which not only one's own future desires but the desires of others may enter. Yet if the conduct of the psychopath Hare describes is not irrational, it is hard to imagine what kind of conduct would be.

ii. Asperger's Syndrome as Evidence of Normative Reasons Motivating

Just as some defenders of Hume's view have argued that the existence of psychopaths shows that morality is based on emotions rather than reason, so Jeanette Kennett has suggested that the example of people with Asperger's syndrome, a form of autism that is compatible with functioning at a high level in some respects, supports her Kantian view that the essence of moral agency is 'the concern to act in accordance with reason' and that 'reverence for reason is the core moral motive, the motive of duty'.[33] People with autism typically have difficulty in understanding people's expressions—they often cannot tell whether someone else is angry or offended, or whether they are serious or joking. This can go so far that they cannot recognize that other people have minds. On the other hand, people with Asperger's syndrome appear to have some capacity for making moral judgments, and for acting morally.

The psychologist Simon Baron-Cohen supports the claim that people with Asperger's syndrome can understand moral judgments:

My own experience of people with high-functioning autism or Asperger's syndrome is that they are certainly not just capable of morality, but may even be hyper-moral, wanting all of us to follow the rules in a precise way and to the nth degree. Some become the whistle-blowers when they spot the rules being broken. While many 'neurotypical' people arrive at their morality via a very visceral empathic route, responding emotionally to another person's distress, other people (and this includes many with Asperger's syndrome) arrive at their moral code through a logical route based on rules (systemising). 'Treat others as you would

---

[33] Kennett, 'Autism, Empathy and Moral Agency', 355. We owe this reference to McGeer, 'Varieties of Moral Agency'. See also Kennett, 'Reasons, Reverence and Value' and Kennett, 'Reasons, Emotion and the Psychopath'.

have them treat you' is an example of a moral code that is rule-based and can be arrived at by appreciating its logic and that it works. In this way morality can be like mathematics: Pythagoras' theorem that $a^2+b^2=c^3$ [*sic*] has a logic that works for any right-angled triangle. [34]

Temple Grandin, a prominent animal welfare consultant and one of the best-known people with autism, gives her own example of this way of thinking:

Many people with autism are fans of the television show *Star Trek*. I have been a fan since the show started. When I was in college, it greatly influenced my thinking, as each episode of the original series had a moral point. The characters had a set of firm moral principles to follow, which came from the United Federation of Planets. I strongly identified with the logical Mr. Spock, since I completely related to his way of thinking.

I vividly remember one old episode because it portrayed a conflict between logic and emotion in a manner I could understand. A monster was attempting to smash the shuttle craft with rocks. A crew member had been killed. Logical Mr. Spock wanted to take off and escape before the monster wrecked the craft. The other crew members refused to leave until they had retrieved the body of the dead crew member. To Spock, it made no sense to rescue a dead body when the shuttle was being battered to pieces. But the feeling of attachment drove the others to retrieve the body so their fellow crew member could have a proper funeral. It may sound simplistic, but this episode helped me finally understand how I was different. I agreed with Spock, but I learned that emotions will often overpower logical decisions, even if these decisions prove hazardous.[35]

Utilitarians, and many non-utilitarians too, will agree with Grandin (and Spock) that it is not worth endangering people's lives in order to retrieve the body of a crew member. Grandin's reaction could be similar to what Baron-Cohen claims to have experienced, namely that some people lacking in empathy can go beyond a set of rules and use reason to appreciate the logic of a principle like 'Treat others as you would have them treat you'. This also resembles the more calculating (and consequentialist) morality of the minority of subjects who, in experiments conducted by Joshua Greene and others, are prepared to push a stranger off a bridge to stop a runaway trolley, if that is the only way to save five other strangers from being killed by the trolley. Most people, Greene showed, refuse to do this, because they have a negative emotional response to the idea of pushing a stranger to his death (whereas they have no such emotional response to throwing a switch

---

[34] Baron-Cohen, 'Does Autism Need a Cure?'
[35] Grandin, *Thinking in Pictures*, 132–3, cited by McGeer, 'Varieties of Moral Agency', 232.

to divert the trolley down a branch line, even though this will also kill one stranger who is on that line).[36]

If this is what is really happening, then we might be led to conclude that at least some high-functioning people with autism are close to Sidgwick's imaginary 'rational beings as such' and this would indicate that at least some human beings can be moved to action by reason alone, without even the need for a 'normal emotional concomitant'. Victoria McGeer, however, has challenged this account. She accepts that some high-functioning people with autism are moral agents, and agrees with Kennett that the moral agency of people with autism 'seems far less permeated by affect, and more deeply governed by reason' than the moral agency of most people, but she suggests that individuals with autism are still motivated by a non-rational passion—specifically, a passion for order, which enables them to make sense of the otherwise baffling social world, and to participate in it.[37] There are, she suggests, three spheres of moral concern: one related to the well-being of others, a second with social structure and social position, and a third with something larger that she labels 'cosmic structure and cosmic position' which is about the nature of the universe, the existence of a god (or not) and the meaning and significance of our life. In most people, the first two are dominant, but for people with autism, who have more difficulty in empathizing with others and find social structures puzzling, the third becomes dominant. The cognitive abilities of high-functioning people with autism enable them to work with this aspect of morality more satisfactorily than with the others, but their interest in doing so also has an affective element. McGeer may be right, but it seems likely that if 'cosmic structure and cosmic position' defines the major sphere of the moral concern of people with Asperger's syndrome, then the use of reason to grasp this structure comes first, and the affective element follows, perhaps as what Sidgwick would call an 'emotional concomitant' of the reasoned judgment.

---

[36] Greene, *Moral Tribes*, 113–28; for an entertaining discussion of the trolley problem, see Edmonds, *Would you Kill the Fat Man?*

[37] McGeer, 'Varieties of Moral Agency', 244ff.

iii. A Sidgwickian Answer

In the final chapter of *The Methods* Sidgwick distinguishes feelings of sympathy from the 'strictly moral feelings' that are the 'normal emotional concomitant or expression' of accepting a moral judgment. He acknowledges that feelings of sympathy and strictly moral feelings are so intertwined that it is difficult for him to say, even when he analyzes his own consciousness, what force sympathetic feelings would have, if separated from the strictly moral feelings. He suggests that the exact proportions of the two feelings will vary between individuals and at different times in the life of a single individual.

Recent research by the psychologist C. Daniel Batson and his colleagues confirms Sidgwick's speculation that, in most people, both moral feelings and sympathy are present, and sheds some light on the balance between them. Batson is known as the leading proponent of the 'empathy-altruism hypothesis'—that is, the not altogether surprising view that when someone has feelings of sympathy and compassion towards another person, that provides a powerful motivation to help them.[38] (The term 'empathy' came into use only after Sidgwick's death, but as currently used it is very close to what he meant by sympathy.) Batson and his co-workers have also shown that empathy can lead to wrongdoing. In one experiment, students heard an interview with Sheri, a 10-year-old child with a slowly progressing terminal illness. Half the students were instructed to remain objective while listening to the interview, and the other half were instructed to imagine Sheri's feelings. All the students were then given a chance to help Sheri by moving her off a waiting list and into an immediate-treatment group ahead of other children who either had more severe terminal illnesses or had been waiting longer for treatment. Only 33 per cent of those who had been instructed to remain objective chose to move Sheri off the waiting list, whereas 73 per cent of those instructed to imagine her feelings did so. Significantly, all the participants agreed that partiality is less fair and less moral than impartiality, but most of the students who had been led to care about Sheri departed from this principle. It seems that, for many of the

[38] Batson, *Altruism in Humans.*

participants, empathy for Sheri overpowered their strictly moral feelings. The experiment supports Sidgwick's contention that some people are motivated merely by grasping the moral truth that we should not act partially or unfairly, for 27 per cent of the participants who had been instructed to imagine Sheri's feelings nevertheless did not move her off the waiting list.[39] The fact that only a minority kept her on the waiting list is in line with Sidgwick's comment that, in human beings, the impulse to which a moral cognition gives rise is only one motive among others and not always and perhaps not usually predominant (*ME* 34).

In the concluding chapter of *The Methods* Sidgwick mentions another kind of feeling that can arise from understanding a moral truth, when he says that a selfish person is likely to feel, 'in a thousand ways...the discord between the rhythms of his own life and of that larger life of which his own is but an insignificant fraction' (*ME* 501). This sounds very much like the emotional state that psychologists know as 'cognitive dissonance'—a state of unease or discomfort caused by holding conflicting beliefs. The Swedish sociologist Gunnar Myrdal invoked this idea in his celebrated 1944 study of race relations in America, *An American Dilemma*. As Myrdal put it, all Americans—including Southern whites who at the time openly defended racial segregation—accepted the 'American Creed' of equality and democracy. The tension between this moral stance and the reality of race relations in the South would, Myrdal believed, come to a head, and be resolved in favour of equality. His prediction was accurate, although this does not prove that he had correctly diagnosed the cause of the change.

Self-esteem is an important human need that contributes to personal happiness. Believing that something is the right thing to do, while knowing that one is not doing it, is likely to undermine one's self-esteem. Richard Keshen, in *Reasonable Self-Esteem*, argues that reasonable people gain self-esteem by knowing that their beliefs are in accord with the relevant evidence, and their values are not open to

---

[39] Batson, *Altruism in Humans,* 197–8; for the full report of the study, see Batson *et al.*, 'Immorality from Empathy-Induced Altruism'.

reasonable criticism by others. For Keshen, a reasonable person is one whose defining commitment is to have reasonable beliefs about the world, about what is in her interests, and about what she ought to do.[40] The concept of values not open to reasonable criticism by others begins with not being influenced by biased thinking, but Keshen takes this further by arguing that at the core of the reasonable person's ethical life is the recognition that others are like us, and therefore in some sense, their lives and their well-being are of equal significance to our own. The reasonable person cannot have self-esteem while ignoring the interests of others whose well-being she recognizes as equally significant. (We will see in Chapter 5 that Keshen's argument here has points of contact with Sidgwick's arguments for his principle of universal benevolence.) Keshen argues that the reasonable person can see herself as part of a tradition stretching from Aristotle through Galileo to our own times—and he includes Sidgwick among the exemplars of this tradition, not only because of Sidgwick's commitment to reason in his philosophical work, but also because of the way he demonstrated his commitment to live according to reason when he resigned his fellowship because of his inability to accept the articles of faith of the Church of England.[41] The reasonable person can therefore see herself as belonging to a worthy tradition, and this can enhance her sense of self-respect.

Cognitive dissonance and reasonable self-esteem are not simply unmotivated desires or emotions that happen to us, as hunger does, but desires or emotions that are motivated by beliefs that involve our ability to reason. It would be very difficult to be a rational being and remain completely indifferent to inconsistency; nor can one have reasonable self-esteem while knowing that one's actions are very far from one's values, or that one is acting on principles that do not have a sound basis that a reasonable person could accept. These motives for acting ethically therefore fit well with Sidgwick's notion that accepting a moral judgment has a normal emotional concomitant or expression.

We can now summarize Sidgwick's account. Moral motivation begins with the rational judgment that an act is right. This judgment

---

[40] Keshen, *Reasonable Self-Esteem*, 7.
[41] Keshen, *Reasonable Self-Esteem*, 98–99.

then has its concomitant desires or impulses that provide motivation for doing what is right. These are motivated desires, in Nagel's sense of the term, and are motivated by the moral judgment itself, against the background that we are reasonable beings capable of cognitive dissonance, to whom reasonable self-esteem matters. They may be specific to that judgment—as Sidgwick suggested when he indicated that, for the utilitarian, they might be a blend of the impulse 'to do what is judged to be reasonable as such' with 'sympathy and philan-thropic enthusiasm'—or they might be, like avoiding cognitive dis-sonance and maintaining reasonable self-esteem, moral feelings that apply more generally to doing what one understands to be right.

This account of moral motivation preserves the objectivity of moral judgments and their ability to motivate reasonable beings like us. In contrast to Hume's insistence that reason is and ought to be the slave of desires, Sidgwick's view makes reason the master, at least over the 'strictly moral feelings'. The rational judgment that an act is right comes first, and gives rise to the feelings that are its normal concomi-tant or expression and which provide the motivation to do what one believes to be right. This view is also distinct from the Kantian view that reason can act directly on our will, although one could see some hints of something like the position we are attributing to Sidgwick in Kant's statement that 'Duty is the necessity of an action from respect for the law' or his claim that 'the moral law *inevitably humbles* every man when he compares the sensuous propensity of his nature with the law'.[42] We do not claim to have proven Sidgwick correct, nor to have refuted Hume, but we have shown, drawing on Sidgwick as well as on Parfit's arguments in *On What Matters,* that there is an alterna-tive to Hume's view that holds open the possibility of reason play-ing a more foundational role in human conduct.[43] In the following chapters, we hope to fill out, in various ways, a broadly Sidgwickian account of the role that reason plays in ethical theory and practice.

[42] Kant, *Groundwork for the Metaphysics of Morals,* 16; Kant, *Critique of Practical Reason,* bk 1, ch. 3, §6.

[43] We agree with Robert Shaver that the view that beliefs can cause desires has had too lit-tle discussion. Shaver notes, in his illuminating essay 'Moral Motivation in Sidgwick', 10: 'It is hard even to find much discussion of whether beliefs can cause desires.'

3

Intuition and the Morality of Common Sense

1. Sidgwick on the Stages of Intuitionism

Intuitionism, as a method of ethics, is the subject of book III of *The Methods*—and it really is a book in itself, consisting of 14 chapters, and more than 200 pages. Sidgwick begins by saying that, in the widest usage of the term, an intuition is 'an immediate judgment as to what ought to be done or aimed at' (*ME* 97). He notes that philosophers often oppose 'intuitive' or '*a priori*' morality to 'inductive' or '*a posteriori*' morality. (He would have had in mind the opposition between Mill, who tried to base his utilitarianism on induction, and William Whewell, who argued against Mill that we know some truths a priori.) This opposition rests, Sidgwick claims, on a confusion because the two are seeking to show different things. The 'inductive' moralist can tell us that certain kinds of action are likely to increase happiness, while the 'intuitive' moralist asserts that certain kinds of action are right. Therefore there is 'no proper opposition'. Then, in an obvious reference to Mill, Sidgwick adds that, if the hedonist asserts that pleasure is the only reasonable ultimate end of human action, he cannot know this by induction, for experience 'can at most tell us that all men always do seek pleasure as their ultimate end...it cannot tell us that any one ought so to seek it' (*ME* 97–8).

Intuitionism, according to Sidgwick, can have different forms. Some people believe that the most trustworthy 'intuitions' are given by conscience, which generally operates at the level of particular actions: *this* is what I should do, in the particular situation in which I now find myself. It does not refer to any general rules or principles. Sidgwick calls this form of intuitionism 'ultra-intuitional' because it relies on the immediate judgment alone, making no appeal to more general rules or to any kind of moral reasoning.

Although all of us experience such moral intuitions, Sidgwick thinks that few people are satisfied with reliance on these immediate judgments of particular situations. We find ourselves doubting them, and noticing that the intuitions we reach at different times may not be consistent with one another, even though the circumstances are not relevantly different. Moreover, different people, apparently equally competent to judge, will have different intuitions. To set these doubts at rest, we seek something that can be more firmly based on widespread acceptance. This leads us to the second version of intuitionism, the fundamental assumption of which is 'that we can discern certain general rules with really clear and finally valid intuition'. Sidgwick calls this form of intuitionism the 'Morality of Common Sense' and discussion of it occupies most of book III. Philosophers who regard common sense morality as the correct method of doing ethics believe that these general rules are implicit in the everyday moral reasoning of ordinary people. The philosophers then see it as the role of the moralist to present these rules in a precise and systematic fashion, without vagueness and with some way of preventing conflict between different rules (*ME* 101).

Sidgwick points out that common sense morality is not fully satisfying because we want to know not only what we ought to do, but why we ought to do it. So even if we generally agree that what common sense morality directs us to do is the right thing to do, we also feel a need for some more sophisticated justification of these rules. This demand leads us to a third phase of intuitionism which seeks to find a basis for the morality of common sense by resting it, perhaps with some slight modification, on a principle or principles that are 'more absolutely and undeniably true and evident' (*ME* 102). Thus intuitionism as a method of ethics has three phases, each one more philosophically developed than its predecessor: first there is the 'voice of conscience' which Sidgwick sometimes calls 'ultra-intuitional' and sometimes 'Perceptional Intuitionism'; second there is the Morality of Common Sense, which Sidgwick also refers to as 'Dogmatic Intuitionism'; finally there is the third phase, which Sidgwick calls 'Philosophical Intuitionism'.

It is worth noting here that this initial discussion of intuitionism and its phases gives rise to a problem that will become clearer in the following chapters. In one sense of the term, to describe a method as 'intuitionism' is to refer to the way in which an ethical judgment is reached, rather than to the content of that judgment. In this sense of intuitionism, however, the label is too wide to constitute a distinctive method of ethics. Rather, in this sense 'intuitionism' is what Broad called 'an epistemic principle of classification'. Philosophical Intuitionism is not in itself a normative theory, but a mode of justifying a normative theory—and the same could be said of Perceptional Intuitionism, for in so far as people may have very varying intuitions about what to do in any given situation, it too does not have any specific normative content. Yet Sidgwick thought that this kind of epistemological intuitionism is, in the end, the only sound way of acquiring knowledge of what it is right for us to do, whether that knowledge leads us to aim at doing our duty for its own sake, or at bringing about certain consequences, as suggested by egoistic and universal hedonism.

The narrower definition of intuitionism allows for a clear separation of normative intuitionism from hedonistic theories. Here the division rests on, to use Broad's words again, 'whether some types of action are intrinsically right or wrong, or whether the rightness or wrongness of actions always depends on their conduciveness to certain ends'. In discussing the division Sidgwick made, Broad introduced a new terminology, the distinction between deontological and teleological theories, which has become one of the most widely used distinctions in normative ethical theory.[1]

---

[1] Broad, *Five Types*, 206–7. Broad writes: 'Deontological theories hold that there are ethical propositions of the form: "Such and such a kind of action would always be right (or wrong) in such and such circumstances, no matter what its consequences might be". This

Once this division is made clear, it may be hard to see why Sidgwick claimed that these stages of intuitionism 'may be treated as three stages in the formal development of Intuitive Morality' (*ME* 102). At first glance, the use of the term 'intuitionism' to refer to the content of our moral judgments seems unrelated to the use of the term to indicate that we reach our judgments by means of intuition.[2] We might think that here Sidgwick is simply following in the footsteps of earlier philosophers, like the 18th-century Scottish philosopher Thomas Reid, who was a great proponent of the philosophy of 'common sense' and was an intuitionist in the epistemic sense too. If this were the case, then Sidgwick's acceptance of the morality of common sense as a form of intuitionism would best be explained historically, rather than philosophically or conceptually. This could be part of the explanation for the way in which he uses the term, but there is also a philosophical link between intuitionism in the wider sense, as a view about the immediate manner in which we grasp moral truths, and intuitionism in the narrower sense that refers to the morality of common sense, with its demand for obedience to rules irrespective of the consequences. As Sidgwick puts it: 'Writers who maintain that we have "intuitive knowledge" of the rightness of actions usually mean that this rightness is ascertained by simply "looking at" the actions themselves, without considering their ulterior consequences' (*ME* 96). It is precisely because the moral rules accepted by common sense morality require us to tell the truth, to keep our promises, not to steal or kill the innocent, and to do justice even if the sky falls, irrespective of the consequences of our action, that we can claim to know that these actions are right simply by understanding the nature of the actions themselves; that is, immediately, without any calculation of the consequences of following them. It is not surprising, therefore, that many of those who believe that we can achieve moral knowledge through our intuition

division corresponds with Sidgwick's Intuitionism in the narrower sense. Teleological theories hold that the rightness or wrongness of an action is always determined by its tendency to produce certain consequences which are intrinsically good or bad. Hedonism is a form of teleological theory.'

[2]   See, for instance, the discussion in Phillips, *Sidgwickian Ethics*, 95.

also believe that certain actions are right or wrong, irrespective of the consequences. If they did not, they would have to admit that calculating the consequences plays an important role in determining what is right or wrong, and this calculation is not something that intuition can do. Here is Sidgwick himself on the link between the idea that some actions are right, and others wrong, irrespective of their consequences, and the idea of intuition as a method of acquiring moral knowledge:

> The moral judgments that men habitually pass on one another in ordinary discourse imply for the most part that duty is usually not a difficult thing for an ordinary man to know, though various seductive impulses may make it difficult for him to do it. And in such maxims as that duty should be performed 'advienne que pourra,' ['come what may'] that truth should be spoken without regard to consequences, that justice should be done 'though the sky should fall,' it is implied that we have the power of seeing clearly that certain kinds of actions are right and reasonable in themselves, apart from their consequences... And such a power is claimed for the human mind by most of the writers who have maintained the existence of moral intuitions; I have therefore thought myself justified in treating this claim as characteristic of the method which I distinguish as Intuitional. (*ME* 200)

Nevertheless, Sidgwick notes that common sense morality is not completely consistent about excluding calculations of consequences, because it generally includes prudence and benevolence among the virtues, and they necessarily take account of the consequences of our actions[3] (*ME* 96, 200).

2. Sidgwick on Testing the Morality of Common Sense

Sidgwick observes that, in the thinking of ordinary people, the different phases of intuitionism cannot be clearly distinguished. Many people trust their particular intuitions, but they also believe that there are general rules that tell us what is right in different areas

---

[3] In addition to the pages from *The Methods* cited in the text, see also Sidgwick's essay 'Professor Calderwood on Intuitionism in Morals', 563–6, reprinted in Henry Sidgwick, *Essays on Ethics and Method*. In that essay, Sidgwick concedes that 'No intuitionist ever maintained that *all* our conduct can be ordered rightly without any calculation of its effects on human happiness' but notes that this calculation is limited to certain principles, such as prudence and benevolence, and shut out from other areas of conduct.

of our lives. At the same time they think that these rules can be deduced from a smaller number of fundamental principles, and thus justified (*ME* 102–3). Can the morality of common sense supply that set of general principles against which our intuitions in particular cases can be tested? Sidgwick defines the morality of common sense as a collection of general rules 'regarded as a body of moral truth, warranted to be such by the *consensus* of mankind,—or at least of that portion of mankind which combines adequate intellectual enlightenment with a serious concern for morality' (*ME* 215). Many philosophers, Sidgwick notes, assume that this morality is able to present us with some self-evident principles or fundamental intuitions that are the basis for a philosophically sound system of ethics. Sidgwick therefore plans a detailed study of the demands of common sense morality to see if they are clear and precise, and are based on self-evident axioms. Before setting out on this examination, however, he explains that the rules of common sense morality express notions of virtue and of duty. To understand a rule and to be sure that it expresses precisely the ideas that lie behind it, it is important to get clear about these two notions. We will say more about them in Chapter 11; it is enough for now to say that Sidgwick defines a virtue as 'a quality exhibited in right conduct'. This definition allows him to sort the major forms of right conduct under headings drawn from the particular virtues, as they are commonly understood (*ME* 219 n.).

Sidgwick then begins his examination of the different virtues of common sense morality, including wisdom, self-control, benevolence, justice, good faith, veracity, prudence, purity, and courage. In each case, he begins by trying to make explicit a rule that encapsulates what the virtue teaches us to do. He seeks to define its terms and content, show what kind of problems we can have with its application, and indicate what kind of exceptions to such a rule common sense morality is ready to accept.

To show how Sidgwick constructs his critique of common sense morality, we have selected just two of these examinations of the rules of common sense morality: the rule of benevolence and the rule of veracity, or truthfulness.

i. Benevolence

The virtue of benevolence is commonly defined, Sidgwick says, in terms of a rule that 'we ought to love all our fellow-men', or 'all our fellow-creatures', but there is no agreement about the meaning of the word 'love' in this context. Kant, according to Sidgwick, understood the virtue of benevolence not in terms of an 'emotional element' like love or kindness, which we cannot be directed to feel, but rather as 'the determination of the will to seek the good or happiness of others'. Sidgwick agrees that it is impossible to order someone to feel an emotion, but at the same time he would not get rid of the emotional element completely. Benevolence requires us to cultivate love and affections, as far as it is possible for us to do so, towards those we are under some obligations to benefit (*ME* 239).

What is the nature of the acts in which benevolence is shown? They are usually called 'doing good'; but this immediately raises another problem because there is no agreement what the good really is. Some define it as happiness, some as perfection. Sidgwick takes the common sense view to be that benevolent acts seek to promote the happiness of others. Next he asks who these others are. Do we owe benevolence only to human beings, or to animals too? Here he points out that, although Bentham thought that the pain of animals is in itself something to be avoided, 'intuitional moralists of repute' have held that the only reason we should treat animals kindly is as a means of cultivating kindness towards humans. (Sidgwick may be thinking of Kant, and of William Whewell, whom Mill rebuked for taking this view.) Sidgwick thinks that, on this point, common sense rejects the 'hard-hearted paradox' of thinking that we ought to be kind to animals, not for the sake of the animals themselves, but only for the sake of humans, and instead accepts Bentham's view that pain is in itself something to be avoided, whether it is in humans or animals. Sidgwick then considers an important difference between the utilitarian view and common sense morality. Utilitarianism encourages us to aim at happiness generally 'and so consider the happiness of any one individual as equally important with the equal happiness of any other' (*ME* 241). This is still compatible with us promoting the happiness of some more than others, as practical circumstances dictate, but this inequality is secondary and derives from the overall principle of equal consideration, coupled with the particular circumstances in which we seek to promote happiness overall. Common sense morality, on the other hand, takes it as immediately apparent that we have special duties to others who stand in some special relation to us (*ME* 242). But when there are doubts about the significance of some of these special relations for our benevolent duties, or conflicts of duties to different people, how are these doubts to be resolved? Are there independent and self-evident principles that can guide us, or must we appeal to utilitarian considerations? This is a crucial question on which the method of intuitionism and the method of utilitarianism differ.

Sidgwick enumerates the duties of benevolence that, according to common sense morality, we have to others:

We should all agree that each of us is bound to show kindness to his parents and spouse and children, and to other kinsmen in a less degree: and to those who have rendered services to him, and any others whom he may have admitted to his intimacy and called friends: and to neighbours and to fellow-countrymen more than others: and perhaps we may say to those of our own race more than to black or yellow men, and generally to human beings in proportion to their affinity to ourselves. And to our country as a corporate whole we believe ourselves to owe the greatest sacrifices when occasion calls...And to all men with whom we may be brought into relation we are held to owe slight services, and such as may be rendered without inconvenience: but those who are in distress or urgent need have a claim on us for special kindness. (*ME* 246)

The problem is that, once we try to become more precise about the extent of our obligations to people in each of these categories, we begin to differ, and such differences can be shown to vary greatly between people of different cultures and periods. We can see this even in the difference between Sidgwick's time and our own, for it could not be said today that common sense morality tells us that we have greater obligations of benevolence to those of our own race than to others less like ourselves. Sidgwick was aware of recent changes in his own culture too. Not long before the time in which Sidgwick was writing, a man was considered morally bound to leave his money to his children unless they had done something seriously wrong, and if he had no children, to leave it to other close relatives. By Sidgwick's time, a childless man could do what he liked with his money, unless his brothers and sisters were in poverty. Sidgwick predicted that 'in a future age' a man would not be considered morally obliged to leave his money to his children, unless they are in need. For some people, at least, this prediction seems to have been fulfilled. We do not think badly of Warren Buffet who, while surely not leaving his children in poverty, has given the overwhelming majority of his fortune to charity.

Sidgwick considers the argument that our duties may really be relative to custom, in the sense that, if in a society it is customary to do something, then that is what we should do. He responds that we can see that custom changes and it changes because people find it inexpedient. But if we admit that custom should change when it is inexpedient, we are using a utilitarian method of reasoning. This tells us that the common sense reading of the rule of benevolence is not self-evident at all, for the limits to the allegedly independent and self-evident principles are not given, even implicitly, by the intuition that reveals the principle, but by the entirely different principle of utility (ME 247).

ii. Truthfulness

When he turns to the virtue of truthfulness, Sidgwick starts with the problem that, while we may all agree with the broad principle that we ought to tell the truth and avoid lying, when we get down to specific cases, this agreement collapses. If a robber asks us if we have any jewellery, are we bound to tell the truth? Can we lie to deceive our enemies? Must a lawyer, in defending his client, avoid creating false beliefs in the jury? If both telling the truth and refusing to answer will let others guess something that we are entitled to keep secret, must we be truthful? Is it incompatible with truthfulness to take part in religious ceremonies that require us to utter words that we believe to be literally false?

Some moralists defend the view that 'Speak the truth' is an ethical axiom that has no exceptions. Common sense morality, however, is, Sidgwick tells us, less clear about truth-telling. It does not tell us that truth-speaking is an absolute duty, to be obeyed in all circumstances, and it also does not demonstrate that it is an independent duty, free of any need for support from any other principle. It is not absolute, because it holds that there is a general right to have others tell us the truth, unless there are special circumstances in which we may forfeit this right, or it may be suspended. For example, it isn't clear that we do wrong if we lie to protect ourselves against 'a palpable invasion of our rights'—after all, we can be justified in killing in self-defence, so it would be paradoxical if we cannot lie in self-defence (*ME* 315). Then there are cases when we lie because it is in the interests of the person to whom we deny the truth. Common sense does not regard it as wrong to tell a lie to someone who is gravely ill, if telling the truth is likely to produce a shock that is dangerous to that person's health. Common sense also allows us to lie to children, when we think it better for them that they not know the truth. But if this kind of 'benevolent deception' is permitted in some cases, how are we to decide in which cases it is justifiable? Only, Sidgwick suggests, 'by weighing the gain of any particular deception against the imperilment of mutual confidence involved in all violation of truth' (*ME* 316). In other words, the justifiability of exceptions to the principle of telling the truth is resolved by an appeal to the quite distinct principle of utility. Hence the principle of telling the truth is not an independent principle.

It is also less clear than it seems, Sidgwick points out, in what the virtue of veracity consists. For instance, where keeping a secret is important for the well-being of society, it is often said that we can legitimately conceal the truth by any means short of uttering an actual falsehood. To protect a secret from a probing question, may we 'turn the question aside' with an answer that, while not strictly false, still leads, and is intended to lead, the enquirer to form a false belief? Is this contrary to the virtue of truthfulness? Common sense is, Sidgwick believes, divided on this point, with some saying it is a form of deception, and thus contrary to truthfulness, and others saying that, since we did not tell a lie, we have not violated our duty to tell the truth.

After considering these and other difficulties in defining in what the principle of truthfulness consists, and whether there are exceptions to it, Sidgwick sums up his argument to this point:

On the whole, then, reflection seems to show that the rule of Veracity, as commonly accepted, cannot be elevated into a definite moral axiom: for there is no real agreement as to how far we are bound to impart true beliefs to others: and while it is contrary to Common Sense to exact absolute candour under all circumstances, we yet find no self-evident secondary principle, clearly defining when it is not to be exacted. (*ME* 317)

Before accepting this conclusion, however, Sidgwick considers an argument that truth is an absolute duty which, if sound, would show that the common sense exceptions to the duty to tell the truth are a result of 'inadvertence and shallowness of thought'. Sidgwick does not name the author of this argument, but he clearly has Kant in mind. The argument is that, if we allow people to tell lies under some circumstances, and this rule becomes generally accepted, lies told under these circumstances will become useless, because no one will believe them. But a moralist cannot lay down a rule that, if generally accepted, would be self-defeating.

To this argument Sidgwick presents three objections. First, he doesn't think that complete trust is always for the best; he believes that under certain 'peculiar circumstances' it is good for people not to be able to trust the answers they get. For instance we should not, he says, 'be restrained from pronouncing it lawful to meet deceit with deceit, merely by the fear of impairing the security which rogues now derive from the veracity of honest men'. Granted, the ultimate result of such a rule would be that lies are no longer told to known rogues— because, anticipating that people would lie to them, they would not bother asking the questions that under a different rule would have led to them knowing some truth useful to them. But since this is not an undesirable outcome, the prospect of it gives us no reason against telling useful lies (*ME* 318). Second, since we are not purely rational beings, even if we know that there are rules telling us that in certain circumstances lying is not wrong, lies may still have an effect, and therefore may still be told. Sidgwick's example here is the skilful lawyer who persuades a jury that he sincerely believes his client to be innocent, even though the members of the jury are well aware that the lawyer regards it as his duty to say, as plausibly as possible, whatever he has been instructed to say on behalf of his client, whether or not he believes it to be true. Sidgwick's third point challenges the assumption behind the entire Kantian argument: 'it cannot be assumed as certain that it is never right to act upon a maxim of which the universal application would be an undoubted evil' (ME 318). It is true that if an act is right for me it must be right for all other people in similar circumstances. But that rule does not exclude the possibility that an act will be right if its maxim is not universally accepted, and it will not be widely imitated, and it can then be right for all people in the relevantly similar circumstance that their act will not be widely imitated. One way in which this might be the case is if the act is done secretly. Here Sidgwick is hinting at the controversial idea of 'esoteric morality' to which we will return in Chapter 10.

3. Perceptional Intuitionism

Sidgwick's three stages of intuitionism have modern parallels. We will discuss them in turn.

The name perceptional intuitionism suggests that we just 'see' what is right or wrong, in much the same way that we see a red object in front of us. Our perception of what is right or wrong appears immediately when we are faced with a situation in which we have to make moral judgments, and we can rely on that perception.

Today the closest approximation to this view that is taken seriously in moral philosophy is known as 'particularism' and its best-known advocate is Jonathan Dancy.[4] Dancy denies that moral judgment needs to draw on moral principles.[5] Unlike Sidgwick's perceptional intuitionists, however, Dancy is not committed to the idea that we just look at a situation and see what is right or wrong. As we shall see, he leaves room for reflection and deliberation.

Generalists claim that moral reasons are determined by general principles and do not vary. If we have a principle that tells us not to lie, the fact that saying something would be a lie is a reason for us not to say it. Now suppose that we are in a situation in which by lying I will save someone's life. For a generalist who is also an absolutist,

---

[4] The term 'particularism' appears to stem from R. M. Hare, *Freedom and Reason*, 18. We owe this reference to Selim Berker, 'Particular Reasons', 111 n. 3; Berker is, however, astray when he also remarks that 'the possibility of such a position was first pointed out' by Hare.

[5] Dancy, *Moral Reasons*, 74.

like Kant, we should not lie, even in this situation, as the principle still provides an overriding reason for action. For a softer general-ist like W. D. Ross, for whom the rule against lying is a prima facie duty, we now have two different reasons for action, stemming from two different duties—one about not lying and the other about doing good—that point in different directions. According to a particularist, however, both Kant and Ross have it wrong because particularists hold that when deciding what we should do in a particular case, gen-eral moral principles are useless. The fact that a statement is a lie may count against it in one situation, but in a different situation not count against it at all or even count in favour of it. Similarly, the fact that an action will save a life may count in favour of it in one situation and against it in another.

Dancy presents similar examples in his book *Moral Reasons*. Here is one: 'I borrow a book from you, and then discover that you have stolen it from the library. Normally the fact that I have borrowed the book from you would be a reason to return it to you, but in this situ-ation it is not. It isn't that I have *some* reason to return it to you and more reason to put it back in the library. I have no reason at all to return it to you.'[6]

Dancy believes that examples like this show that reasons are holis-tic. According to holism about reasons: 'a feature that is a reason in one case may be no reason at all, or an opposite reason, in another'.[7] Dancy offers a non-moral example: normally the fact that some-thing looks red to me is a reason for believing that it is red and against believing that it is blue. But if I have just taken a drug that makes red things look blue and blue things look red, then the fact that some-thing looks red to me is a reason against believing that it is red, and a reason for believing that it is blue. Similarly, in the case of reasons for action, the fact that an action is against the law may sometimes be a reason against doing it, but in other cases—for instance, when pro-testing against a bad law—it is a reason for doing it.[8] When we decide what to do, we should be open to an idea that different things at dif-ferent times become reasons and cease to be reasons.

---

[6] Dancy, *Moral Reasons*, 60.   [7] Dancy, *Ethics without Principles*, 73.
[8] Dancy, 'Moral Particularism'.

Dancy admits that this may make moral judgment seem to be 'a mess'. He asks: 'Are we reduced to looking at the case before us and hoping that the complex interrelations between the various features that happen to be relevant here will just strike us, somehow?' That is, he acknowledges, a possibility, but not the only possibility for particularists. They can take moral experience into account and so 'are not reduced to just gazing vacantly at the case before them and coming up with an answer that somehow seems appropriate'. They can say that a certain feature of a situation—for example, that it involved cruelty—mattered in one case, and so it might well matter in the present case. What they cannot say is that because it mattered in another case, it *must* matter in the present case.[9]

A particularist deciding what to do has to *see* in what direction the moral reasons point. She may see that in one situation saving a life is a reason for telling a lie, but since there is no principle that says 'The good of saving an innocent life outweighs the wrong of telling a lie', there could also be situations in which saving a life is not a reason for telling a lie. Indeed, according to Dancy, the particularist cannot assume that the fact that telling a lie will save an innocent life is even going to count in favour of telling the lie. It might, for all the particularist can know, count against telling the lie. The same is true of the fact that you stole the book that I then borrowed from you. In some situations the fact that you stole it from a library is a reason for me not to return it to you, but presumably in a different situation the fact that you stole the book from the library would be a reason for me to give it back to you. How could this be?

The natural response to this question is that, if in some situation the fact that an act saves an innocent life counts against that act, there must be some further feature of the situation that explains why this is so. For instance, the life may be that of a child who has a genetic condition that means she will suffer horribly for a few more weeks and then die. Suppose now that a person repeatedly makes decisions in situations that are similar to this in respect of the quality of the life that is at stake (as a neonatal intensive care specialist

---

[9] Dancy, 'Moral Particularism'.

might do). This person, even if she does not initially act on the basis of any principle, is likely to notice a pattern to her decisions in a set of similar cases. A reflective person will wonder if the pattern indicates that there is a rule in the offing. If there cannot be rules because there are too many varying factors and the rules would become too complicated, then either a prima facie principle or a considerations about the values at stake may help her reach well-considered decisions. She may, for instance, conclude that a life full of suffering and lacking other redeeming features is of negative, rather than positive, value. But then she seems to have adopted a principle, namely that the fact that an action will lead to a life full of suffering is a reason against doing that action. She may base this principle on a view of the significance of suffering as a (negative) value. If the particularist answers that there are many values, not just this one, she could respond that then she will reach a final decision by weighing the relevant values—which is already some distance from particularism. Again, a reflective person would then ask herself whether life is of intrinsic value, or of only instrumental value, and if there is more than one intrinsic value, how we are to rank them or trade them off against each other. If the judgments of particularists form patterns and can be brought under rules, principles, or theories of value, even if very complicated ones, the distinction between particularism and any other rule-based normative ethical theory—including what Sidgwick calls the morality of common sense—seems to have vanished.

If, on the other hand, the particularist rejects all resort to rules, principles, or theories of value, it is hard to see how she can learn from experience about the special factors that could lead to the fact that an act will save an innocent life counting *against* doing the act, or the fact that a person stole a book from a library operating *in favour of* returning it to him. What would learning that be like? Remember, it can't be a matter of deriving, from a range of particular cases, a common moral element that makes some of these acts right and others wrong. That would be the derivation of a principle. Is it, then, impossible to know what is right or wrong until we actually find ourselves in a situation in which the morally relevant factors apply? Then it does seem that, despite Dancy's denials, the particularist is reduced to 'just gazing vacantly at the case' and wondering if she will just *see* that *this* is such a case.

We are familiar with people varying their behaviour in matters of taste. We have no objection to someone saying: 'At this restaurant the pea soup is excellent, but today I don't feel like soup.' But we are likely to object to someone saying: 'I don't usually return books to people who steal them from libraries, but today I don't feel like help-ing the library to regain its property', and we surely would condemn a lifeguard who noticed that a toddler had fallen into the pool he was supervising and said 'I usually rescue drowning children, but today I don't feel like doing so'. At least in serious matters, morality requires that we do not let such feelings affect our judgment of what we ought to do. Our point is not that particularists base their judgments on subjective feelings. They do not. They regard themselves as seeing objectively wrong-making or right-making features of situations. But the idea that a reason could in one case count in favour of an action, and in another case against an action, without any rule, principle, or theory of value justifying the change, is uncomfortably close to a change in a matter of taste, and morality demands more explanation of this change than the particularist is willing to offer.

Here Dancy's examples serve only to highlight the problem. In the case of colour perception after taking the drug, we know exactly what principle will lead us to the correct beliefs: 'After taking a drug that makes blue things appear red, and red things appear blue, if some-thing appears red to you, believe that it is blue and if it appears blue to you, believe that it is red.' Similarly, there are many possible principles that might guide obedience to the law. One might be: 'Obey the law when doing so will have the best consequences for all those affected by your action.' But there could also be others. Neither of these exam-ples gives us any clue to how a reason for a belief or an action could 'change direction' *except* on the basis of some general principle that would explain or justify the change. In the absence of any such prin-ciple, and on the assumption that we are not talking about a matter of taste or subjective feelings, the change of direction is utterly mysteri-ous. As Selim Berker puts it, 'The very notion of a reason for action depends on there being a certain level of constancy either in the connection between reasons and what grounds them or in the connection between reasons and one's overall duties, and when particularists posit as much variability as they do, we lose our grip on what they could mean when they call something a "reason for action."[10]

When we are thinking about what we ought to do, we seek something more satisfying to our intellect that explains *why* in some situations saving a life is a reason for doing an act, and in other situations it is not. This search leads straight to the kind of rules and principles that make up common sense morality.

4. Common Sense Morality

Common sense morality was established as a philosophical theory in Scotland in the latter part of the 18th century, as a response to Hume's scepticism. Thomas Reid, the main figure in this school, believed that moral knowledge is within the reach of everyone, for we can all grasp, by intuition, the basic set of self-evident truths that constitute the foundations of moral knowledge. Richard Price was another important 18th-century defender of this view, which received further development at the hand of the 19th-century theologian and philosopher William Whewell, and in the first half of the 20th century, from W. D. Ross. Today some of the key elements of this tradition can be discerned in the work of such philosophers as David McNaughton, Michael Slote, and Bernard Gert.

We will focus on Ross, and then turn to the views of Bernard Gert, a more recent defender of common sense morality, before closing this section by comparing Sidgwick's account of common sense morality on lying with Sissela Bok's study of the same topic.

i. W. D. Ross

As we have already noticed, Ross is, in contrast to Dancy, a generalist who holds that moral reasons derive from general principles. Unlike Kant, however, he does not think that these principles are

---

[10] Berker, 'Particular Reasons', 112. For a defence of Dancy against Berker, see Lechler, 'Do Particularists have a Coherent Notion of a Reason for Action?'

absolute. He thinks that we have a variety of prima facie duties; specifically, duties of fidelity, reparation, gratitude, justice, beneficence, and self-improvement and non-maleficence.[11] In almost every case where we have one of these duties, however, it will conflict with at least one other duty. We have, for example, promised to meet a friend at a certain time and place, but on our way we come across an accident, and can do more good by helping the victim, although we will then break our promise. In such a situation, Ross says, we do not simply calculate what will have the best consequences—will the victim suffer more if we do not help than our friend will suffer by being kept waiting? That is the wrong question to ask. Instead, we should weigh the stringency of the conflicting duties, in order to decide what is our all-things-considered duty. Perhaps by aiding the accident victim we may save his life. In that case, the duty of beneficence outweighs the duty of fidelity, which is the basis of our obligation to keep our promise. We would then do wrong to keep our promise; but this does not mean that we were not under such an obligation, or that this obligation is null and void. (To this extent, Ross acknowledges, the use of the term prima facie is misleading, because it suggests that the duties are only duties 'at first glance,' and that subsequently, given the circumstances, they turn out not to have been duties at all. Some contemporary philosophers therefore use pro tanto instead of prima facie.) On Ross's view, the obligation to keep our promise remains real and valid even when it is outweighed. We may recognize our breach of this obligation by apologizing to our friend, and offering to make it up to her in some way.

A.C. Ewing regarded Ross's idea of prima facie duties as one of the most important discoveries in 20th-century moral philosophy. Philip Stratton-Lake, the editor of a recent edition of *The Right and the Good,* acknowledges that this assessment may be 'over the top' but nevertheless considers Ross's doctrine 'an important step in our

---

[11] Ross, *The Right and the Good,* 20–2. In the following pages he suggests that the duties of justice, beneficence, and self-improvement can all be regarded as aspects of a single duty, to promote the maximum aggregate good.

understanding of morality'.[12] There is no doubt that the idea of duties providing reasons, but not conclusive reasons, for action softens the rigour of an ethic of exceptionless moral rules or duties, and so makes it more plausible. It is also true that it does this in a way that does not collapse into utilitarianism. For suppose that, in the case previously described, stopping to help the accident victim would not save a life, but would only reduce, to a modest degree, the suffering of the victim. Imagine that we are able to weigh this suffering against the unhappiness of our friend that results from breaking the promise. Imagine, too, that we then add into the calculation any negative effects that will flow from the breach of promise, not only to our friend, but also to anyone else who might be affected by any tendency that our breach has to weaken the valuable practice of promise-keeping. Suppose that, after doing this calculation, we find that the net benefits of keeping our promise amount to 1,000 happiness units, whereas the net benefits of breaking our promise add up to 1,001 happiness units. Then, Ross will say, we ought to keep our promise, because the prima facie duty to keep a promise carries its own weight, and this will outweigh the prima facie duty of beneficence, when the increased happiness brought about by doing what is in accord with the duty of beneficence is very small.

Ross's theory is grounded in our intuitive knowledge of right and wrong. Ross writes:

I should make it plain at this stage that I am *assuming* the correctness of some of our main convictions as to *prima facie* duties, or, more strictly, am claiming that we know them to be true. To me it seems as self-evident as anything could be, that to make a promise, for instance, is to create a moral claim on us in someone else. Many readers will perhaps say that they do not know this to be true. If so, I certainly cannot prove it to them; I can only ask them to reflect again, in the hope that they will ultimately agree that they also know it to be true. The main moral convictions of the plain man seem to me to be, not opinions which it is for philosophy to prove or disprove, but knowledge from the start; and in my own case I seem to find little difficulty in distinguishing these essential convictions from other moral convictions which I also have, which are merely fallible

---

[12] See Ewing, *Second Thoughts in Moral Philosophy*, 126; we owe this reference, and the quote from Stratton-Lake, to the latter's introduction to W. D. Ross, *The Right and the Good*, p. xxxvii.

opinions based on an imperfect study of the working for good or evil of certain institutions or types of action.[13]

Ross's theory is thus a version of what Sidgwick called 'dogmatic intuitionism' or 'the morality of common sense'. Sidgwick takes a very different view of the moral convictions to which Ross refers. He sees them as 'precepts to which custom and general consent have given a merely illusory air of self-evidence' and adds:

I know by direct reflection that the propositions, 'I ought to speak the truth', 'I ought to keep my promises'—however true they may be—are not self-evident to me; they present themselves as propositions requiring rational justification of some kind. (*ME* 383)

This may seem like a mere clash of intuitions, about which no further progress can be made. But Sidgwick does not simply rely on 'direct reflection' and he is not, in this passage, stating his full case against the morality of common sense. He has, in earlier sections of book III of *The Methods,* raised many difficulties against common sense morality. Ross's introduction of the notion of prima facie duties overcomes some of the difficulties, but not others. It avoids the implausibility of Kant's view that it is wrong to tell a lie even if by doing so one saves the life of an innocent person, and it does point to a possible manner of resolving conflicts between duties without resorting to calculations of consequences.

There are, however, other difficulties on which Ross's innovation makes no impression. As we have seen, Sidgwick argues that the universal support enjoyed by many of the principles that make up common sense morality lasts only as long as the principles remain vague. Regarding the principle that we ought to keep our promises, for example, we can shatter the consensus simply by asking whether our promise is binding when it is made as a result of false statements; or, even in the absence of falsehood, if some important circumstances were concealed; or if we were led to believe (perhaps without any malicious intentions) that the consequences of keeping the promise would be very different from what they now turn out to be; or if we made the promise under some form of coercion; or if the

---

[13] Ross, *The Right and the Good*, 20–1 n. 1.

circumstances have changed in an unexpected but materially relevant way; or if we now see that keeping the promise will impose a very
serious loss on ourselves, completely out of proportion to the benefit
it confers on the person to whom we made the promise; or if we learn
that keeping the promise will actually harm the person to whom it
was made, although he is unable to see this. Without deciding about
these cases, we cannot know that our promise will have even prima
facie weight.

Similarly, when it comes to our duty to tell the truth, we can ask
whether it is wrong to lie to a robber about whether we have any
jewellery, or wrong for a lawyer to tell members of a jury facts that,
although true, do not present a complete picture of the actions of his
client and therefore will create in their minds a misleadingly favourable belief about those actions. Simply raising these points, Sidgwick
asserts, shows that the confidence with which most people assert that
we ought to tell the truth, or that promises ought to be kept, is due to a
failure to give adequate thought to the issue.

Decades after Sidgwick made his claim about the inadequate
thought that lies behind the confidence with which most people
assert that promises ought to be kept, it was again proven correct when, shortly after the publication of Ross's *The Right and
the Good,* W. A. Pickard-Cambridge published a critique of Ross's
position in which he presented a range of examples of promises
that raised problems like those Sidgwick had described. Ross
subsequently responded to these examples, indicating the cases
in which he thought a promise does give rise to a prima facie
obligation to keep it, but his responses merely show how much
room there is for disagreement about which promises generate
even a prima facie obligation.[14]

Even if we were to grant Ross his set of prima facie duties, we would
still need to know how we are to decide what our actual duty is when

---

[14] See Pickard-Cambridge, 'Two Problems about Duty (II)', 158–66; and Ross,
Foundations of Ethics, 94–101. We owe these references to Skelton, 'William David Ross'.
Skelton, who is in general quite sympathetic to Ross, also finds his response on these points
inadequate.

two or more prima facie duties conflict. Ross acknowledges that 'Our judgements about our actual duty in concrete situations have none of the certainty that attaches to our recognition of the general principles of duty.'[15] Those general principles are self-evident, but judgments of our actual duty in particular circumstances are not. All we can do is 'reflect to the best of our ability on the *prima facie* rightness or wrongness of various possible acts in virtue of the characteristics we perceive them to have', and in this way we are more likely to do the right act than if we act without this kind of reflection.[16] Ross does not, however, offer any real guidance as to how we should go about this kind of reflection, and at this point, it seems, he falls back into perceptional intuitionism, or particularism, because the final decision is a judgment made in each particular situation. It is not easy to see what that judgment can be, other than a distinct intuition about the 'weight' of each of the prima facie duties as they apply to the specific situation. Some of the difficulties of that approach will therefore apply, at this point, to Ross as well, especially the pressure to systematize the various individual decisions that we make, and bring them under some more general rule, such as 'saving the life of an innocent person always outweighs breaking a promise'. But Ross does not embrace this kind of move.

In defending this aspect of his theory, Ross advances an *ad hominem* argument against his main rival, utilitarianism. If we favour a pluralistic form of utilitarianism that embraces as intrinsically valuable not just pleasure, but other goods such as knowledge, then he says that there is no logical basis for deciding that one of these goods is greater than the other, and 'we can only fall back on an opinion'. Even if we take a monistic theory such as hedonistic utilitarianism, 'the infinite variety of the effects of our actions in the way of pleasure' make it illusory to claim that the theory gives us a readily applicable criterion we can use to decide what is the right thing to do.[17]

---

[15] Ross, *The Right and the Good*, 30.   [16] Ross, *The Right and the Good*, 32.
[17] Ross, *The Right and the Good*, 23–4.

Ross is surely right to point out that consequentialist theories with more than one intrinsic value are in similar difficulty in telling us how to balance conflicting values as his own theory is in telling us how to decide when there are conflicting prima facie duties. A monistic form of utilitarianism, like hedonistic utilitarianism, is in principle in a better position, because if all the facts were known, we would know which action would produce the greatest net increase in pleasure for all affected, and we would know what we ought to do. In practice, it has to be admitted that we never know this, and there are many situations in which reasonable hedonistic utilitarians can differ about what we ought to do. Nevertheless, monistic utilitarianism at least gives us an 'in principle' way of resolving the question, which Ross's theory lacks. If our ability to predict the consequences of our actions improves, utilitarianism will yield more determinate guidance. In contrast, there seems no way of eliminating the indeterminacy that is at the heart of Ross's ethic of prima facie duties.

We have not yet discussed the foundations of Ross's defence of common sense morality. As we have seen, his ethic of prima facie duties is grounded on the 'main moral convictions of the plain man'. Can we really take the moral convictions of ordinary people as a source of moral knowledge? We have postponed asking this question because we are not yet in a position to discuss the same inquiry about Sidgwick's own method of arriving at moral knowledge. We therefore postpone further discussion of this foundational question until we discuss, in the next chapter, how Sidgwick justifies his claim that some normative principles are self-evident.

First, however, we turn to a more recent version of common sense morality.

ii. Bernard Gert

The American philosopher Bernard Gert, who died in 2011, wrote more than a century after Sidgwick, but there are strong parallels between his view and common sense morality as Sidgwick discussed it. Gert's philosophy is based on some kind of natural law, rather than on intuition, but his main focus is on morality understood as a shared phenomenon that develops among rational beings. We can start with his understanding of morality:

Morality is an informal public system applying to all rational persons, governing behavior that affects others, and includes what are commonly known as the moral rules, ideals, and virtues and has the lessening of evil or harm as its goal.[18]

Essential to Gert's conception of morality is the idea that it is known to, and could be chosen by, every rational person. No one has any special knowledge of it, not even—or perhaps especially not—philosophers. Gert believes that for all moral philosophers the starting point should be common morality, but he does not think of this as the promptings of the 'unsophisticated conscience'—on the contrary, he believes that it is often underestimated by thinkers who fail to appreciate how sophisticated it can be. Philosophers should not put forward their own guides to what we ought to do, because 'these cannot differ in any significant way from that offered by the common moral system'. Instead philosophers should 'explain and justify, if possible, the common moral system'.[19] If they put forward suggestions for how we are to live that do not overlap sufficiently with the common moral system, they will end up with 'general guides to conduct or philosophies of life' rather than with moral theories.

Gert thinks that it is possible to show that all rational persons should support common morality. There are, in his view, both weak and strong forms of justification. The weak justification shows that all rational persons *could* support a public system of common morality. The strong justification shows that it *would* be supported by all rational persons. Common morality can be strongly justified to people who 'seek agreement with other rational persons and use no beliefs not shared by all moral agents'.[20]

Morality, according to Gert, takes the form of rules that every rational person knows, and can and should follow. He groups the moral rules into 10 main ones that tell us not to kill, not to cause pain, not to disable, not to deprive of freedom, not to deprive of pleasure, not to deceive, to keep one's promise, not to cheat, to obey the law,

---

[18] Gert, *Morality*, 14.   [19] Gert, *Morality*, 18.   [20] Gert, *Morality*, 19.

and to do our duty. He believes that, towards all of those rules, all rational persons would take the following attitude:

Everyone is always to obey the rule, except when a fully informed, rational person can publicly allow violating it. Anyone who violates the rule when a fully informed, rational person cannot publicly allow such a violation may be punished.[21]

Hence in Gert's understanding of common morality, rules are not absolute, but when we want to justify breaking a rule, we need to show that 'all suitably qualified rational persons can or would publicly allow this kind of violation of a moral rule'.[22] There is, however, a significant difference between justifying rules and justifying violations, for Gert believes that we can all agree on the moral rules, but we will not agree on their violations. Gert considers it especially important that the procedure of justifying violations of rules must be a part of a public system, which means that everyone must be able to understand it and it cannot be irrational for people to use it.

In setting out Sidgwick's critique of common sense morality, we chose, as an example of the many rules he discussed, the rule 'Do not deceive' and Gert's approach to this rule is significant in that it shows yet another way in which this rule can be understood. For Gert deceiving is an action that leads someone to have false beliefs. Although lying is limited to intentional actions, he believes that one could deceive someone unintentionally, and this would also be a violation of the rule against deceiving, although possibly an excusable one. It isn't clear here what Gert may have had in mind, but he could be thinking of a case in which I foresee that, as an unintended consequence of an intentional action of mine, someone will be led to have a false belief.[23] This could still count as a violation of the rule against deception.

Gert observes that what will count as being deceived may be viewed differently by different societies. Much depends on what rights people have in specific situations. If a patient has a right to know what his medical tests show, then, Gert says, a doctor who stays silent violates the rule against deception.[24] This is a surprising view, especially

---

[21] Gert, *Morality*, 219.   [22] Gert, *Morality*, 221.
[23] We thank Walter Sinnott-Armstrong, a former colleague of Gert, for suggesting this explanation.
[24] Gert, *Morality*, 188–9.

if the doctor does not imply anything about the information, other than that she is unwilling to release it to the patient. The more fundamental question, however, is what attitude a rational person would have towards the rule against deception. Gert claims that, because being deceived 'increases the chances of suffering evils', a rational person will want not to be deceived.[25] Gert believes that a rational person would want everyone else to comply with the rule so she was not deceived. This is what he calls 'the egocentric attitude' because it focuses on the person's own gain or loss. But a similar moral attitude would also be taken by people who 'seek agreement with other moral agents, or consider the rule as part of a public system that applies to all moral agents'.[26]

Though rational persons have this attitude towards the rule, it does not mean that they would never allow the rule to be violated. Gert believes that some deception can be strongly justified and that 'all rational persons will publicly allow deception when it is done with the consent of the deceived and for their benefit'.[27] Deception is also justified, Gert tells us, when it can prevent 'death and other serious harms to innocent parties'. As these examples show, Gert considers that the costs and benefits of deception are highly relevant to deciding when it is right to deceive. Thus just as, in Sidgwick's view, the rule against lying in Victorian England relied on an assessment of the consequences of lying in various situations, both to delineate the scope of the rule—what counts as lying or deception—and to provide the grounds for justifying or excusing violations of the rule, so too Gert's rule against deception looks to the consequences of deception both to define the scope of the rule 'Do not deceive' and to justify the exceptions to it.

iii. Sissela Bok

Further confirmation that Sidgwick's observations about the rule of veracity still apply today comes from Sissela Bok's widely read *Lying*, which is in some respects a more detailed 20th-century version of Sidgwick's study of the same topic. Bok investigates many different

---

[25] Gert, *Morality*, 189. [26] Gert, *Morality*, 189. [27] Gert, *Morality*, 189.

situations in which lying may be justified, including white lies, social science research that can only be done by deceiving the research subjects, lies to protect the confidentiality of clients, lies told to liars or to enemies, lies told by politicians for the public good, and lies told to the sick and dying. Basing her argument on our common moral intuitions, Bok considers and rejects the view that lying is always wrong. Instead she points out that many of our common practices, including social relationships and education, are based on trust. We believe that other people tell us the truth—about them, about us, and about the world. Hence it is important for us to try to build and maintain a strong 'foundation of respect for veracity'. Bok's grounds for this are thoroughly consequentialist. Trust and integrity are, she says, 'precious resources, easily squandered' and deceptive practices can fuel other wrongs. Lies often have harmful consequences, yet there are occasions when the consequences of a lie are more helpful than harmful, and the lie can be justified. Bok's analysis of lying would have fitted neatly into Sidgwick's argument that no self-evident principle of veracity can explain when we do, and when we do not, think lying is justified, and instead we need to appeal to some kind of utilitarian view to support the judgments we typically make about lying.

5. Conclusion

The rule against lying can be taken as typical of the rules of common sense morality, all of which need further justification. Common sense morality is, Sidgwick tells us, 'unconsciously Utilitarian' (*ME* 424). Because it is only unconsciously so, common sense morality leaves us feeling a need for some sort of 'rational synthesis' or 'deeper explanation' of *why* the conduct we commonly judge to be right really is right. This demand generates 'a third species or phase of Intuitionism, which, while accepting the morality of common sense as in the main sound, still attempts to find for it a philosophic basis which it does not itself offer' (*ME* 102).

We have looked at some contemporary ethical theories that in important respects represent Sidgwick's perceptional intuitionism and his common sense morality. In discussing his philosophical intuitionism we will take a different approach. As we have seen, the term 'philosophical intuitionism' does not refer to one particular normative theory. It is rather a view about how we can obtain knowledge of truths about morality. Sidgwick believes that we can grasp very general moral axioms that can provide the basis of different normative theories. For this reason we have divided the discussion of philosophical intuitionism into two separate chapters, one on the methodology of justification and the other on the content of the principles we are justified in reaching. In the following chapter we will compare Sidgwick's philosophical intuitionism with its major rival as a form of justification in contemporary ethics, the model of reflective equilibrium. In Chapter 5 we present the axioms that are the substantive conclusions of Sidgwick's philosophical intuitionism.

4

Justification in Ethics

1. Sidgwick on Justifying Ethical Principles

In book III Sidgwick sets out certain methodological conditions that any significant self-evident rule should fulfil if it is to achieve 'the highest degree of certainty attainable' and so serve as the premise of reasoning that 'is to lead us cogently to trustworthy conclusions'. These conditions are (*ME* 338–42):

1. 'The terms of the proposition must be clear and precise.'
2. 'The self-evidence of the proposition must be ascertained by careful reflection.' The importance of this condition comes from the fact that we often mistakenly take for self-evident intuitions either our 'impressions and impulses', 'opinions' that we have got used to by hearing them often, or rules that 'we have a habitual impulse to obey'. Sidgwick proposes 'a Cartesian method of testing the ultimate premises of our reasoning, by asking ourselves if we clearly and distinctly apprehend them to be true'. He does not, however, claim that this method will guarantee an error-free outcome.
3. 'The propositions accepted as self-evident must be mutually consistent.' If there is a conflict between two intuitions that we take as self-evident, at least one of them must be erroneous. Sidgwick says that many writers treat this condition too lightly, putting it aside as a problem that can be solved later. He is, however, adamant that 'such a collision is absolute proof that at least one of the formulae needs qualification'. Once

suitably qualified, however, it may no longer present itself as self-evident at all.

4. To the extent that other equally competent judges deny the truth of a proposition that I hold, my own confidence in the truth of that proposition should be reduced, and if I have no more reason to suspect that the other judges are mistaken than I have to suspect that I am mistaken, this should lead me, at least temporarily, to 'a state of neutrality'.

For Sidgwick, this condition comes from understanding that truth is essentially the same for everyone. Hence if any of my judgments conflict with those of another, at least one of us must be mistaken. It remains only to find on which side the error lies.

Sidgwick concludes that none of the rules of common sense morality he considered in book III meet these four conditions. When we consider these rules in general terms, he suggests, they seem obvious to everyone, but they lack clarity and precision. As soon as we try to define them more precisely, they cease to be obvious. In other situations, the rules of common sense may leave us with equally plausible alternatives, and no way of choosing between them. In some cases there is no definite rule that seems able to cover the moral notion that common sense morality accepts, and in yet other cases there are disparate moral elements that cannot be brought under any single rule, except something very broad like the principle of utility. Thus the rule that we should tell the truth fails the first condition—it is not clear enough what 'telling the truth' involves. When we try to make it more precise, for instance as to whether it applies to each of the variety of cases that Sidgwick discussed, any answer we give will lead to a rule that fails the fourth condition—competent judges will disagree as to whether the more precise rule is right.

Sidgwick does not take his critique of common sense rules as showing that they are unsuitable 'to give practical guidance to common people in common circumstances'. The general rule applying to the central cases can still have force, even if the rule is not an absolute and independent principle, and even if for each rule there is 'a margin of conduct involved in obscurity and perplexity'. Sidgwick sees his review of the morality of common sense not as wholly destructive of that morality, but as showing that it cannot be elevated into a system of intuitionist ethics (*ME* 360–1). The next stage of his search for a sound method of ethics must therefore be to seek clear and self-evident moral principles that meet his four requirements for leading us cogently to trustworthy moral conclusions. We will pursue that topic in the next chapter.

2. Reflective Equilibrium

i. *Rawls on Justification in Ethics*

Philosophers who ask how we can justify our beliefs can be divided into two rival camps according to how they answer. On one model, knowledge must start from some foundation that we cannot doubt. Descartes is the standard example of a foundationalist. Do I know that I am sitting here at a desk, typing? I could be dreaming, or an evil demon could be deceiving me, planting illusions in my brain, if I even have a brain. But I am thinking, so some thinking substance must exist and I am that substance. This 'I think therefore I am' is, for Descartes, the foundation on which he seeks to build all knowledge. Other philosophers, however, do not think that we can test any single belief in isolation. Suppose that we try to test a scientific theory in an experiment, and the data we get are not what the theory predicted. Have we refuted the theory? Not necessarily. If the theory itself fits with other well-established theories, we may reject the validity of the data rather than reject the theory. We may, for instance, take the view that our instruments must have malfunctioned, or that we have overlooked some confounding features of the situation that could explain the aberrant data. In general, these philosophers argue, what we take to be knowledge in a particular case will be what coheres best with our overall set of beliefs, and the most coherent possible set of beliefs will be what we regard as knowledge as a whole. Hence this view is known as coherentism.

In ethics a form of coherentism called reflective equilibrium became popular after John Rawls used it in his highly influential book, *A Theory of Justice.* In that book Rawls proposes that we start by regarding a moral theory as 'the attempt to describe our moral capacity'.[1] This description is not just a list of the moral judgments we make, but rather an attempt to formulate a set of principles that, together with our factual beliefs, would lead us to make these judgments. For example, in the specific case of justice, Rawls writes, 'A conception of justice characterizes our moral sensibility when the everyday judgments we do make are in accordance with its principles.' He compares the moral philosopher's task with Noam Chomsky's attempt to formulate the principles underlying the judgments we make about which sentences in our native language are grammatical and which are not.

To this, so far entirely descriptive, account of the task of moral philosophy, Rawls then introduces an important further idea: that of 'considered judgments'. These are the judgments 'in which our moral capacities are most likely to be displayed without distortion' and, therefore, the judgments about which we are most confident, and which we make without being unduly swayed by our own interests. They are, in other words, the judgments we make under conditions that are favourable for judging well. Rawls then sets out his classic statement of the method of reflective equilibrium:

When a person is presented with an intuitively appealing account of his sense of justice (one, say, which embodies various reasonable and natural presumptions), he may well revise his judgments to conform to its principles even though the theory does not fit his existing judgments exactly. He is especially likely to do this if he can find an explanation for the deviations which undermines his confidence in his original judgments and if the conception presented yields a judgment which he finds he can now accept. From the standpoint of moral theory, the best account of a person's sense of justice is not the one which fits his judgments prior to his examining any conception of justice, but rather the one which matches his judgments in reflective equilibrium. As we have seen, this state is one reached after a person has weighed various proposed conceptions and he has either revised his judgments to accord with one of them or held fast to his initial convictions (and the corresponding conception).[2]

Rawls sees our considered judgments as facts, and a moral theory as analogous to a scientific theory. A scientific theory seeks to

---

[1] Rawls, *A Theory of Justice,* 41.   [2] Rawls, *A Theory of Justice,* 42–3.

match observational data—and if some data do not fit an otherwise attractive theory, we may question the reliability of the data. 'I wish to stress...', Rawls writes, 'that a theory of justice is precisely that, namely, a theory' and he adds: 'There is a definite if limited class of facts against which conjectured principles can be checked, namely, our considered moral judgments in reflective equilibrium.'[3]

Reflective equilibrium has become the dominant procedure for justifying a normative theory. Brad Hooker observes that 'most philosophers currently accept this theory' and T. M. Scanlon has gone so far as to say that reflective equilibrium is not only 'the best way of making up one's mind about moral matters' but 'the only defensible method: apparent alternatives to it are illusory'.[4]

Rawls did not claim to have invented the method of reflective equilibrium. On the contrary, he thought it had been used by many great philosophers of the past, including Aristotle and 'most classical British writers through Sidgwick'.[5] The suggestion that Sidgwick had used the method of reflective equilibrium did not meet with general approval from admirers of Sidgwick, and a lively discussion sprang up on whether Sidgwick was a foundationalist or a coherentist.[6] The interpretive issue is interesting, but the difference of opinion on this issue is revealing, not only about Sidgwick, but also about these two methods of justification. If philosophers can place Sidgwick in what seem to be two radically different camps on the issue of justification, isn't it possible that those two methods of justification are less distinct than has generally been assumed? Our main aim in this section will be to show that, though initially the two methods seem sharply distinct, some current readings of reflective equilibrium and foundationalism in ethics, as of coherentism and foundationalism in philosophy more generally, have led to a narrowing of the gap between the two approaches.

[3] Rawls, *A Theory of Justice*, 44.
[4] Scanlon, 'Rawls on Justification'.
[5] Rawls, *A Theory of Justice*, 45.
[6] For discussion, see Singer, 'Sidgwick and Reflective Equilibrium'; Sverdlik, 'Sidgwick's Methodology'; Brink, 'Objectivity and Dialectical Methods in Ethics'; Skelton, 'Henry Sidgwick's Moral Epistemology'; Crisp, 'Sidgwick and the Boundaries of Intuitionism'; Phillips, *Sidgwickian Ethics*, ch. 3.

ii. Wide Reflective Equilibrium

The method of reflective equilibrium has developed since *A Theory of Justice*, most notably in the distinction now drawn between narrow and wide reflective equilibrium. Although this distinction can be traced to *A Theory of Justice*, Rawls first named these two ways of understanding reflective equilibrium in his 1974 article on 'The Independence of Moral Theory'[7] and he describes the distinction most clearly in his late work, *Justice as Fairness: A Restatement*. With the idea of a conception of justice in mind, he explains that we adopt a narrow reflective equilibrium if we choose the conception of justice that leads to 'the fewest revisions' in our initial judgments and 'proves to be acceptable when the conception is presented and explained'. We then accept other judgments that match this conception. If, however, we carefully consider other conceptions of justice and the arguments that stand behind those conceptions, weighing the force of the various reasons for and against these conceptions, we adopt wide reflective equilibrium. Rawls acknowledges that 'wide and not narrow reflective equilibrium is plainly the important concept'.[8] We agree and will take wide reflective equilibrium as the only form worth discussing.

The idea of wide reflective equilibrium has been developed most fully by Norman Daniels. As he puts it, seeking wide reflective equilibrium amounts to 'the process of bringing to bear the broadest evidence and critical scrutiny we can, drawing on all the different moral and nonmoral beliefs and theories that arguably are relevant to our selection of principles or adherences to our moral judgments'.[9] Daniels describes the procedure as follows:

We collect the person's initial moral judgments, which may be particular or general, and filter them to include only those of which he is relatively confident and which have been made under conditions generally conducive to avoiding errors of judgment. We propose alternative sets of moral principles which have varying degrees of 'fit' with the moral judgments. Rather than settling immediately for the 'best fit' of principles with judgments, which would give us only a narrow

---

[7] Rawls, 'The Independence of Moral Theory'.
[8] Rawls, *Justice as Fairness: A Restatement*, 31.
[9] Daniels, *Justice and Justification*, 1–2.

equilibrium, we advance philosophical arguments that reveal the strengths and weakness of the competing sets of principles...Assume that some particular set of arguments wins and the moral agent is thus persuaded that one set of principles is more acceptable than the others...The agent may work back and forth, revising his initial considered judgments, moral principles, and background theories, to arrive at the equilibrium point...[10]

iii. Criticisms of Reflective Equilibrium

From the moment it was introduced, the idea of reflective equilibrium faced criticism. R. M. Hare started the discussion in his review of *A Theory of Justice* when he argued that Rawls's use of the method of reflective equilibrium means that his theory is a form of intuitionism that relies on common agreement about what is right and wrong. Rawls, he said, disguises this fact by calling intuitions 'considered moral judgments'. Hare argued that agreement is not proof of anything, and what we believe to be right may be a result of self-interest, cultural upbringing, or other biases. Hare summed up his view of reflective equilibrium by recalling the words of Plato: 'If a man starts from something he knows not, and the end and middle of his argument are tangled together out of what he knows not, how can such a mere consensus ever turn into knowledge?'[11] R. B. Brandt took up the same general line of criticism, asserting that 'The fact that a person has a firm normative conviction gives that belief a status no better than fiction. Is one coherent set of fictions supposed to be better than another?'[12]

Daniels believes that behind such objections there are really two distinct claims: first that reflective equilibrium merely systematizes a set of moral judgments that has in some way been previously determined, and second that an ethical theory should rest on a firmer foundation than considered moral judgments.[13] In response to the first charge, Daniels emphasizes the way in which, in seeking wide reflective equilibrium, all of our judgments can be revised, and

---

[10] Daniels, *Justice and Justification*, 82.
[11] Plato, *The Republic*, 533c, quoted by R. M. Hare in 'Rawls' Theory of Justice—I', 146–7.
[12] Brandt, *A Theory of the Good and the Right*, 20.
[13] Daniels, *Justice and Justification*, 27.

no type of judgment is immune to revision.[14] This is clearly different from Rawls's original conception of a 'definite if limited class of facts against which our conjectured principles can be checked'.[15] In response to the second claim, that considered judgments are insufficiently credible to serve as the foundation for a normative theory, Daniels makes an even more significant revision, allowing a crucial role for a sound moral theory. To say that there is no credibility in moral judgments in wide reflective equilibrium is, Daniels says, 'at best premature', adding that it is plausible to think that only when we have developed an acceptable moral theory and therefore have 'an answer to our puzzlement about the kind of fact (if any) a moral fact is' that we will be able to distinguish 'initially credible' and 'merely initially believed' moral judgments, and explain the difference between them. We might then also have a better understanding of why people agree on some moral views and disagree on others. It might turn out that some of the agreement is a matter of shared culture or ideology, but it might also be the case that the agreement results from the truth of some shared background theories, on which the moral judgments are based. Daniels acknowledges that we do not yet have an account of what makes moral judgments credible, but adds that 'we also have no reason to think it impossible or improbable that we can develop such an account once we know more about moral theory'.[16] This is consistent with Rawls's acceptance, in 'The Independence of Moral Theory', of the possibility that, in the procedure of reflective equilibrium, 'one [moral] conception may unanimously win out over all the rest and even suffice to limit quite narrowly our concrete moral judgments'. He adds that 'it is natural to suppose that a necessary condition for objective moral truths is that there be a sufficient agreement between the moral conceptions in wide reflective equilibrium, a state reached when people's moral convictions satisfy certain conditions of rationality'—although he then declines to consider whether this supposition is correct.[17]

[14] Daniels, *Justice and Justification*, 28.
[15] Rawls, *A Theory of Justice*, 44.
[16] Daniels, *Justice and Justification*, 33.
[17] Rawls, 'The Independence of Moral Theory', 9.

iv. Can Wide Reflective Equilibrium Lead us to Moral Truth?

If we contrast a foundationalist theory of ethics, which we can think of as building a theory on a solid bedrock, with a coherentist theory like reflective equilibrium, then it is plausible to think that the foundationalist project will—if it can succeed—deliver objectively true ethical judgments, while the coherentist theory will produce only inter-subjective agreement between those who have an overlapping moral consensus, and thus share enough considered moral judgments to reach the same reflective equilibrium.

It is instructive here to compare the different ways in which Ross and Rawls based their different normative theories on moral convictions. Ross, as we saw in the previous chapter, takes the 'main moral convictions of the plain man' as the foundation of his theory. Like Rawls, he draws an analogy with scientific method, and sees that not all moral convictions are equally valid: 'the moral convictions of thoughtful and well-educated people are the data of ethics just as sense-perceptions are the data of a natural science'. He even proposes something that looks very much like trying to find an equilibrium: 'The verdicts of the moral consciousness of the best people are the foundation on which [the moral theorist] must build; though he must first compare them with one another and eliminate any contradictions they may contain.'

Despite these parallels, there is a crucial difference between Ross and Rawls. For Ross, our main moral convictions, presumably cleansed of contradictions, are 'knowledge from the start'. The moral order expressed in our convictions about our prima facie duties is 'just as much part of the fundamental nature of the universe (and, we may add, of any possible universe in which there were moral agents at all) as is the spatial or numerical structure expressed in the axioms of geometry or arithmetic'.[18] In contrast, Rawls describes his own view as a form of 'constructivism', indicating that he takes the best moral view to be something we construct, not a truth we discover that is part of any possible universe with moral agents.

---

[18] Ross, *The Right and the Good*, 29–30.

What then would Rawls say if he were to encounter people from a different culture with a very different set of moral convictions? Presumably the theory that they would construct from their considered moral judgments would be very different from that which he would construct from the considered moral judgments of his own culture. If there is no truth to be found beyond the achievement of reflective equilibrium, this leads to moral relativism. Rawls acknowledges this in his 1980 essay 'Kantian Constructivism in Moral Theory', when he directly contrasts his approach with that of Sidgwick:

We have arrived at the idea that objectivity is not given by 'the point of view of the universe' to use Sidgwick's phrase. Objectivity is to be understood by reference to a suitably constructed social point of view, an example of which is the framework provided by the procedure of the original position.[19]

Here he seems to have rejected the possibility that he had envisaged 6 years earlier, in 'The Independence of Moral Theory', of unanimous agreement based on conditions of rationality—which would provide a kind of objectivity that might well be described, with a little extra colour, as taking the 'point of view of the universe'. Another 5 years on, in 'Justice as Fairness: Political, Not Metaphysical', Rawls writes that his theory of justice 'presents itself not as a conception of justice that is true, but one that can serve as a basis of informed and willing political agreement between citizens viewed as free and equal persons'. He sees this as a way of 'avoiding philosophy's longstanding problems', such as 'the problem of truth and the controversy between realism and subjectivism about the status of moral and political values'.[20] But to say that objectivity is to be understood by reference to something that is socially constructed is not to avoid the controversy between realism and subjectivism in ethics: it is to take one side in this controversy.

Daniels accepts that there is evidence in Rawls's writing that he took an 'eliminative' view of moral truth,[21] but Daniels's own view is that the issue of whether reflective equilibrium is compatible with the idea

---

[19]   Rawls, 'Kantian Constructivism in Moral Theory', 570.
[20]   Rawls, 'Justice as Fairness: Political, Not Metaphysical', 230.
[21]   Daniels, *Justice and Justification*, 45 n. 30.

of objective truth in ethics is more complicated. We need, he says, to distinguish two definitions of 'objective'. We may say that something is objective if there is sufficient intersubjective agreement about it, or we may say that something is objective if it expresses 'truths relevant to the area of inquiry'.[22]

That reflective equilibrium can lead to intersubjective agreement is obvious, but that isn't what most people mean by objectivity or truth. As Daniels aptly puts it: 'The fear here is that intersubjective agreement will be taken as *constitutive* of moral truth or as eliminative of any fullblown (realist) notion of objective moral truth.' He then goes on to suggest that, although the fact that we reach agreement in wide reflective equilibrium is neither a necessary nor a sufficient condition for claiming that we have reached objective moral truth, 'such convergence may constitute *evidence* we have found some'.[23] Whether it does will depend on whether the convergence can be explained by showing that the agreement is the result of some similar set of biases, perhaps resulting from a similar culture. Conversely, even if there is no convergence, if we can explain the failure of convergence by pointing to 'a provincial feature of human psychology or biology', then we might construct a 'modified and *idealized* "agreement" on principles' and that idealization might 'be a good candidate for containing objective moral truths, even though it is *not* accepted in any actual wide equilibrium'.[24]

This passage, with its acceptance of the idea that there could be objective moral truths that are not accepted in wide equilibrium, indicates that Daniels's version is significantly different from Rawls's version, and closer to the position taken by Sidgwick, Ross, and all those who want to talk about the possibility of ethical principles that are objectively true, whether the majority accept them or not. Before we investigate how far Daniels's conception of wide reflective equilibrium is from Sidgwick's foundationalist approach, however, we need to pause to consider a more radical defence of reflective equilibrium that may be closer to Rawls's original idea.

[22] Daniels, *Justice and Justification*, 33.
[23] Daniels, *Justice and Justification*, 35.
[24] Daniels, *Justice and Justification*, 36, italics in the original.

v. Mikhail and the Linguistic Analogy

As we have seen, in *A Theory of Justice* Rawls compared the task of a moral philosopher seeking to defend a moral theory with the linguist's task in proposing a theory of grammar that explains which sentences we find grammatical. This analogy is clearly tenuous, and potentially very misleading. Native speakers of a language have a very high degree of agreement as to what constitutes a grammatical sentence in that language, whereas it is easy to think of moral issues on which there is very widespread disagreement. More importantly, the standard of grammar in a language is just what native speakers of that language judge to be a correctly formed sentence. Native speakers of Polish construct Polish sentences without using the definite article where English native speakers constructing a similar English sentence would use the definite article, but no one would suggest that this means that either the Polish or English speakers are mistaken; whereas if one culture practises slavery and another does not, we may very well suggest that the one that practises slavery is doing something morally wrong. In ethics, we believe there is a standard beyond what most people judge to be right. In grammar, there is no such standard.

John Mikhail takes the linguistic analogy very seriously, and he believes that Rawls did too. In *Elements of Moral Cognition* Mikhail writes: 'Rawls' early writings contain the germs of a scientific theory of moral cognition that far surpasses the work of psychologists like Jean Piaget and Lawrence Kohlberg in terms of depth, coherence, and analytical rigor.'[25] If this is true, then Rawls was engaged in a very different enterprise from that which occupied Sidgwick, who at the outset of *The Methods* made it clear that 'an attempt to ascertain the general laws or uniformities by which the varieties of human conduct, and of men's sentiments and judgments respecting conduct, may be explained, is essentially different from an attempt to determine which among these varieties of conduct is right and which of these divergent judgments valid' and indicated that it was the latter attempt on which he was engaged (*ME* 2).

[25] Mikhail, *Elements of Moral Cognition*, 10–11.

In responding to criticism, from Hare and from one of us, of the attempt to draw normative conclusions from data about the judgments most people make,[26] Mikhail maintains that 'the problem of empirical adequacy' has been central in the history of moral philosophy. He refers to Rawls's claim that 'most classical British writers through Sidgwick' used reflective equilibrium and adds that 'it becomes clear that these writers placed this problem at the very center of their inquiries'.[27] This may be true of most British philosophers before Sidgwick—Mikhail cites, in particular, Hume, Price, and Smith—but as we have seen, it is emphatically not true of Sidgwick, and we would also question whether it is true of Price. If the historical claim about earlier writers is accurate, however, all this does is highlight Sidgwick's historic significance in turning moral philosophy decisively and permanently from empirical to normative questions. Similarly, if Mikhail is correct in his interpretation of Rawls and how we should understand reflective equilibrium, then Sidgwick would have firmly rejected reflective equilibrium, on grounds similar to those on which he rejected Mill's attempt to use inductive methods to establish hedonism. We cannot establish what we ought to do by establishing what we desire to do, or even what most people think it right to do.

Mikhail's reply is to question the idea of a standard of what is right that is external to our existing moral sense. The idea of such an objective standard is, he says, 'complex, controversial, and possibly unintelligible' and 'may be an inappropriate and unattainable ideal for moral philosophy'. He thinks that Rawls was right not to let questions of this kind 'stand in the way of the problems of descriptive and normative adequacy as he has framed them, which are perfectly intelligible and which present both difficult challenges and fruitful opportunities in their own right'.[28] We grant that it may be possible and worthwhile to develop adequate descriptive theories of our moral sense without resolving the complexities and controversies raised by the idea of an

---

[26] Hare, 'Rawls' Theory of Justice—I'; Singer, 'Sidgwick and Reflective Equilibrium'.

[27] Mikhail, *Elements of Moral Cognition,* 312.

[28] Mikhail, *Elements of Moral Cognition*, 223, 226.

objective standard, but we agree with Sidgwick that we cannot reach a normatively adequate theory in that way.

Mikhail concludes his discussion of the objection that Rawls's conception of moral theory, as he presents it, is insufficiently normative by saying that Rawls's critics 'have not identified and defended a more cogent metaethical alternative...It takes a theory to beat a theory.'[29] Sidgwick did identify a meta-ethical alternative, and this book defends it.[30] In any case, one cannot just say that the problem is complex and difficult, and then go on to claim normative adequacy for an entirely different conception against which Sidgwick, Moore, Parfit, and many others have already pressed powerful arguments. These arguments need to be met, and in our view, they cannot be. Our argument in Chapter 7 will indicate a further ground for resisting the approach Mikhail defends, for there we shall argue that, even with moral judgments that do not vary with differences of culture, and are virtually universally accepted, the explanation for this near-universal acceptance, far from leading us to accept the judgments as valid, should lead us to reject them.

3. Foundationalism

The plausibility of foundationalism with regard to knowledge arises from the difficulty of finding any other way of avoiding an infinite regress that would lead to scepticism. Suppose that I believe that Napoleon invaded Russia because I read it in a biography of Napoleon, and I believe that the biography is reliable because the author is a history professor at a renowned university, and I believe that the author is a history professor at a renowned university because I heard him lecture there recently... eventually, if I am to really know anything at all, this chain of reasoning must come to a stop. It can't be infinite, because beings with finite lives cannot follow infinite chains of reasoning. Nor can it be circular, because circular reasoning does not justify a belief—it could all be false. To avoid circularity, the chain

---

[29] Mikhail, *Elements of Moral Cognition,* 227.
[30] For a fuller defence, see Parfit, *On What Matters,* and Parfit's contribution to Singer, *Does Anything Really Matter?*

of justification must start from a belief that I am justified in holding directly, on the basis of experience or reason, without inferring it
from any other beliefs. Foundationalists hold that all justification has
this structure of having one or more basic beliefs that are the foundation of everything that we know.

The chief objection to foundationalism concerns the basic beliefs.
How can we know that they are true? We can say that they are
self-evident, but if someone else does not regard them as self-evident,
it seems that we have nothing more to say, except to reassert the truth
of the beliefs—and this strikes opponents of foundationalism as
unacceptably dogmatic.

In contrast to the foundationalist view that all our knowledge of
the world ultimately rests on a small number of basic beliefs, coherentism holds that it is our entire set of beliefs that constitutes what
we know about the world, and what counts as knowledge depends
on what fits best with all of our beliefs. Can this view escape relativism or scepticism? Couldn't different people, or people from different
cultures, or perhaps rational aliens from another planet have sets of
beliefs that are different from ours, but just as coherent? If so, could
these conflicting beliefs all be knowledge? Doesn't this really mean
that none of them is knowledge? And if that is so, then even in the
absence of anyone with a divergent but equally coherent set of beliefs,
coherence alone does not justify our attributions of knowledge.

We do not need to resolve this problem in epistemology here, but
we do want to note—because it will prove useful when we turn to
the parallel problem in ethics—a recent restatement of foundationalism that addresses the problem of dogmatism. Susan Haack defends
a middle position between foundationalism and coherentism, coin-
ing the awkward term 'foundherentism' for her combination of the
empirical foundations of our knowledge and the mutual dependence
of our beliefs.[31] Robert Audi draws a useful distinction between strong
and modest foundationalism. Strong foundationalism is exempli-
fied by Descartes's search for a foundation that is beyond doubt.
Modest foundationalism accepts the possibility of error regarding

---

[31] Haack, *Evidence and Inquiry*.

foundational beliefs. The justification of such beliefs is 'at least typically defeasible'. In addition, beliefs that are not foundational need not derive all of their justification from foundational beliefs, 'but only enough so that they would remain justified if any other justification that they have (say, from coherence) were eliminated'.[32] Modest foundationalism allows a role for coherence, or at least for incoherence, as incoherence with other beliefs may defeat even the justification for a foundational belief—Audi's example is that my justification for believing that I may be hallucinating prevents me from remaining justified in believing that there are books in front of me. Justification does not owe its existence to coherence, but it can be undermined by incoherence. Modest foundationalists can also accept that coherence can enhance justification. The more mutually coherent independent factors we believe to support the truth of a proposition, the stronger our justification for believing it, other things being equal. The difference between modest foundationalism and coherentism is that, for modest foundationalists, coherence between beliefs is a necessary consequence of their truth, whereas for coherentists either it is constitutive of the truth, or it is seen as constitutive of justification, and truth is seen as something unknowable, because we can never get beyond beliefs that are justified in terms of their coherence with each other. As Audi writes: 'what modest foundationalism denies regarding coherence is only that it is a basic source of justification'.[33]

i. Foundationalism in Ethics

Roger Ebertz has drawn on Audi's work to distinguish 'classical ethical foundationalism' from 'modest ethical foundationalism'. Whereas the classical ethical foundationalist holds that some ethical beliefs are 'directly justified and unrevisable because they are self-evidently true', and the rest of one's ethical beliefs are justified because they are based on these directly justified self-evident beliefs, the modest ethical foundationalist is committed only to holding that some ethical beliefs have a 'prima facie direct justification' and all other ethical

---

[32] Audi, 'Foundationalism, Coherentism and Epistemological Dogmatism', 417–18.
[33] Audi, 'Foundationalism, Coherentism and Epistemological Dogmatism', 418–19, 425, 429–30.

beliefs are justified in a way that depends on their relationship to these directly justified beliefs.[34]

With this distinction in mind, let us take an example of ethical foundationalism. My aunt knitted a cardigan and sent it to me for my birthday. My mother, who knows that the cardigan isn't in a style I wear, tells me that I should tell my aunt that I like it. I ask my mother why she thinks it is right to lie, and she says it is right when it is the only way of avoiding making someone unhappy. I ask why we should avoid making people unhappy, and she says that one should not make people unhappy if no one will be better off as a result. When I ask her why not, she says: 'I do not know. I cannot find a reason for that, but I just know that it is wrong to make people unhappy when no one will be better off if you do.' If my mother holds that this judgment is unrevisable, she is a classical ethical foundationalist. If, however, she regards it as something she knows directly, but could, conceivably, abandon—perhaps because she recognizes that her judgments are fallible, and it could became clear that this judgment is incoherent with other beliefs that she also believes she knows directly—she is a modest ethical foundationalist.

Sidgwick's position is not too far from that of the mother in this exchange. In his autobiographical sketch, he wrote that 'the supreme rule of aiming at the general happiness, as I had come to see, must rest on a fundamental intuition, if I was to recognise it as binding at all' (ME p. xxi). This remark suggests that Sidgwick is a foundationalist rather than a practitioner of the method of reflective equilibrium. The 'fundamental intuition' that Sidgwick is referring to here is the intuition that a proposition is self-evident, but we will postpone to the next chapter a discussion of the details of the ethical propositions Sidgwick considered self-evident. Here we will instead pose the obvious objection that can be made to any foundationalist: how do you know that what you take to be self-evident really is self-evident? What if you and I do not find the same claims self-evident? In the face of disagreement, when you admit that you cannot infer your belief from anything else, isn't it simply dogmatic to assert that you are right?

---

[34] Ebertz, 'Is Reflective Equilibrium a Coherentist Model?', 200–1.

Dogmatism is often associated with having a closed mind, and with asserting one's claims with greater confidence than is warranted. We do not think that anyone familiar with Sidgwick's approach could consider him closed-minded, nor as a writer with excessive confidence in his conclusions. Consider, for instance, this passage:

> I wish therefore to say expressly, that by calling any affirmation as to the rightness or wrongness of actions 'intuitive,' I do not mean to prejudge the question as to its ultimate validity, when philosophically considered: I only mean that its truth is apparently known immediately, and not as the result of reasoning. I admit the possibility that any such 'intuition' may turn out to have an element of error, which subsequent reflection and comparison may enable us to correct; just as many apparent perceptions through the organ of vision are found to be partially illusory and misleading: indeed the sequel will show that I hold this to be to an important extent the case with moral intuitions commonly so called. (*ME* 211)

This sounds like a modest ethical foundationalist, rather than a classical one, in Ebertz's terminology. Sidgwick does not assume that the intuitions he takes to be self-evident must be so; on the contrary, he is open to objections, and unusual in his willingness to see difficulties with his own position. At the conclusion of *The Methods* he even acknowledges that he has found 'an ultimate and fundamental contradiction in our apparent intuitions of what is Reasonable in conduct'—that is, in the very intuitions that he has been defending—and that from this contradiction it seems to follow that the reasoning that has led him to these judgments is 'illusory' (*ME* 508). This is consistent with him being a modest foundationalist whose conclusions can be put in doubt by incoherence between them and another belief. We can conclude that dogmatism is not a necessary element of foundationalism.[35]

Nevertheless, we appear to have a direct conflict between Sidgwick, who is a foundationalist, and Scanlon, who writes that there is no alternative to the method of reflective equilibrium. Sidgwick even argues, against Mill's attempt to base hedonism on induction from what people want, that if it is claimed that we ought to see happiness as the only reasonable ultimate end of human action, this proposition

---

[35] Audi concludes that modest fundamentalists are not necessarily dogmatic. See 'Foundationalism, Coherentism and Epistemological Dogmatism', 432–9.

'must either be immediately known to be true,—and therefore, we may say, a moral intuition—or be inferred ultimately from premises which include at least one such moral intuition' (*ME* 98). So, on the one hand we have the idea that there is no alternative to using reflective equilibrium, and on the other the idea that there is no alternative to founding ultimate moral principles on intuitions. Can these two views be reconciled?

Sidgwick would have regarded the original concept of reflective equilibrium outlined in *A Theory of Justice* as resting on an illegitimate inference from a description of people's moral judgments to a conclusion of a quite different type, about what we ought to do. Can the move to wide reflective equilibrium overcome this flaw? In some formulations—those that allow philosophical arguments in support of particular normative moral theories—it may. The question is, however, whether wide reflective equilibrium does not then become so wide that there is no longer a contrast between it and any other way of justifying normative theories, including foundationalism.

We have already seen that Daniels accepts that wide reflective equilibrium allows us to 'advance philosophical arguments that reveal the strengths and weakness of the competing sets of principles'. He is also willing to accept the possibility of objective moral truth, meaning by that a truth that is not constituted merely by the convergence of views in reflective equilibrium. Suppose, then, that after investigating many different moral theories, it turns out that the only acceptable one is that moral facts are objective truths discoverable by reason. Suppose, too, that it turns out that philosophical arguments show us which moral facts are objectively true and that all true ethical judgments can be derived from a very small number of objective moral truths discoverable by reason—perhaps even just one. (Daniels could exclude this possibility by limiting the scope of the philosophical arguments he will allow to be advanced, so that they refer only to normative theories, and not to the basis on which we may claim to know that such theories are justified. But this would beg the question against objectivism, and would be unacceptably *ad hoc*.) As this example shows, whether wide reflective equilibrium and foundationalism can be distinguished depends on the substance of the 'acceptable moral theory' and on what the philosophical arguments allow us to conclude. Without knowing which moral theory is acceptable and whether there are philosophical arguments that reveal which moral judgments are objectively true, we cannot exclude the possibility that, once we have found the soundest moral theory and the best philosophical arguments, we will be able to demonstrate that none, or virtually none, of our existing moral judgments are credible; and the strength of the reasoning in support of this theory may be such that we can confidently reject all, or virtually all, of our current moral judgments, and replace them with the judgments that follow from the moral theory. (If you have trouble imagining an acceptable moral theory that is so sweeping in its rejection of widely held moral judgments, we ask you to suspend judgment until you have read the next three chapters.) In that case, the distinction between wide reflective equilibrium and foundationalism has narrowed to a vanishing point. It would then be true, but trivial, that when we do normative ethics, there is no alternative to the method of reflective equilibrium. There would be no alternative because wide reflective equilibrium is so wide that it includes all possible methods, including foundationalism. (Moral particularism, discussed in the previous chapter, might seem to be an exception, since it appears to eschew theory, and even coherence, altogether.[36] But in so far as advocates of particularism offer reasons for their approach—for example, that our immediate intuitions are more reliable than ethical judgments derived in any other manner—then it too is a position that we might reach by means of wide reflective equilibrium.)

We are not the first to deny that there is a clear distinction between reflective equilibrium and foundationalism. Ebertz argues that unless one assigns some credibility to the initial moral judgments then it is far too easy for anyone using reflective equilibrium to obtain coherence in his or her moral beliefs. All we have to do is select any moral theory that fits our background theories, derive a set of moral judgments from it, and substitute them for whatever moral judgments we held previously. Once we do assign some credibility to initial

[36] Tersman, 'The Reliability of Moral Intuitions', 400.

moral judgments, however, they function as foundational beliefs, and reflective equilibrium becomes a form of modest ethical foundationalism.[37] No wonder that Sidgwick cannot easily be placed in one camp or the other.

Folke Tersman has attempted to defend the distinctiveness of reflective equilibrium. He responds to Ebertz's argument by doubting that 'it is psychologically possible to just forget about one's initial considered judgements and replace them with the implications of the theory one explores'.[38] Whether that is so will no doubt vary from individual to individual, but is not relevant to the question we are trying to answer, which is about what we ought to do, not what we can do without psychological difficulty. An atheist who was raised as an orthodox Jew may find it psychologically impossible to enjoy pork, even though he now sees no sound reason for observing Jewish dietary laws, but that has nothing to do with whether he would be justified in eating it.

Tersman makes a further objection to Ebertz: replacing the initial judgments has to be justified, he writes, by 'the theories of reliability that account for the credibility of considered judgements in the first place'. It isn't clear what these theories of reliability might be, especially as Daniels thinks that we cannot have such theories of reliability until we have an acceptable moral theory. In the following chapter, however, we shall see how Sidgwick seeks to establish reliability in moral judgments, and in Chapter 7 we shall also consider a theory of reliability—or perhaps better, a theory of unreliability—that explains both why people hold certain moral beliefs, and why many of these beliefs are unreliable.

---

[37] Ebertz, 'Is Reflective Equilibrium a Coherentist Model?', 204.
[38] Tersman, 'The Reliability of Moral Intuitions', 399.

5

The Axioms of Ethics

1. Sidgwick's Axioms

If common sense morality does not yield clear and self-evident ethical principles, can such principles be found elsewhere? In asking this question, Sidgwick moves to the third phase of the intuitionist method, 'Philosophical Intuitionism', which is also the title of chapter 13 of book III of *The Methods*. Many philosophers claim to have found self-evident principles that can serve as the basis for a moral theory, but Sidgwick does not think that any of them achieved more than partial success. A supposedly self-evident principle such as 'we ought to give every man his own' appears plausible only as long as we do not ask what is meant by 'his own'. Once that question is asked, it emerges that this means 'what it is right that he should have'. But then the principle is really a tautology and gives us no new information. In other cases the circle of reasoning that brings us back to our original starting point is larger, but the upshot is the same.

So is it possible to have self-evident principles or intuitions that really tell us something? On the one hand Sidgwick thinks that common sense gives us a 'strong instinct' to believe in the existence of such principles. On the other hand, when we study human history and observe human behaviour in different times and places, it seems harder for us to believe that there could be a code of absolute rules that applies to all human beings irrespective of the different circumstances in which people live. Sidgwick thinks that there is some truth in both of these perspectives, and they can be reconciled by the view that there are some principles which, once stated explicitly, we can see to be true, but these principles are so abstract and universal in their scope that we cannot use them to derive, in any direct or immediate manner, what we ought to do in particular situations. For that derivation, we need to use some other method (*ME* 379).

What then are these abstract and universal self-evident principles? For those brought up in the Judeo-Christian tradition, the first that would come to mind is the Golden Rule, 'Do to others as you would have them do to you'. But this lacks precision, because there may be differences in the nature or circumstances of two individuals, A and B, such that it would be wrong for A to treat B in the way that B may properly treat A. The self-evident element of the Golden Rule expresses something that is independent of any particular historical tradition, and should instead be stated, Sidgwick maintains, in a negative form, as follows:

It cannot be right for A to treat B in a manner in which it would be wrong for B to treat A, merely on the ground that they are two different individuals, and without there being any difference between the natures or circumstances of the two which can be stated as a reasonable ground for difference of treatment. (*ME* 380)

Sidgwick acknowledges that this principle is not much of a guide to what we ought to do. Its effect is, he says, to throw the burden of proof on anyone who claims that it is right for him to treat someone else in a manner to which he would object if it were done to him. But taken in this way it is recognized by common sense as being of practical significance and, Sidgwick says, 'its truth, so far as it goes, appears to me self-evident'.

Sidgwick also formulates the principle as an aspect of our common notion of justice:

whatever action any of us judges to be right for himself, he implicitly judges to be right for all similar persons in similar circumstances. Or, as we may otherwise put it, 'if a kind of conduct that is right (or wrong) for me is not right (or wrong) for someone else, it must be on the ground of some difference between the two cases, other than the fact that I and he are different persons.' (*ME* 379)

This principle has an application in the administration of law, and thus is an important element in our standard idea of justice. It requires that rules should be applied impartially as far as mere difference of persons is concerned. Once again, to know this is not enough as it doesn't tell us anything about the content of just rules, and hence does not say *what* rules should be applied impartially. A rule requiring people to provide for their own children is impartial in this sense, although it also requires them to be partial between their own children and the children of strangers. But Sidgwick's principle does tell us to exclude one kind of partiality from government and, Sidgwick writes, 'from human conduct generally'.

Sidgwick notes that the principle of justice 'is obtained by considering the similarity of the individuals that make up a Logical Whole or Genus' (*ME* 380). Another such 'whole' is the 'good on the whole' of an individual person. This thought leads Sidgwick to his second self-evident axiom. He first mentions the proposition 'that one ought to aim at one's own good', which he refers to as one way in which the principle of 'Rational Self-love or Prudence' can be stated. But he again points out that this can be a tautology, if we define 'good' as 'what one ought to aim at'. Instead he takes as self-evident the view that one ought to aim at 'one's own good on the whole'. This is not tautologous because it requires us to have 'impartial concern for all parts of our conscious life', or as Sidgwick also puts it: 'Hereafter *as such* is to be regarded neither less nor more than Now' (*ME* 381). The phrase '*as such*' is intended to guard against the counterargument that a present good may reasonably be preferred to a future good on the grounds that the present good is more certain than the future one. That is no objection to the principle Sidgwick is defending. Similarly, a week sometime in the future may be more important to me than a week now, because I expect that my ability to enjoy it will increase during the interim, but that is different from saying that one week is more important than another simply because it is nearer or further away in time. Since we tend to be more strongly attracted to pleasures or other goods that are present or in the near future than goods that are in the more distant future, the form in which the principle is of practical relevance to most people is that, allowing again for differences in certainty, 'a smaller present good is not to be preferred to a greater future good'.

Stated thus, this principle falls short of supporting egoism. Impartial concern for all parts of our conscious life is compatible with having impartial concern for all parts of everyone's life, and with having no greater concern—or possibly even less concern—for one's own life than for the lives of others. Granted, this discussion of the avoidance of bias in favour of one period of time over another should be understood within the context of the principle that Sidgwick mentioned at the outset of his discussion of this axiom, namely that one ought to aim at one's own good on the whole. But a utilitarian will accept that one's own good is a part of the universal good. The question is, ought one to aim at one's own good on the whole, even if that would put one in conflict with aiming at the universal good? That is what egoism requires. In his chapter on 'Philosophical Intuitionism', Sidgwick does not put forward any self-evident principle that indisputably shows that one ought to do this—indeed, he claims that he has put forward an argument for utilitarianism (*ME* 388). (In the next chapter, we will examine other passages from *The Methods* in which he discusses the relationship between egoism and utilitarianism.[1])

---

[1] A scholarly dispute exists over whether what Sidgwick calls the 'axiom of prudence' expresses the idea of egoism. The form of the axiom that he offers in bk III, ch. 13, is, as we have noted, about having equal concern for all moments of our existence over time and not about preferring our own good to the good of others (*ME* 381, 383). In the autobiographical preface to the 6th edn, however, Sidgwick has in mind a distinct principle when he says that 'the rationality of self-regard seemed to me as undeniable as the rationality of self-sacrifice'(*ME* xviii). It is to this distinct principle, the principle of rational egoism, that he refers when in the concluding chapter he sets up the problem of the dualism of practical reason (*ME* 497–8). Parfit has suggested (e-mail to the authors, 25 June 2012) that the fact that Sidgwick does not include the principle of rational egoism among the axioms he discusses in bk III, ch. 13, could be taken as evidence that he grasped that rational egoism is in some way less secure or undeniable than the axioms he does endorse in that chapter. This leads us to a view slightly different from that taken by J. B. Schneewind, who argues that to understand why Sidgwick believed that there is a dualism of practical reason, we should understand the axiom of prudence as 'my own greatest happiness is the rational ultimate end for me' (*Sidgwick's Ethics and Victorian Moral Philosophy*, 290–7). Here we are in agreement with Mariko Nakano-Okuno, who sees rational egoism as a distinct principle and not the 'axiom of prudence' defended in bk III, ch. 13. Although we recognize that in his concluding chapter Sidgwick does refer to the principle of egoism as 'the maxim of Prudence' and puts it on a par with 'the maxim of Rational Benevolence' (*ME* 498), this must be a rare example of loose writing in *The Methods,* because egoism includes the axiom of prudence, but goes significantly beyond it. As Nakano-Okuno points out, egoism requires one to maximize one's own happiness, whereas the axiom of prudence does not require maximization, nor does it refer to happiness, but demands only impartiality over time. See her

Sidgwick reaches the third of his principles by pointing out that, just as we can talk about the good on the whole of an individual person, summing up parts of the good in his life, so too we can talk about universal good as a sum of particular goods of all individuals. In this way we reach a further self-evident principle:

the good of any one individual is of no more importance, from the point of view (if I may say so) of the Universe, than the good of any other; unless, that is, there are special grounds for believing that more good is likely to be realised in the one case than in the other.

Sidgwick then makes a further claim:

And it is evident to me that as a rational being I am bound to aim at good generally,—so far as it is attainable by my efforts,—not merely at a particular part of it.

From these two rational intuitions, Sidgwick deduces what he calls 'the maxim of Benevolence, in an abstract form':

each one is morally bound to regard the good of any other individual as much as his own, except in so far as he judges it to be less, when impartially viewed, or less certainly knowable or attainable by him. (*ME* 382)

Strictly speaking, this maxim is not an axiom, because it is deduced from the two self-evident intuitions we have just mentioned. In subsequent passages Sidgwick does, however, refer to it as an axiom, and we will do the same.

Sidgwick notes, in a fine piece of understatement, that the duty of benevolence, as recognized by common sense morality, 'seems to fall somewhat short' of what his maxim of benevolence requires. He explains the discrepancy by pointing out that, in practice, people will do better to concern themselves with promoting the good of a limited number of people, especially those to whom they are close, than to attempt to promote the good of everyone. In that way they are likely to have greater success in promoting good generally, even from

Sidgwick and Contemporary Utilitarianism, 103–7, 112–13. Doubts about whether Sidgwick's axiom of prudence is an axiom of egoism go back as far as von Gizycki's review of '*The Methods of Ethics,* by Henry Sidgwick', and more recently have been expressed by Shaver, *Rational Egoism,* 74–7; Schultz, *Henry Sidgwick: Eye of the Universe,* 213; and Skorupski, 'Three Methods and a Dualism', 61–82. See also Phillips, *Sidgwickian Ethics,* 138–9.

a universal perspective. (We discuss Sidgwick's views on this issue in Chapter 11.) Suppose, though, Sidgwick continues, that we were to ask an ordinary person to consider this question: would it be morally right for you to seek your own happiness if doing so meant sacrificing the greater happiness of another human being, with no counterbalancing gain to anyone else? Sidgwick asserts—perhaps rather optimistically—that if such a person were to consider this question fairly, as a matter of conscience, the answer would be 'unhesitatingly in the negative' (*ME* 382).

Sidgwick believes that he has demonstrated that, in the generally accepted principles of justice, prudence, and benevolence, 'there is at least a self-evident element, immediately cognizable by abstract intuition'. He sees this as vindicating the common belief that 'the fundamental precepts of morality are essentially reasonable'. When Sidgwick reflects on propositions like 'I ought not to prefer a present lesser good to a future greater good' and 'I ought not to prefer my own lesser good to the greater good of another', he finds that he cannot deny them. They are self-evident to him, in much the same way as he can see the self-evidence of mathematical propositions such as 'if equals be added to equals the wholes are equal'. In contrast, although 'custom and general consent' may have given 'a merely illusory air of self-evidence' to other principles such as 'I ought to speak the truth' and 'I ought to keep my promises', when we reflect on these principles we see that they are not really self-evident, but require some other kind of rational justification (*ME* 383).

After presenting his self-evident axioms Sidgwick observes that they are not specific to intuitionism in the narrower sense in which he has used this term to refer to a morality that, like common sense morality, is based on rules that require obedience irrespective of the consequences. The axiom of prudence is 'implied in Rational Egoism as commonly accepted', while the axiom of justice belongs as much to utilitarianism as to intuitionism in the narrower sense, and the axiom of rational benevolence is 'required as a rational basis' for utilitarianism. To demonstrate that the self-evidence of the axiom of benevolence is the *only* way in which utilitarianism can be put on a rational basis, Sidgwick takes us on a short tour of the deficiencies of John Stuart Mill's 'proof' of the principle of utility.[2]

Sidgwick's conclusion, then, is that utilitarianism is 'the final form into which Intuitionism tends to pass, when the demand for really self-evident first principles is rigorously pressed'. He acknowledges, however, that the argument thus far still falls short of taking us from intuitionism to utilitarianism. That is because the axioms, including the axiom of rational benevolence, talk about aiming at what is 'good' for individuals, but leave untouched the question of the nature of that good. Utilitarianism, on the other hand, at least in the classical form in which Sidgwick understands it, takes pleasure or happiness as the ultimate good. We therefore still need an argument to show that the ultimate good is happiness.

2. The Axiom of Justice

We begin our discussion with Sidgwick's axiom of justice. It does seem to be true that morality does not allow us to make exceptions for ourselves. If I claim that you ought to give to the poor, I must either agree that I too ought to give to the poor, or I must give a reason for the difference in what we ought to do. Perhaps you are a billionaire and I am struggling to pay for the nursing care that my elderly mother needs. That might justify my differing moral judgments. But I cannot simply say that you ought to give to the poor but I do not have to give to the poor because if I give away my money then *I* will have less to spend on *my*self and I don't want that, whereas if you give away your money, then *you* will have less to spend on *your*self, and I don't mind that. I cannot, to use Sidgwick's words, simply say that different judgments apply because you and I are 'different persons'.

Sidgwick writes that the axiom of justice is part of utilitarianism and of intuitional ethics—pointedly omitting any mention of rational egoism (*ME* 386–7). It is therefore worth asking whether rational egoism is consistent with the axiom of justice. The answer depends on how we formulate egoism. If it is phrased in the grammatical first

---

[2] The now notorious 'proof' occurs at the beginning of ch. 4 of Mill's *Utilitarianism*.

person, as the view that 'Everyone ought to do what is in *my* inter-ests', then it draws a distinction between myself and others that vio-lates the axiom of justice. On the other hand, if we think of it in the third person, as the view that 'Everyone ought to do what is in *his or her* interests', then the principle does not refer to any particular indi-viduals, and so there is no inconsistency with the axiom of justice.[3] Presumably those who defend egoism as a principle of rational action are defending the third person version of it. Because it may be bet-ter for me if you are more concerned about the interests of others (of whom I am one) than you are for your own interests, rational egoism may lead egoists to deny, when speaking publicly, that it is rational to be an egoist, although that is what they continue to believe. As we shall see in Chapter 10, something similar may also be true of utili-tarianism, though perhaps in more limited circumstances.[4]

The axiom of justice may seem undeniable, but could that be because it is in fact part of the meaning of moral terms like 'right' and 'ought'? That is what R. M. Hare, whose views on the meaning of the moral terms we already encountered in Chapter 1, would have argued. Moral judgments are, Hare said, universalizable prescrip-tions and this means that, in Hare's words: 'if I say "This is what ought to be done; but there could be a situation exactly like this one in its non-moral properties, but in which the corresponding person, who was exactly like the person who ought to do it in this situation, ought not to do it", I contradict myself'.[5] To examine whether Sidgwick's axiom of justice can be defended in this way, we need to understand Hare's position, and the major objection that has been made to it.

Hare held that moral language requires universalizable judg-ments, but there is no logical requirement that one use moral lan-guage, or guide one's life by universalizable principles. Amoralists who refuse to be guided by universalizable judgments need not, in his view, be inconsistent or irrational—indeed, since Hare thought that there are no objective reasons for action, he could not claim

  [3] See Shaver, *Rational Egoism*, 80–1.
  [4] For a discussion of the implications of a principle such as consequentialism being self-effacing, see Parfit, *Reasons and Persons*, 150ff.
  [5] R. M. Hare, 'Universal Prescriptivism', 456. See also Hare, *Freedom and Reason*, 10ff.

that universalizability is a requirement of reason.[6] Taking this view weakens the significance of any conclusions that we may be able to reach by drawing out the implications of universalizability, since people can always escape those conclusions by refusing to make moral judgments. Nevertheless, many of us do want to use terms like 'ought' and 'right', so the possibility of rational amoralism does not render pointless the exercise of exploring the implications of universalizability, and seeing what normative conclusions may follow from its application.

For Hare, when I prescribe something, using moral language, my prescription commits me to a substantive moral judgment about all relevantly similar cases. This includes hypothetical cases in which I am in a different position from my actual one. So to make a moral judgment, I must put myself in the position of those affected by my proposed action. Whether I can accept the judgment—that is, whether I can prescribe it universally—will depend on whether I could accept it if I had to live the lives of all those affected by the action. Although in his early work Hare treats this as a formal requirement that cannot bind anyone to any particular ethical conclusion, by 1976, when he wrote 'Ethical Theory and Utilitarianism', he had decided that putting yourself in the position of others affected by your action means giving their desires and preferences as much weight as your own, and therefore a proper understanding of the implications of the moral terms leads us to the conclusion that the only moral judgments we can prescribe universally are those that do the most to satisfy the interests and desires of all those affected by our actions. Thus universalizability leads to a form of utilitarianism based on the maximal satisfaction of interests or desires—commonly known as preference utilitarianism.[7]

To get such a strong conclusion from a merely formal claim about moral language looks suspiciously like the philosophical equivalent of getting a rabbit out of an empty hat. Among those critical of it was

---

[6] In *Moral Thinking*, Hare discusses amoralism, but does not reject it on the grounds that the amoralist is necessarily involved in a contradiction. Instead he appeals to prudential considerations as a reason for not being an amoralist. See esp. 186.

[7] See 'Ethical Theory and Utilitarianism'; repr. in R. M. Hare, *Essays in Ethical Theory*; and *Moral Thinking*, esp. chs. 5 and 6.

John Mackie, who thought that Hare had failed to distinguish three different stages of universalizability:

1. The irrelevance of numerical differences.
2. Putting oneself in the other person's place.
3. Taking (equal) account of different tastes and ideals.

Mackie was ready to grant that universalizability, in some sense, is part of the meaning of the moral terms, but said that, if so, this will be no more than the first, or at most the first two, of these stages of universalizability, and no substantive moral principles, whether utilitarian or not, will follow from either of these two stages. Hare, however, needs to appeal to the third stage for his argument to succeed. That is a problem for his argument, because moral language appears to allow me to commit myself to an ideal that is independent of my own desires. For example, there seems to be no contradiction in saying: 'Let justice be done although we all perish, because rather than perpetrate injustice, I am willing to sacrifice everything that is dearest to me.' If that is not a contradiction, we cannot treat moral language as having the logical implication that every moral question is simply a matter of weighing up desires or interests. Mackie asserts that the moral terms allow me to assume that my ideals are *true* and ought to prevail over any mere aggregation of interests, including my own. Mackie sees this as the fatal weakness in Hare's attempt to draw substantive moral conclusions—and specifically, utilitarian conclusions—from universalizability. His verdict has been widely shared.

Sidgwick would have seen Mackie's objection to Hare as akin to his own warning that we must not confuse tautologies with substantive moral principles. According to Hare, to say that I ought to do X is to say that X is the only act I can prescribe when I give equal weight to the interests of all those affected by my act. On Hare's own analysis, however, this is true in virtue of the meaning of 'ought'. The judgment therefore provides guidance only to someone who has already decided to do what she 'ought' to do, using 'ought' in the sense that Hare describes. Such a person must, however, have previously committed herself to doing what she can prescribe when she gives equal weight to the interests of all affected by her actions. If we are using the word 'ought' in this way, then the principle that I ought to give equal weight to the interests of all those affected by my acts is a tautology. Tautologies lead, Sidgwick said, only to 'sham-axioms' (*ME* 374). But does Hare's claim that universalizability is built into the meaning of the moral terms mean that Sidgwick's own axiom of justice is, after all, a tautology rather than a substantive ethical principle? There are two passages in *The Methods* that seem to suggest that Sidgwick and Hare are doing something very similar. In the first, Sidgwick says that 'by reflecting on the general notion of rightness' we can reach the 'practical rule' that 'We cannot judge an action to be right for A and wrong for B, unless we can find in the natures or circumstances of the two some difference which we can regard as a reasonable ground for difference in their duties' (*ME* 208–9). In the second, he discusses, in book IV, the rational process— he says that it is only by a stretch of language that it can be called a 'proof'—by which an egoist might be persuaded to accept utilitarianism. He acknowledges, however, that this proof requires that 'the Egoist should affirm, implicitly or explicitly, that his own greatest happiness is not merely the rational ultimate end for himself, but a part of Universal Good' and adds that the egoist can refuse to say this, and so avoid the proof of utilitarianism (*ME* 497–8; see also 420–1). In the first of these passages, Sidgwick appears to be deducing a practical conclusion from a moral concept, and in the second, there seems to be a striking parallel with Hare's amoralist, who can avoid both utilitarianism and self-contradiction by refusing to use moral language.

It is implausible that Sidgwick would have forgotten his own forceful insistence that a tautology can lead only to a 'sham-axiom' and not to a rule of practical significance. It therefore seems best to understand the phrase 'reflecting on the general notion of rightness' as referring, not to the formal concept of rightness, but rather to a widely shared substantive view of it. (This phrase does, after all, occur at the start of his discussion of the morality of common sense.[8])

Regarding Sidgwick's treatment of the egoist and Hare's treatment of the amoralist, there are important differences.[9] For Hare there is

---

[8]   We owe this point to Skelton, 'Sidgwick's Philosophical Intuitions', 198–9.

[9]   For an account of these differences and an argument similar to that made here, see Nakano-Okuno, *Sidgwick and Contemporary Utilitarianism*, ch. 8, esp. pp. 180–8.

a specific form of discourse that he refers to as 'moral' whereas for Sidgwick, as we have seen, ethics encompasses any rational procedure by which we decide what we ought to do, or what it is right to do.[10] For Hare, reasoning about how to live can take place outside the sphere of morality, and without using moral terms, whereas for Sidgwick any such reasoning occurs within ethics. Sidgwick's egoist does not need to avoid moral language in order to avoid the 'proof' of utilitarianism— indeed at one point Sidgwick describes him as one who 'strictly confines himself to stating his conviction that he *ought* to take his own happiness or pleasure as his ultimate end' (*ME* 420; our emphasis). The issue, for Sidgwick, is not what language we use, but what we have most reason to do. If, as we have argued in Chapter 2, there are objective reasons for action, then Sidgwick is right to take what we have most reason to do as the important question. Nevertheless, as we shall see in Chapter 6, it is a question Sidgwick was unable to resolve, and he therefore ends up no better able to overcome the egoist than Hare was able to overcome the amoralist. At least, though, Sidgwick's question allows us to see what the task of vindicating the rationality of ethics requires: an argument to show that the egoist (or the amoralist) is not acting on the best reasons available. Whether such an argument exists is the subject of Chapter 7.

3. The Axiom of Prudence

Sidgwick's second axiom is that 'Hereafter *as such* is to be regarded neither less nor more than Now', which he also puts as saying that we should have 'impartial concern for all parts of our conscious life' or that 'a smaller present good is not to be preferred to a greater future good'. The most fundamental form of the axiom is the one that requires impartial concern for all parts of our conscious life, since that implies that we should not give more or less weight to 'now' than to any future moment. This principle has been challenged in two distinct ways that correspond to the difference between the more fundamental form of the axiom, and the form that focuses on avoiding giving greater weight to the present

---

[10] See Ch. 1.

than to the future. Bernard Williams asserts the primacy of the present moment, while Michael Slote denies the more fundamental form of the axiom, holding that we are justified in thinking of some times of life as more important than others. The rejection of Sidgwick's axiom of prudence is also implicit in the view, widely held among economists, that we should discount the future. But this raises different issues that we shall postpone to Chapter 12 when we discuss Sidgwick's views about how utility should be distributed. Here we are focusing on discounting within a single person's life, rather than discounting the future in general.

i. The Dominance of Now

Bernard Williams describes the view that it is rational to have equal consideration for all moments of one's existence as seeing one's life as 'a given rectangle that has to be optimally filled in'. But, Williams claims, this conception (which he also attributes to John Rawls and Thomas Nagel) omits the perspective of how much of that rectangle I care to cultivate. In his view, 'the correct perspective on one's life is *from now*'.[11] Williams thinks that we have 'projects', a term he uses to describe a set of desires or concerns. Among these projects are some that are closely related to a person's existence and 'to a significant degree give a meaning to his life'. These Williams calls 'ground projects' and he regards them as 'the condition of my existence' because 'unless I am propelled forward by the conatus of desire, project and interest, it is unclear why I should go on at all'. A person's 'ground projects' provide him with the motive force that 'propels him into the future'.

Williams is here taking a Humean approach to practical reason. He does not consider that an act could be in accordance with our desires, projects, and interests, and yet nevertheless irrational. We argued against this view of practical reason in Chapter 2, where we saw that giving supremacy to present desires can lead to incoherence in one's decision-making. Here is another example, suggested by John Broome, that is less bizarre than Parfit's example of the person with Future Tuesday Indifference. Suppose

---

[11] Williams, 'Persons, Character and Morality', esp. 206–9.

that I have time to go to just one movie this week. When I buy the ticket on Monday, I can choose between a less good movie on Wednesday or a better one on Friday. Even though I know I will enjoy the Wednesday movie less than the Friday one, because I am taking the perspective 'from now' and I now desire my pleasures to come sooner rather than later, I rank a smaller good on Wednesday above a greater good on Friday, and so I buy the ticket for Wednesday's movie. From my present perspective this is the correct decision, but I can predict that on Friday, I will—again, correctly—regret that I made that decision—for by then I will be at a different 'now' and will be sorry that I have not maximized value for myself. It is as if each decision I make is being made by a different 'I' with values that change continually as he or she moves through time. As Broome says: 'A theory that says you can act rightly even though you know that you will later correctly judge that you acted wrongly is not consistent with living a coherent life.'[12] John Rawls makes a similar point when he writes that it is a guiding principle of rationality that 'a rational individual is always to act so that he need never blame himself no matter how his plans finally work out'.[13] On Williams's view, if our desires, projects, and interests change—and even if, as in Broome's example, they change in entirely predictable ways—we would often regret having made the wrong decision.

Dean Buonomano, in *Brain Bugs*, describes a study of college students who were asked to draw lines on a computer to represent periods of time varying from 3 to 36 months. The relationship between the length of line and the period of time was not linear, suggesting that the difference between 3 months and 6 months seemed much longer than the difference between 33 months and 36 months.[14] The students had a focus from 'now' rather than judging 'hereafter as such' as 'neither less nor more than now'. There are also many studies showing that people make irrational choices about the future. For example, they prefer to take a sum of money offered now rather than a larger sum a month later, even when the difference between the sums is an effective annual interest rate

[12]   Broome, *Climate Matters*, 151.
[13]   Rawls, *A Theory of Justice*, 371.
[14]   Loftus *et al.*, 'Time went by so slowly', 3–13; we owe this reference to Buonomano, *Brain Bugs*, 103–4.

of 345 per cent.[15] Buonamano offers a plausible explanation for our bias towards the present. For our ancestors, he points out, life was shorter and the future less certain than it is for those of us living in developed countries today. To obtain food and survive in the immediate future was more important than thinking about months or years ahead. As a result, he suggests, we developed brains with a built-in 'bug' that leads us to discount the future in ways that, given the circumstances of people living in developed countries today, are irrational.[16]

ii. The Importance of Happy Endings

Michael Slote has some sympathy with Williams's preference for the present, but his distinctive argument against giving equal weight to all periods of our life draws more from Aristotle, and treats human beings as organisms with a natural life-cycle.[17] On that basis, he suggests, 'we typically and naturally think of some times of life as more important than others'. For example, we give less weight to childhood. We do not consider that someone who had a wonderful childhood but then had a disappointing adulthood had as good a life as someone who had a miserable childhood and a fulfilling adulthood.[18] In determining how good a life is, Slote suggests 'what happens late in life is naturally and automatically invested with greater significance and weight'.[19] To persuade us to share this intuition, he asks us to think of two politicians, one of whom spends a long time in the political wilderness, and then achieves power and does much good, dying while still in office, at a decent old age. The other politician achieves success much earlier in life, winning office while still young, holding it just as long as the first politician, and doing a similar amount of good. Then he loses power and although he too lives to a decent old age, he dies

---

[15] Thaler, 'Some Empirical Evidence on Dynamic Inconsistency', 201–7.

[16] Buonomano, *Brain Bugs*, 118–19.

[17] Slote, *Goods and Virtues*, 21, 36.

[18] Slote, *Goods and Virtues*, 13ff.

[19] Slote, *Goods and Virtues*, 23. Others to hold that what happens later in life typically matters more include Brentano in *The Foundation and Construction of Ethics*, 196–7; Lewis, *An Analysis of Knowledge and Valuation*, 488; Velleman, 'Well-Being and Time'; and Richard Chappell, 'Value Holism'.

without ever regaining it. Our natural response is, Slote says, to judge the first life as more fortunate.

To the view that what happens late in life matters more than what happens early in life, Slote adds what appears to be a distinct claim: that the prime of life matters more than any other period. Outstanding success at the senior citizen shuffleboard competition does not make up for failure in one's prime. Childhood and senescence make, Slote says, 'a rather negligible contribution to what seems to matter most in a total human life'. Larry Temkin might agree with Slote's judgment about the lives of the two politicians. In *Rethinking the Good*, he urges that we should reject Sidgwick's conception of individual self-interest in favour of one that pays attention to the direction or pattern of a life. To illustrate this, he asks us to consider two scenarios:

In the first, one's life starts out poorly and steadily improves, so that at the end of one's life one is very well off. For simplicity, let's just divide the life into five twenty-year segments and say that as the life progresses, one's levels would be 10, 30, 50, 70, and 90, respectively. In the second scenario, the pattern is reversed. The life starts out very well off and steadily worsens, so that the life ends poorly. Specifically, as the life progresses, one's levels would be 90, 70, 50, 30, and 10, respectively. On the simple additive approach, the two lives are equally good, and if, in fact, the second life ended at level 12 instead of level 10, then that life would be better than the first all things considered. But I think relatively few people would actually choose a life plan for themselves, or a loved one, in accordance with this position.[20]

Similar issues apply to both Slote's and Temkin's pairs of lives. If Slote's politicians experienced the same amount of bitterness and frustration when out of office, and the same feelings of elation and achievement when in office, we do not have any confidence in the intuitive judgment that one life is better or worse than the other. Similarly, in considering Temkin's example, we are liable to imagine that the person whose happiness level declines experiences disappointment that things are getting steadily worse. She may feel frustrated at her inability to reverse this trend, and she will have little to look forward to. No wonder that we would not choose for ourselves a life plan like hers! But because the numbers that Temkin provides are levels of overall

---

[20] Temkin, *Rethinking the Good*, 111.

well-being, these feelings must already be factored into them; that means that, apart from these factors, the life of the person whose happiness level declines must be significantly *better* than the life of the person whose happiness level increases. If we keep this in mind, we may well feel that the two lives are equally good.

Temkin considers this type of response, and does not deny that there are 'kernels of psychological truth' in it. But he rejects it because 'it amounts to the view that either people's judgments about such alternatives are unreflective, or even on reflection people can't accurately assess the alternatives presented'. Temkin says that he finds such a view 'both deprecating and dubious'.[21] We shall return to this response shortly.

Some of the intuitions to which Slote appeals can be explained in ways that are compatible with Sidgwick's axiom. One reason why we give less weight to childhood and senescence may simply be that they are normally shorter than the period between them. To be miserable for 12 or even 16 years is bad, but not as bad as being miserable for 50 years. We can therefore defend the idea that each year of a miserable childhood or decrepit old age makes one's life as a whole worse by the same amount as a miserable year of adulthood, while still accepting that the quality of one's childhood or one's senescence makes a smaller contribution to how well one's life goes than a miserable adulthood.

If, in addition to giving less weight to childhood or senescence as a whole, people typically give less weight to each year of these periods of life than they do to adulthood, this may be explained by the fact that, when people are in their prime, their abilities to enjoy their life, and to savour their achievements, are much greater than at earlier or later stages. A 4 year old, for instance, is not likely to remember very vividly what he achieved; a 20 year old may remember her greatest moments for the rest of her life, and feel pleased that she had those experiences. From an altruistic perspective, too, what people achieve in their prime typically contributes more to others—to those they love and care for, and to society as a whole—than what people

---

[21] Temkin, *Rethinking the Good*, 112.

achieve in childhood and senescence. These reasons may justify us in giving greater weight to what people achieve in their prime, without departing from the view that the same amount of good should be given the same weight, whenever it occurs.[22]

Slote comes close to this account of the greater emphasis we give to what people achieve in the prime of life, but his explanation differs in an important way from the view we have just described. On Slote's view, we think of humans as organisms that exist in order to develop their various capacities and talents. The 'prime of life' is when our capacities are at their greatest, and that is why it has greater significance.

We are organisms, but that does not justify the view that there is some special value to the time of life at which our capacities are at their greatest, apart from the contribution these capacities and talents make to our happiness and the happiness of others. Aristotle may, as Slote suggests, have held that there is special value in this period of life because he believed that everything exists for a purpose, and the purpose for which humans exist is to develop their capacities, especially the capacity to reason. That anyone living before Darwin should hold a teleological view of the universe, and of human existence, is understandable; it is, nevertheless, mistaken. Because this way of thinking still permeates some religious views of the world, it may still influence popular thought. It is odd, though, that a contemporary philosopher should take this pre-Darwinian conception of our existence as a ground for rejecting the view that, in considering the quality of a life, it is rational to give equal consideration to the same amount of good at each moment of that life.

Finally, in reacting to the pairs of lives presented by both Slote and Temkin, we may be under the sway of a different kind of phenomenon explored by the psychologist Daniel Kahneman who has shown that our attitudes to experiences are greatly influenced by the way they end. We tend to prefer an experience that caused us more pain over one that caused us less pain, as long as the pain in the final moments of the more painful experience was not as bad as the pain at

---

[22] We thank Mariko Nakano-Okuno for this point.

the final moment of the less painful experience. Kahneman considers this one form of the well-known 'focusing illusion' which he states as 'Nothing in life is as important as you think it is when you are thinking about it.'[23] To give one well-known example, if you ask Americans if they think they would be happier if they moved to California, they tend to focus on the better climate that California has, in comparison to most parts of the United States, and answer in the affirmative. But climate makes very little difference to how happy people are, so their answers are likely to be astray. In the case we are considering, people tend to think about how the experience ends, neglecting its duration.

Kahneman's research is particularly relevant to the issues of assessing happiness that we will discuss in Chapter 9 and we will therefore postpone a fuller account of it to that chapter. For now it suffices to say that the judgments on which Slote and Temkin rely are of a type that appears to lead to false judgments in a variety of other contexts. More generally, Kahneman's findings suggest that we should not be greatly influenced by what 'we typically and naturally think' about some times of life being more important than others. Our typical and natural feelings may be mistaken. If Temkin finds this 'deprecating' then, unless Kahneman's findings can be shown to be mistaken, deprecation can be avoided only at the cost of overlooking errors to which we are demonstrably prone.

4. The Axiom of Rational Benevolence

The essence of Sidgwick's principle of rational benevolence is that we are 'morally bound' to have as much concern for the good of any other individual as we have for our own good. Sidgwick derived the principle of rational benevolence from two self-evident principles, the first that from the point of view of the universe, the good of one individual is of no more importance than the good of any other (unless there are special reasons for thinking that more good is likely to be realized one case rather than in the other), and the second that 'as a rational being I am bound to aim at good generally' rather than

---

[23] Kahneman, *Thinking Fast and Slow,* 402.

at just a part of it. These two principles lay the foundation from which 'we may deduce, as a necessary inference', the principle of rational benevolence. Taking the point of view of the universe is an essential part of the ground for the principle of rational benevolence. The requirement to aim at good generally will not lead us to the principle of rational benevolence unless we have accepted that our own good is of no more importance than the good of any other—without that, it would be possible to take our own good as the general good, and therefore to aim predominantly or even exclusively at our own good. We see that our own good is of no more importance than the good of any other when we take the point of view of the universe. We will therefore begin our discussion of the principle of rational benevolence by considering Bernard Williams's objection to the very idea of taking the point of view of the universe.

i. Is Evaluation from the Point of View of the Universe Conceivable?

When Sidgwick introduces the idea of taking 'the point of view of the Universe' he adds a parenthetical 'if I may say so', which suggests that he has some reservations about ascribing a point of view to the universe. This is of course understandable, if the expression is taken literally. Pantheists, nowadays, are rare, and for the rest of us the universe has no point of view. Sidgwick clearly intended the idea as a metaphor, to suggest detachment not only from the perspective of one's own good, but from the various other possible partial stances that one might take, such as 'the point of view of my country' or 'the point of view of my race'. Bernard Williams correctly understands what Sidgwick is doing:

The model is that I, as theorist, can occupy, if only temporarily and imperfectly, the point of view of the universe, and see everything from the outside, including myself and whatever moral or other dispositions, affections or projects, I may have; and from that outside view, I can assign to them a value.

But Williams regards this as an impossibility:

The difficulty is...that the moral dispositions, and indeed other loyalties and commitments, have a certain depth or thickness; they cannot simply be regarded, least of all by their possessor, just as devices for generating actions or states of affairs. Such dispositions and commitments will characteristically be what gives one's life some meaning, and gives one some reason for living it...There is simply no conceivable exercise that consists in stepping completely outside myself and from that point of view evaluating *in toto* the dispositions, projects and affections that constitute the substance of my own life.[24]

Williams thinks this exercise is inconceivable because, when we evaluate something, we can only do so from the basis of our own dispositions, projects, and affections.

We readily grant that, as a matter of psychological fact, it is extremely difficult, and perhaps for most people impossible, to put aside those aspects of one's capacity for evaluation that are particular to oneself. But why does Williams think that it is inconceivable? The answer, surely, is that he rejects the idea of normative reasons for action that are independent of our own dispositions, projects, and affections. Williams thinks that all reasons for action are 'internal reasons' and denies that there are any 'external reasons' that give people reasons for action that do not depend on their motives or anything that they care about.[25] If, as Sidgwick believes and we argued in Chapter 2, there are objective reasons for action, independent of our desires or motivations, then we can see why, contra Williams, evaluating the world from a point of view outside one's own dispositions, projects, and affections is conceivable.

Williams's claim that we can only see things from a perspective that already starts from our own dispositions, projects, and affections is related to his well-known claim that utilitarianism destroys the integrity of the moral agent. The objection is commonly understood as a normative objection to utilitarianism: to demand that the agent focus on maximizing overall utility is to require her to violate her own integrity, and this is wrong. We will consider this interpretation, but before doing so we note that it may be a misunderstanding of Williams, who may simply be making, in other terms, the point we have already considered and rejected, namely the impossibility of abandoning one's own projects and dispositions and taking the point of view of the universe.[26] In making his point about integrity, Williams draws on two well-known examples. The first concerns

---

[24] Williams, 'The Point of View of the Universe', 191.
[25] Williams, 'Internal and External Reasons', 101–13.
[26] See T. Chappell, 'Bernard Williams'.

Jim, who is invited to shoot an innocent person, and knows that if he declines, 20 innocent people (including the one he was invited to shoot) will be shot. We shall pass over this case, however, for we think that Williams's second example makes a clearer case for the integrity objection. This example concerns George, a chemistry Ph.D. struggling to find a job. George learns of a position in a laboratory that does research into chemical weapons. (The example was written before such weapons were outlawed by international agreement, so let us assume that there is no illegality involved.) George is opposed to such weapons, but is told by someone who knows the laboratory in question that, if he refuses, the position will go to another candidate who will be particularly zealous in pursuing the research, with consequences that may be much worse than if George were to take the position.[27] The goal of maximizing utility therefore suggests that George should take the job and hide his objections to chemical weapons, while ensuring that his research leads nowhere.

Williams sees the problem as stemming from the utilitarian view of negative responsibility, which holds us responsible not only for what we directly cause, but also for what we allow or fail to prevent. On such a view, Williams says, our projects are not really ours to choose in accordance with our particular commitments and values. I should choose only what leads to the greatest expected good, and therefore must be ready to abandon every project that does not do so. There is a sense in which a utilitarian cannot have 'commitments' to projects that he will stick with, irrespective of the circumstances. As Williams puts it, 'how can a man, as a utilitarian agent, come to regard as one satisfaction among others, and a dispensable one, a project or attitude round which he has built his life, just because someone else's projects have so structured the causal scene that that is how the utilitarian sum comes out'? It is, Williams claims, 'absurd to demand of such a man, when the sums come in from the utility network which the projects of others have in part determined, that he should just step aside from his own project and decision and acknowledge the decision which utilitarian calculation requires'. To do so is to alienate him from his

---

[27] Williams, 'A Critique of Utilitarianism', 95–8.

actions and his own convictions, with which he identifies, and is, 'in the most literal sense, an attack on his integrity'.[28]

If by 'absurd' Williams here means 'inconceivable' then our earlier discussion of the conceivability of taking the point of view of the universe applies. If, on the other hand, by 'absurd' Williams means that it is absurd to think that it would be right to make this demand, then our response is that we reject Williams's account of what integrity is, and the idea that it is an overriding value. Elizabeth Ashford has pointed out that if Williams is relying on a notion of subjective integrity, then it is open to a serious objection. To free one's slaves may be contrary to the project or attitude around which a white Southern slave-owner built his life during the first half of the 19th century, but no one today would accept that he would have been justified in resisting the moral requirement to do so on the grounds that it would be a violation of his integrity.[29] Integrity may be a character trait that we admire, but it is like loyalty in that, just as we do not value loyalty in the soldiers of evil regimes, so we do not value integrity when it is based on indefensible values or projects. It is only if our projects and attitudes are defensible that we can justifiably resist moral pressure to change them. But then we need to consider whether it is defensible to have projects that do not maximize the good, and that of course is the question at issue in this chapter and this book. Williams's use of the notion of integrity is, as R. M. Hare put it, remarkable for 'the boldness of the persuasive definition by which he labels the self-centred pursuit of one's own projects "integrity" and accounts it a fault in utilitarianism that it could conflict with this'.[30]

ii. Does Taking the Point of View of the Universe Ignore 'the Separateness of Persons'?

In *A Theory of Justice,* John Rawls presents his own position as an alternative to utilitarianism, adding that the form of utilitarianism with which he will contrast his theory is 'the strict classical doctrine which receives perhaps its clearest and most accessible formulation

---

[28] Williams, 'A Critique of Utilitarianism', 116–17.
[29] Ashford, 'Utilitarianism, Integrity, and Partiality', 423–4.
[30] R. M. Hare, 'Ethical Theory and Utilitarianism', 219n.

in Sidgwick'. He goes on to say that 'the most natural way' of arriving at utilitarianism 'is to adopt for society as a whole the principle of rational choice for one man'. This way of thinking leads, Rawls argues, to a conception of social justice as 'the principle of rational prudence applied to an aggregative conception of the welfare of the group.' The underlying problem, Rawls thought, is that 'Utilitarianism does not take seriously the distinction between persons.'[31]

Since the publication of A Theory of Justice, this alleged failure to take seriously the distinction between persons has come to be seen as a crucial objection to utilitarianism. Rawls himself seems to have in mind, in the lines just quoted, the way in which Sidgwick moves from the axiom of prudence to the axiom of rational benevolence. Sidgwick's reference to 'the point of view of the universe' can also be seen as an example of this failure, because a single point of view is being used as a means of deciding what it is right to do when our actions affect many individuals, each with their own distinct point of view.

Someone who did not see that human beings are distinct individuals would have to be mentally ill, or to have achieved the state of cosmic consciousness that, according to some Buddhist teachings, is supposed to come after long years of meditation. Regarding Sidgwick, it is enough to mention a passage we shall discuss more thoroughly in the next chapter, in which he writes: 'It would be contrary to Common Sense to deny that the distinction between any one individual and any other is real and fundamental...' So why would Rawls think that Sidgwick did not take this distinction seriously?

Nozick suggests that the problem is that utilitarians imagine the sum of all individuals adding up to some kind of organic whole. As individuals, each of us may be willing to incur a present or future cost for a greater benefit at some other time, so 'Why not, *similarly*, hold that some persons have to bear some costs that benefit other persons more, for the sake of the overall social good?' Nozick answers his own question: 'But there is no *social entity* with a good that undergoes

---

[31] Rawls, A Theory of Justice, 20–4. Rawls was not, however, the first to make this point; that honour appears to go to Gauthier, Practical Reasoning, 123–7.

some sacrifice for its own good.'[32] Again, though, it is obvious that utilitarians know this. It is Hegelians and their intellectual descendants, not utilitarians, who are liable to take the kind of holistic view to which Nozick refers.

Perhaps, though, what utilitarians have failed to appreciate is that when we properly recognize the separateness of persons, it is no longer possible to add up the sum of the good or bad things that may happen to each of them. After all, where one person is concerned, she can choose whether to make some sacrifice now, for instance by not buying something she would like to buy, in order to gain a benefit later, such as having enough money to go hiking in Patagonia. It makes sense for her to say that the initial sacrifice was worth it, because it was outweighed by the gain. But can we say this when separate people are involved? John Taurek denies that we can. In his essay 'Should the Numbers Count?' he argues that we should refuse to take seriously 'any notion of the sum of two persons' separate losses' and he is willing to draw from this the implication that if we have a choice between saving one person and saving five people—and everything else is equal— we have no reason to choose to save the five rather than the one. When we deny the possibility of adding up gains and losses across different people, this will remain true no matter how large the number we can save gets: 'The numbers, in themselves, simply do not count…'[33]

Summing up the gains and losses of two separate persons and concluding that in some situations, to use Nozick's words, 'some persons have to bear some costs that benefit other persons more' is not always difficult to do. Consider this example, adapted from Parfit:

You are searching for survivors in the remains of a building that collapsed in an earthquake. You see two people, trapped in the rubble, both unconscious but alive. The only way to rescue White, and save her life, is to push aside a piece of concrete that will fall across Black's toe, breaking it. But you will then be able to rescue both White and Black, saving their lives. If you don't do this, you will be able to rescue Black, who will be uninjured, but White will die.[34]

[32] Nozick, Anarchy, State, and Utopia, 32–3, italics in original.
[33] Taurek, 'Should the Numbers Count?', 308, 310. Parfit's 'Innumerate Ethics' is a convincing rebuttal to Taurek's arguments.
[34] Parfit gives several such examples in On What Matters, Volume One, Part Two. Our example is closest to his Third Earthquake, on 222.

If it is never justifiable to impose costs on one person so that another benefits, you will have to leave White to die. That would be wrong. The fact that individuals are distinct does not debar us from weighing up the costs and benefits of our actions to different individuals.

Nozick, after suggesting that his opponents must believe in some illusory social entity, changes tack and instead accuses them of a moral failing: 'To use a person in this way does not sufficiently respect and take account of the fact that he is a separate person, that his is the only life he has.'[35] For this objection to be made to stick, however, we need an account of what is involved in respecting individuals as separate persons. Hare has offered a utilitarian account (using the term 'concern' instead of 'respect'):

> To have concern for someone is to seek his good, or to seek to promote his interests; and to have equal concern for all people is to seek equally their good, or to give equal weight to their interests, which is exactly what utilitarianism requires... To do this is not to fail to 'insist on the separateness of persons'.[36]

If Hare is correct, then the 'separateness of persons' objection to taking the point of view of the universe collapses. But is Hare right? In reply, it is often said that giving equal weight to the interests of separate people fails to show respect for the interests of those who are worse off. We should, on this view, give some weight to individual rights, or to equality or to priority for the worse-off, in a form that goes beyond what a utilitarian can endorse. Such replies transfer the debate about the separateness of persons to other normative issues, about the role of rights, or the issue of how we should distribute welfare or resources. We say something about individual rights in Chapter 10, and we discuss issues of distribution in Chapter 12, so we will leave further discussion of these objections to utilitarianism to those chapters.

---

[35] Nozick, *Anarchy, State, and Utopia*, 33.

[36] R. M. Hare, 'Rights, Utility, and Universalization: Reply to J. L. Mackie', 80. We owe this reference to Richard Chappell, 'Sacrifice and Separate Persons'; see also Richard Chappell, 'Value Receptacles'. For a general defence of utilitarianism against the separateness of persons objection, see Alastair Norcross, 'Two Dogmas of Deontology: Aggregation, Rights, and the Separateness of Persons', *Social Philosophy and Policy*, 26 (2009), 76–95.

iii. The Maximization Principle

One alternative to the view that we ought to do the most good we can is a morality that leaves room for supererogation. This term first appears in the Latin version of the New Testament, in regard to the parable of the Good Samaritan, who is described as going beyond what was due.[37] Roman Catholic theologians later developed this distinction between what is due, and what lies beyond that, into the idea that there are some things that are our duties, which are obligatory, and other things that are good to do, but not obligatory. In the 20th century J. O. Urmson revived philosophical discussion of the topic with an influential article called 'Saint and Heroes', arguing that heroic actions, like throwing oneself on a hand grenade to save the lives of one's comrades, cannot be our duty.[38] Urmson's example relies on the intuition that it would be impossibly harsh to say that someone who does not throw himself on a hand grenade has done something wrong. It would also mean that those we praise as heroes are simply doing their duty, and that too seems odd. We seek to explain this oddity when we discuss the demandingness of morality in Chapter 11.

Because maximizing consequentialism leaves no room for supererogation, and seems to be extremely demanding, some consequentialists have developed an alternative form of consequentialism known as 'satisficing' consequentialism. The idea of 'satisficing' comes from economics, and in particular from Herbert Simon's 1955 paper 'A Behavioral Model of Rational Choice'. Simon argued that the requirement to maximize expected utility demands knowledge-gathering and calculations that are beyond human abilities.[39] To overcome this, he suggested that one could rationally choose outcomes that are satisfactory, or 'good enough' rather than those that are best, or have the highest expected utility. This kind of satisficing is not really a challenge to maximizing, however, because if we include the value of the resources that would be spent in trying to improve our knowledge and calculative abilities in order to make the best choice, we can

[37] Heyd, 'Supererogation'.
[38] Urmson, 'Saints and Heroes'.
[39] Simon, 'A Behavioral Model of Rational Choice'.

see that the choice that maximizes expected utility may be one that cuts off the knowledge-gathering and calculating at some point and says: 'Enough! The time you are spending on making the decision is likely to be more valuable than anything you will gain from making a better-informed decision.'[40]

Michael Slote argues that moral satisficing is different from this kind of rational satisficing. Common sense morality accepts, he argues, that, as long as we do *enough* good, we do not need to always do the *most* good we can. If a poor family travelling by car have a breakdown at night outside a motel and the manager offers them a room at no charge, the manager is under no obligation, Slote says, to offer them the *best* vacant room. A doctor who wants to relieve human suffering and finds India a particularly interesting country in which to live and work does nothing wrong if he chooses to go to India—where he can relieve a great deal of suffering—without investigating whether he could relieve even more suffering if he went somewhere else.[41] Thus satisficing consequentialism can accommodate supererogation. It would be supererogatory for the doctor to go to, say, Mali, simply because he can relieve even more suffering there, when he would greatly prefer to be in India.

In responding to Slote, Philip Pettit points out that moral satisficing also faces a conceptual problem. On the satisficing view, as long as what we do satisfies the demands of morality, we are not under any obligation to do more, even though we could choose to do better things, and it would be no trouble at all for us to choose them. 'It is not clear', Pettit writes, 'what it can mean to rank A above B if when other things are equal one insists on choosing B'.[42]

It is not clear to us whether that objection can be met; but if it can be, we would next need to ask if satisficing is really to be preferred to

---

[40] R. B. Brandt argues along these lines, defending a satisficing strategy on the grounds that 'there is rough background information that other plans are likely to be only slightly better and . . . it is not worth the time to canvass possibilities further when the most that can be hoped for is a minor improvement'. *A Theory of the Good and the Right*, 73.

[41] These examples are from Slote, 'Satisficing Consequentialism', 149, 156. See also Slote, *Beyond Optimizing*.

[42] Pettit, 'Satisficing Consequentialism', 173.

maximizing. For those who are troubled by the demandingness of maximizing utilitarianism, satisficing does offer, as its name implies, a standard that is easier to satisfy, at least when the level of doing good that satisfies the requirement is sufficiently moderate. On the other hand, if this level is too low, then satisficing leads to the opposite objection: it lets us off too easily. Once we have met the standard, whatever it is, we have no obligation to do more. So if we do whatever is required to meet the standard, and then an opportunity arises to save many lives, at no cost to ourselves, but we do nothing, a satisficing utilitarian will have to say that we have done nothing wrong. That conclusion may be just as hard to accept as the maximizing conclusion that we are required to do what, on a satisficing view, would be supererogatory.

Slote claims to detect in Sidgwick's treatment of motives something like 'an embryonic form of *satisficing* motive utilitarianism'.[43] He points out that Sidgwick and other consequentialists often accept that we may act from such motives as the love of parents for one's children, even though this may not promote the greatest good, and suggests that this reveals a satisficing standard for motives, which is in tension with a maximizing standard for acts.

Moral satisficing may appear to be more in accord with common sense morality than maximizing utilitarianism, but we think this can be explained in a manner that is consistent with the maximizing view. Maximizing may seem greedy, and contrary to Solon's injunction 'nothing in excess', but Solon can also be seen as offering a strategy that, by reducing our endless striving for imaginary or minimal extra benefits, maximizes our expected utility.[44] As for the objection that utilitarianism is too demanding, we will, as already mentioned, respond to that in Chapter 11. What Sidgwick says about motives, and how this and some of the judgments of common sense morality on which Slote relies follow from a maximizing form of consequentialism, applied to beings with limited capacities for universal benevolence, will then become clearer.

---

[43] Slote, 'Satisficing Consequentialism', 159, italics in original.
[44] We owe the reference to Solon to Pettit, 'Satisficing Consequentialism'.

5. The Unfairness Objection

We saw in Chapter 3 that Sidgwick denied that the principles of common sense morality—for example, 'I ought to speak the truth' and 'I ought to keep my promises'—are truly self-evident. Now that we have seen the axioms that Sidgwick does regard as self-evident, the obvious question is whether Sidgwick is justified in asserting that his axioms are truly self-evident in some sense in which the principles of common sense morality are not. Many philosophers—and not only supporters of common sense morality, but also some who are broadly sympathetic to Sidgwick's views—argue that he is not, because he fails to apply to his own views the very standards by which he judged the principles of common sense morality to fail the test of self-evidence. As David Phillips puts what he calls 'the unfairness objection': 'Sidgwick insists that common-sense principles meet a standard of determinacy from which he exempts his own favored utilitarian principles. And that is unfair.'[45]

Let's look more closely at the case for holding that Sidgwick is unfair to the proponents of the morality of common sense. First, here again are the standards he sets for the principles of common sense morality to meet in order to be accepted as valid self-evident principles:

1. the proposition must be clear and precise
2. its self-evidence must be ascertained by careful reflection
3. the propositions must be mutually consistent; and
4. there should be agreement by other equally competent judges.

(*ME* 339–42)

These conditions do not mention 'determinacy', which Phillips singles out as the basis for his charge of unfairness. But Sidgwick does make that a central part of his criticism of the principles of common sense morality:

When, however, we try to apply these currently accepted principles, we find that the notions composing them are often deficient in clearness and precision. For

---

[45] Phillips, *Sidgwickian Ethics*, 101; R. Crisp, 'Sidgwick and Intuitionism', 74; Shaver, 'Sidgwick's Axioms and Consequentialism'; for a deontologist making a similar point, see Alan Donagan, 'Sidgwick and Whewellian Intuitionism'.

instance, we should all agree in recognising Justice and Veracity as important virtues; and we shall probably all accept the general maxims, that 'we ought to give every man his own' and that 'we ought to speak the truth': but when we ask (1) whether primogeniture is just, or the disendowment of corporations, or the determination of the value of services by competition, or (2) whether and how far false statements may be allowed in speeches of advocates, or in religious ceremonials, or when made to enemies or robbers, or in defence of lawful secrets, we do not find that these or any other current maxims enable us to give clear and unhesitating decisions. And yet such particular questions are, after all, those to which we naturally expect answers from the moralist. For we study Ethics, as Aristotle says, for the sake of Practice: and in practice we are concerned with particulars. (*ME* 215)

In speaking about more specific duties, such as those of parents to their children, or the duties of gratitude, Sidgwick sometimes points out that they are indeterminate; and speaking more generally, he finds a 'high degree of indeterminateness' in the common notions of duties (*ME* 347, 349, 360). There can be no doubt, therefore, that in his view one of the reasons why the principles of common sense morality are unsatisfactory is that they are not clear or precise enough to answer our questions about what we ought to do in particular situations. Nor can this deficiency be overcome by reformulating these principles to make them more precise because then, as we saw in our discussion of the morality of common sense, the consensus as to what is the right principle breaks down, and this violates the fourth standard, requiring agreement by other competent judges. Similarly, as we saw above (Chapter 3, section 4) Ross's use of prima facie duties also does not get around the problem of imprecision, for if we are to take account of the prima facie duty to tell the truth (for example), we first need to know which acts of evasive or misleading speech count as lies.

Now we must ask whether Sidgwick relaxes these standards for the principles he considers self-evident, which of course are the ones we have been considering in this chapter. As we have seen, Phillips focuses on Sidgwick's rejection of common sense principles on grounds of indeterminacy, and he does so because this makes it possible for him to point to what appears to be a damning admission that Sidgwick makes, in introducing the principles that he considers self-evident: they are, Sidgwick says, 'of too abstract a nature, and too universal in their scope, to enable us to ascertain by immediate application of them what we ought to do in any particular case; particular duties have still to be determined by some other method' (*ME* 379).

How can Sidgwick reject the principles of common sense morality because they do not tell us what we ought to do in particular cases, and then go on to accept as the basis of utilitarianism a principle—the principle of rational or universal benevolence or the two self-evident principles from which it is derived—when he acknowledges that these principles are too abstract and too universal to do just what he has demanded the principles of common sense morality do? This looks bad, and the admission cannot be dismissed as mere loose writing, of which even Sidgwick is occasionally capable. He could scarcely deny that the axioms we have examined in this chapter are incapable of telling us what we ought to do. The axiom of justice can at most tell us what we ought *not* to do; that is, we ought not to do an act that we would not judge to be right if another person were to do it in circumstances that were relevantly similar to those in which we are acting. The axiom of prudence tells us to have impartial concern for all parts of our conscious life, but does not tell us how to balance concern for our own conscious life against concern for the conscious lives of others; and while the principle of rational benevolence does answer this question, by telling us to have as much regard for the good of others as we have for our own good, it still does not tell us what this good is. That comes only in the next chapter of *The Methods* (to be discussed in our Chapters 8 and 9, on ultimate good), and for the argument of that chapter, Sidgwick does not claim self-evidence.[46] Without knowing whether the good is pleasure, or virtue, or the satisfaction of desires, or perhaps some combination of goods, the principle of rational benevolence is no better—and perhaps in some cases

---

[46] Here we agree with Phillips, *Sidgwickian Ethics*, 102. Anthony Skelton believes that Sidgwick must base his hedonism on a self-evident intuition, although he admits that Sidgwick does not explicitly claim that it is self-evident that happiness is the sole ultimate end. We give our exposition of the process by which Sidgwick reaches hedonism in Chs. 8 and 9. We grant that he appeals to intuition, but we would distinguish this from a claim of self-evidence; it is, rather, an appeal to what is, on balance, the more plausible view. For Skelton's argument to the contrary, see his 'Sidgwick's Philosophical Intuitions', 191–3.

worse—at yielding determinate conclusions about what we ought to do than the principles of common sense morality.

Nevertheless, we think Sidgwick is not guilty of unfairness. To see this, we must first remind ourselves of the differences between the methods of common sense morality and of utilitarianism, and therefore of the different roles played in those methods by the principles that Sidgwick rejects and those that he accepts. Take first the passage in which Sidgwick introduces the morality of common sense. As we outlined in Chapter 3, he begins his discussion of intuitionism with perceptional intuitionism, the view that every individual discovers what is right to do by consulting his or her intuitions, or conscience, in each particular situation. The doubts that inevitably arise about the validity of each person's particular judgments lead us, however, 'to general rules, more firmly established on a basis of common consent' (*ME* 100). This is the morality of common sense, which Sidgwick also refers to as 'dogmatic intuitionism'. Later he describes it as the view according to which the right moral principles are 'the moral generalities that we obtain by reflection on the ordinary thought of mankind'. So 'common consent' or 'the ordinary thought of mankind' is the basis of these rules, and without it there is nowhere else to go. Sidgwick mentions that this is the reason why even if the rules of common sense morality fitted together perfectly, did not conflict with each other, and answered every practical question, across the whole field of human conduct, 'philosophic minds' would find it an unsatisfying 'accidental aggregate of precepts' and would see a need for some deeper rational justification (*ME* 102). But the morality of common sense can offer no such deeper justification. That is why it has an absolute need for common consent to its principles. Once that consent breaks down—as Sidgwick has demonstrated it does, when we try to make its principles precise enough to offer determinate answers to practical questions—this method of ethics collapses like a pricked balloon.

The method of utilitarianism is different, in that it has resources that go beyond its self-evident principles. These self-evident principles should still be clear and precise, their self-evidence must stand up to careful reflection, they should be mutually consistent, and they should meet the acceptance of other equally competent judges—but note that these four standards do not include the requirement that they should yield determinate answers to questions about what we ought to do. As Sidgwick tells us in introducing these standards, they apply to valid self-evident propositions. Of course, any method of ethics must, in the end, give us determinate answers about what we ought to do, but that does not mean that the self-evident principles on which the method is based need, by themselves, yield such results.[47] They do not, because utilitarianism, in contrast to the morality of common sense, has other resources. The particular duties, as Sidgwick says, 'have still to be determined by some other method' (*ME* 379). This remark, like the entire chapter we have been discussing, is still part of book III. The 'other method' to which Sidgwick is referring is, it seems reasonable to assume, the subject of book IV, namely the method of utilitarianism.

---

[47] This is, we believe, where Phillips goes wrong. He considers the possibility that it is not simply the principles Sidgwick believes to be self-evident, but utilitarianism itself, that gives determinate answers, but he rejects this response, saying that then Sidgwick must claim that utilitarianism passes the fourth standard, of universal acceptance—which of course it does not. But the standards (as Sidgwick makes clear when he introduces them, *ME* 338) apply to propositions that are candidates for being self-evident, and we have already noted that we agree with Phillips that Sidgwick does not assert that hedonistic utilitarianism is self-evident.

6

The Profoundest Problem of Ethics

1. Sidgwick's Dualism of Practical Reason

Sidgwick sought a coherent set of self-evident principles that could be used as a basis for practical reasoning that would tell us what we ought to do. He found three such principles that he considered axioms: the principles of justice, prudence, and universal benevolence. All three are, he claimed, found by means of reason, or more specifically, by direct insight into their self-evidence. They are non-natural normative truths, discovered by the method of philosophical intuitionism, but normatively, they are distinct from the intuitions of common sense morality which turn out not to be self-evident. Common sense morality, Sidgwick shows, faces problems that it cannot overcome without appealing to the principle of utility. On the other hand, utilitarianism must ultimately rest on an appeal to principles or axioms that we intuitively grasp as self-evident. Hence, Sidgwick says, we must discard the common antithesis between intuitionists and utilitarians. Intuitionism is not really incompatible with utilitarianism; rather, intuitionism leads to the self-evident moral principles that form a rational basis for utilitarianism (*ME* 496).

That still leaves us with the two remaining theories: can we reconcile egoism and utilitarianism? In practice, we often can. Aiming at my own happiness, I add to the general happiness. Thinking of others and acting to promote their happiness makes me happy. But on some occasions, this harmony fails. If I have to choose between my own happiness and the happiness of others, is it rational for me to choose one rather than the other? Sidgwick regarded this—the relation of rational egoism and rational benevolence—as 'the profoundest problem of ethics' (*ME* 386 n. 17).

Strictly speaking, Sidgwick's axioms are silent on this question. As we saw in the last chapter, what he calls the 'axiom of prudence' can be interpreted as leaving open the question whether one should aim at one's own good in preference to the good of others. But at various places in *The Methods*, he does address this question, often indicating what he takes the common sense view to be. In book I, he refers to one of his favourite philosophers, saying that it is 'in accordance with common sense to recognize—as Butler does—that the calm desire for my "good on the whole" is authoritative; and therefore carries with it implicitly a rational dictate to aim at this end' (*ME* 112). A few pages later, in discussing egoism in book II, he writes: 'it is hardly going too far to say that common sense assumes that "interested" actions, tending to promote the agent's happiness, are prima facie reasonable: and that the onus probandi lies with those who maintain that disinterested conduct, as such, is reasonable' (*ME* 120). But the first explicit discussion of whether reason requires us to be utilitarian occurs in book IV, when Sidgwick is discussing a possible 'proof' of utilitarianism. Here he refers to the earlier chapter in which he sought to establish his ethical axioms, and then comments:

It should be observed that the applicability of this argument depends on the manner in which the Egoistic first principle is formulated. If the Egoist strictly confines himself to stating his conviction that he ought to take his own happiness or pleasure as his ultimate end, there seems no opening for any line of reasoning to lead him to Universalistic Hedonism as a first principle; it cannot be proved that the difference between his own happiness and another's happiness is not for him all-important.

In that case, Sidgwick says, all the utilitarian can do is try to persuade the egoist that seeking the universal happiness will also be in his own interests—which if successful would not amount to a proof of utilitarianism, for the egoist would be pursuing universal happiness only as a means to his own happiness. But Sidgwick then continues:

When, however, the Egoist puts forward, implicitly or explicitly, the proposition that his happiness or pleasure is Good, *not only* for him but from the point of view of the Universe,—as (e.g.) by saying that 'nature designed him to seek his own happiness,'—it then becomes relevant to point out to him that his happiness cannot be a more important part of Good, taken universally, than the equal happiness of any other person. And thus, starting with his own principle, he may be brought to accept Universal happiness or pleasure as that which is absolutely and without qualification Good or Desirable: as an end, therefore, to which the action of a reasonable agent as such ought to be directed. (*ME* 420–1)

Sidgwick returns to this question in the concluding chapter, titled 'The Mutual Relations of the Three Methods'. Here, turning again to the relationship between egoism and utilitarianism, he reminds the reader of the passage just quoted, and repeats that the egoist may avoid the proof of utilitarianism by declining to affirm that 'his own greatest happiness is not merely the rational ultimate end for himself, but a part of Universal Good'. He then follows this with a passage from which we quoted in the previous chapter:

It would be contrary to Common Sense to deny that the distinction between any one individual and any other is real and fundamental, and that consequently 'I' am concerned with the quality of my existence as an individual in a sense, fundamentally important, in which I am not concerned with the quality of the existence of other individuals: and this being so, I do not see how it can be proved that this distinction is not to be taken as fundamental in determining the ultimate end of rational action for an individual.

This passage is followed by one that comes very close to suggesting that the principle of prudence, interpreted not merely as requiring equal concern for all parts of one's own existence, but as supporting rational egoism, is an axiom with the same standing as the axiom of rational benevolence:

And further, even if a man admits the self-evidence of the principle of Rational Benevolence, he may still hold that his own happiness is an end which it is irrational for him to sacrifice to any other; and that therefore a harmony between the maxim of Prudence and the maxim of Rational Benevolence must be somehow demonstrated, if morality is to be made completely rational. This latter view, indeed (as I have before said), appears to me, on the whole, the view of Common Sense: and it is that which I myself hold. (*ME* 498)

Sidgwick calls this opposition between prudence and benevolence, which underlies the opposition between egoism and utilitarianism, 'the dualism of practical reason'. He cannot say that we should simply accept this dualism, because at the outset of *The Methods of Ethics* he stated that he would take as 'a fundamental postulate of ethics' that 'so far as two methods conflict, one or other of them must be modified or rejected' (*ME* 6). He also took it as 'a postulate of the Practical Reason, that two conflicting rules of action cannot both be reasonable' (*ME* 12). Now, therefore, he is left with 'a fundamental contradiction in one chief department of our thought' (ME 508). The language with which Sidgwick closed the first edition of *The Methods of Ethics* reflected his dismay at the conclusion he had reached:

the Cosmos of Duty is thus really reduced to a Chaos, and the prolonged effort of the human intellect to frame a perfect ideal of rational conduct is seen to have been foredoomed to inevitable failure. (*ME* 1st edn, 473)

The ending of the 7th edition is not quite so pessimistic, but it is clear that Sidgwick still cannot find a rationally defensible way out of the problem. We are forced to admit, he says, 'an ultimate and fundamental contradiction in our apparent intuitions of what is Reasonable in conduct' and this means that 'the apparently intuitive operation of the Practical Reason, manifested in these contradictory judgments, is after all illusory'. This does not require us to 'abandon morality altogether' but we do have to 'abandon the idea of rationalising it completely' (ME 508).

Sidgwick tries to resolve the deadlock in several ways, none of which he thinks is really successful. As we have seen, he thought that the egoist who declines to assert that his own good is a part of some universal good is immune to the argument that establishes the axiom of rational benevolence, because this argument requires one to take the point of view of the universe. The egoist who limits himself to saying that his own happiness is the rational ultimate end for himself seems, to Sidgwick, to have put himself in a rationally impregnable position.

Another option that has already been mentioned is to try to convince the egoist that aiming at the general goodness is the best path to happiness for himself. This line of argument was taken up by J. S. Mill, who pointed to the especially important role that sympathy plays both in making moral decisions and in gaining happiness for ourselves. Sidgwick admits that empirical observation shows that many people who think of others, rather than only of themselves, are happier than those who concentrate only on their own pleasures, and that an egoist misses many enjoyments and satisfactions of life. As a result, in Sidgwick's words:

it seems scarcely extravagant to say that, amid all the profuse waste of the means of happiness which men commit, there is no imprudence more flagrant than that of Selfishness in the ordinary sense of the term,—that excessive concentration of attention on the individual's own happiness which renders it impossible for him to feel any strong interest in the pleasures and pains of others. (*ME* 501)

Sidgwick describes the selfish man as missing 'the sense of elevation and enlargement given by wide interests', as well as 'the more secure and serene satisfaction' likely to result from activities that focus on more stable ends than one's own happiness. And as we noticed in Chapter 2, Sidgwick refers to what would now be called cognitive dissonance as indicating that those who are selfish are likely to experience 'discord'. Yet while Sidgwick is ready to say that concentrating only on your own pleasures will often bring unhappiness, he finds himself unable to treat this as universally true. 'Some few thoroughly selfish persons', he observes, 'appear at least to be happier than most of the unselfish'. And then he points out that there are others who, while not selfish, find their chief happiness in activities that are not directed towards human happiness (*ME* 501 n. 3).

Nor, in Sidgwick's opinion, is the feeling of sympathy able to lead to 'a perfect coincidence between Utilitarian duty and self-interest' (*ME* 502). It is enough to imagine that we face a situation in which we have to sacrifice our health or even life. There are people so close to us that we would think we can make such a sacrifice in order to gain good for them. But the situation would change if we were called upon to sacrifice an important part of our happiness for those that we do not know at all. Very few people would feel, towards people that they do not know at all, a degree of sympathy that is at all comparable with their concern for their 'wife or children or lover or intimate friend'. So the feeling of sympathy would not give most people a sufficient reason to act in accordance with the utilitarian principle. Indeed, utilitarianism may require us to sacrifice not our own good but the good of those we love. Then sympathy acts *against* what utilitarianism requires. Thus the connection between the happiness that we may cause and the happiness that we feel because of our act will often not hold. In general, therefore, Sidgwick concludes that it is impossible to satisfactorily demonstrate, on empirical grounds, that there is an 'inseparable connexion' between maximizing one's own happiness and doing as utilitarianism directs.

Finally, Sidgwick considers utilitarians who seek to combine universal hedonism with religion. The religious proponents of utilitarianism Sidgwick has in mind hold that the moral code is given by God, who commands people to aim at general happiness and promises that those who obey his laws will be rewarded and those who do not will be punished. (Though he mentions no names, Sidgwick probably has William Paley, a late 18th-century clergyman, philosopher, and early utilitarian, in mind.) Sidgwick agrees that the promise of a divine reward or threat of a divine punishment would be sufficient motive for a rational egoist to live according to the principle of utilitarianism; given that there is so much unhappiness in the actual world, and that God is supposed to be omnipotent, however, Sidgwick wonders whether, if God is really the source of moral law, it would be a law directed towards universal happiness. If that difficulty can be overcome, then another arises: whether there really is a God who will reward or punish us for obedience to his laws. Sidgwick finds no way of showing, from our understanding of ethics, that such a being exists. There could, however, be proofs of the existence of God from outside ethics. At the conclusion of *The Methods*, that question is left open.

Hence Sidgwick has failed to find any argument with sufficient power to convince an egoist that he must act impartially. Elsewhere he writes: 'I do not hold the reasonableness of aiming at happiness generally with any stronger conviction than I do that of aiming at one's own' (*ME* p. xii).

***

2. Morality and Self-Interest

Recent research has confirmed Sidgwick's view that those who concern themselves with the well-being of others are more likely to find happiness than those who live more self-centred lives. There is experimental evidence that happy people give more to charity, and that those who give to others are happier.[1] An analysis of Gallup Poll data from 136 countries showed that, in 122 of them, there was a positive correlation between subjective well-being and giving an affirmative answer to the question: 'Have you donated money to charity in the last month?' The results were controlled for household income, so this was not simply a case of wealthier people being both happier and more likely to donate. In fact, donating to charity had the same positive impact on subjective well-being as a doubling of household income.[2] Researchers have also looked at what happens in people's brains when they do good things. They gave $100 to 19 female students who, while undergoing magnetic resonance imaging, were given the option of donating some of the money to a local food bank for the poor. To ensure that any effects observed came entirely from making the donation, and not from knowing that others would think well of you, the students were informed that no one, not even the experimenters, would know which students made a donation. The research found that, when students donated, the brain's 'reward centers'—the parts of the brain that respond when you eat something sweet or see attractive faces—became active.[3]

These and other studies make the connection between helping others and personal happiness (and even both mental and physical health) quite strong.[4] Even the most enthusiastic advocate of this connection, however, would have to accept that Sidgwick's cautiously phrased assessment still stands: the connection cannot be empirically demonstrated to be 'inseparable'. Self-interest and morality can, and often do, point in different directions.

What is it rational to do when self-interest clashes with morality? That question goes back—at least—to ancient Greece. In *The*

---

[1] Dunn *et al.*, 'Spending Money on Others Promotes Happiness'; Anik *et al.*, 'Feeling Good about Giving'.

[2] Aknin *et al.*, 'Prosocial Spending and Well-Being'.

[3] Harbaugh *et al.*, 'Neural Responses to Taxation and Voluntary Giving Reveal Motives for Charitable Donations'.

[4] For a wider perspective, see also Post, *Altruism and Health*.

Republic Glaucon reminds Socrates of the story of the shepherd Gyges, who found a magic ring that made him invisible, and used it to kill the king and take the crown for himself. Why, Glaucon challenges Socrates, wouldn't everyone behave unjustly, as Gyges did, if they knew they could get away with it? Greek ethics is often characterized as more in harmony with human nature than modern ethics, which typically sees reason as in conflict with our desires, and also sees a tension between the interests of individuals and those of the larger group. Glaucon's question shows, however, that in ancient Greece justice and self-interest were already thought of as opposed to each other.[5]

Today's discussion of the dualism has been greatly influenced by Parfit, who refers in turn to Sidgwick and his understanding of 'the profoundest problem in ethics'.[6] The conflict between self-interest and impartiality is a central concern of Parfit's two major works, *Reasons and Persons* and *On What Matters*. In *Reasons and Persons*, Parfit focused his criticism on what he calls 'the Self-interest Theory' which he states as: 'For each person, there is one supremely rational ultimate aim: that his life go, for him, as well as possible.' Self-Interest Theory leaves open the question of what it means for someone's life to go well. Sidgwick argues that this should be understood hedonistically, as meaning the greatest possible surplus, for the person whose life it is, of pleasure over pain. Thus Sidgwick's method of rational egoism is one version of Self-Interest Theory.

Parfit compares the Self-Interest Theory with two others. One is similar to Sidgwick's axiom of universal benevolence. According to this view—which in *On What Matters* Parfit refers to as Impartialism—for each person, the one supremely rational ultimate aim is that everyone's life go as well as possible. Impartialism is neutral in respect of both time and persons, telling us to have equal concern for all moments of existence, whether they are present or future, ours or someone else's. The third theory, Present-Aim Theory, rejects neutrality in respect of both time and persons: it tells everyone to

---

[5]   See White, *Individual and Conflict in Greek Ethics*, 172–3.
[6]   Parfit takes this quote from Sidgwick in *On What Matters*, i. 142.

do whatever will best achieve his or her present aims. Self-Interest Theory, on the other hand, is a hybrid: it claims that it is irrational to give priority to our present lesser good over our greater future good, but at the same time it requires that we give priority to our own lesser good over someone else's greater future good. It is neutral with regard to time but not with regard to persons.[7] This means that Self-Interest Theory 'can be charged with a kind of inconsistency' and 'can be attacked from both directions'.

The point Parfit is making here—as he himself acknowledges—may be one that Sidgwick mentions but leaves undeveloped when, in setting out to discuss what kind of proof could be given for utilitarianism, he remarks:

I do not see why the axiom of Prudence should not be questioned, when it conflicts with present inclination, on a ground similar to that on which Egoists refuse to admit the axiom of Rational Benevolence. If the Utilitarian has to answer the question, 'Why should I sacrifice my own happiness for the greater happiness of another?' it must surely be admissible to ask the Egoist, 'Why should I sacrifice a present pleasure for a greater one in the future? Why should I concern myself about my own future feelings any more than about the feelings of other persons?' (ME 418)

Parfit's puts his argument this way:

In rejecting Neutralism, a Self-interest Theorist must claim that a reason may have force only for the agent. But the grounds for this claim support a further claim. If a reason can have force only for the agent, it can have force for the agent only at the time of acting. The Self-interest Theorist must reject this claim. He must attack the notion of a time-relative reason. But arguments to show that reasons must be temporally neutral, thus refuting the Present-aim Theory, may also show that reasons must be neutral between different people, thus refuting the Self-interest Theory.[8]

Before considering the conclusion Parfit draws from this argument, we should note that Sidgwick's undeveloped idea about questioning prudence can also be seen as a precursor of Thomas Nagel's argument in *The Possibility of Altruism*. Nagel argues that if, for instance, I know that I will be in Rome in 6 weeks, and will then want to be able to speak Italian, that gives me a reason, now, to start to learn Italian. To reject the idea that reasons are timeless, in this sense, is a

---

[7] Parfit, *Reasons and Persons*, 140–4.
[8] Parfit, *Reasons and Persons*, 144.

form of dissociation with one's future self, a failure to see the present as a stage in the life of a persisting individual, and hence a failure to regard oneself as a person who exists over time.[9] Nagel then goes on to explain altruism—that is, the view that the interests of others provide us with reasons for action—as a rational requirement. I am just one person among others. If my interests give me reasons to act, then anyone's interests also give me reasons to act. Just as reasons for action are timeless, Nagel argues, so they cannot be restricted to one person. To fail to see this is to fail to grasp that other people are real in the same sense that we are. It is a form of solipsism.[10]

If Nagel were right, this would resolve the problem of the dualism in favour of some form of Impartialism; but Sidgwick would no doubt have thought that Nagel has not overcome the problem that he himself was unable to resolve, namely that of showing why, given the 'real and fundamental' nature of the distinction between individuals, I should not be 'concerned with the quality of my existence as an individual in a sense, fundamentally important, in which I am not concerned with the quality of the existence of other individuals'.

Parfit's use of the same type of argument is less ambitious than Nagel's. He concludes that we should reject Self-Interest Theory, but not necessarily in favour of Impartialism. Present-Aim Theory remains untouched by his argument. This has led some commentators to assume that in *Reasons and Persons* he was defending a subjectivist desire-based theory, of the kind that he argues against in *On What Matters*.[11] But the man with Future Tuesday Indifference had already made his appearance in *Reasons and Persons*, and so Parfit had powerful arguments for holding that no matter how well informed we might be, or how carefully we might deliberate, we can have desires that are simply irrational.[12] In *Reasons and Persons* Parfit therefore proposes another version of the Present-Aim Theory, the Critical Present-Aim Theory, which holds: 'What each person has most reason to do is whatever will best achieve those of his present aims that

[9]   Nagel, *The Possibility of Altruism*, 58–62.
[10]   Nagel, *The Possibility of Altruism*, 87–8, 104–7.
[11]   Parfit, e-mail to de Lazari-Radek, July 2012.
[12]   Parfit, *Reasons and Persons*, 124–6.

are not irrational.'[13] This raises the key question of which present aims might be rational and which irrational. Parfit's discussion of Critical Present-Aim Theory therefore points towards the issue more fully discussed in *On What Matters*: do we have both self-interested and impartial reasons for action, and if so, does reason provide any guidance when they are in conflict?

Before moving to that issue, however, we will briefly digress to note that in *Reasons and Persons* Parfit presents another possible basis for questioning Self-Interest Theory, and therefore egoism. This argument too is suggested in the passage from Sidgwick we quoted previously in which he mentions that the egoist can be challenged with the question 'Why should I sacrifice a present pleasure for a greater one in the future?' After the lines we have already quoted, Sidgwick continues by saying that those who hold Hume's view of personal identity will find the challenge particularly difficult to repudiate:

Grant that the Ego is merely a system of coherent phenomena, that the permanent identical 'I' is not a fact but a fiction, as Hume and his followers maintain; why, then, should one part of the series of feelings into which the Ego is resolved be concerned with another part of the same series, any more than with any other series? (*ME* 419)

The question Sidgwick is raising here is: Do I have a special connection with my future self, in a way that I do not have with another person, that makes it more rational for me to care for my future self? Suppose that I am 20 years old, and my main interest is in going to parties, drinking, listening to loud music, and having fun. I know that very probably, as I get older, my tastes will change, and I will adopt values and a lifestyle more like that of my parents. At the moment, however, I despise their values and their way of living. Do I now have any reason to care more about the 70-year-old person who will be physically continuous with me, and have my genes, my name, and my date of birth, than I have to care about anyone else? Parfit holds a view of personal identity that shares some features of Hume's view, and in particular he holds that, from a self-interested point of view, the extent to which it makes sense to care

---

[13] Parfit, *Reasons and Persons*, 94.

about my future self depends on the psychological connectedness that my future self has to me, and this is a matter of degree. I am the same person today as I was yesterday, because the connectedness of memory, beliefs, personality, values, and other psychological characteristics is very tight; but I am bound to be less psychologically connected to the being I will become in 50 years. Then I will have different beliefs, values, and memories.

Egoism assumes that when Emma, who is 20, saves for her retirement, she is caring for her own interests in just the same sense as she does when she plans what she will do in the coming summer. Egoism doesn't take into account that the person who, 50 years on, will benefit from Emma's savings will be less tightly connected to Emma than the person who will enjoy Emma's next summer vacation. Egoism's view about what matters from a self-interested perspective may seem just common sense but it is, Parfit believes, mistaken. Personal identity is not as deep a fact as the common sense view takes it to be. On Parfit's view, there is a sense in which the person Emma will become in 50 years is a different person to the one she is now, or will be next summer, and therefore the relationship between Emma and her distant future self is in some respects similar to the relationship between Emma and someone else.[14]

If Parfit is right about this, then Sidgwick is open to criticism for accepting the common sense view that 'the distinction between any one individual and any other is real and fundamental', and this flaw undermines his conviction that an egoist might be justified in taking this distinction as fundamental in determining what it is rational for him to do. To pursue this way of resolving the dualism would, however, take us more deeply into theories of personal identity than we think appropriate for this book, and because on Parfit's theory we are very closely connected with our immediate future self, it would in any case yield at most a partial resolution of the problem.

Parfit's arguments against the Self-Interest Theory in *Reasons and Persons* lead to a modification of Sidgwick's problem of the dualism

---

[14] Parfit's argument for his view of personal identity can be found in *Reasons and Persons*, 198–217.

of practical reason. Parfit puts this more clearly and straightforwardly in *On What Matters*. There he rejects both rational egoism,
which states that 'we always have most reason to do whatever would
be best for ourselves' and rational impartialism, which claims that
'we always have most reason to do whatever would be impartially
best'. Closer to the truth than either of these, he says, is Sidgwick's
dualism of practical reason:

> We always have most reason to do whatever would be impartially best, unless some
> other act would be best for ourselves. In such cases, we would have sufficient rea-
> son to act in either way. If we knew the relevant facts, either act would be rational.[15]

On Sidgwick's view these two reasons for action are wholly incomparable—when they conflict, neither reason can be stronger than the
other. Parfit rejects this. If we have a choice between saving ourselves
from mild discomfort and saving a million people from death or
agony, Parfit claims, it is obvious that we would have a decisive reason
to choose our own slight discomfort. He later leaves it open whether
we could rationally save one of our fingers if that would involve failing to save the lives of several strangers. In other circumstances we
may have sufficient reason to act on the basis of either self-interested
or impartial reasons. Parfit also modifies Sidgwick's dualism by adding, to self-interested and impartial reasons, what he calls 'partial reasons'; that is, reasons to benefit people 'such as our close relatives and
those we love'.

This reformulation of Sidgwick's dualism leads Parfit to what he
calls a 'wide value-based objective view':

> When one of our two possible acts would make things go in some way that would
> be impartially better, but the other act would make things go better either for our-
> selves or for those to whom we have close ties, we often have sufficient reasons to
> act in either of these ways.[16]

The word 'often', as Parfit himself admits, leads to difficult decisions,
as there is no appropriate calculator to tell us when we have sufficient
reasons and when we have decisive reasons for actions. I may have
sufficient reasons to save my own life rather than the lives of a few

---

[15] Parfit, *On What Matters*, Volume One, 130–1.
[16] Parfit, *On What Matters*, Volume One, 137.

strangers, and I may have sufficient reasons to save myself from a serious injury rather than to save the life of a stranger, but I may have a decisive reason to save a million strangers from agony rather than to save myself from slight pain. There is no clear boundary that would tell us that, from some specific point, we have decisive reasons to act in one way rather than sufficient reasons to act in either way.

3. Does the Dualism Undermine Morality?

When we wonder what to do, Parfit states, we may pose two questions: 'What do I have most reason to do?' and 'what ought I morally to do?' According to those who define 'morality' narrowly, so as, for example, to exclude egoism, these two questions could have different answers. Although Sidgwick did sometimes refer to morality in this narrow sense, on the whole he sticks to the view that 'any rational procedure' for determining what we ought to do will count as ethical, and he is interested in what is ethical, rather than what is moral in the narrower sense of that term (*ME* 1). If it turns out that egoism is rational, egoism will be ethical. Parfit claims that, if the two questions *often* had conflicting answers, so that we often had decisive reason to act wrongly, morality would be undermined. 'For morality to matter,' he writes, 'we must have reasons to care about morality, and to avoid acting wrongly.' We could try to claim that though it is rational to act contrary to morality, these acts would still be wrong, and hence morality would not be undermined. But this does not save the importance of morality:

It could be similarly claimed that, even if we had no reasons to follow the code of honour, or the rules of etiquette, this code and these rules would not be undermined.

It would still be dishonourable not to fight some duels, and still be incorrect to eat peas with a spoon. But these claims, though true, would be trivial. If we had no reasons to do what is required by the code of honour, or by etiquette, these requirements would have no importance. If we had no reasons to care about morality, or to avoid acting wrongly, morality would similarly have no importance. That is how morality might be undermined.[17]

This sets up a problem to which Parfit fails to give a compelling answer. He claims that for morality not to be undermined we must

---

[17] Parfit, *On What Matters*, Volume One, 147.

have reasons to care for morality and to avoid acting wrongly. But if the reasons to avoid acting wrongly are merely sufficient but not decisive, so that they do not make it irrational to act contrary to morality, is that enough? Parfit writes: 'Morality might have supreme importance in the reason-implying sense, since we might always have decisive reasons to do our duty, and to avoid acting wrongly.' A few lines later he says: 'we can plausibly assume that we do have strong reasons to care about morality, and to avoid acting wrongly'.[18] Parfit's use of 'might' to go with 'decisive' contrasts with 'can plausibly assume' to go with 'strong' and indicates that Parfit is not arguing that we always have *decisive* reasons to act morally. He provides the following example.[19] Suppose I stole some stranger's life raft, so that I could save one of my children but the stranger would be unable to save two of her children. Parfit agrees that I would be acting wrongly, but he nevertheless says: 'I cannot believe that I would be acting irrationally.' Parfit could, of course, add that I also have reasons to act morally and not steal the life raft. But if I have sufficient reasons to act morally and sufficient reasons to act immorally, that can still undermine morality. On this view, though I always choose to act wrongly, on at least some of these occasions—and perhaps on many of them—I am not acting contrary to any decisive reason. If we compare this to a situation in which, when I choose to act wrongly, I am always acting contrary to a decisive reason, it seems clear that, in the second of these situations, morality has much greater importance.

We therefore conclude that any form of the dualism of practical reason undermines morality. Parfit's wide value-based objective view, which can allow that we often have decisive reasons to do what morality requires, is less damaging to the importance of morality than Sidgwick's 'wholly incomparable reasons' view. Nevertheless, if we want morality to be truly important, we need to be able to do better in overcoming the dualism.

From Plato to the present, many philosophers have tried to argue that egoism does not conflict with morality. If this were true, the

[18] Parfit, *On What Matters*, Volume One, 148.
[19] Parfit, personal communication, 15 Jan. 2010. Parfit has indicated that he is reconsidering his view on this issue.

dualism would cease to be a practical problem, and if morality were to reduce to egoism, there would be no dualism at all. We will discuss two contemporary philosophers who have taken different paths in order to reach these distinct conclusions: David Brink and David Gauthier.

4. Brink's Metaphysical Egoism and Personal Identity

Brink's aim is to reconcile the demands of morality and practical reason by showing that acting in accordance with morality is a reliable way to promote one's own interest. To achieve this aim, he makes use of a distinctive concept of personal identity that gives everyone an interest in the welfare of others. Brink calls this 'metaphysical egoism' because it rests on a view of people's interests that makes them metaphysically, and not just causally, interdependent with the interests of others. Acting morally then is a reliable way for each of us to promote our interests. Brink traces the roots of this way of defending the convergence of self-interest and morality to Plato and Aristotle, as well as to Sidgwick's contemporary, T. H. Green.

Brink starts with John Locke's distinction between a person and a human being. The former is a normative concept: a person is a responsible being who can deliberate upon what to do. Brink holds that capacities for deliberation—including formulating, assessing, choosing, and implementing projects or goals—are essential to being a person.[20] To persist in being a person is different from persisting as a human organism, and requires psychological continuity. For Brink, though, I can have this psychological continuity not only with myself, but also with others with whom I interact. The people with whom I am intimate, and interact on a regular basis, help shape my mental life, as I help to shape theirs: 'in such relationships, the experiences, beliefs, desires, ideals, and actions of each depend in significant part upon those of the others'.[21] Brink acknowledges that this kind of continuity

---

[20]   Brink, 'Self-Love and Altruism', 136.
[21]   Brink, 'Self-Love and Altruism', 141.

is a matter of degree, and that I'm more continuous with myself than with my intimates, and more continuous with my intimates than with those who are more distant to me. Nevertheless he suggests that the web of connections between people is bigger than we may think. Who I am depends on many different relations between people and therefore 'each can and should view the other as one who extends her own interests in the same sort of way that her own future self extends her interests'.[22]

Brink believes that these psychological interactions mean that the concern that we have for others is also a concern for our own interests. Thus he hopes to have reconciled self-interest with a morality based on concern for others. There are, however, several objections to his argument. First, we can ask: why should I cultivate interpersonal relations at all? Why not spend my time and resources just on myself, and not on others? Brink's answer is that interpersonal self-extension promotes my well-being, which he understands in terms of the ancient Greek concept of 'eudaimonia'. Drawing on Aristotle, he argues that 'it is in my interest to exercise those capacities that are essential to the sort of being I essentially am'.[23] If I am essentially a person, then, Brink claims, exercising my deliberative capacities must be a principal element of my welfare. But to exercise my deliberative capacities, I need to interact with others, who can help me understand myself better, and give me a different perspective from which I can better understand what is good for me. To build up these relationships, I may have to make some short-term sacrifices, but they are justified because they promote my overall good. Concern for the welfare of others with whom I am in these psychological relationships is part of my own overall good.[24]

Sidgwick would reject the conception of the good that Brink uses to reach this conclusion. For hedonists, what is good for me is not determined by what I am 'essentially', but by what gives me the greatest surplus of pleasure over pain. Perhaps the fact that I am a deliberative being is what is distinctive about me, as compared to, say, other mammals, but this does not prove that what is important to my well-being

---

[22] Brink, 'Self-Love and Altruism', 142.
[23] Brink, 'Self-Love and Altruism', 144.
[24] Brink, 'Self-Love and Altruism', 147–8.

is my deliberative capacities, rather than other capacities that I share with other mammals; for example, being close to my children. We prefer Sidgwick's view of the good to Brink's, for reasons we develop in Chapters 8 and 9.

We could grant that Brink's argument does show that everyone has egoistic reasons for being concerned with the welfare of those close to them, and with whom they are in frequent communication, but it is hard to see how his account gives the average person living in, say, North America, any reason to be concerned with the welfare of a person living in a rural village in Africa, whom she will never meet and who will not have any influence on her. Brink might, of course, simply accept this conclusion, and deny that we have obligations to distant strangers. Utilitarians who think that we have such obligations, at least given certain factual assumptions, would not find this view appealing, and nor do we, for it is contrary to the axiom of benevolence we defended in the previous chapter. In any case, Brink does appear to want his account to provide egoistic reasons for helping strangers because he argues that, when I help someone, I become involved in his life and earn my 'share, however small, of his happiness, much the way care and nurture of my children grounds posthumous interests I have in their continued well-being'.[25] But even if we accept Brink's initial, and in our view dubious, claim about our interests being determined by our distinctive nature as deliberative beings, it would still be the case that, to most people, harms to others to whom they are not closely connected are insignificant compared with some similar harm to themselves. Thus the need to choose between duty and self-interest returns in the form of a need to choose between one's own good and the good of others. In response, Brink concedes that he does not believe that all conflicts between the interests of different people can be resolved by his metaphysical brand of egoism. Our good has, he acknowledges, both 'other-regarding' and 'more self-confined' aspects, and these can be 'distinct and at least potentially conflicting'.[26] It follows that, at least in some situations,

[25] Brink, 'Self-Love and Altruism', 152.
[26] Brink, 'Self-Love and Altruism', 154.

practical reason still points in two different directions and the dualism is not resolved.

5. Gauthier's Contractarian Argument

Like Thomas Hobbes, David Gauthier holds that reason tells us to do what is in our own interests. In contrasting his own view of rationality with what he calls the 'universalistic' conception, Gauthier points out that both agree that when one has to decide what to do, and only one's own interests are affected, it is rational to do what is in one's own greatest interest. If then we add to this situation that the interests of others are involved in one's choice, on the universalistic conception, of course, everything is changed, and the rational thing to do now is to try to satisfy all the interests affected. On the view of reason that Gauthier defends, in contrast, 'essentially nothing is changed; the rational person still seeks the greatest satisfaction of her own interests'.[27] If Gauthier is right, there is no dualism of practical reason: rational egoism subsumes morality. Egoism and morality are compatible, Gauthier argues, because 'the acceptance of duty is truly advantageous'.[28]

Gauthier also follows Hobbes in understanding morality as the outcome of an agreement between self-interested individuals: each agrees to constrain the pursuit of his or her interests in certain circumstances, and thereby all gain the benefit of living in a just society.[29] This hypothetical agreement, or social contract, forms the basis of morality. The result of such an agreement is, Gauthier tells us, that 'to choose rationally, one must choose morally'.[30]

To this Hobbes has already stated the obvious objection, putting it in the mouth of an opponent he calls 'The Foole'. The Foole, drawing on Hobbes's own view that reason directs us to pursue our own interests, says that 'to make, or not make; keep, or not keep Covenants, was not against Reason, when it conduced to one's benefit'.[31] Hobbes's

---

[27] Gauthier, *Morals by Agreement*, 7.   [28] Gauthier, *Morals by Agreement*, 2.
[29] Gauthier, *Morals by Agreement*, 2.   [30] Gauthier, *Morals by Agreement*, 4.
[31] Hobbes, *Leviathan*, ch. 15, quoted by Gauthier, *Morals by Agreement*, 160–1.

reply is, essentially, that the agreement must include a sovereign with the power to enforce it and ensure that no one can reasonably expect to benefit by breaking it. But this is a flawed solution: no sovereign can be so omnipotent as to make sure that crime never pays, and if such a sovereign were possible, it would be a dangerous form of tyranny.

Gauthier therefore seeks a different solution. He acknowledges that, although the overall agreement is to everyone's advantage, it does require that people sometimes do what is contrary to their interests.[32] How can this be rational? Gauthier's answer depends on a reinterpretation of the standard self-interested conception of rationality so that it applies at the level of dispositions, rather than individual acts. On his interpretation, a disposition is rational 'if and only if an actor holding it can expect his choices to yield no less utility than the choices he would make were he to hold any alternative disposition'. ('Utility' here means the individual utility of the actor.) Particular choices are then rational if they express a rational disposition.[33]

To meet the Foole's objection, Gauthier must show that to develop a disposition to keep one's agreements can be expected to yield more utility for oneself than not developing such a disposition. He begins by introducing the idea of 'the just person' as one who has internalized the idea of mutual benefit to such an extent that his first thought is to bring about the best cooperative outcome. Only if he cannot reasonably expect to do this will he choose to maximize his own utility.[34] Gauthier also refers to such a person as a 'constrained maximizer' and contrasts this approach with that of a 'straightforward maximizer'; that is, someone who is always ready to do what is in her or his interest. Gauthier argues that the straightforward maximizer cannot enjoy benefits from cooperation that are available to the constrained maximizer. To cooperate with others we should be ready to develop a disposition to cooperate, to be just, to be truthful, and so on. If we have the right dispositions, others will cooperate with us and will trust us, which will be beneficial for us. Only the just person

---

[32] Gauthier, *Morals by Agreement*, 9; see also Gauthier, 'Morality and Advantage', 254–5.
[33] Gauthier, *Morals by Agreement*, 182–3.
[34] Gauthier, *Morals by Agreement*, 157.

who has internalized the idea of mutual benefit is 'fit for society'.[35] If we focus on any given individual action on its own, the constrained maximizer may gain less utility than the straightforward maximizer would in that situation, but the dispositions of constrained maximizers allow them to gain more utility overall. On rare occasions constrained maximizers will suffer disadvantages so serious that it would have been better for them not to have made the agreement in the first place and not to have developed the disposition to be a just person; but, according to Gauthier, it is not reasonable to plan one's life on the expectation of such bad luck; it is reasonable for everyone to expect that entering the agreement and developing the disposition of a just person will be in one's best interests. Hence, Gauthier claims, 'such a person is not able, given her disposition, to take advantage of the "exceptions"; she rightly judges such conduct irrational'.[36]

Why, though, would the rational strategy not be to make the agreement, and appear to be a just person, while secretly being a straightforward maximizer and violating the agreement whenever it is clearly in one's interests to do so? If our intentions and dispositions were transparent, such secrecy would be impossible, but we are not transparent. Gauthier thinks, however, that a more realistic assumption is sufficient for his purposes: we are neither transparent nor opaque, he says, but 'translucent'. This is a pre-condition for morality—if we were opaque and could reliably conceal our intentions and dispositions, Hobbes would be right, and it would not be rational to enter into an agreement that could not be enforced. Given translucency, however, others can tell what our intentions and dispositions are, 'not with certainty, but as more than mere guesswork'. Hence only those who are 'truly disposed to honesty and justice' can expect to get the full benefits of being accepted as people with whom others will cooperate in arrangements that rest on honesty and voluntary compliance with the principles of justice.[37] This, in brief, is Gauthier's defence of the view that to act morally is in harmony with acting in accordance

[35] Gauthier, *Morals by Agreement*, 157.
[36] Gauthier, *Morals by Agreement*, 182.
[37] Gauthier, *Morals by Agreement*, 182.

with rational self-interest. Gauthier says that, if this defence fails, 'we must conclude that a rational morality is a chimera, so that there is no rational and impartial constraint on the pursuit of individual utility.'[38]

i. Problems for Gauthier's Defence

Gauthier's defence of morality rests on several assumptions of fact, of which the most critical is that we cannot reasonably expect to be able to hide our disposition to act unjustly when doing so would clearly benefit us. But people vary in their ability to disguise their intentions and dispositions. If, before my disposition to act justly is fully formed, I discover that I am unusually good at persuading people that I am trustworthy, why should I develop a trustworthy disposition? It seems that I can gain the benefits of having such a disposition without incurring the possible costs. I can then be a straightforward (but deceitful!) maximizer of my interests, and for me to be a just person would be irrational.

Even among those who are translucent, and for whom it is therefore rational to develop the disposition and intentions of a just person, it can be rational to act unjustly. Let us accept that generally speaking it is good to have a disposition to tell the truth so others can trust and rely on us. In deciding whether to develop such a disposition, we could reasonably disregard improbable circumstances in which, by unjustly deceiving others and putting them at risk of death, I can save my own life or the life of someone I love. Such incidents are so rare that the tiny probability of their occurring is not enough to outweigh the benefits of developing a disposition to tell the truth. But now, having developed that disposition, by extraordinarily bad luck, I find myself in one of those rare situations. Wouldn't I be rational to act contrary to my disposition? Gauthier seems to be committed to denying this, because he holds that it is rational to act upon dispositions that we acquired when we reasonably believed that doing so would further our interests. But to take this view is to abandon the link between rationality and self-interest. Granted, given my disposition, it may be very difficult, perhaps even impossible, for me to carry

---

[38] Gauthier, *Morals by Agreement*, 158.

out this unjust deception. But if I am able to do it, and if it is rational for me to do what is in my interest, it cannot be irrational for me to do it.[39]

A related assumption—but one of fact, rather than about what it is to be a rational agent—is that if we adopt a disposition, we cannot abandon it if circumstances change. Perhaps, for example, people in the village where I live know me and will remember whether I am trustworthy. In the village, then, it will be advantageous for me to develop the disposition to act justly. In the big city, however, no one knows me. It would seem that the best disposition for me to develop is one that makes me just in my relations with my fellow-villagers, and ready to cheat strangers in the city when it will benefit me to do so. There is nothing impossible about this—that there is 'honour among thieves' is well known, and there are many cultures in which one does not cheat those who are part of the family or tribe, but may cheat or steal from outsiders.

This leads to another problem: even if we accept Gauthier's arguments, his morality is of a strictly limited kind, especially when compared with Sidgwick's. For Sidgwick, as we shall see in more detail in Chapter 12, utilitarianism requires us to consider the interests of those who cannot enter into mutually advantageous agreements with us, such as future generations and non-human animals. Gauthier's ethic does not. As he says: 'Animals, the unborn, the congenitally handicapped and defective, fall beyond the pale of a morality tied to mutuality.'[40] Sometimes Gauthier suggests that our feelings may have an impact on how we treat members of these categories; for instance, regarding animals, he says that we 'may be affected by particular feelings for certain animals'. But if we don't have such feelings, or we have them only for cats and dogs and not for pigs or cows, does that mean that nothing we do to the animals for whom we have no feelings could be morally wrong? So it seems: 'In grounding morals in

---

[39] Parfit has suggested other counter-examples to Gauthier's view of rationality, and considered a comprehensive set of responses that Gauthier either has made, or could make. He shows that none of them save Gauthier's position. See Parfit, *On What Matters*, Volume One, appendix B, pp. 433–47.

[40] Gauthier, *Morals by Agreement*, 268.

rational choice, Gauthier says, 'we exclude relations with non-human creatures from the sphere of moral constraint.'[41]

Something similar may be the case with future generations. At one point Gauthier writes: 'an individual does his descendants no injustice in not concerning himself with them. If the world is not left a fit place for their habitation, much less their well-being, this merely characterizes the circumstances in which they find themselves; their rights are not affected.'[42] To mitigate this harsh verdict, Gauthier again suggests that we could 'explore the morality of feeling'. But how far will that get us? It is easy to see how our love for our children and grandchildren could lead us to ensure that they inherit a world that can provide them with a decent life—although our current failure to reduce our greenhouse gas emissions suggests that when this love has to compete with our present comforts and conveniences, it may not prevail. When we consider such questions as the disposal of radioactive waste that will be deadly for thousands of years, however, it is hard to see how our feelings could lead us to invest in the much more expensive storage structures that will outlast the radioactivity of the waste, rather than in cheaper structures that will outlast the lives of our great-grandchildren.

Gauthier also appeals to the fact that generations overlap. As he says: 'The generations of humankind do not march on and off the stage of life in a body, with but one generation on stage at any time.' The need to continue an agreement as some of the parties to the agreement die, and others are born, means that 'among rational persons, the terms must remain constant'. This leads Gauthier to suggest that: 'No matter when one lives, one should expect the same relative benefits from interaction with one's fellows as were enjoyed by one's predecessors and as will be enjoyed in turn by one's successors.' This seems to be a distinct moral principle, not grounded in mutual advantage, and it is difficult to see how it can be a principle of reason, understood as doing what is in one's own best interests. If, as Sidgwick and utilitarians generally believe, we have obligations to

---

[41]   Gauthier, *Morals by Agreement*, 285.
[42]   Gauthier, *Morals by Agreement*, 298.

nonhuman animals and to future generations that do not depend on our emotional ties to them, then we need to look beyond Gauthier's theory of morality for a foundation for these obligations.

6. Conclusion: The Unresolved Dualism

It would be very comforting if there were no conflict between morality and self-interest. But current empirical studies do not allow us to reach such a strong conclusion, and neither Brink nor Gauthier have succeeded in putting forward good philosophical arguments for taking this view. Like Sidgwick, we believe that the cracks in the coherence of ethics caused by the dualism of practical reason are serious, and threaten to bring down the entire structure. We need to face them. In the next chapter, we show how this can be done.

7

The Origins of Ethics and the Unity of Practical Reason

1. Sidgwick and Darwin

One way of attacking the objectivity of ethics is to suggest that an understanding of the origins of our moral judgments casts doubt on their reliability. If, for example, our moral judgments result from our upbringing in a particular culture, and others brought up in different cultures have contrary moral judgments, this may be seen as discrediting all such judgments. The appearance of Darwin's theory of evolution gave rise to a distinctive form of this type of critique, resting on the claim that the judgments we hold have evolved to enhance our prospects of surviving and reproducing. If different judgments had improved these prospects, we would have had different moral beliefs.

The first edition of *The Methods of Ethics* appeared in 1874, just 3 years after Charles Darwin's *The Descent of Man*. It did not take long for some readers of Darwin to draw from his theory the conclusion that our moral intuitions are not a reliable guide to moral truth. In this chapter we shall see how Sidgwick responded to that claim, and whether his response is still valid against a contemporary version of it. This response is of course important for anyone seeking to defend the objectivity of ethics, and readers may therefore wonder why we have postponed our discussion of it until after the previous chapter on the dualism of practical reason. The answer is that these two problems—the evolutionary critique of objectivity in ethics and the dualism of practical reason—are linked. Though Sidgwick himself failed to see it, we believe that his response to the evolutionary critique provides a basis for a solution to his own, very different, worry about the dualism of practical reason and its dismaying implications for the project of putting ethics on a rational footing.

Although there is no explicit mention of Darwin in any edition of *The Methods*, Sidgwick does ask whether knowledge of the origins of our intuitions can help us to decide whether they are valid. He also published an essay on 'The Theory of Evolution in its Application to Practice', in the first volume of the journal *Mind*, in 1876, and the arguments of that essay are similar to those he uses in *The Methods* when discussing the significance of the origins of our intuitions.[1]

Both intuitionist moralists and their opponents, Sidgwick observes, often assume that 'if our moral faculty can be shown to be "derived" or "developed" out of other pre-existent elements of mind or conscious-ness, a reason is thereby given for distrusting it' and, conversely, if our moral faculty 'can be shown to have existed in the human mind from its origin', then 'its trustworthiness is thereby established'. About this Sidgwick says flatly: 'Either assumption appears to be devoid of foun-dation.' He cannot see why we should reject an intuition that seems to be self-evident, only on the ground that it was 'caused in known and determinate ways'. He goes further still, denying that those who affirm the truth of judgments that we intuitively grasp as self-evident need even to demonstrate that the causes of these judgments are of a kind that is likely to lead to true judgments. That requirement would, Sidgwick argues, lead to a kind of infinite regress that would make it impossible ever to find certainty about anything, for 'the premises of the required demonstration must consist of caused beliefs, which as having been caused will equally stand in need of being proved true, and so on ad infinitum'. In other words, if all our beliefs are equally the effect of some prior causes, this fact alone cannot show any of them to be invalid. If it did, it would equally show all of our beliefs to be invalid, thus committing us to total scepticism about everything (*ME* 212–13). As he puts the point in 'The Theory of Evolution in its

---

[1] We owe the reference to 'The Theory of Evolution in its Application to Practice' to Hallvard Lillehammer, 'Methods of Ethics and the Descent of Man', 364 (Lillehammer slightly mis-states the title of Sidgwick's article).

Application to Practice', accepting the line of argument that, because our moral faculty is the outcome of evolution, it is unreliable, 'would leave us with no faculty stable and trustworthy: and would therefore destroy its own premises'.

The burden of proof therefore falls on the other side. Those who appeal to the origins of moral intuitions in order to challenge their validity need to show not merely that the intuitions are caused in a certain way, 'but that these causes are of a kind that tend to produce invalid beliefs'. But no theory about the causes of the development of our moral faculty could, Sidgwick asserts, prove the invalidity of our fundamental ethical concepts, such as 'right' or 'good' or 'what ought to be done' or 'what it is reasonable to desire and seek', and therefore no such theory could prove that 'all propositions of the form "X is right" or "good" are untrustworthy'. In support of this claim, Sidgwick appeals to the distinction between 'is' and 'ought', saying that ethical propositions are about something 'fundamentally different from that with which physical science or psychology deals', and so 'cannot be inconsistent with any physical or psychological conclusions' (*ME* 213).

Although Sidgwick thus firmly defends ethics from a general sceptical attack grounded on any theory of the origins of our moral intuitions, he does then acknowledge that a more limited claim could be successful: 'It may, however, be possible to prove that some ethical beliefs have been caused in such a way as to make it probable that they are wholly or partially erroneous.' He then says that it will 'hereafter' be important to consider whether any ethical intuitions that we are disposed to accept as valid are open to attack on such grounds, but that his 'present' concern is only to deny the more general argument against the trustworthiness of the moral faculty. The 'hereafter' comes towards the end of book III, when Sidgwick has presented the three moral principles or axioms—the principles of justice, prudence, and benevolence—which he takes to be self-evident. After satisfying himself that we can know some moral truths by intuition, Sidgwick explains why he refrained from a lengthy discussion of the origins of our moral intuitions. The reason is, he says, that no theory of the origins of our moral intuitions has ever been put forward that

professes to discredit the axioms that he finds self-evident by showing that they were produced by causes that have a tendency to make
them false. On the other hand, an argument that targeted any of our
other moral intuitions on these grounds in order to show that they
are not absolutely true would be superfluous, since the kind of direct
reflection that has occupied him in book III has already led us to this
conclusion. Finally, Sidgwick adds, if a theory of the origins of our
moral rules viewed them as existing because they are broadly means
to the ends of improving the welfare of either individuals or of the
larger community, then this would tend to confirm the results that
he has reached by a different method, since they show that the rules
of common sense morality are subordinate to the principles of prudence and benevolence (*ME* 383–4).

Since this discussion in *The Methods of Ethics* about the ethical relevance of theories of the origins of morality is relatively brief, we will
mention one other comment Sidgwick makes on this topic. Sidgwick
wrote a review of a *Darwinism in Morals, and Other Essays*, by
Frances Power Cobbe, a formidable Irish social reformer, advocate of
votes for women, and founder of the British Union for the Abolition
of Vivisection. In the essay that gives the book its title, Cobbe refers to
the following passage in *The Descent of Man*:

If…men were reared under precisely the same conditions as hive bees, there can
hardly be any doubt that our unmarried females would, like worker bees, think it
a sacred duty to kill their brothers, and mothers would strive to kill their fertile
daughters; and no one would think of interfering.[2]

This passage, in Cobbe's view, 'aims…a deadly blow at ethics' because
it suggests that our moral sense comes from a source 'commanding no
special respect' and that its judgments are 'merely temporal and provisional' rather than answering to some eternal reality. On Darwin's
view, Cobbe continues, the 'provincial prejudice' of our world 'would
be looked upon with a smile of derision by better-informed people
now residing on Mars'.

Sidgwick denies that Darwin's comment is destructive of all ethics. He points out that the well-being of the bee community would

---

[2] Darwin, *The Descent of Man*, 151–2.

seem to depend on the habits Darwin described. He grants that, 'in the conscience of an average member of the hive', these habits would be seen as moral rules (presumably Sidgwick is referring to Darwin's imaginary human hive, rather than imputing a conscience to bees). But he also thinks Darwin mistaken, because 'a superior bee, we may feel sure, would aspire to a milder solution of the Population question'. Sidgwick adds that Cobbe fails to see that the principle of utilitarianism can accept 'almost any degree of variation in actual rules' without giving up the idea of absolute moral duties.[3] Thus accepting Darwin's claim would not undermine our belief that there are some things that we ought to do. So ethics as a whole is not threatened by the theory of evolution. Nevertheless, since Sidgwick says that the superior bee would 'aspire' to a milder solution—a choice of words that allows for the possibility that no other solution is available—he appears to accept that our particular set of moral rules does not hold for all ways of living. In very different circumstances, killing one's brother or daughter could be the right thing to do. That would mean that Cobbe's objection that Darwin's view makes the judgments of our moral faculty 'temporal and provisional' is sound, in so far as it applies to rules like 'Do not kill your brother', but mistaken about ultimate principles like 'Do what is best for the well-being of all'.

In later editions of *The Descent of Man*, Darwin responded, in a footnote, to Sidgwick's comment. He thought that Sidgwick's belief that the 'superior bee' would solve the population problem by a milder method was optimistic, and pointed to 'the habits of many or most savages' as indicating that the problem was more likely to be solved by such measures as female infanticide, polyandry, and 'promiscuous intercourse'. Darwin didn't explain how the last of these solves the population problem.[4]

---

[3] Sidgwick, 'Review of Cobbe's Darwinism in Morals', cited in Lillehammer, 'Methods of Ethics and the Descent of Man', 366.

[4] Darwin, *The Descent of Man*, 152 n. 6, quoted in Lillehammer, 'Methods of Ethics and the Descent of Man', 366.

2. The General Evolutionary Objection to the Objectivity of Ethics

Since Sidgwick's day, and especially over the past 40 years, an extensive literature has developed on the origins of morality and of our moral intuitions, much of it informed by a considerable body of empirical research.[5] It is not surprising that this body of theory should lead to further discussion of the implications of our understanding of evolutionary theory for morality. The most widely discussed and philosophically sophisticated contemporary argument for the kind of view that Sidgwick rejected is Sharon Street's claim that a 'Darwinian Dilemma' faces those who hold a realist theory of value.[6] Street starts from a premise that we fully accept: 'Evolutionary forces have played a tremendous role in shaping the content of human evaluative attitudes.' She then argues that those who defend objective moral truth face a choice between two uncongenial possibilities. The first possibility is that evolutionary forces have no tendency to lead to the selection of beings who hold objectively true evaluative attitudes. In this case, objectivists will have to admit that most of our evaluative judgments are unjustified. The second possibility is that evolutionary forces did favour the selection of those who are able to grasp objective moral truths. But this, Street argues, is contrary to a scientific understanding of how evolution works.

To take the first horn of the dilemma and accept that evolutionary forces have no relation to objectively true evaluative attitudes means, Street suggests, that our prospects of having evaluative attitudes that lead us to moral truths are like the prospects of sailing to Bermuda while allowing our boat's course to be determined by the winds and tides. We would be incredibly lucky to reach Bermuda, and if we did, it would be a remarkable coincidence. Barring such a coincidence, however, the realist has to accept what Street considers a 'far-fetched skeptical result', namely that 'most of our evaluative

---

[5] See e.g. Hamilton, 'The Genetical Evolution of Social Behaviour. I'; and 'The Genetical Evolution of Social Behaviour. II'; Trivers, 'The Evolution of Reciprocal Altruism'; Wilson, *The Moral Sense*; Wright, *The Moral Animal*; Ridley, *The Origins of Virtue*; and Haidt, *The Righteous Mind*. Also relevant is J. D. Greene, 'The Secret Joke of Kant's Soul'.

[6] Street, 'A Darwinian Dilemma for Realist Theories of Value'.

judgments are off-track due to the distorting pressure of Darwinian forces'.

Those taking the second horn of the dilemma fare no better. They make a claim that is unacceptable on scientific grounds. Street offers a list of some of the judgments we make, which includes, for example: 'We have greater obligations to help our own children than we do to help complete strangers.' Such judgments are conducive to reproductive success, so it is easy to see how evolutionary forces would lead us to make them. It is not so easy to see how evolutionary forces would lead us to make only judgments that are objectively true. Why should the truth of a judgment be something that evolution favours? As Street says, it is more scientifically plausible to explain human evaluative attitudes as having evolved because they help us to survive and to have surviving offspring, than because they are true.

To show how evolution could shape our evaluative judgments, Street asks us to suppose that we had evolved as a different kind of being. Social insects, for example, have a stronger orientation towards the welfare of the community than to their own individual survival, and male lions kill offspring that are not their own. Assuming that in some way we could be intelligent, but with reproductive patterns more like those of social insects or lions, we would, she claims, have different basic evaluative attitudes that would lead us to make different reflective evaluative judgments. Since not all these judgments could be true, wouldn't it be a remarkable coincidence if we just happened to have evolved as the kind of beings that make true evaluative judgments?

Street's speculation about intelligent social insects echoes the one that Darwin made, which so troubled Frances Power Cobbe, about what we would take to be our duties if we were reared in conditions like bee-hives. As we have seen, Sidgwick was willing to accept that our particular set of moral rules does not hold for all ways of living, but he insisted that an ultimate principle like 'Do what is best for the well-being of all' would hold in all conceivable circumstances. Hence ethics as a whole is not threatened by the theory of evolution. This suggests that Sidgwick, if armed with a modern understanding of evolutionary psychology, could reach a verdict not far from what Street describes as the 'far-fetched skeptical result' that 'most of our evaluative judgments are off-track due to the distorting pressure of Darwinian forces'. Sidgwick and Street could argue about whether it is 'most' or only 'many' of our common moral judgments that are off-track, but a contemporary Sidgwick might be closer to Street than the historical one. Sidgwick thought that what he calls 'the morality of common sense'—that is, the set of moral rules that we intuitively assume to be true—tends to produce actions that maximize utility, though it does so imperfectly. If he shared our modern scientific understanding that evolutionary forces operate at the level of the gene or the individual, or at most the community, rather than at the level of the species (and certainly not at the level of all sentient beings), he would surely have been open to the possibility that these evolutionary forces have produced evaluative attitudes that fail to conduce to ultimate moral truths such as 'Do what is best for the well-being of all'. To the extent that our common moral judgments are affected by these evolutionary forces, it would then have been consistent with Sidgwick's own approach to the morality of common sense for him to reject the particular judgments to which these forces led, while maintaining the validity of the more general principle that we should do what is best for the well-being of all. This is, after all, what he already does in book III of *The Methods* with many of the particular judgments of common sense morality. (In saying that Sidgwick would have rejected these judgments, we mean that he would not have taken them to state true moral principles. As we shall see in Chapter 10, whether they should continue to be included among the set of moral rules that people are encouraged to follow would, for Sidgwick, depend on whether continuing to include them would have better consequences than dropping them.)

The position we have just attributed to Sidgwick avoids Street's dilemma by accepting its first horn, for many of our common moral judgments. Street would no doubt then try to press her argument against the ultimate principle. How do we reach it, if it has no relation to our evolved basic evaluative attitudes? Was it sheer coincidence, like our drifting boat reaching Bermuda? When it comes to an ultimate principle like doing what is best for the well-being of all, however, Sidgwick has a good response to this argument. He believes we come to understand such principles by the use of our reason.

At this point Sidgwick could take the second horn of Street's dilemma. Street focuses on the question whether evolution is likely to lead us to have a capacity to recognize objective moral truths. If our moral beliefs are evolutionarily advantageous, then the advantages they confer on us in surviving and reproducing have nothing to do with their truth. So why would evolution have led us to have a capacity to recognize moral truth? Street correctly points out that a specific capacity for recognizing moral truths would not increase our reproductive success. But a capacity to reason would tend to increase our reproductive success. It may be that having a capacity to reason involves more than an ability to make valid inferences from premises to conclusions. It may include the ability to recognize and reject capricious or arbitrary grounds for drawing distinctions, and to understand self-evident moral truths—what Sidgwick referred to as 'rational intuition'. In other words, we might have become reasoning beings because that enabled us to solve a variety of problems that would otherwise have hampered our survival, but once we are capable of reasoning, we may be unable to avoid recognizing and discovering some truths that do not aid our survival.[7] That can be said about some complicated truths of mathematics or physics. It can also, as Parfit has suggested, be the case with some of our normative epistemic beliefs; for instance, the belief that when some argument is valid and has true premises, so that this argument's conclusion must be true, these facts give us a decisive reason to believe this conclusion. Parfit argues that this normative claim about what we have decisive reason to believe is

---

[7] McGinn suggests this explanation of why evolution has not eliminated moral behaviour in 'Evolution, Animals and the Basis of Morality', 91. One of us has defended a similar view in Singer, *The Expanding Circle*, ch. 5, and also in Singer, 'Ethics and Intuitions'. Derek Parfit makes a related argument against Street in *On What Matters*, Volume Two, 492–7. A broader application of this view can be found in Pinker, *The Better Angels of our Nature*, where Pinker draws on *The Expanding Circle* as well as history, psychology, and cognitive science to make the case that our capacity to reason (which he sees as having been enhanced by the invention of printing and subsequent social developments) is partly responsible for the decline in violence in recent times. See esp. *The Better Angels of our Nature*, 642–70, 689–92.

not itself evolutionarily advantageous, since to gain that advantage, it would have been sufficient to have the non-normative beliefs that the argument is valid, and has true premises, and that the conclusion must be true. Hence this and other normative epistemic beliefs are not open to a debunking argument.[8] This may also hold for some of our moral beliefs. One such moral truth could be Sidgwick's axiom of universal benevolence: 'each one is morally bound to regard the good of any other individual as much as his own, except in so far as he judges it to be less, when impartially viewed, or less certainly knowable or attainable by him' (*ME* 382).

It may be objected that if some aspects of our capacity to reason conferred an evolutionary advantage, while other aspects were disadvantageous in that respect (perhaps because they lead us to act more altruistically than we would otherwise have done), then these other aspects would have been selected against, and would have disappeared. (They might also have disappeared even if they were merely neutral, neither advantageous nor disadvantageous, because of evolutionary drift, but obviously the more a trait or capacity disadvantages the being who possesses it, the more rapidly it is likely to disappear.) It appears to be the case, however, that we have retained capacities to reason that do not confer any evolutionary advantage, and may even be disadvantageous. How can that be? A possible explanation of the existence of these capacities is that the ability to reason comes as a package that could not be economically divided by evolutionary pressures. Either we have a capacity to reason that includes the capacity to do advanced physics and mathematics and to grasp objective moral truths, or we have a much more limited capacity to reason that lacks not only these abilities, but others that confer an overriding evolutionary advantage. If reason is a unity of this kind, having the package would have been more conducive to survival and reproduction than not having it. We acknowledge that there are grounds for questioning whether our ability to reason is likely to have evolved as a package, rather than in the more piecemeal fashion in which evolution tends to proceed, resulting in the evolution of distinct modes

---

[8] Parfit, *On What Matters*, Volume Two, 492, and Parfit, e-mail to the authors, 16 Aug. 2011.

of reasoning, which would not have included the capacity to grasp moral truths, if that were disadvantageous in evolutionary terms. The fact that mathematical reasoning takes place in a different part of the brain from deductive reasoning (and so may have had a separate evolutionary origin) would also lead one to expect moral reasoning to be at least as distinct. It is possible that further research will eventually clarify this question, and if it can be shown that there is no 'package' of the kind we have postulated, that would undermine the argument we are making here.[9]

Street discusses the objection that our capacity to grasp objective moral truths could be a by-product of some other evolved capacity. She argues that this capacity must be a highly specialized one, 'specifically attuned to the evaluative truths in question'.[10] Therefore those who make this proposal face the Darwinian dilemma once again, this time with respect to the relationship between the specialized capacity to grasp objective moral truths and the other more basic evolved capacity. Either there is no relationship between the evolution of the basic capacity and the independent moral truths—in which case it is a remarkable coincidence that the basic capacity had, as a by-product, a capacity to grasp objective moral truths—or there is some relationship between the evolved basic capacity and the capacity to grasp independent moral truths. We have taken the second horn of this dilemma. Those who take this course, Street says, must claim that the evolved capacity 'involves at least some basic sort of ability to grasp independent evaluative truths, of which our present-day ability to grasp evaluative truths is a refined extension, in much the same way that our present-day ability to do astrophysics is presumably a refined extension of more basic abilities to discover and model the physical features of the world around us'. She then adds: 'But at this point the realist has to give some account of how this more basic sort of ability to grasp independent evaluative

---

[9] See Kroger *et al.*, 'Distinct Neural Substrates for Deductive and Mathematical Processing'. We owe this reference to Adam Lerner, who has pressed this objection against us, in his 'Fine-Tuning Evolutionary Debunking Arguments'.

[10] Street, 'A Darwinian Dilemma', 143.

truths arose.'[11] Indeed, that is true: but given that philosophers like Sidgwick have long said that it is our capacity to reason that enables us to grasp moral truths, and given that we can explain why a capacity to reason would have been evolutionarily advantageous, it is odd that Street does not directly confront the idea that the capacity to grasp moral truths is simply an application of our capacity to reason, which enables us to grasp a priori truths in general, including both the truths of mathematics and moral truths. For if the ability to grasp moral truths is an aspect of our ability to reason, it is easy to give an account of how it arose.

3. The Particular Objection: How Universal Benevolence Survives the Evolutionary Critique

We saw earlier in this chapter that Sidgwick believes that no theory of the origins of our moral intuitions 'has ever been put forward professing to discredit the propositions that I regard as really axiomatic, by showing that the causes which produced them were such as had a tendency to make them false'. We can now ask: is it still true, after all the work that has been done on the origins of our moral intuitions since Sidgwick wrote, that no theory has been put forward professing to discredit the propositions that he regards as really axiomatic? Remarkably, we believe that it is, at least for the all-important axiom of universal benevolence. After all, that axiom contradicts the very evaluative attitudes that Street offers as examples of judgments that are likely to lead to reproductive success, such as 'We have greater obligations to help our own children than we do to help complete strangers'. Evolutionary theorists have long had difficulty in explaining how pure altruism is possible. They tend to explain it in terms of more limited forms of altruism, such as altruism toward kin, which can be explained because it favours the survival of those with whom we share genes, and reciprocal altruism, which can be explained because it enables the development of mutually beneficial cooperative relationships. Some theorists also accept the possibility of

---

[11] Street, 'A Darwinian Dilemma', 144.

altruism toward one's own group. It is, however, difficult to see any evolutionary forces that could have favoured universal altruism of the sort that is required by the axiom of universal benevolence. On the contrary, there are strong evolutionary forces that would tend to eliminate it.

There is a popular misconception that altruism can arise because it is 'for the good of the species'. Modern evolutionary theorists point out that, while species go in and out of existence only over very long periods of time, individuals are much more short-lived. This means that individuals who behave altruistically would be likely to be selected against, and eliminated from the population, before they could become common enough to have any impact on the survival of the species as a whole. Richard Dawkins has argued—as the title of his early work, *The Selfish Gene*, suggests—that actions that involve sacrificing an organism's prospects of surviving and reproducing have evolved because they benefit the organism's genes, largely through favouring kin. He does not hesitate to draw the conclusion that 'Much as we might wish to believe otherwise, universal love and the welfare of the species as a whole are concepts that simply do not make evolutionary sense.'[12] Pierre van den Berghe has said flatly, and no doubt too bluntly: 'we are programmed to care only about ourselves and our relatives'.[13] Richard Alexander, in *The Biology of Moral Systems*, writes:

I suspect that nearly all humans believe it is a normal part of the functioning of every human individual now and then to assist someone else in the realization of that person's own interests to the actual net expense of those of the altruist. What this greatest intellectual revolution of the century [i.e. the individualistic perspective in evolutionary biology] tells us is that, despite our intuitions, there is not a shred of evidence to support this view of beneficence, and a great deal of convincing theory suggests that any such view will eventually be judged false.[14]

In *Unto Others*, Elliot Sober and David Sloan Wilson have forcefully challenged this individualistic perspective in evolutionary theory.

---

[12] Dawkins, *The Selfish Gene*, 2. For a summary of the debate on this issue, see Okasha, 'Biological Altruism'.

[13] Van den Berghe, 'Bridging the Paradigms'.

[14] Alexander, *The Biology of Moral Systems*, as quoted by Sober and Wilson, *Unto Others*, 5–6.

They argue that evolution could have selected for actions that benefit groups to which individuals belong, rather than for actions that benefit the individuals themselves. For the argument we are about to make, therefore, it is vital to understand that, while Sober and Wilson are challenging the views of Dawkins, van den Berghe, and Alexander, they do not argue that evolution could have selected for the kind of benevolence required by Sidgwick's axiom. As they put it:

> our goal in this book is not to paint a rosy picture of universal benevolence. Group selection does provide a setting in which helping behavior directed at members of one's own group can evolve; however it equally provides a context in which hurting individuals in other groups can be selectively advantageous. Group selection favors within-group niceness and between-group nastiness.[15]

This was Darwin's own view. He thought that the 'moral faculties' had spread because tribes that were ready to aid and defend each other would be victorious in conflicts with other tribes. Samuel Bowles has shown that Darwin could be right, because the genetic differences between human groups are sufficient for 'lethal intergroup competition' to account for the evolution of altruism.[16] This leaves us as far as ever from an evolutionary explanation of why people should go out of their way to help complete strangers, especially in ways that mean they never know who they have helped, and those who are helped never know who helped them. Moreover, even if 'altruism for the good of the species' somehow were the product of our evolution, that would still not go far enough, for the principle of universal benevolence bids us to have concern not only for the good of our own species, but for all sentient beings.

Street argues that an evolutionary account of the origins of morality is incompatible with moral realism. We have seen that Sidgwick has good reasons for denying that such an argument undermines the normative truth that each of us ought to give as much weight to the good of anyone else as we give to our own good. On the other hand, an evolutionary understanding of the origins of our ethical

---

[15] Sober and Wilson, *Unto Others*, 9, emphasis in the original.

[16] Bowles 'Group Competition, Reproductive Leveling and the Evolution of Human Altruism'. Darwin makes the argument to which Bowles refers in ch. 5 of *The Descent of Man*, esp. 199.

judgments does seem to undermine some of our ethical judgments, at least to the extent of suggesting that we should not take them for granted merely because we intuitively judge them to be sound. Guy Kahane puts it like this: 'if only some of our evaluative beliefs are susceptible to the relevant kind of evolutionary explanation, and we can at least roughly gauge the degree of this evolutionary influence on various beliefs, then what we should get isn't evaluative skepticism but a proportional lowering of justification'.[17]

Consider, for instance, the judgment that incest is wrong, even when those involved are adult siblings. Among our ancestors, for millions of years, such sexual relationships carried an increased risk of abnormal offspring, and hence diminished prospects of reproductive success, as compared to sexual relationships between unrelated couples. Hence the almost universal negative evaluative attitude towards incest—which becomes less universal when the degree of consanguinity, and hence the risk of abnormal offspring, is reduced—is easily explained as part of our evolutionary heritage. But today we can separate sex and reproduction, so this reason for rejecting incest in the circumstances described is no longer always applicable. Thus the judgment that incest is always wrong can be seen to be the product of a cause that, in at least some cases, produces judgments likely to be in error.[18] Something similar may be true of the widespread, though not universal, attitude that homosexuality is wrong, since it is even less likely than incest to lead to reproductive success.

Roger Crisp, in *Reasons and the Good*, offers a further example of an intuition for which an evolutionary explanation is available:

On Monday I blind a stranger to prevent his buying the last copy of a CD I want to buy. I buy the CD. On Tuesday I buy another CD, knowing that I could have given the money to Sight Savers International and prevented the blindness of at least one person.[19]

---

[17]   Kahane, 'Evolutionary Debunking Arguments', 119.

[18]   Haidt, 'The Emotional Dog and its Rational Tail', citing Haidt *et al.*, 'Moral Dumbfounding'.

[19]   Crisp, *Reasons and the Good*, 21. Harman offers a similar explanation of the distinction—with the more specific proviso that moral attitudes derive from implicit agreement, and whereas everyone would benefit from an agreement not to harm others, the rich and strong would not benefit from an agreement to help others. See his 'Moral Relativism Defended', 12.

Crisp points out that most people would think that the blinding is wrong, but the failure to prevent blinding is not, although the consequences of both are largely the same. He adds that this is the kind of morality that we would expect to result from evolution, because 'It is clear that a group cannot function well if its members are permitted to harm one another, whereas the survival value of a prohibition on allowing others to suffer is more dubious.'

As we have already mentioned, Street uses, as an example of how our judgments coincide with intuitions likely to lead to reproductive success, the judgment: 'We have greater obligations to help our own children than we do to help complete strangers.' The common intuition that this judgment is true may be the result of the fact that those who accept it would be more likely than those who do not accept it to leave surviving offspring to carry on their genes. In reviewing common sense morality, Sidgwick writes that, when we consider the duty of parents to their children as such, without taking into consideration psychological and social aspects of how best to bring up children, it is not at all self-evident 'that we owe more to our own children than to others whose happiness equally depends on our exertions'. In support of this view, Sidgwick asks us to imagine that my family and I land on a desert island where I find an abandoned child. It is not, he seems to think, self-evident that I have a lesser obligation to provide for the subsistence of this child than I do to provide the same for my own children (*ME* 346–7). This is not to say that the judgment that we have greater obligations to help our own children than to help strangers cannot, in particular cases, be justified, but rather that if it is to be justified, it needs a form of justification that does not start from the idea that, because we strongly feel that it is right, it must be true. For instance, it may be the case that our nature is such that the most reliable way of raising happy, well-adjusted children is to raise them in a close, caring family, united by natural ties of love and affection. If so, then this would provide an indirect justification of the judgment that we have greater obligations to our own children than to the children of strangers. Given the kind of creatures we are—not social insects, but mammals with children who are dependent on us for many years—loving our own children and helping them more than we help the children of strangers would, on this view, be justified in terms of the more ultimate principle that Sidgwick mentioned, that it is good to do what is best for the well-being of all.

Crisp accepts what he calls 'the Self-Interest Principle', which states, in effect, that any agent has a reason to do what makes her life go better, the strength of the reason varying in proportion to the extent to which her well-being will be improved.[20] But this principle can itself be debunked, in much the way that Crisp debunked the acts and omissions distinction. As Folke Tersman writes (using 'SI' to stand for the Self-Interest Principle):

A debunking explanation of SI can be given along the following lines. It is safe to assume that at least some concern for one's self-interest is the result of evolution-ary pressure, and the conviction that we have a reason to act self-interestedly can be seen as a way of verbalizing that concern, given the role of such judgments in planning and deliberation. The universal element of SI—the part that entails that it holds for everyone—needs another explanation. But then we can appeal to the cognitive processes mentioned above. We search for generality and coherence, and try to find relevant similarities and ignore irrelevant differences. If we restrict the scope of SI, we need an explanation in terms of relevant differences between the persons for whom it holds and those for whom it does not hold. The universal ver-sion does not require such complexity, and is therefore attractive for the reflective mind that seeks simplicity. So, the fact that reflection on SI can prompt us to accept it comes as no surprise.[21]

Tersman's point is that the fact that a cognitive process is involved in the formation of an intuition does not show that the intuition can-not be debunked. Just as we cannot trust the conclusion of a valid deductive argument if it starts from premises not known to be true, so we cannot trust the conclusion of an intuition reached by a cogni-tive process unless we know that the starting point of the process is true. Guy Kahane makes a similar point against the claim that one of us (PS) has previously made, that an evolutionary debunking argu-ment strengthens the case for utilitarianism. Kahane says that if evo-lution has selected for a disposition to altruism towards one's kin and those with whom one is in reciprocal relationships, then we should suspect not only principles that support altruism towards kin and

---

[20] Crisp, *Reasons and the Good*, 73.
[21] Tersman, 'The Reliability of Moral Intuitions', 403.

cooperating partners, but also the 'reasoned extension of such partial forms of altruism to universal altruism'. Otherwise, he says, we
risk being like a person who comes upon a madman counting the
blades of grass in his backyard, and tells him that because the distinction between his backyard and anyone else's backyard is arbitrary, he
should instead be counting blades of grass everywhere in the world.[22]

We accept that if a starting point can be debunked, it cannot lend
support to a more general or less arbitrary version of itself. But in
The Methods Sidgwick did not develop the case for his axiom of
universal benevolence by arguing for a reasoned extension of egoism or partial altruism. Instead, as we saw in Chapter 5, he claimed
that it is self-evident that a mere difference in time does not give
some moments of our own existence greater significance than any
other moments. This is, for Sidgwick, the 'self-evident element' in
the principle of prudence, and he goes on to argue that the reasoning which enables us to see this as self-evident also enables us to see
as self-evident that 'the good of any one individual is of no more
importance, from the point of view (if I may say so) of the Universe,
than the good of any other'. He then adds that it also seems to him
to be self-evident that 'as a rational being I am bound to aim at good
generally,—so far as it is attainable by my efforts,—not merely at a
particular part of it'. It is only in other passages of *The Methods* that
Sidgwick explicitly states the 'maxim of Prudence' (*not* the 'axiom of
Prudence') in a form that implies egoism, and this is not part of his
argument for the axiom of universal benevolence.

We can agree with Tersman's debunking explanation of the
Self-Interest Principle without thereby being compelled to accept a
similar debunking explanation of the principle of universal benevolence. The Self-Interest Principle extends the idea that I have a reason to act in my own interests only by granting that others have
similar reasons to act in their own interests. This modest extension
can be seen as inherent in the very concept of what it is to have a
reason—it is the 'first stage' of universalization that, as we saw in

---

[22] Kahane, 'Evolutionary Debunking Arguments', 119, referring to Singer, 'Ethics and
Intuitions', 350–1.

Chapter 5, J. L. Mackie described as 'the irrelevance of numerical differences'. Mackie was prepared to accept that this minimal stage of universalization is inherent in the meaning of 'ought' and other moral terms. On the other hand he rejected R. M. Hare's contention that this notion of universalizability is sufficient to get us to a form of utilitarianism. That, Mackie said, involves a substantive moral claim, not to be found in the meanings of the moral terms, nor in the bare concept of what it is to have a reason.[23] We agree and, as Sidgwick said, the same is true of the principle of universal benevolence: 'If the Egoist strictly confines himself to stating his conviction that he ought to take his own happiness or pleasure as his ultimate end, there seems no opening for any line of reasoning to lead him to Universalistic Hedonism as a first principle' (*ME* 420–1). It is only when the egoist makes the distinct claim that his pleasure is good, not only for himself but from the point of view of the universe, that Sidgwick's argument gets a hold. This is a substantive claim that we cannot get to from egoism merely by seeking, in Tersman's words, 'generality and coherence' or Kahane's 'reasoned extension'. There is nothing incoherent in accepting the principle of self-interest while rejecting the principle of universal benevolence. Even if there were such an incoherence, however, the fact that, as we have shown, there is another way of reaching the principle of universal benevolence would suffice to establish that it is not founded on a contaminated starting point.

Tersman contends that, to avoid general scepticism about ethics, 'one must show that there are intuitions for which no debunking explanation can be given or where the debunking explanations are inferior to non-debunking ones'. He then adds:

Let us say that if an explanation of an intuition entails that it is true or likely then it is 'validating'. In my view, if an explanation appeals to the way the intuition was formed, it is validating only if combined with an account of *why* the fact that it was so formed makes it true or significantly likely. And that account must both be described in some detail and have some degree of independent plausibility—not just any *ad hoc* story would do. [Emphasis in original][24]

---

[23] Mackie, *Ethics: Inventing Right and Wrong*, ch. 4.
[24] Tersman, 'The Reliability of Moral Intuitions', 403–4.

We suggest that this is indeed the case with the principle of universal benevolence. We form the intuition as a result of a process of careful reflection that leads us to take, as Sidgwick puts it, 'the point of view of the universe'. This idea is not specific to any particular cultural or religious tradition. On the contrary, the leading thinkers of distinct traditions have independently reached a similar principle and have regarded it as the essence of morality. In addition to the well-known Jewish and Christian versions of the Golden Rule, we find similar ideas in the Confucian, Hindu, and Buddhist traditions. Admittedly, these rules do not require us to adopt universal benevolence, but they do require impartiality. Significantly, the Golden Rule does not merely advocate reciprocity. It tells us to do unto others as we would have them do unto us, whether or not these others actually do treat us as well as we treat them. The words of the *Mahabharata* are especially clear on the distinction between self-interest and concern for others: 'One should not behave towards others in a way which is disagreeable to oneself. This is the essence of morality. All other activities are due to selfish desire.'[25] Finally, there is no plausible explanation of this principle as the direct outcome of an evolutionary process, nor is there any other obvious, non-truth-tracking explanation. Like our ability to do higher mathematics, it can most plausibly be explained as the outcome of our capacity to reason. The absence of good rival explanations for our intuitive grasp of the principle of universal benevolence does not prove that it is a substantive normative truth, but we consider it makes that a reasonable hypothesis to hold, at least until a better explanation is offered.

Crisp accepts that universal benevolence is not vulnerable to debunking based on an understanding of our evolutionary origins, but he thinks that this is equally true of the principle of egoism, because it too is contrary to kin altruism, which is what evolutionary theory would lead us to expect. Improving the prospects of one's kin surviving and reproducing is somewhere in the middle between

---

[25] *The Analects of Confucius*, also known as *The Selected Sayings of Kongfuzi*, 15.23; *Mahabharata*, Anusasana Parva 113.8; For Buddhism, see *Samyutta Nikaya*, v. 353. For a comprehensive list of such ideas in many different texts and civilizations, see Terry, *Golden and Silver Rules of Humanity*.

the wider principle of universal benevolence and the narrower principle of egoism, hence Crisp thinks that, as far as immunity from evolutionary debunking explanations is concerned, universal benevolence and egoism are on a par.[26] This is, however, a misleading map of the locations of the three principles. Kin altruism is much closer, from an evolutionary perspective, to egoism than it is to universal benevolence. Evolution explains altruism towards kin by seeing it as promoting the survival of the genes we carry. We can do this in many ways, but in normal circumstances, we will do it best by living a long life, finding a mate or mates, having children, and acquiring the resources, status, or power that will improve the prospects of our children and other close kin surviving, reproducing, and in turn promoting the survival of their children. Most of this looks remarkably similar to what an egoist would do anyway, at least on standard conceptions of self-interest. Moreover, because most humans care about their children, it is normal to think that whether a person's children are flourishing is a significant component of how well that person's life is going. Thus the behaviour we would expect to result from kin altruism will overlap very considerably with the behaviour that would result from following the principle of egoism. In contrast, following the principle of universal benevolence would lead to altruism towards distant and unrelated members of our species, and even to sentient members of other species. This is much more at odds with kin altruism and we do not see how evolution can explain it.

In correspondence on an earlier version of this chapter, Tersman agreed that, as far as Sidgwick's principle of rational benevolence is concerned, 'we presently don't have a fully satisfactory and well-established (evolutionary) debunking explanation of it'. He indicated that such a debunking explanation might, in time, emerge. We accept that this is possible. Tersman added that the line of argument we have developed in this chapter is 'vulnerable to possible falsification by future empirical results and empirical theorizing'. We agree, but we also think Tersman is correct when he goes on to

---

[26] Crisp, critical précis for *Ethics* Discussions at PEA Soup: Katarzyna de Lazari-Radek and Peter Singer, 'The Objectivity of Ethics and the Unity of Practical Reason'.

say that, although this vulnerability to future possible falsification should motivate some humility, on the part of both sceptics and non-sceptics, about their conclusions, it is not a drawback or fault. On the contrary, as Tersman puts it: 'more philosophers should try to articulate their positions in a way that makes them vulnerable in this way'.[27] Our judgment as to how well grounded a moral principle is should be sensitive to our best understanding of how we have come to accept that principle.

There are thus three elements in the process of establishing that an intuition has the highest possible degree of reliability:

1. careful reflection leading to a conviction of self-evidence;
2. independent agreement of other careful thinkers; and
3. the absence of a plausible explanation of the intuition as a non-truth-tracking psychological process.

If the third requirement were not met—if the intuition could be explained as the outcome of a non-truth-tracking process—that would not show the intuition to be false, but it would cast some doubt on its reliability. The agreement of others would not put this doubt to rest, for this agreement could be explained by the fact that the others share the same biological nature. This would raise the possibility that, in thinking that the intuition is self-evident, we are deceiving ourselves. Because the intuition plausibly could arise as part of our evolved nature, it would be, as Street argues, a coincidence if it happened to also be true. Coincidences do sometimes happen, but if an intuition that met the first two requirements but not the third were to clash with an intuition that met all three, we would have a ground for preferring the intuition for which there was no evolutionary explanation.

On the other hand, if an intuition does not meet the first two requirements, the fact that it meets the third would not help it. The ideal of celibacy serves as an example. Celibacy seems likely to diminish, rather than enhance, reproductive fitness, although if it brings sufficient power or prestige, the benefits that the celibate

---

[27] Tersman, e-mail to the authors, 25 July 2011.

might confer on his or her kin conceivably could outweigh the loss of direct descendants. The widespread support for celibacy during many centuries of the Christian era suggests that our moral ideas are not always responses to evolutionary pressures, but in the absence of some specific religious beliefs, few regard celibacy as an ideal, and certainly not as a self-evident one. Still, one might ask why celibacy has not generally met with the opprobrium often given to homosexuality, given that it seems equally likely to diminish reproductive success. We do not know the answer, but could it be that in order to be celibate, most humans have to be persuaded, against the urgings of a strong desire, that it is the right thing to do, whereas this is not the case for those whose sexual orientation is towards their own sex?

We have argued that Sidgwick's axiom of universal benevolence passes this test, but we are not claiming that it is the only principle to do so. Other principles, including deontological principles, might be equally impartial—for instance, the principle that lying is wrong, whether one is lying to strangers or to members of one's own community. Ethical principles of respect for human rights might also be thought to be impartial in the same way, but to be fully impartial, they would need to be freed from any specific association with members of our species, and instead to be reformulated as rights that are possessed by all beings with certain capacities or characteristics.

As we mentioned earlier, the principle that the good of one individual is of no more importance, from the point of view of the universe, than the good of any other, tells us nothing about what this good may be. The principle of universal benevolence needs a theory of well-being, or else it is empty of content. Sidgwick is, of course, aware of this. That is why the chapter in which he defends the axioms is followed by a chapter (to be discussed in our next chapter) in which he argues that the Ultimate Good is pleasure, and the absence of pain. Our next two chapters discuss whether Sidgwick succeeds in that endeavour. Our primary aim in this chapter is to show that partial reasons can be debunked and that, whatever the ultimate good may be, we have overriding reasons to aim at it impartially.

4. Resolving the Dualism of Practical Reason

Now that we have prepared the ground, it is not difficult to see the implications of our argument for the problem of the dualism of practical reason which we discussed in the previous chapter. As we saw there, it is, Sidgwick believes, 'in accordance with common sense to recognize—as Butler does—that the calm desire for my "good on the whole" is authoritative; and therefore carries with it implicitly a rational dictate to aim at this end'. This may indeed be Butler's view (although on this point Butler appears to contradict himself[28]) and it may also be in accordance with common sense, but here common sense seems likely to have been formed by the evolutionary influences we have been discussing. Since the claim that egoism is rational clashes with the principle of universal benevolence, we have precisely the situation described in the previous section, and we have grounds for supporting the intuition for which there is no evolutionary explanation rather than the one for which there is an evolutionary explanation. If the rationality of egoism can thus be put in doubt, we can tentatively conclude that all reasons for action are impartial, and the dualism that led Sidgwick to fear 'an ultimate and fundamental contradiction in our apparent intuitions of what is Reasonable in conduct' can, at least on the level of rationality, be dissolved.

This may seem too paradoxical to take seriously. But our reluctance to admit that all reasons for action are impartial may stem from the assumption that a reason for action must provide the person for whom it is a reason with a motivation for acting. Denying the rationality of egoism leaves reason detached from our strongest sources of motivation, namely our desires to further our own interests and those of our family. If, however, we recall the distinction we noticed in Chapter 2 between normative reasons and motivating reasons, the paradoxical nature of our claim is reduced.[29] The distinction, which offers an alternative to Hume's view that all reasons for action must be based on desires, is implicit in Sidgwick's objectivist, reason-focused,

---

[28] On the interpretation of Butler on this point, see Garrett, 'Joseph Butler's Moral Philosophy'.

[29] See Nagel, *The View from Nowhere*, ch. 8; Scanlon, *What we Owe to Each Other*, ch. 1; Dancy, *Practical Reality*, ch. 1; Parfit, *On What Matters*, Volume One, 37.

non-naturalist meta-ethics. More recently it has been developed by Thomas Nagel, Thomas Scanlon, Jonathan Dancy, and Derek Parfit. In Chapter 2, we had the example of the person who knows that if he does not go to the dentist now, his tooth will cause him pain in a few days, but he does not care about that. He has a reason to go to the dentist, but it is a normative, not a motivating reason. We may also have a motivating reason without having a normative reason. Parfit gives the example of someone who acted in order to get revenge. We may say: 'His reason was to get revenge, but that was no reason to do what he did.'[30] A discussion of a person's motivating reasons is relevant to understanding why people act as they do, but not to how they ought to act. We can have normative reasons for action, irrespective of whether we like them, agree with them, or desire to act in accordance with them.

Given Parfit's insistence on the normative rather than the psychological nature of practical reason, our argument suggests that he could have gone further and rejected what he refers to as personal and partial reasons. Why then does Parfit accept the validity of personal and partial reasons, rather than say that they are very common motivating reasons, but—as with the desire for revenge—not normative reasons? One possibility is that, as we saw in Chapter 4, he accepts the model of reflective equilibrium made popular by John Rawls, and this leads him to be reluctant to reject too many of our common moral judgments.[31] But Parfit interprets reflective equilibrium widely so that the process of reaching an equilibrium takes into account both scientific theories and normative theories. Among the scientific theories to be taken into account is evolutionary theory, along with the argument that it undermines the credibility of some of our most widely shared moral intuitions. Parfit, in particular, is well aware of this, for he stated it with his usual clarity in *Reasons and Persons*:

if some attitude has an evolutionary explanation, this fact is neutral. It neither supports nor undermines the claim that this attitude is justified. But there is one exception. It may be claimed that, since we all have this attitude, this is a ground

---

[30] Parfit, *On What Matters*, Volume One, 37.
[31] Parfit, *On What Matters*, Volume One, 367.

for thinking it justified. This claim is undermined by the evolutionary explanation. Since there is this explanation, we would all have this attitude even if it was not justified; so the fact that we have this attitude cannot be a reason for thinking it justified. Whether it is justified is an open question, waiting to be answered.[32]

Parfit, and other proponents of reflective equilibrium, widely interpreted, could therefore draw on evolutionary theory, as well as on Sidgwick's normative arguments in order to reject many widely shared moral intuitions, while retaining the principle of universal benevolence. Although those who make use of reflective equilibrium in normative and applied ethics typically assume that they should try to achieve an equilibrium between a plausible normative theory and most, or at least many, of our commonly accepted moral judgments, there is no need for them to make this assumption. They could reject the commonly held view that it is rational to do what is in one's own interests (even though people may have strong motivating reasons to act in this way) and accept that when one of two possible acts would make things go impartially better, that is what we have decisive normative reason to do.

[32] Parfit, *Reasons and Persons*, 308; we owe this reference to Kahane, 'Evolutionary Debunking Arguments', 110.

8

Ultimate Good, Part I: Perfectionism and Desire-Based Theory

1. Sidgwick on Ultimate Good

We saw that the rules of common sense morality, even if at first apparently self-evident, could be made more precise only by referring to the principle of prudence or the principle of benevolence. Both of those principles require us to aim at something good—either the good on the whole of an individual or the universal good of everyone. But what is this good at which we have an obligation to aim? In the *Methods,* Sidgwick discusses this question in two widely separated chapters. In the ninth chapter of book I he tells us that he will examine 'the import of the notion "Good" in the whole range of its application'. His concern here is with the conceptual question of what we mean by the term 'good', rather than with the substantive question of what is good. Then in book III, chapter 14—after setting out the axioms we have just considered—he develops and defends his own answer to the substantive question 'What is the ultimate good?'

In discussing the meaning of 'good' Sidgwick first rejects the view that to say something is good is implicitly to say that it is a means to pleasure. He offers some examples of common usage to show that this cannot be what we mean by 'good'—for example, to say that someone has 'good taste' in wines or art is not at all the same as saying that he derives the greatest enjoyment from them. Moreover, while we regard individuals as the final judge of what gives them the greatest pleasure, the idea of 'good taste' assumes a 'universally valid standard' to which the judgment of those who we say have good taste comes near (*ME* 108–9). The most important objection Sidgwick makes to any attempt to define 'the good' as equivalent to 'pleasure' or 'happiness', however, is one that anticipates G. E. Moore's 'naturalistic fallacy' argument. Sidgwick points out that, when hedonists affirm that pleasure or happiness is their ultimate good, they imply that the meaning of 'pleasure' or 'happiness' differs from the meaning of 'the good'. Otherwise, what they are saying would not be a significant proposition, but a tautology (*ME* 109).

After rejecting the view that we can simply define good in terms of pleasure or happiness, Sidgwick examines a definition that links a person's good with what he or she desires. He traces this view to Hobbes, who wrote: 'whatsoever is the object of any man's Desire, that it is which he for his part calleth Good, and the object of his aversion, Evil'.[1] Sidgwick begins his discussion of this view with the obvious point that 'a man often desires what he knows is on the whole bad for him'. One example is a desire for revenge when you know that reconciliation would be much better for you. Moreover, what we desire may appear to be good, but turn out to be, as Sidgwick puts it, 'a "Dead Sea apple", mere dust and ashes in the eating' (*ME* 110). Another argument against Hobbes's definition of goodness is that we call some things good even though nothing we can do will enable us to achieve them. Sidgwick's examples are 'fine weather, perfect health, great wealth or fame'. We may even try to suppress our desire for them, so that wanting what we cannot have does not make us unhappy; but any success we have in doing so will not lead us to judge these things as less good.

Sidgwick therefore suggests that a more plausible way of interpreting the notion of a person's good in relation to his or her desires would involve identifying it not with what people actually do desire,

---

[1] Hobbes, *Leviathan*, ch. 6 (Sidgwick slightly misquotes Hobbes. The original reads: 'whatsoever is the object of any man's appetite or desire, that is it which he for his part calleth good; and the object of his hate and aversion, evil').

but rather with what they would desire under certain conditions, namely:

what would be desired, with strength proportioned to the degree of desirability, if it were judged attainable by voluntary action, supposing the desirer to possess a perfect forecast, emotional as well as intellectual, of the state of attainment or fruition. (*ME* 111)

Yet even this is not an adequate definition of a person's 'good on the whole'. For one thing, it does not require 'an equal regard for all the moments of our conscious experience', although for Sidgwick that is, as we saw in Chapter 5, rationally required. The definition is also vulnerable to cases in which a person desires something that he will not regret having, but only because his choice will change his preferences—and change them for the worse. For example, a person who might have had a rich and rewarding life, perhaps even achieving great things, may instead indulge in pleasures so that 'he is never roused out of such a condition and lives till death the life of a contented pig, when he might have been something better'. To avoid this objection, Sidgwick suggests a further modification, so that we say that:

a man's future good on the whole is what he would now desire and seek on the whole if all the consequences of all the different lines of conduct open to him were accurately foreseen and adequately realised in imagination at the present point of time. (*ME* 111–12)

The notion of 'good' at which Sidgwick has now arrived is a very complicated one, and he acknowledges that there is something paradoxical about the claim that this is 'what we commonly mean' when we say that something is 'good on the whole' for a person. Still, he says, it could be seen 'as giving philosophical precision to the vaguer meaning' with which the word 'good' is ordinarily used, when used as a noun. But Sidgwick remains dissatisfied. The notion of 'good' we have reached is in one sense an idealized notion, because no one ever does have such fully informed desires, but it is nevertheless a notion that refers only to facts about the world and 'does not introduce any judgment of value, fundamentally distinct from judgments relating to existence'. (Had Sidgwick put this in the terminology later introduced by Moore, he might have said that it is a naturalistic definition of good.) Sidgwick thinks, however, that the common sense notion of a person's good on the whole includes in it some kind of judgment of value, rather than of fact, and even a 'dictate of reason'—to be specific, a rational dictate to aim at my 'good on the whole'.

It may help to make Sidgwick's argument clearer if we put it more formally:

(1) The idea of 'my good on the whole' carries with it the idea that it is something at which I am rationally required to aim.
(2) What I would desire under ideal conditions of the sort described above lacks the normative element required to generate any such rational requirements
Therefore
(3) What I would desire under ideal conditions of the sort described above cannot be what is my good on the whole.[2]

Thus Sidgwick concludes this discussion by suggesting that we take 'ultimate good on the whole for me' to mean 'what I should practically desire if my desires were in harmony with reason, assuming my own existence alone to be considered'. And if we move from the ultimate good for me to simply 'ultimate good on the whole', then we should take this to mean 'what as a rational being I should desire and seek to realise, assuming myself to have an equal concern for all existence' (*ME* 112). With this definition, Sidgwick in effect reduces the meaning of 'good' to 'what ought to be desired'—'ought', as we saw in Chapter 2, being the elementary notion that cannot be further broken down into constituent parts, and 'good' therefore being explained in terms of it.

The question now is what exactly is this good at which we should aim? Thus, Sidgwick reminds us, we have arrived at the question that was posed at the very beginning of philosophical ethics in Europe (or more specifically, ancient Greece): 'What is the ultimate good for man?' Sidgwick does not, in fact, limit his inquiry to what is good for males, nor to members of our own species, but the reference to 'good for' does indicate that he cannot take seriously the idea that something can be ultimately good unless it is also 'good for' someone. He begins his inquiry into this question with the claim that when we think about what we judge to be good, everything that can survive

[2] We thank Theron Pummer for suggesting this way of putting Sidgwick's argument.

the scrutiny of careful reflection has some connection to 'human existence, or at least to some consciousness or feeling' (*ME* 113). He considers possible counter-examples to this claim, noting that we commonly judge inanimate objects or scenes to be good because they are beautiful, or bad because they are ugly. Yet no one, he claims, 'would consider it rational to aim at the production of beauty in external nature, apart from any possible contemplation of it by human beings' (*ME* 114).

Next Sidgwick turns to the objection that, even if such things as beauty and knowledge are only good in some relationship to human beings, or at least to minds of some kind, it would be reasonable to be concerned with producing beauty or knowledge for their own sake, and to take them as ultimate ends, irrespective of who may come to contemplate the beauty or gain in knowledge. If we think carefully about such allegedly 'ultimate goods', however, Sidgwick believes that we will come to see that it is reasonable to seek them only if they lead either to happiness (presumably defined in the way suggested elsewhere in *The Methods*, as the surplus of pleasure over pain) or to 'the Perfection or Excellence of human existence' (*ME* 114).

With these last remarks of book I, chapter 9, Sidgwick has strayed beyond conceptiual analysis of the meaning of 'good' and into the more substantive considerations about what is ultimately good that are the subject of book III, chapter 14, entitled 'Ultimate Good'. He has narrowed the possible candidates for ultimate good to either happiness or perfection. Perfection as ultimately good may sound strange to modern ears, but perfectionism as a theory of value has its roots in ancient Greece. Aristotle can be interpreted as identifying the good with the perfection of our human essence. So if we are essentially rational beings, or beings who pursue knowledge, or who care for others, or who are courageous warriors, or who strive to do what is right, then the ultimate good for us will be a life that has the essential characteristics to the highest possible degree.

Sidgwick starts the chapter on 'Ultimate Good' by discussing the variant of perfectionism that links human perfection specifically to living virtuously. He observes at once that 'to say that "General Good" consists solely in general Virtue...would obviously involve us in a logical circle' (*ME* 392). Virtue is commonly understood as 'a quality exhibited in right conduct' (*ME* 219 n.). But to know what kind of quality this is, we have to know first what right conduct is. And to know what right conduct is we have to define what the good is. The problem can be most clearly illustrated by considering some specific virtues. How do we decide when frugality (which was considered a virtue in Sidgwick's day) passes over into the vice of meanness? Or when the virtue of courage becomes mere foolhardiness? When do candour, generosity, and humility become excessive? We need to appeal to a notion of what is good in order to answer such questions, and without such a notion of the good, virtue theory is seriously incomplete. The only virtues that have no such corresponding vices or excesses, Sidgwick says, are wisdom, universal benevolence, and justice, but each of them already has an intrinsic reference to the good—wisdom is insight into what is good and how to get it, benevolence is shown in purposively doing good, and justice consists in the distribution of what is good (or evil) impartially and according to the right rules. So we still need an independent notion of the good, which must consist in something other than wisdom, benevolence, or justice.

If we try to cut this discussion short by saying that virtue consists in conformity to the rules and principles of common sense morality, this too will not avoid the circularity problem. For the outcome of Sidgwick's examination of these rules and principles was that we cannot make these rules sufficiently precise, nor decide how to act when they conflict, without an understanding of what consequences—that is, what ultimate good—we ought to be aiming at. Hence regarding virtue, in the sense of conformity to these rules and principles, as the ultimate good will again lead us into the same logical circle.

Proponents of virtue as ultimate good might object that by 'virtue' they mean a quality of character, rather than one of conduct: 'Be this' rather than 'Do this'. Sidgwick has anticipated this objection. From a practical perspective, he is willing to agree that it can be important to urge people to aim to have an ideal character. But he cannot see how character and its elements—some dispositions or habits—could constitute Ultimate Goodness. On the contrary, he points out that a disposition is a tendency to act under some special conditions and so it is not valuable on its own but rather 'for the acts and feelings in which it takes effect, or for the ulterior consequences of these' (*ME* 393).

Sidgwick also considers a view associated with Kant, who famously opens the first section of his *Groundwork* by writing: 'There is nothing...that can be held to be good without limitation, excepting only a good will.'[3] On this view, we are to seek what is right, but this right-seeking is itself the sole ultimate good, and there is no other end to seek, except the end of seeking what is right. So, for instance, on this view, if doing right involved feeding the starving, there would be nothing good about the fact that people who were starving now had food; the good would consist only in the fact that the person providing the food had done what she believed was right. This is, in Sidgwick's words, 'a palpable and violent paradox'.

Of course, from the individual's own perspective, Sidgwick acknowledges, there can be no higher rule than to do what you judge to be right, because from your own perspective, when you think about what you ought to do right now, you cannot distinguish between doing what you judge to be right, and doing what is objectively right. But the distinction is one we make all the time when we consider the actions of others, and we often judge an action to be subjectively right—that is, we judge the person to be doing what he or she takes to be right—but we nevertheless regard the action as objectively wrong. This is, for example, the case with fanatics who dedicate themselves to acting in accordance with what they see to be right, even though the rest of us can clearly see that what the fanatic takes to be right is in fact wrong. To intend to do the right thing is not enough. That it is good at all only makes sense against the background of a belief that there is something objectively right to do or good to aim at.

There is also another argument that Sidgwick presents for rejecting a good will as the Ultimate Good. In his review of the morality of common sense (book III, chapter 9) Sidgwick noted that 'rational

---

[3] Kant, *Groundwork for the Metaphysics of Morals*, 9.

ends are sometimes better attained by those who do not directly aim at them as rational'. As an example, he suggests the view that 'marriage is better undertaken as a consequence of falling in love than in execution of a tranquil and deliberate design'. There are also services that, if springing from spontaneous affection, will possess an excellence that they would lack if done from a sense of duty (*ME* 345). Now he reminds us of this point and adds that this makes the extent to which it is good that people act on the basis of moral choice, rather than for some other motive, a practical question. But the fact that this is even an admissible question implies that 'conscious rightness of volition is not the sole ultimate good' (*ME* 395).

If human perfection does not consist in virtue, could it consist in 'the other talents, gifts, and graces which make up the common notion of human excellence or Perfection'? We have already offered our own examples of such talents: rationality, the pursuit of knowledge, caring for others, and showing courage in battle. But, Sidgwick says, no matter how much we admire such talents, 'reflection shows that they are only valuable on account of the good or desirable conscious life in which they are or will be actualised, or which will be somehow promoted by their exercise' (*ME* 395).

Sidgwick takes his argument to have shown that ultimate goodness is good or desirable conscious or sentient life. Not all of consciousness is desirable, though, for it includes both pain and pleasure, and what is painful is not desirable. Sidgwick says that if all life were 'as little desirable' as some parts of his own experiences have been—and he thinks that most people have had such experiences—then the preservation of life would be 'unmitigatedly bad'. If we regard the preservation of life as generally good, it is because we regard human life 'even as now lived' as having, on average, a positive balance of happiness. The 'mere existence of human organisms, even if prolonged to eternity', does not appear to Sidgwick in any way desirable. So it is not even conscious life as such that is ultimately good but only life that is accompanied by consciousness that is 'on the whole desirable'. Sidgwick thus reaches an important conclusion: 'it is therefore this Desirable Consciousness which we must regard as ultimate Good' (*ME* 397).

Acting virtuously may still be part of that ultimate good, because the conscious experiences that come with it may be desirable for the virtuous person. But could we say that 'Virtuous life would remain on the whole good for the virtuous agent, if we suppose it combined with extreme pain' (*ME* 397)? That is 'a paradox from which a modern thinker would recoil'. Though a martyr may have a duty to suffer torture for a greater good, we cannot say that the period spent undergoing torture is itself good for the martyr, no matter how virtuous the martyr is during this period. Hence virtuous actions, good as they are as means to desirable consciousness, cannot be good in themselves.

The question now remains: what forms of consciousness are desirable? In the section on pleasure and egoism, Sidgwick defined pleasure as 'a feeling which, when experienced by intelligent beings, is at least implicitly apprehended as desirable or...preferable' (*ME* 127). So Sidgwick seems to agree with utilitarians who regard pleasure as the ultimate good and he acknowledges that, at this stage of his argument, it may seem inevitable that we will identify desirable consciousness with pleasure or happiness. But he does not see himself as justified, yet, in drawing that conclusion. If we say that the ultimate good is happiness or pleasure, he points out, we are implying, first, that *nothing* is desirable except desirable feelings, and secondly, that the desirability of each feeling is something that can be known only by the individual, at the time of feeling it—in other words, the individual's judgment is final, regarding the extent to which each element of the feeling has the quality of being ultimately good (*ME* 398). Before accepting this, we need to consider alternative views such as that the consciousness of knowing something true is desirable in a way that the consciousness of believing something false is not, even if the subjective experiences are identical; or that having, say, the will to be free, or to be virtuous, is good in itself and not because it brings about desirable consciousness.

Sidgwick accepts that we ordinarily think that knowing the truth is to be preferred to believing what is false, on grounds other than the greater pleasantness of the knowledge of the truth. Often this can be explained by the better effects on future consciousness of knowing the truth, but that is not the only possibility. He offers the example of someone who prefers to know the truth, even when knowing it may be more painful than remaining in ignorance, and independently of any expected future effects on his or her consciousness. What such a person really prefers, Sidgwick says, is not the conscious state of knowing the truth, but the fact that what is known is true—and that, of course, depends on the relation between the state of mind and something else, namely the objective state of the world. For imagine that this person later learns that what she believed to be true is in fact false. She would then feel that her preference for the state she believed to be knowledge was mistaken. If her preference had really been for one state of consciousness rather than another—considering the two states purely as consciousness, lasting only while we are experiencing them—it is hard to understand why a subsequent discovery should show us that our choice was mistaken (*ME* 399).

Similarly, a man may want to be free though in poverty, instead of being a slave living in luxury. It is not that 'the pleasant consciousness of being free outweighs in prospect all the comforts and securities that the other life would afford' (*ME* 399). Rather, Sidgwick explains, that person has a strong aversion to the idea that his will is a slave to somebody else's will. The same applies to a philosopher who chooses so-called 'inner freedom' and does not surrender to his appetites though he knows that, considered merely as feelings, they would be more desirable. In both these cases, if this person were to be persuaded that 'his conception of Freedom or self-determination was illusory', he would think of his choice as mistaken (*ME* 400).

We could, Sidgwick allows, 'take "conscious life" in a wider sense, so as to include the objective relations of the conscious being implied in our notions of Virtue, Truth, Beauty, Freedom' (*ME* 400). Should we take this view, and therefore pursue, as the ultimately desirable ends for everyone, not just pleasure or happiness, but also these 'ideal goods' as Sidgwick calls them, of living virtuously, knowing the truth, contemplating beauty, and living in freedom? To that possibility Sidgwick responds in a manner typical of his approach to bedrock questions. He appeals to 'the sober judgment of reflective persons'. As he did when arguing that the common moral rules should not be thought to be independently valid, irrespective of their consequences, he begins by asking the reader to reflect upon his 'intuitive judgment after due consideration of the question when fairly placed before it'. Although he admits that we do experience preferences for states of affairs that are not merely conscious experiences, when we reflect on this, he claims, we can only justify to ourselves the importance we give to any of these objects 'by considering its conduciveness, in one way or another, to the happiness of sentient beings' (*ME* 401).

The second appeal Sidgwick makes is to the 'ordinary judgments of mankind'. This argument is, he acknowledges, more difficult to make completely cogent, as even some 'cultivated persons' are in the habit of judging knowledge, art, and virtue as ends to be sought independently of the pleasure we may get from them. But Sidgwick believes that common sense shows that such things as beauty, knowledge, and freedom do make us happier, and moreover that they gain our approval roughly in proportion to the extent to which they do so. Would common sense support freedom if it had no tendency to promote the general happiness? The pursuit of knowledge, too, receives the greatest support from common sense when the knowledge we gain brings benefits; although we often accept the value of scientific inquiry that brings no immediate benefits, because we know from past experience that knowledge that appears useless may become unexpectedly useful. Moreover, when the legitimacy of a branch of science is contested—Sidgwick gives the example of experiments on animals—the debate is always conducted on a utilitarian basis; that is, the proponents of the form of inquiry under attack always appeal to the benefits of the knowledge they are seeking, rather than to the value of gaining knowledge for its own sake.

Finally, the example of virtue is especially interesting. Normally, encouraging people to have virtuous impulses and dispositions is so obviously desirable that it is odd to even raise the question whether encouragement to virtue can go too far. But there are rare examples when concentrating on the cultivation of virtue leads to moral fanaticism, which tends to reduce the general happiness. If we admit this possibility, then we should also agree that the criterion for deciding how far the cultivation of the virtues should go must be, not the intrinsic value of virtue, but whether in the particular circumstances the further cultivation of virtue is likely to increase or decrease the general happiness.

Sidgwick has to concede that common sense shows some aversion to the idea that the sole ultimate end of our actions, and the standard of right and wrong, is happiness, in the sense of maximizing pleasures; but he thinks this aversion is due to some misunderstandings. He mentions four of them.

First of all, in ordinary usage the word pleasure is often used narrowly, to suggest 'the coarser and commoner' feelings that we desire to have, rather than the more elevated desirable states of consciousness, which would be less likely to produce aversion. Moreover, we know that some pleasures will lead to great pain or the loss of more important pleasures. Since in many cases we have moral or aesthetic instincts warning us against such 'impure' pleasures, we do not want to even think that they could be part of ultimate goodness.

Second, we should remember that we will be able to achieve many important pleasures only if we desire something other than pleasure, and do not directly aim at pleasure. This means that 'the very acceptance of Pleasure as the ultimate end of conduct involves the practical rule that it is not always to be made the conscious end' (*ME* 403). Hence the reluctance of common sense to take pleasure as the only thing desirable can be justified on the grounds that people are less likely to be happy if they concentrate only on their own happiness. The pleasures of being benevolent, for example, presuppose that we have genuine impulses to bring about the happiness of others.

Third, the aversion of common sense to the idea that pleasure is the ultimate good may result from the assumption that this means that each individual should pursue his or her own pleasure. The truth is that it is to egoism that common sense is really averse, not to 'Universal Happiness, desirable consciousness or feeling for the innumerable multitude of sentient beings, present and to come', which, Sidgwick says, 'seems an End that satisfies our imagination by its vastness, and sustains our resolution by its comparative security' (*ME* 404). Finally, the point made about finding our own pleasure only if we have other direct goals also applies, Sidgwick tells us, from the universal point of view. The general happiness is more likely to be achieved if in many circumstances we do not consciously aim at it. So to aim at such ideal objects as 'Virtue, Truth, Freedom, Beauty, etc., *for their own sakes*, is indirectly and secondarily, though not primarily and absolutely, rational' (*ME* 405–6).

Thus Sidgwick takes himself to have shown that common sense is not really opposed to the idea that the ultimate good is pleasure. But before concluding his argument, he offers one more consideration for accepting this view. If we reject it, he says, can we frame any coherent account of ultimate good? If we do not take universal happiness as the proper common goal of human activities, on what other basis can we systematize our ends? How, for example, can we compare the values of the different ends, other than hedonism, with each other and with the value of happiness? For in practice, we need to decide not only whether we should pursue truth rather than beauty or freedom, but how far we should seek any of these if we foresee that doing so will lead to more pain, or less pleasure, for humans or other sentient beings. Sidgwick tells us that he has failed to find 'any systematic answer to this question that appears to me deserving of serious consideration'. As a result, he concludes that rigorously applying the method of intuitionism leads us to universalistic hedonism, or in a word, utilitarianism.

2. Theories of the Good

For Sidgwick, the major challenge to hedonism comes from perfectionism. Today, hedonism and perfectionism still have their defenders, but so does the view that Sidgwick considered only as an account of the meaning of 'good for', namely that what is good for conscious beings is determined by what they desire, or what they would desire under specified conditions. Why when Sidgwick went on to discuss, in his chapter on Ultimate Good, substantive normative theories of the good, like perfectionism and hedonism, did he not also consider a desire-based account expressly advocated—as such theories are advocated today—as a normative theory? A clue may lie in what

Sidgwick says against this theory as an account of the meaning of 'good'. He pointed out that the account of 'good for' remains at the level of description, and so fails to capture the normative element of a judgment of value. This is certainly the natural reading of the passage in Hobbes with which, as we have just seen, Sidgwick begins his discussion of accounts of the meaning of 'good for' in terms of desires. The assumption that a desire-based theory is a descriptive account of human behaviour would have been easy to accept, given that none of Sidgwick's contemporaries clearly advocated a normative theory that resembles a modern desire-based view. (And indeed, as we are about to see, even in our own day Parfit considers that desire-based theories of the good are descriptive rather than normative.)

Most contemporary discussion of theories of the good is over the merits of these theories as theories of welfare—that is, as accounts of what makes a life go best for the being living it—rather than as theories of what is ultimately or intrinsically good in general. We will focus on theories of what makes a life go best for the being living it, before turning to the question of the bearing that our answer has on what is good 'from the point of view of the universe'.

Theories of what is good for a conscious being, also known as theories of welfare, or theories of self-interest, have been classified in various ways, none of them free of problems. In *Reasons and Persons* Parfit uses three categories: hedonistic theories, desire-fulfilment theories, and objective list theories. Parfit's tripartite classification has been widely followed, but it can lead to confusion. 'Objective list theories' is a catch-all for infinitely many different kinds of theory that have in common only that they hold that certain things are good or bad for us irrespective of our attitudes towards them. Hedonism can be seen as an objective list theory with just one item—pleasure—on the list. Parfit explains the difference between a desire theory and an objective list theory by saying that the former appeals only to what a person prefers, or would prefer under certain conditions and therefore gives 'an account of self-interest which is purely descriptive—which does not appeal to facts about value'. He contrasts this to an objective list theory which he says 'appeals directly to what it claims to be facts about value.'[4] But a desire theory does not have to be merely descriptive: it is possible to hold that it is a fact about value that what is objectively good for conscious beings is that their desires should be satisfied. This may or may not be a plausible normative claim, but it cannot be ruled out of court on meta-ethical grounds and it would make desire theory, defended in this way, a form of objective list theory. In failing to consider this possibility of a normative interpretation of desire theory, Parfit here seems to be making the same mistake as Sidgwick when he did not include such a theory in his discussions of Ultimate Good. In *On What Matters* Parfit does allow for a normative interpretation of desire theory that makes the fulfilment of desires an objective value.[5]

L. W. Sumner points to a more fundamental distinction when he distinguishes subjective and objective theories. He regards a theory of welfare as subjective if it treats 'my having a favourable attitude toward something' as a necessary condition of that thing being intrinsically good for me. Objective theories deny this, holding—like Parfit's objective list theories—that something can be directly and immediately good for me 'though I do not regard it favourably, and my life can be going well despite my failing to have any positive attitude toward it'.[6] The terms 'subjective' and 'objective' are used in many different ways, however, and we have already used them in a different way in this book. In the way we have used these terms in our discussion of subjective and objective theories of practical reason and of ethics, it would be possible to argue that a world in which everyone gets what they desire, or have a favourable attitude toward, is objectively good. To describe this as a subjective theory of welfare therefore seems liable to induce confusion.

Peter Railton captures the core of Sumner's subjective/objective distinction when he writes that for something to be intrinsically

---

[4] Parfit, *Reasons and Persons*, 499. Christopher Woodard argues, on grounds that are distinct from those we suggest here, that Parfit's distinction is confusing because it conflates distinct issues, and unduly narrow because it excludes some possible theories. See his 'Classifying Theories of Welfare'.

[5] Parfit, *On What Matters*, Volume One, 74.

[6] Sumner, *Welfare, Happiness and Ethics*, 38.

valuable for a person, it 'must have a connection with what he would find in some degree compelling or attractive'. Railton refers to this as 'internal resonance', a term taken up by Chris Heathwood who writes: 'It is hard to believe that showering a person with goods which in no way resonate with him is of any benefit to him.'[7] We will follow Railton and Heathwood in speaking of what Sumner calls subjective theories of welfare as theories that incorporate a 'resonance constraint'. We will describe theories with such a constraint as 'internalist theories' to indicate that they are based on or at least linked to the internal perspective of the conscious being whose good we are discussing; whereas objective theories, as Sumner defines them, do not, so we will refer to them as externalist theories, since for them what is good is external to the perspective of the being whose good it is.[8] We begin with the group of theories that most clearly incorporates the resonance constraint.

3. Desire-Based Theories

i. The Roots of Modern Desire-Based Theories of the Good

Hobbes's theory of the good took 300 years to become mainstream. As we saw in Chapter 1, during the 1930s many philosophers held that moral judgments should be understood as expressions of attitudes or emotions. As such, it seemed pointless to discuss which moral theories are true or false, or better or less well justified. Instead the task of philosophy was seen as limited to the morally neutral work of clarifying concepts and analyzing the meanings of words, and many philosophers offered analyses of words like 'good' in terms of 'pro-attitudes', which was really another way of saying desires.[9]

Similar influences persuaded economists that to establish their field as a science they should eliminate references to unobservable and unquantifiable mental states and instead focus on observable

---

[7] Railton, *Facts and Values*, 47; Heathwood, 'Subjective Desire Satisfactionism'.

[8] Note that these terms, externalism/internalism, can also be used differently. See e.g. Sumner, *Welfare, Happiness, and Ethics*, 87–91.

[9] See, for instance, Nowell-Smith, *Ethics*.

behaviour. Thus references to happiness or pleasure were replaced by 'revealed preferences'—for example, the preferences people reveal when they go shopping. If for the same price I could buy an orange or an apple, and I buy the orange, this reveals my preference, at the time of purchase, for the orange, and from this the economist would conclude that my utility is increased more by an orange than by an apple. On the other hand, if apples were half the price of oranges and I bought two apples rather than one orange, this would show that two apples increase my utility more than a single orange. The switch from unobservable mental states like pleasure to observable choices that were supposed to reveal a being's preferences meant an important shift in the nature of the value that economists assumed should be maximized. Though it was still referred to as 'utility' it was no longer happiness or pleasure: it was, instead, the satisfaction of preferences or desires. The shift was accepted without much challenge at the time, perhaps because most philosophers thought value-judgments cannot be true or false anyway, and so individual preferences are as good a basis for value as anything else, and perhaps also because to insist on a conception of well-being not based on the preferences of the individual seemed paternalistic. This view remains dominant in economics.

Philosophers returned to normative ethics in the 1960s and 1970s, but many of them were still inclined to favour some form of non-cognitivism, such as C. L. Stevenson's emotivism or R. M. Hare's universal prescriptivism. For Hare, as we saw in Chapter 5, to make a moral judgment is to prescribe that something be done in all relevantly similar circumstances, and this requirement leads to preference utilitarianism. Hare rejected alternative views, such as views based on claims that some things are objectively good, irrespective of whether people prefer them, on the grounds that 'as soon as we start asking what it is for a moral quality or fact to exist in the world, we get lost'.[10] One of us (PS) was for many years sufficiently persuaded by this reasoning to accept preference utilitarianism as, at least, 'a first base

---

[10]   Hare, 'Universal Prescriptivism', 451; for discussion of the way in which Hare's position must rely on the claim that there are no objective moral truths, see Peter Singer, 'Reasoning Towards Utilitarianism', 147–59.

that we reach by universalising self-interested decision making' and hence a view that requires minimal presuppositions. To go beyond preference utilitarianism, he claimed, 'we need to be provided with good reasons for taking this further step'.[11]

In Chapter 2 we argued that there are objective non-natural ethical truths, such as the truth that agony is just as bad when it happens on a future Tuesday as when it happens on any other day. If there are such objective truths, desire-based theories of the good lose the default position that they had on Hare's meta-ethical view. It can no longer be argued that desire-based theories are metaphysically minimalist, whereas other theories must make problematic claims to objective moral truth. The satisfaction of desires *could* still be an ultimate objective good, or even the only ultimate objective good, but now there are many rivals that stand, initially, on an even footing with the desire-based theory. Proponents of desire theories need to show, by reasoned argument of the kind that Sidgwick uses to argue for hedonism, that we should regard the satisfaction of desires as the ultimate good, just as the proponents of any other theory of what is ultimately good need to show why we should regard their candidate as ultimately good. They also need to decide on which version of the desire theory they wish to defend.

ii. Varieties of Desire Theory

There are many varieties of desire theory, so supporters of such theories need to decide which version they wish to defend. The most basic form holds that my good consists in the fulfilment of whatever desire I have right now. The strength of this theory is that it wholeheartedly embraces the resonance constraint. Whatever the theory holds to be good for me will necessarily resonate with me, because what is good for me now is what I now want. The most obvious problem with this basic version, as Sidgwick observed, is that I may now have

---

[11] Singer, *Practical Ethics*, 1st edn (1979), 13; the same passage appears in the 2nd (1993) edn, but in the 3rd (2011) edn, an additional paragraph on p. 14 notes some objections to the idea that the satisfaction of preferences should be our ultimate end, and refers to arguments for hedonistic utilitarianism and other moral theories, before putting the issue aside with the comment that this is 'a topic for a different book.' You are now reading that book.

a desire that I will later regret satisfying. I may, for example, now have an intense desire for revenge on someone I believe to have wronged me, although if I do take revenge, it will lead to a spiral of violence that will rebound on me and lead me to wish I had never done it. Sidgwick therefore considered also an 'informed desire' theory in which we suppose that the desirer has a 'perfect forecast' of all the consequences of satisfying her present desire. But even this is not enough, since there may have been alternatives open to the desirer that would have led her to form different desires from which she would have attained greater satisfaction. If we accept that this would have been a better outcome, we must switch to a theory that says that my good consists in the fulfilment of the desires I would have under conditions of full information about all the different lines of conduct open to me and the impact that these would have on the fulfilment of the desires I would then come to have, over my lifetime, or perhaps it would be better to say, over all the different lifetimes that I could live.

Even under such fantastically complicated ideal conditions of full information, however, someone might choose against what would satisfy her desires on the whole—she might, for example, give little weight to the future, or she might, like Parfit's man with Future Tuesday Indifference, have no desire for what happens to her on a particular day of the week. So even this fully informed desire theory of the good is inadequate, since—as we saw in Chapter 5—there are grounds for holding that it is a requirement of reason that I have equal concern for all the moments of my conscious experience. If, however, desire theory must give consideration to whether a person's desires are rational, in a sense that goes beyond whether they are fully informed, then a new and independent standard has been brought into the decision, and the resonance constraint has been abandoned, or at least severely weakened.

Desire theorists could try to find a more minimalist way of dealing with the problem of the person who fails to give full weight to the satisfaction of her future desires. They might say that what is ultimately good for me is not the satisfaction of my present desires but the greatest possible satisfaction of desires over my whole life. This is still a form of desire theory, for it denies the existence of any goods apart from the satisfaction of desires. It suggests that we should take into account all of someone's desires, actual and hypothetical, over the different alternatives open to her. We could then assign a positive number to a fulfilled desire and a negative number to an unfulfilled one, with the numbers reflecting the intensity or importance of the desire. A simple sum would then tell us which alternative yields the 'greatest total net sum of desire-fulfilment'.[12]

There is, however, another, more general problem about desire theories that sum up desire satisfaction over one's entire life. Richard Brandt has pointed out that desires may change over time, and vary in intensity: 'Some occurrence I now want to have happen may be something I did not want to have happen in the past, and will wish had not happened, if it does happen, in the future.'[13] Suppose, for example, that your friend has been, for most of his life, an atheist who would have been appalled at the thought of a priest being present at his death bed. When he is dying, however, he becomes afraid of hell-fire and asks for a priest. The question is: should we ignore the desire that he had most of his life, and call for the priest, or should we ignore the desire he has right now? It would seem that a summative theory would require us to give greater weight to desires held for many years than to a desire held for only a few hours. But it seems odd to bind the present self by the desires of the past self. Ulysses' sailors were right to reject his calls to be untied, when he heard the song of the sirens, but that was because they knew—as he knew when he ordered them to bind him to the mast and block their own ears—that the sirens lead you to act on irrational desires, and sail onto the rocks. In deciding whether to call the priest, do we need to form a view as to whether your dying friend's fear of hellfire is irrational?[14]

Desires might be not only unstable, but intransitive or cyclical. In some studies, people have been shown to prefer A to B, B to C, and C to A. It is hard to know what a desire theorist could make of that. Since there is then no fact of the matter about which of A, B, or C a person desires, one response would be to ignore all such desires. But

---

[12] Parfit, *Reasons and Persons*, 496.
[13] Brandt, *Morality, Utilitarianism, and Rights*, 169.
[14] Brandt, *Morality, Utilitarianism, and Rights*, 171–2.

if all of a person's desires were cyclical, that would provide a strong reason for abandoning desire theory and moving to a different theory about what is good for that person.[15]

Parfit has another objection to 'summative' desire theories. Suppose I offer to make you addicted to a drug. Taking the drug itself is neither pleasant nor painful, but when you wake up each morning you have a strong desire for the drug. Fortunately, you will always be able to satisfy this desire because supplies of the drug are readily available at no cost. Becoming addicted to this drug will therefore increase your desire satisfaction throughout your life—but note, this is not because you get any pleasure from satisfying your desire for the drug. On a summative desire theory, becoming addicted to the drug increases your well-being. This, Parfit suggests, is not plausible.

A desire theorist might try to deal with Parfit's addiction example by thinking of unfulfilled desires as debits in a moral ledger. You don't get wealthy by borrowing money and then repaying it, and similarly, you do not give someone a better life by creating a desire in them and then giving them the means to satisfy it.[16] On this view, only the satisfaction of existing desires, or desires that will exist anyway, makes someone's life go better. This approach has its own difficulties, however, for surely we may improve someone's life by stimulating in them a desire for, say, reading Jane Austen. The difference between this case and Parfit's addiction example may be that reading Austen is a pleasurable experience, whereas becoming addicted to the imaginary drug is not. But that difference points towards a hedonistic theory of the good, not a desire theory.

The problem for the debit version of desire theory gets even worse if there are enjoyable experiences linked to a predictably unsatisfied desire. Suppose that, as a result of your urging, your friend develops a desire to read one of Austen's novels. She reads it, enjoys it immensely, and then desires to read another, which she does, after which she wants to read another, and so on, until—too soon!—she has read them all, and is left with an unsatisfied desire to read more.

---

[15] Mark Alfano drew our attention to this point. See his 'Wilde Heuristics and Rum Tum Tuggers' and his 'Some Normative Implications of Indeterminate and Unstable Preferences'.
[16] See Singer, *Practical Ethics*, 114.

Nevertheless she is very happy to have encountered Austen's work. From time to time she thinks about her favourite scenes from the novels, always with great pleasure, tinged with regret that Austen did not write more. According to the debit version of desire theory, it was wrong to stimulate in her a desire to read Austen, because now she has an unsatisfied desire she would not otherwise have had. That seems implausible.

Parfit himself suggests that defenders of desire theory could respond to his addict example by switching to a 'global' version of desire theory which takes into account only the desires a person has for 'some part of his life, considered as a whole, or about his whole life'. If a person prefers not to be addicted to this drug, either for his whole life or for some part of his life, that is the only desire to be counted.[17] This global version, however, leads to its own difficulties. One is that in situations that are the mirror image of the drug addiction case, the global version gives us the wrong result. Suppose that because of your strict puritanical upbringing you have a preference, looking at your life as a whole, that you never engage in frivolous activities like dancing. Nevertheless, you often see other people dancing and when you do, you experience a strong desire to join in. Invariably, you yield to this desire and when you do, always enjoy dancing. At the end of an evening's dancing, you feel relaxed, you have no frustrated desires, and because you are not given to dwelling on your sins, you feel no regret or guilt. You are not the reflective type, and so these enjoyable episodes have no impact on your overall preference for a life without dancing. This desire, on the global version of desire theory, is the one that matters. Your desire to dance is a desire to do something *now*, not a desire for your life as a whole. Your life would have gone better for you if you had never yielded to your desire to dance. We find this verdict implausible.

A further problem for the global version of desire theory is that it gives us no way of saying what is good for beings who lack the intellectual capacity to envisage their existence over extended periods of time, and so to form preferences for such periods. Yet the life of

[17] Parfit, *Reasons and Persons*, 497.

a baby, or a person with dementia, or a non-human animal, can go well or badly, even without this capacity. It seems odd that we need a completely separate account of the good for such beings. Yet if the global desire theory allows us to take into account *only* desires for one's whole life, or for a part of one's life, considered as a whole, there appears to be no overlap between what is good for a being capable of such desires, and what is good for a being incapable of them.

iii. The Awareness Requirement

So far, we have been thinking of situations in which the fulfilment of my desire will have a positive effect on me; but this is not a necessary element of desire theory. Suppose that I desire that Barcelona should win the UEFA Champions League. I watch every match Barcelona plays. When it finally clinches the championship, I am thrilled and have a happy feeling for several weeks afterwards. My desire has been satisfied. But now suppose that at the start of the season, I am transferred to a job on a remote island where I cannot get any football news. As before, Barcelona wins the championship, but this time, I don't know about it. Nevertheless, my desire that Barcelona wins has been satisfied—in one sense of the term. We can refer to this as a 'state of the world requirement'—I desired that the world be in a certain state (Barcelona winning, its players exuberant, the team's name on the trophy) and the world is in that state. But the standard form of desire theory has no 'awareness requirement', and so the fact that I am unaware of the result of the match, and that my mental state is exactly the same as it would have been if the result had been reversed, is irrelevant. Perhaps I will never know—I may die before the news reaches me. If I do, did Barcelona's victory make my life go better? That seems implausible.[18]

---

[18] Parfit raised this problem with his 'Stranger on the Train' example: you meet a stranger who tells you that he is ill, and you want him to be cured. You never meet again, but unknown to you, he is cured. Parfit thinks that it is implausible to say that the stranger's improved health has made your life go better. See *Reasons and Persons*, 494. Kagan, in *Normative Ethics*, 37, considers the example of someone who is keen on prime numbers, and desires that the number of atoms in the universe is prime. Does his life go better if this is the case, even though he can never know it?

The obvious solution to this problem is to add an awareness requirement to desire theory, so that it asserts that what is good for a person is not merely that what she desires occurs, but that she is aware of the fact that it has occurred. Such a modification has been mentioned in passing by both Richard Brandt and Wayne Sumner. Chris Heathwood has pointed out that this view still makes my welfare depend on a state of the world that I may know nothing about; namely, whether an event has really taken place. For suppose, in the example we have been discussing, a friend of mine on the island, knowing that I do not have long to live, tells me that his wife managed to get a message to him that Barcelona won. In fact he has not received any such message, but I die happy in the firm belief that my team is the victor. If my friend now wishes to assess how well my life has gone, does he have to wait until he can find out which team really won? Heathwood would say that he does not. Hence he makes a further modification of desire theory, dropping the state of the world requirement altogether. On his 'subjective desire satisfactionism' theory, it is the belief that one's desire has been satisfied that matters, not whether it really has been satisfied. Since you cannot, strictly speaking, be aware of something that has not occurred, we can also say that he has replaced the awareness requirement with a belief requirement.[19]

Subjective desire satisfactionism is no longer a pure desire theory, in a sense that is easy to distinguish from mental state theories like hedonism, which we will be considering in the next chapter. Heathwood knows this and sees his theory as combining the strengths of both desire theory and hedonism. Yet this also raises the question of whether subjective desire satisfactionism retains the resonance constraint. We will postpone further discussion of this view until our examination of hedonism, where the same question arises. Meanwhile we return to our assessment of forms of desire theory that do not have an awareness or belief requirement, and which are prepared to stand by the implication that my life goes better if the state

---

[19] See Heathwood, 'Subjective Desire Satisfactionism'; an earlier version is Heathwood, 'Desire Satisfactionism and Hedonism.' For Brandt and Sumner, see Brandt, 'Two Concepts of Utility,' 172, and Sumner, *Welfare, Happiness, and Ethics,* 127–8. We owe these references to Heathwood, 'Subjective Desire Satisfactionism'.

of the world is as I desire it to be, even if I never become aware of this fact and it does not impinge on my consciousness in any way.[20]

If how well people's lives go depends on whether their desires are satisfied, even when the satisfaction of their desires will make no difference at all to any of their mental states, does it matter whether they are alive at all when their desires are satisfied?[21] This question has important practical implications for such issues as the weight we give to deceased people's wishes about their funeral arrangements, or the disposal of their personal papers. Our willingness to respect such wishes might, however, also be justified by the positive difference that this practice makes to people's lives, while they are still living them. They are likely to be happier if they can have confidence in their wishes being followed after they die. We can imagine examples in which this consideration does not apply. Suppose that a friend who lives by herself has asked you to visit her because she is ill. You find her much worse than you expected: she is dying. She raises herself from her pillow to hand you a thick manuscript. It is, she tells you, a novel into which she has poured all of her creative energy during the past 5 years. She knows that she will never see it published, but she does not want her work to have been in vain. 'Please,' she says, 'See that it gets published. I want it to be read.' Before you can reply, she falls back, dead. Should you do as she asked? You flick through the pages, and judge that the novel is publishable, but not so different from many others that publishing it would add much to the happiness of the world, although it would not detract from it either. Despite this, many people would be uneasy at the idea that it is perfectly fine for you to throw the manuscript in the recycling bin.

Some desire theorists see it as a virtue of their theory that it can explain why this would be wrong, and therefore also give a direct justification of our practice of giving weight to the wishes of the dead, without resorting to the indirect explanation that this is for the benefit of those still living. On the other hand, there are wishes of the dead

---

[20] For a discussion of the difficulties faced by Hare in defending a pure desire theory, and a vindication of Sidgwick's views, see Nakano-Okuno, *Sidgwick and Contemporary Utilitarianism*, 196–202.

[21] Parfit discusses this question in *Reasons and Persons*, 494–5.

that seem to carry no weight at all. If we excavate an ancient Roman tomb and find an inscription indicating that the person buried there desired that, in 2,000 years, a lamp would be lit on his grave, does that give us any reason to light a lamp there? It might be a neat thing to do, but would it be wrong not to do it? How is the desire theorist to explain the apparent difference between this case and the previous one? Does the moral weight of the desires of a deceased person decline as the years pass? Why should it?

iv. Informed Desires

Even if we confine ourselves to the living, we have not resolved the problem Sidgwick raised, whether desire theorists should take into consideration only present desires, or present informed desires, or the sum of all a person's desires over her entire life. We have seen some of the problems of the summative view, and of its global variant. Contemporary desire theorists usually agree with Sidgwick that the most plausible forms of desire theory refer to the desires people would have if fully informed and rational. Peter Railton, for example, writes: 'an individual's good consists in what he would want himself to want, or to pursue, were he to contemplate his present situation from a standpoint fully and vividly informed about himself and his circumstances, and entirely free of cognitive error or lapses of instru mental rationality'.[22] Harsanyi goes so far as to say: 'It would be absurd to assert that we have the same moral obligation to help other people in satisfying their utterly unreasonable wants as we have to help them in satisfying their very reasonable desires'.[23]

There are two problems with this switch to informed desires. One is the resonance requirement which, as we have seen, Railton himself described as essential to a defensible notion of what is good for someone, saying that for something to be of intrinsic value for a person, it 'must have a connection with what he would find in some degree compelling or attractive'. This passage continues, though,

---

[22] Railton, *Facts and Values*, 54; Railton elucidates his position further—and arguably, modifies it in the direction of hedonism—in his 'Reply to John Skorupski' (see esp. p. 235).

[23] Harsanyi, 'Morality and the Theory of Rational Behaviour', 55.

'at least if he were rational and aware'.[24] The qualification 'at least if he were rational and aware' opens the way for a conception of someone's good that may not be at all 'compelling and attractive' to a person who is *not* rational and aware, and perhaps never will be sufficiently rational to appreciate that what he has been given is what he would have wanted if he were rational and aware.[25] It's like giving a 5 year old a birthday present that she would want if she were 10, except this 5 year old may never grow up and change her tastes. An informed desire theory does not really meet the resonance requirement, or meets it only accidentally.

We have already had a glimpse of the second problem for fully informed desire theories. When Sidgwick argues that we should take into account only desires that are in harmony with reason, he is in fact rejecting a desire theory of the good, and opening the way for its replacement by a hedonistic account. Harsanyi's suggestion that we count only 'reasonable desires' clearly risks the same fate. Kagan observes that this is a more general problem for all informed desire theories:

> what exactly is it that explains why it is only ideal desires whose satisfaction will contribute to well-being? Why does having what we want leave us better off in those cases—but only in those cases—where the desires in question are ideal desires?... A tempting thought is this. Having the things we would want—if only we were fully informed, rational, free from bias, and so forth—is valuable, because these are the things that are truly worth having! That is, if we were fully informed, and so on, we would be in an ideal position to *recognize* which things have value and which things do not. And then our preferences would follow accordingly: we would prefer to have what has more value over what has less.[26]

As Kagan suggests, in attempting to make desire theories more attractive by incorporating a proviso for full information and rationality, one can slide into a theory that says that the good for us is determined by whether our lives contain things that are objectively good for us, independently of our wants and desires. Accepting a requirement that desires be substantively rational would mean that we are unable

---

[24] Railton, *Facts and Values*, 47.
[25] Heathwood makes this point in his 'Subjective Desire Satisfactionism'.
[26] Kagan, *Normative Ethics*, 39; Yew-Kwang Ng presses a related argument against Harsanyi in much more detail in his 'Utility, Informed Preference, or Happiness?'

to determine in what a person's ultimate good consists until we have decided whether there are some objective goods that it is rational to desire. This is no longer a desire-based theory.

Desire-based theories of value have been defended because, for those with sceptical views about the role of reason in determining our ends, they seemed the only metaphysically viable option, other than nihilism. If we can accept objective normative reasons for action, we have other options. Some philosophers favour desire-based theories because they satisfy the resonance requirement, but this is most clearly true for the basic theory, which implies that if we want revenge now for an imagined wrong done to us, then revenge is good for us, even if we will later regret having that desire. The more we strive to make a desire-based theory plausible by putting constraints on the desires that we accept as determining what is good for us, the less well the theory does in terms of fulfilling the resonance requirement.

4. Externalist Theories of the Good

According to Sidgwick, the proper question to ask, if I am seeking my good on the whole, is not what I do desire, but what as a rational being I should desire (*ME* 112). Sidgwick is therefore willing to countenance abandoning the resonance requirement, for what I should desire as a rational being may have no resonance at all with what I actually do desire. The question then becomes: what is it rational to desire? Sidgwick held, as we saw in the first section of this chapter, that there is only one thing that it is rational to desire, namely pleasure. Whether this is truly an externalist theory is a question that we will postpone to the next chapter, after we have had a chance to examine in more detail what Sidgwick means by pleasure. Some other philosophers, including G. E. Moore, Hastings Rashdall, and W. D. Ross, have suggested that there are several things that are good and rational to desire. They are pluralists. If we limit this discussion to what is good for someone, rather than simply good, one list of plausible candidates is provided by Parfit: moral goodness, rational activity, the development of one's abilities, having children and being a good parent, knowledge, and the awareness of true beauty.[27] Chris Heathwood offers a longer list of possible intrinsic values: enjoyment, freedom, happiness, being respected, knowledge, health, achieving one's goals, friendship, getting what one wants, being a good person, being in love, creative activity, contemplating important questions, aesthetic appreciation, and excelling at worthwhile activities.[28]

i. The Paternalism Objection

These theories cannot claim a necessary internal connection between what a person wants—even if she is fully informed and thinking clearly—and what is good for her. It may be thought that this objection is especially damaging because it implies that paternalism would be justified, to induce or compel people to have what is really good for them, even if they do not want it.[29] That makes it sound as if externalism is liable to lead to support for totalitarian or at least authoritarian states. 'No government', we may indignantly exclaim, 'should decide what is good for me, without even asking me what I want!'

This objection to externalist theories is muddled. There is no necessary inference from the claim:

What is good for a person is independent of what she desires or would desire if fully informed.

to political or social paternalism, which we state as:

The state (or some other institution or social group or individual) is justified in coercing or putting social pressure on people to live in ways that they do not desire nor would desire if fully informed.

It is not difficult to imagine externalist theories of value that would, either always or in most circumstances, lead to the rejection of political paternalism. For instance, one might hold that freedom of thought and action is a fundamental, or even an overriding, value, whether or

---

[27] Parfit, *Reasons and Persons*, 499.

[28] Heathwood, 'Subjective Theories of Wellbeing'.

[29] Sumner mentions paternalism as an objection to all mental state theories in *Welfare, Happiness and Ethics*, 98. See also Hooker, *Ideal Code, Real World*, 41.

not people have a pro-attitude towards it.[30] (Are we then paternalistically imposing freedom of thought on people who do not want it?) Or a hedonistic utilitarian might judge that people do, in fact, experience more pleasure if they are allowed to follow their own desires, without coercion or social pressure. Hence the justifiability of political or social paternalism is a separate issue from the justifiability of external values. The real issue with externalist theories of value is therefore not so much whether they are, as a whole, paternalist, but whether it is plausible to believe that there are external values such that what is good for conscious beings can be independent of their own preferences. If this can be shown, and those values provide grounds for opposing paternalism, then there is no problem of paternalism for externalist theories based on these values. If, on the other hand, values that *do* imply paternalism can be shown to be justified, then paternalism itself is justified. So, either way, paternalism is not a problem for externalist theories of value.

ii. Perfectionism

Sidgwick, as we have seen, rejects perfectionism, which is the clearest example of an externalist theory that he considers, because he thinks that goods like knowledge and virtue are only valuable when they contribute in some way to a desirable state of consciousness. Sidgwick's contention did not convince G. E. Moore, who in *Principia Ethica* referred to Sidgwick's claim that no one 'would consider it rational to aim at the production of beauty in external nature, apart from any possible contemplation of it by human beings' (*ME* 114). Moore said that he *did* think this rational, and sought to persuade his readers to share his view by asking them to imagine two worlds, one exquisitely beautiful and the other simply 'one heap of filth', without one redeeming feature. Granted that no human being can ever see either world, Moore wrote, it would nevertheless be rational to hold that it is better for the beautiful world, rather than the ugly world, to

---

[30] See Hooker, *Ideal Code, Real World,* 42. Hooker notes that to accept an objective list theory does not mean that we have to reject autonomy as one of the values to promote. 'Therefore, the list theory itself might prohibit what we intuitively think of as objectionable paternalism.'

exist.[31] To this we respond that in imagining the two worlds, we find the beautiful world more pleasing—but then, that is because we are, in a sense, *seeing* the two worlds, in our mind's eye. If we can put that distorting effect aside, we can see no reason for *thinking it better* that the beautiful world exist. Moore himself eventually thought better about his contrary opinion, because in his subsequent book *Ethics,* he abandoned it and agreed with Sidgwick that nothing is intrinsically good unless it has some relation to consciousness.[32] Admittedly, this is a distinct point from the question whether *awareness* of beauty has some value other than the desirable consciousness it can bring. Would there be value in someone being aware that they were seeing something beautiful, but not finding the conscious state that this brought about in any way desirable? Here too, we cannot see value in anyone being aware of beauty unless that awareness either is, or has some tendency to bring about, a desirable conscious state.

iii. Parfit's Composite Thesis

Parfit has suggested that arguments like Sidgwick's rest on a questionable assumption. Sidgwick asked his readers to reflect on whether states of mind like knowledge, or awareness of beauty, would be good if they brought no enjoyment and if the person in those states did not desire that they continue. Sidgwick answered that question in the negative, and therefore concluded that knowledge and awareness of beauty are valuable only because of their tendency to lead to states of consciousness that are desirable. But, Parfit suggests, this argument rests on the assumption that the value of a whole is just the sum of the value of its parts. It might be the case that the value of, say, being in a state of knowledge is a composite of two necessary elements—genuine knowledge, and the enjoyment of it—so that what is good for someone is to be in a state of knowledge *and* to desire to be in this state or enjoy being in it.[33] Either of these, without the other, Parfit suggests, might have 'little or no value'. But this 'Composite Thesis' is, as Theron

---

[31] Moore, *Principia Ethica*, 135–6.
[32] Moore, *Ethics*, 103–4, 148, 153.
[33] Parfit, *Reasons and Persons*, 501–2.

Pummer aptly puts it, 'a mere promissory note' until the details are filled in and we are able to see just how the two elements are to be combined to create the value in question.

There are various ways in which different values, like enjoyment and knowledge, might be combined to make a whole that is more than the sum of the value of its parts, but, Pummer shows, it is surprisingly difficult to do this in a plausible way. Parfit's claim is that both genuine knowledge and enjoyment of knowledge are necessary for there to be value in being in a state of knowledge. So if Alex possesses vast knowledge but gets no enjoyment at all from it, her knowledge is of no value. Suppose that Ben knows as much as Alex, and gets a tiny amount of enjoyment from it—just enough to make him, for one minute each day, slightly more cheerful than he would otherwise be. Is Ben's tiny amount of enjoyment enough to give full value to his state of knowledge, so that it is as valuable as the state of knowledge of Carla, who knows as much as Ben and Alex and constantly delights in it? That would suggest, Pummer says, that the value of being in a state of knowledge is hypersensitive to the amount of enjoyment one receives from it—a tiny bit of enjoyment makes all the difference. That doesn't seem plausible. What if the value of the state of knowledge is the mathematical product both of the amount of knowledge one has and the amount of enjoyment one gets from it? David knows only one-tenth as much as Ben, but the knowledge he has makes him slightly more cheerful for 10 minutes every day. Is his state of knowledge as valuable as Ben's? That still seems to leave the value of a state of knowledge too sensitive to modest changes in the amount of enjoyment one gets out of it, while being insufficiently sensitive to a big drop in the amount of knowledge one has. Pummer also considers a 'fixed amount' formula, according to which, for each unit of enjoyment, only a fixed number of units of knowledge would count towards the value of the whole—for example, for each unit of enjoyment we can only count up to 10 units of knowledge. This avoids hypersensitivity, because small differences in enjoyment can only yield small differences in the value of the composite. But now there is the opposite problem of insensitivity, because this formula ignores differences in knowledge beyond the specified limits. This can best be seen by putting numbers on levels of enjoyment and knowledge. In the table below, the composite value of Emma and Fred's knowledge and enjoyment is the same, even though Fred knows 10 times as much, and Emma and Fred's enjoyment is the same.

Fixed Amount View of Composite Value

	Knowledge	Enjoyment	Composite Value
Emma	1,000,000	10,000	100,000
Fred	10,000,000	10,000	100,000

There are, of course, many other possible formulae by which one might link the value of a state of knowledge to the levels of knowledge and enjoyment of the knower, and it is possible that one of them will avoid these problems of hypersensitivity and insensitivity. Until someone finds such a formula, however, we should remain sceptical about the Composite Thesis.[34]

In any case, we do not find ourselves drawn to the view that whether a person's firmly held beliefs constitute knowledge makes a sharp difference to how well her life has gone, if it makes no difference to her enjoyment of that life. Consider the life of the celebrated 17th-century mathematician Pierre de Fermat, who believed that he had discovered an elegant proof of a theorem now known as 'Fermat's Last Theorem'. He made a note to this effect but never wrote out the proof. For more than 350 years after Fermat's death, mathematicians sought to find Fermat's proof. A proof of the theorem eventually was found, but it is so complex that it is certainly not the proof Fermat imagined that he had discovered, and today most mathematicians believe that what he thought to be a proof was fallacious. Assume this is the case, and assume also that Fermat's false belief gave him as much pleasure and satisfaction over the remaining years of his life as he would have had if the proof had been valid. In that case, it would seem that his life

---

[34] The argument of this paragraph comes from Pummer, 'The Problem of Joyless Life'.

would not have been any better, for him, than it would have been if he had proved the theorem. The quality of one's conscious experiences makes an obvious difference to how well one's life has gone. The truth of one's beliefs may not.

We realize that some people will not share our judgment about Fermat's life, and the same people, reflecting on this and on the items on Parfit's and Heathwood's lists, will conclude that some of them are good in themselves independently of their positive effect on the conscious lives of sentient beings. We have no way of proving such a conclusion to be mistaken, but we will present some considerations against it in the next chapter when we discuss the case for hedonism and draw our final conclusions about ultimate good.

iv. Virtue and Perfection

We turn now to the perfectionist theory that the ultimate end for human beings is the perfection of our human essence. Aristotle can be interpreted as holding one version of this theory, and Thomas Aquinas brought this Aristotelian line of thought into Christian thinking, where it continues to have some adherents.

For Aristotle, it is good for us to perfect our nature because that is our function. As he puts it:

For just as for a flute-player, a sculptor, or any artist, and, in general, for all things that have a function or activity, the good and the 'well' is thought to reside in the function, so it would seem to be for man, if he has a function. Has the carpenter, then, and the tanner, certain functions or activities, and has man none? Or as eye, hand, foot, and in general each of the parts evidently has a function, may one lay it down that man similarly has a function apart from all of these? What then can this be?[35]

We have already pointed out (in Chapter 5, when discussing Michael Slote's views about the shape of a life) that Aristotle's view make sense within the framework of a teleological vision of the universe, but without that framework the idea that human beings have a function collapses, and with it Aristotle's foundation for the view that we ought

---

[35] Aristotle, *Nicomachean Ethics*, 1097b23–1098a17. We owe this reference to Hurka, *Perfectionism*, 24.

to perfect traits that are essential to us.[36] Without the idea that we were put on Earth for some purpose, attempts to retain the view that it is good for us to perfect our human nature run the risk of skating over the gap between 'is' and 'ought'. If there are no cosmic purposes, we cannot assume that our nature is suitable to some desirable purpose, or that it is good on the whole and ought to be perfected. Those who try to derive an ethic from human nature often assume that whatever good elements are reflected in our character and our activities are part of our 'true' human nature, while the bad things we do are not part of our nature, but the product of some corrupting influences upon it. There is no basis for such a rosy view of human nature. Waging aggressive war, for example, is arguably more central to human nature than is altruism towards strangers. Which of these traits we should perfect is a moral choice, and not something to be decided by an investigation of human nature.

We could develop a perfectionist account that is explicitly based on morality, or more specifically, on virtue. To perfect human nature, on this view, is to act virtuously. Because knowledge of what it is to act virtuously does not itself come from a mere description of human nature, but from our beliefs about what it is to be virtuous, there is no illicit crossing of the gap between facts and values. This is the form of perfectionism that Sidgwick discusses.

Virtue ethics has undergone a revival recently, but Sidgwick's criticism of the idea that virtue is the ultimate good remains applicable to modern virtue ethics if it claims to offer a comprehensive normative ethical theory. Sidgwick's objection is that to know what qualities are virtues, we need to know what we ought to do; but as his analysis of common sense morality showed, in order to set the limits to a common sense moral principle such as those of benevolence or veracity, we need to appeal to the consequences of our actions, and for that we need an account of what is of ultimate value. Thus to define ultimate good as virtue leads us around in a circle.

It looks, then, as if the idea that there is ultimate value in perfecting our human nature is in bad shape. Its origins in a teleological view of

---

[36] As Hurka agrees, in his *Perfectionism*, 24.

the universe are no longer credible. If it tries to derive moral values from an account of human nature as it is, it illicitly crosses the 'is–ought' gap, and if to avoid that gap it simply assumes that perfecting human nature is to be found in acting in accordance with our common idea of virtue, it becomes circular. It is, surely, time to abandon the entire position.

v. Hurka's Human Nature Perfectionism

Not so fast, says Thomas Hurka, a contemporary philosopher who has argued that human nature perfectionism can survive the demolition of its foundations in Aristotle. He regards talk of a human function not as foundational to the perfectionist view, but as an 'accretion' that can be scraped away, leaving a sounder perfectionism underneath.[37] He understands the difference between evaluation and description, and rejects attempts to derive evaluative conclusions from a purely descriptive account of human nature. Nor does he approve of allowing moral considerations to influence one's concept of which characteristics are, and which are not, part of human nature. For perfectionism to remain a distinct and defensible view it must, he says, 'be serious about human nature', by which he means, it must take an objective look at human nature, warts and all. 'On no admissible account of nature,' Hurka writes, 'does a conventionally good human always develop human nature more than a conventionally bad one.'[38] Hurka considers it understandable that Sidgwick should treat perfectionism as a form of common sense, or intuitionist, morality, because Sidgwick was thinking of such perfectionists as Kant and T. H. Green, and they did see perfection as consisting in living in accordance with the conventional moral sense of virtue. But it is unfortunate, in Hurka's view, that Sidgwick had these models before him, because it meant that he does not consider perfectionism at its best.[39]

---

[37] Hurka, *Perfectionism*, 24. Hurka himself is no longer committed to the views we discuss here, but we think his position remains worth discussing, as it shows how perfectionism can be modified to avoid some of the difficulties we have just discussed, as well as the new difficulties that confront this modified version. See Hurka, *Virtue, Vice, and Value*, p. vii.

[38] Hurka, *Perfectionism*, 30.

[39] Hurka, *Perfectionism*, 20.

What then is perfectionism at its best? It is, Hurka tells us, a 'stripped-down version' that must be free of 'moralism' and so 'must never characterize the good by reference to conventional moral rules, but always non-morally; and in defending its claims about essence, it must likewise appeal only to non-moral considerations'. Moreover, it 'defines its ideal in terms of essential properties without tying those properties to any metaphysical purposes', and does not claim to be true in virtue of the meaning of good or any other concepts. It must be defended by substantive moral argument.[40] This is certainly a thoroughly sanitized version of perfectionism, cleansed of its long-standing fallacies. The next question is: without the support perfectionism had from Aristotle's teleological view of the universe, or from religious beliefs, or from morally loaded accounts of human nature, what reason do we have to accept it?

In defending his stripped-down version of perfectionism, Hurka appeals to reflective equilibrium as his mode of justification. We have discussed reflective equilibrium in Chapter 4 and we will not rehearse our objections here. Hurka claims that 'the goal of developing human nature, or exercising essential human powers, is deeply attractive'. It has 'widespread acceptance', is implicit in non-philosophical talk of living a 'fully human' or 'truly human' life, and is endorsed by writers like Aquinas, Nietzsche, Green, and Marx. Although these thinkers have very different visions of what the good life for a human is, the fact that they all seek to ground their visions in an ideal of human nature shows, Hurka argues, the intrinsic appeal of that ideal.[41]

Hurka provides no evidence that the ideal is widely accepted among non-philosophers. It would be interesting to know how people would choose if offered a choice between a life that is 'fully human' but less happy and an alternative life that is happier but less than 'fully human'. Even if survey results showed that they would choose the 'fully human' life, however, Hurka himself admits that at least some of the support he claims to find could be the result of one or more of the 'accretions' to the perfectionist view, especially the view that God gave us our human

---

[40] Hurka, *Perfectionism*, 20, 30.
[41] Hurka, *Perfectionism*, 31–2.

nature and wants us to develop it. Hurka plays down the influence of such factors, but plainly he does not really know how much support the stripped-down view would retain among people who were clear about the indefensibility of the accretions. (None of the writers Hurka mentions, incidentally, are particularly renowned for the clarity of their thought, except perhaps Aquinas who was under the influence of at least two of the accretions, Aristotelian teleology and Christian theology.)

One way of showing that the ideal of developing human nature is not in itself an attractive ideal is to imagine that human nature were different. Suppose, for example, that being cruel to the weak were an essential element of human nature. Whether it actually *is* an essential element of human nature is not something we will discuss here— much depends on the idea of what is essential to being human. For our purposes, it is enough to imagine that it could be. Would it then be good for us to be cruel? And if the question is turned aside with the claim that it is inconceivable that cruelty to the weak could be an essential part of human nature, let's imagine that being cruel to the weak is an essential element of Martian nature. Would this mean that it is good for Martians to develop their nature? To become more highly refined, perhaps, in inflicting greater and greater agony on all those weaker than they are, and to be sure not to neglect their talents in this area by focusing on non-essential aspects of their nature, like helping the weak or enjoying the warmth of the sun?

Hurka is aware of this objection. Although he does not think it possible that humans could be essentially cruel, he accepts the implications of his view for other species:

A generalized perfectionism does imply that, if essentially cruel beings existed, the development of cruelty in them would be intrinsically good.

He then adds:

This is not a claim that, given the beings' remoteness from our experience, our specific judgements give us good reason to reject. And an attractive general ideal gives us reason to accept it.[42]

---

[42] Hurka, *Perfectionism*, 22.

We should not accept Hurka's suggestion that the remoteness of the beings from our experiences vitiates the reasons we have to reject the claim that, in essentially cruel beings, the development of cruelty would be intrinsically good. How remote are these beings, really? Mark Twain observed: 'Of all the animals, man is the only one that is cruel. He is the only one that inflicts pain for the pleasure of doing it... Man is the Cruel Animal.'[43] That doesn't say that cruelty is essential to human nature, but it does suggest that, were we to encounter beings in whom cruelty was an essential part of their nature, we would not find them as utterly unlike some members of our own species as Hurka appears to be suggesting. In any case, it isn't too difficult to imagine such beings. The appalling implication that it would be intrinsically good for them to develop their capacities for cruelty shows that the general ideal of developing human nature, shorn of its accretions and its favourable view of what is essential to our nature, is not attractive at all.

We should briefly mention a different form of perfectionism. As John Rawls uses the term, a 'strict perfectionist' view is simply the idea that achieving excellence, whether in art, science, or culture, trumps all other values. For a strict perfectionist, if the achievements of the ancient Greeks in art, science, and philosophy were only possible because they had slaves, then slavery in ancient Greece was justifiable.[44] This is not, of course, a view Rawls endorses, and it is not likely to find many defenders today. Rawls also allows for a 'far more reasonable view' which simply gives 'the realization of human excellence in the various forms of culture' some weight in addition to other principles. This more reasonable view is a form of the pluralist externalist view that we discussed at the outset of this section.

5. Looking Ahead

We have found difficulties in the leading internalist and externalist theories. The remaining candidate to consider is Sidgwick's own favoured theory, hedonism. As we shall see, hedonism, as Sidgwick

---

[43] Twain, 'The Lowest Animal', 156.
[44] Rawls, *A Theory of Justice*, 285–6.

understands it, is neither completely internalist nor completely externalist, but intermediate between the two. Before we can properly assess it, however, we need to return to Sidgwick because in following the steps by which he develops his axioms and his account of ultimate good, we have taken only a brief glance at his discussion of the nature of happiness and pleasure. A fuller discussion of his understanding of these concepts is an essential preliminary to an assessment of hedonism.

9

Ultimate Good, Part II: Hedonism

1. Sidgwick on Pleasure and Happiness

Sidgwick, like Bentham and Mill, often wrote of happiness as the ultimate value. By happiness, all three philosophers meant a state of consciousness in which there is a surplus of pleasure over pain. Happiness is thus identified with pleasure, and Sidgwick often writes of 'happiness or pleasure'. In identifying the two, however, the classical utilitarians did not see themselves as simply capturing common usage. Sidgwick notes that the common notions of 'interest' and 'happiness' are vague and ambiguous, and need to be made more precise 'for the purposes of scientific discussion'. He believes that this can be done 'while retaining the main part of their signification' if we understand the term 'greatest possible Happiness' to mean 'the greatest attainable surplus of pleasure over pain', while using 'pleasure' to mean all kinds of 'agreeable feelings' and 'pain' to mean all kinds of disagreeable ones (*ME* 120–1). It is in this sense, Sidgwick argues, that happiness is the ultimate value.

What then is pleasure, for Sidgwick? Sidgwick begins his discussion of pleasure by offering a preliminary definition of it as 'a kind of feeling which stimulates the will to actions tending to sustain or produce it' (*ME* 42). Mill regarded desiring something and finding it pleasant as different ways of describing the same phenomenon, but Sidgwick rejects this view (*ME* 43). On the other hand, Sidgwick also rejects the view that 'there is a measurable quality of feeling expressed by the word "pleasure", which is independent of its relation to volition, and strictly undefinable from its simplicity...like the quality of feeling expressed by "sweet", of which also we are conscious in varying degrees of intensity'. Instead, he tells us, he uses the term 'in the comprehensive sense...to include the most refined and subtle intellectual and emotional gratifications, no less than the coarser and more definite sensual enjoyments' (*ME* 127). He adds that he is unable to find any common quality in these feelings, other than the way in which they relate to 'desire and volition' or the general term 'desirable'.

Mill famously argued that there are differences of quality among pleasures, distinct from differences in the quantity of pleasure. This enabled him to assert that 'It is better to be a human being dissatisfied than a pig satisfied; better to be Socrates dissatisfied than a fool satisfied.'[1] Sidgwick rejects the distinction between quality and quantity of pleasure. He recognizes, as Bentham did, that some pleasures are 'impure', in the sense that experiencing them either has a painful element mixed with it, or has consequences that involve pain. But to the extent that this is the case, no judgment of quality is needed to judge these experiences as containing a smaller net quantity of pleasure than a comparably pleasurable experience that did not have these painful elements or consequences. If, on the other hand, someone asserts that some pleasures are to be preferred to others, even though they are less pleasant, because they are nobler, or involve our intellect rather than our physical senses, then this judgment is based on values distinct from pleasure, and so the basis for this claim cannot simply be hedonism. Thus, in contrast to Mill, Sidgwick is prepared to accept Bentham's remark that, 'quantity of pleasure being equal, push-pin is as good as poetry' (*ME* 94–5).

The idea of taking 'the greatest happiness' as an end of action implies that it is possible to compare pleasures and pains. They must, in Sidgwick's words, have 'determinate quantitative relations to each other' because otherwise it does not make sense to see them as part of a total that we must make as great as possible. All the pleasures and pains that we can experience must therefore be in some finite ratio with each other. Sidgwick mentions two dimensions in particular, intensity and duration, saying that if one pleasure is finite in duration, but greater in intensity than another, then if the less intense

---

[1] Mill, *Utilitarianism*, ch. 2.

pleasure were gradually increased in duration, without a change in its intensity, at some point it would exactly balance the more intense pleasure—and the same would apply to pains. In addition, if pleasure is seen as positive and pain as negative, then there must be a 'hedonistic zero', a neutral state that is the point of transition between pleasure and pain (*ME* 123–4). This neutral state is not, however, in any sense the normal state of human existence. 'Nature', Sidgwick says, 'has not been so niggardly to man as this'. If we can maintain our health and avoid 'irksome toil' then our everyday activities are frequently a source of moderate pleasure, alternating with periods of neutral or near-neutral mental states.

Next Sidgwick turns to the question of measurement of pleasures and pains. As we have seen, he initially accepted the view that pleasure is a state of consciousness that one desires to sustain or gain, and pain is a state of consciousness that one desires to escape or avert. He therefore considers whether we can measure pleasures and pains by the strength of the desire to sustain or escape them, but concludes that we cannot. Knowing the dangers of over-eating, we develop a frame of mind in which the desire to prolong the pleasures of eating ceases before the pleasure itself does. Similarly, we might get used to a pain, like a mild toothache, and take no action to remove it. We might also take no action to sustain the pleasure of resting, because we are only vaguely conscious of the desire to continue resting. In such cases, the stimulus is latent, because if we were asked whether we would like to get rid of the pain, or prolong the pleasures of eating or resting, taking those experiences in themselves and putting aside all other consequences of doing so, we would answer yes. A different phenomenon occurs with what Sidgwick quaintly calls 'exciting pleasures'—the prospect of the pleasure may produce in us a desire that is out of proportion to how great the pleasure is. Then again, there can be sensations like being tickled which lead us to try to stop the sensations, even though they are not painful at all. It is therefore, Sidgwick acknowledges, 'obviously inexact to define pleasure, for purposes of measurement, as the kind of feeling that we seek to retain in consciousness'. Instead he offers a distinct definition of pleasure, to be used 'when we are considering its "strict value" for purposes of quantitative comparison'. In this more exact sense, pleasure is 'a feeling which, when experienced by intelligent beings, is at least implicitly apprehended as desirable or—in cases of comparison— preferable' (*ME* 127). For brevity, Sidgwick often uses the term 'desirable consciousness' as shorthand for his account of pleasure.

This more exact definition immediately leads to a further problem. As we saw when discussing the differences between Sidgwick and Mill on the idea of 'quality of pleasure', one might prefer a lesser pleasure to a greater pleasure because the former is perceived as 'nobler' or 'higher'. But the definition of pleasure just given appears to make this a contradiction. If pleasure is defined as the feeling that is desirable or preferable, then if the experiencing being judges one form of pleasure as preferable to another, it cannot be less pleasurable. Sidgwick's solution is to draw a distinction between preferring one feeling to another *solely on the basis of the quality of the present feeling* as compared with preferring one feeling to another on the basis of appealing to some common standard that others can apply as well as the experiencing individual. When we prefer a less pleasant feeling to a more pleasant one, 'it is not really the feeling itself that is preferred, but something in the mental or physical conditions or relations under which it arises, regarded as cognisable objects of our common thought'. On the other hand, if we contemplate a feeling 'merely as the transient feeling of a single subject', Sidgwick argues, it is impossible to find any quality in it that one might prefer, other than its pleasantness, 'the degree of which is only cognisable directly by the sentient individual' (*ME* 128). Sidgwick builds these elements into his fullest and most precise definition of pleasure as:

feeling which the sentient individual at the time of feeling it implicitly or explicitly apprehends to be desirable;—desirable, that is, when considered merely as feeling, and not in respect of its objective conditions or consequences, or of any facts that come directly within the cognisance and judgment of others besides the sentient individual. (*ME* 131)

Given this more precise definition of pleasure, there may be no outward signs by which one can judge the intensity of a pleasure, as assessed by the experiencing subject at the time of experiencing it. This makes it very difficult to perform, 'with definite and trustworthy results', the kinds of comparisons that are needed to make quantitative judgments of pleasure and pain. Such comparisons, when made, are 'very rough' and also 'liable to illusion, of which we can never measure the precise amount, while we are continually forced to recognise its existence' (*ME* 140). Even our own recollections of our past pleasures, Sidgwick tells us, are unreliable. Drawing on his own experience, he says that he finds some past pleasures or pains much easier to recall than others. Past hardships may, after an interval of time, appear pleasurable, and the gratification of one of our appetites will appear much more pleasurable when that appetite is not satiated than when it is (*ME* 144–5).

Despite all these problems, Sidgwick finds that he himself cannot avoid making comparisons between pleasures and pains, and using these comparisons as a basis for his own practical decisions. He therefore concludes, not that we should reject altogether this method of deciding what will lead to the greatest happiness, but rather that we can have only limited confidence in the conclusions we reach by means of it (*ME* 150).

2. The Definition of Pleasure

Sidgwick is on firm ground when he says that there is no quality of feeling that is common to everything that we call pleasure. I may get pleasure from feeling the warmth of the sun on my back as I lie on the grass on a fine summer's day, and I may get pleasure from following an ingenious argument in a philosophy paper, but it is hard to see anything that these two feelings have in common, other than my positive attitude towards them. Sidgwick's view here is consistent with the most recent neuroscientific understanding of pleasure. As Kent Berridge and Morten Kringelbach, two leading researchers in the field, put it: 'Pleasure is never merely a sensation... Instead, it always requires the activity of hedonic brain systems to paint an additional "hedonic gloss" onto a sensation to make it "liked".'[2]

---

[2] Berridge and Kringelbach, 'Affective Neuroscience of Pleasure', 459.

It would not have been adequate, however, to say, as Sidgwick did in his preliminary attempt to define pleasure, that what the different forms of pleasure have in common is that they are feelings that stimulate us to act in ways that will sustain them, if they are present, or to obtain them, if they are not. Trying to sustain or to obtain a feeling is neither a sufficient nor a necessary condition of something being pleasure. Alex Voorhoeve has offered the example of grief to show that it is not sufficient. If someone we love has died, we may want to sustain our grief, and we may try to do so by, for example, looking at pictures of the person we loved. That does not mean that we are taking pleasure in sustaining our grief. Rather we feel it is the right thing to do. Similarly, trying to sustain a feeling is not a necessary condition for something being pleasure. When we hear of a rival's misfortune, we may experience *Schadenfreude,* but we are ashamed of ourselves for having this feeling. We therefore do whatever we can to avoid feeling it, perhaps by focusing our mind on her good qualities, and trying to feel more empathy for her. This does not prove that what we were feeling was not pleasure. *Schadenfreude* is still *Freude,* even if we would rather not feel it.[3]

Sidgwick could deny that these cases show that pleasure is not a feeling we try to sustain, when we consider it purely as a state of consciousness. We would not try to feel grief, if we did not feel that it was in some way right or appropriate for us to feel it, after the death of the person we love. We may feel that it would be disrespectful to her, for instance, not to feel grief; or perhaps it would even be psychologically harmful to us. Otherwise, the feeling itself is not one we desire to have. We do not try to feel grief when someone we do not know has died. Conversely, the rush of pleasure that we get when we first learn of our rival's misfortune is a feeling we would like to sustain, if we consider it only as a feeling. We seek to eliminate it only because we hold other views that make us think that we should not feel it.

In 1954 J. Olds and P. Milner implanted electrodes in a specific site in the brains of rats, and gave the rats the opportunity to stimulate

---

[3] Voorhoeve, 'Discussion of "A Defense of Hedonism" by Katarzyna de Lazari-Radek and Peter Singer.' The example of *Schadenfreude* is our own.

those sites by pressing a lever. They found that the rats pressed the levers thousands of times, in some cases even to the point of starving themselves to death.[4] The assumption was that the rats were giving themselves pleasure, and the sites in the brain became known as 'pleasure centers'. The experiment was often cited by critics of hedonism who suggested that for hedonists, the ultimate good would be a world in which we all spent our lives pressing levers connected to electrodes in our brains. Further research, including some cases in which stimulation has been given to humans for therapeutic reasons, has led to this assumption being reconsidered. It now appears that the electrodes may cause increased 'wanting' without the reward of pleasure. The human subjects did not say that they experienced pleasure, and their self-stimulation seems rather to have had a compulsive aspect. If motivation is separate from pleasure, Berridge and Kringelbach suggest, then a human or animal may want to press the lever 'without ever gaining significant pleasure or even necessarily having a clear expectation of gaining pleasure'.[5]

This finding confirms that Sidgwick was right to reject Mill's equation of pleasure and desire, and it invalidates Sidgwick's preliminary definition of pleasure as a state of consciousness we try to sustain, but it does not threaten the final form of his definition according to which pleasure is a feeling that is 'at least implicitly apprehended as desirable'. If those with the electrodes implanted in their brains felt a compulsion to stimulate themselves, but did not apprehend the feelings they were getting as desirable, then they were not feeling pleasure, as Sidgwick defines it.

3. The Definition and Significance of Happiness

Fred Feldman attributes to Bentham, Mill, and Sidgwick a view he calls 'sensory hedonism', according to which you can be called happy

---

[4] Olds and Milner, 'Positive Reinforcement Produced by Electrical Stimulation of Septal Area'.

[5] Berridge and Kringelbach, 'Affective Neuroscience of Pleasure', 470–2. We are grateful to William MacAskill and Adam Lerner for drawing our attention to this recent research, and its relevance for Sidgwick's definition of pleasure.

at a given time 'only if you feel more sensory pleasure than pain at that time, and unhappy if and only if you feel more sensory pain than pleasure at that time'. Feldman does not tell us exactly what he means by 'sensory pleasure' but the dictionary definition of 'sensory' is 'relating to sensation or the physical senses; transmitted or perceived by the senses'.[6] In discussing sensory hedonism, Feldman asks us to suppose that sensory pleasure always has 'some phenomenally given sensory intensity' which is a measure of how 'strong, or vivid, or "brilliant" the pleasure is'.[7]

Feldman offers two counter-examples to sensory hedonism, as he conceives it. In his first example, an unfortunate character named Wendell has seen advertisements for an orgasm enhancer that provides amazing 400-hedon orgasms. His friends warn him that the advertisements are a scam, but Wendell buys it anyway. When he tries it, instead of the monster orgasm he is expecting, he gets a pathetic little 12-hedon orgasm. Experiencing it, Wendell is unhappy. But why? Twelve hedons is better than no hedons, so Wendell is experiencing more pleasure than pain. If happiness were just having a positive balance of pleasure over pain, we would have to agree that, at the moment of orgasm, Wendell is happy. Yet anyone observing him can see that he has a pained look on his face, and seems generally unhappy. In Feldman's second example, a woman is in the throes of giving birth without drugs because she wants to be able to experience the birth fully. She is in considerable pain; but with one last push the baby comes out. Later she says that the pain was the worst she has ever felt, much greater than she had expected, but at the same time the birth was the happiest moment of her life. These cases show, Feldman argues, that: 'Hedonism of the Bentham-Mill-Sidgwick variety about happiness is false.'[8]

As we have seen, Sidgwick uses the term 'pleasure' very broadly, to include any type of consciousness that the experiencing subject judges to be intrinsically desirable. Among the pleasures Sidgwick

[6] <http://oxforddictionaries.com/definition/sensory>.
[7] Feldman, *What is This Thing Called Happiness?* 24–5.
[8] Feldman, *What is This Thing Called Happiness?* 32–6; the quote is from 36.

refers to, for example, are 'intellectual exercise', 'scientific apprehension', 'beneficent action', 'aesthetic reception', and 'labour'. This suggests, first, that Sidgwick is not a sensory hedonist at all, as Feldman uses this term; and second, that Sidgwick's view is not troubled by the examples Feldman offers. Sidgwick could almost have in mind someone very like Wendell when he writes of 'the disappointment of the Hedonist, who fails to find self-satisfaction where he seeks for it', adding that this disappointment 'is attended with pain or loss of pleasure' (*ME* 135). A state in which we feel disappointed is not a desirable state of consciousness, and the negative aspects of disappointment could easily outweigh the limited pleasure Wendell gets at the moment of his orgasm—which of course is also the moment at which he realizes he has been the victim of a scam.

The example of the woman giving birth is more complex. One aspect of it is covered by Sidgwick's observation that states in which 'a certain amount of pain or discomfort is mixed with pleasure' are common, and among such states he mentions 'triumphant conquest of painful obstacles' (*ME* 143), which could well describe the process of giving birth after a difficult and painful labour. But the woman's happiness is surely largely due to the fact that she knows that at this moment she has become a mother, and to her expectations about motherhood. The consciousness of entering this new stage of her life gives her so much emotional pleasure that it swamps the physical pain she is experiencing.

Feldman's preferred alternative to sensory hedonism is 'attitudinal hedonism'. To be happy at a given moment, on this view, is not to have a positive balance of pleasurable feelings, but to have a positive balance of 'intrinsic occurrent attitudinal pleasure'. But what does that mean? Feldman tells us that attitudinal pleasures and displeasures are propositional attitudes—and thus more like beliefs than like feelings. I might, for instance, be pleased to learn from a newspaper article that the distribution of bednets by aid agencies has led to fewer children dying from malaria. This does not necessarily mean that I have a warm inner glow, or any other kind of cheery feelings. We can, according to Feldman, take pleasure in things without experiencing any pleasurable sensations. Do I, though, experience the state of consciousness in which I believe that fewer children are dying as desirable? If my belief that fewer children died does not involve *any* positive emotions or feelings and fails to make my own state of consciousness more desirable in any way, we cannot see why this belief should be regarded as contributing to my happiness. As Daniel Haybron points out, this view 'takes the fun out of pleasure'. In response, Feldman gives another example, this time of a friend who was happy as a result of finding a new medication that led to some (but not complete) relief from the severe pain of arthritis. Feldman claims that this person was happy even though he was still in pain and there is no reason to suppose that he had any 'cheery feelings' at this time.[9] Yet, as Feldman describes the example, it seems his friend did have a positive feeling because he hoped that, even if his pain could not be eradicated, it would be reduced to a level at which he would be able to think about philosophy again. That could easily cause him to feel cheerful, at least for a time. So this is not a counter-example that favours Feldman's attitudinal hedonism rather than a form of hedonism that finds intrinsic value in desirable states of consciousness.

Haybron offers a different critique of the hedonistic view of happiness. He argues that some pleasures—like the enjoyment of eating crackers, and, once again, orgasms, though not necessarily all of them—may be too superficial to have any impact on our happiness. As he puts it, these pleasures 'just don't *get* to us'. They 'flit through consciousness and that's the end of it'.[10] They leave our happiness level untouched. Feldman suggests that the sensory hedonist could meet this criticism by saying that such pleasures are so minor that they are unlikely to tip the balance between happiness and unhappiness but they nevertheless contribute *something* to happiness. Haybron, on the other hand, believes that these minor pleasures are just *not relevant* to a person's happiness. To feel pleasure is to be having an experience, whereas to describe people as happy is to say something about their emotional states and moods. Emotional states and moods

---

[9] Haybron, *The Pursuit of Unhappiness,* 64, cited by Feldman, *What is This Thing Called Happiness,* 143–7. Feldman also cites several other critics who have made similar criticisms including Roger Crisp, Elinor Mason, Michael Zimmerman, and Alastair Norcross.

[10] Haybron, *The Pursuit of Unhappiness,* 63.

are dispositions to feel something, rather than present feelings. To say that I am irritable is not to say that I am feeling irritated right now, but rather to say that I am liable to become irritated about trivial things that would not bother someone who was in a more expansive mood. Haybron grants that a person with a generally dour personality might, because of good fortune, be in high spirits for a time, and we could then consider her happy; but this would, he says, be a fragile sort of happiness, unlike the robust happiness of the person who has a propensity to have positive moods and emotions.[11]

We find Haybron's account of happiness plausible, if it is understood as an account of the ordinary meaning of the word 'happiness'. As commonly used, the term does seem to refer to a certain emotional state, rather than to having a positive balance of pleasure over pain. Does this mean Sidgwick and the classical utilitarians are mistaken? Not really, for Sidgwick was aware that he was taking a term that is in common use and giving it more precision in order to make it more useful for scientific discussion. Haybron considers and rejects the idea that we might use the term 'happiness' to stand for *whatever* psychological state best fulfils the role of ultimate value in a utilitarian theory. 'Happiness' is, he insists, a term in common use, and therefore is not 'up for grabs' by theorists who wish to use it for their own purposes. Appropriating the term for whatever we decide is of ultimate value risks leaving us with a notion of happiness that ordinary people would not recognize.[12] Sidgwick is not, however, playing as loosely with the notion as that. He is, as he says, trying to make the concept more precise while retaining the major part of its meaning. Haybron might reply that, in making the concept more precise, Sidgwick has failed to capture the major part of its meaning. To the extent that the popular use of the term really is vague and ambiguous, there may be no clear resolution to that question. But suppose that Haybron's account of happiness gets the concept right, and Sidgwick's account, far from making the ordinary meaning of the term more precise, instead substitutes for it an idea that is significantly different

---

[11] Haybron, *The Pursuit of Unhappiness*, 145.
[12] Haybron, *The Pursuit of Unhappiness*, 45.

from what most people mean when they talk about happiness. What would follow?

Haybron himself is clear that his critique of the hedonistic account of *happiness* has no implications for the hedonistic theory of *value*. All utilitarians need to do, he says, is grant that their theories are about pleasure, and not about happiness.[13] Given Haybron's account of happiness, that is a plausible view. Sidgwick himself argued, as we saw in the previous chapter, that a disposition could not be something that is valuable in itself, and he would surely say the same of Haybron's account of happiness, namely that if happiness is, at least in part, a disposition to have certain feelings under certain conditions, then what would have to be good is not the disposition itself but the feelings that it is a disposition to have.[14]

Admittedly, for utilitarians to speak only of pleasure, and not of happiness, would require a substantial change in vocabulary, but not in what we ought to do. Still, one might feel that the utilitarian view would be less persuasive if it were stated without reference to happiness. It would at least be helpful if utilitarians could explain why, on their view, happiness is important.

Fortunately, Haybron's account of happiness itself provides such an explanation. To be happy, on his view, is to be in a certain emotional state, or set of states, and emotional states have, as he says, 'extremely far-reaching consequences for the character of our lives'. Among these consequences is that emotional states appear to be 'the single most important *determinant* of our hedonic states'.[15] If therefore we combine the classical utilitarian view that the only thing of intrinsic value is pleasure, with Haybron's view that happiness consists of a set of emotional states that determine how pleasant our experiences are, we reach the conclusion that happiness is instrumentally good, not intrinsically good. Pleasure, in the sense of being in a positive hedonic state, is intrinsically good, and happy people are more likely

---

[13] Haybron, *The Pursuit of Unhappiness*, 77.

[14] Compare Sidgwick's argument discussed in our Ch. 8 against the idea that having a virtuous character is intrinsically good, in *The Methods*, 393.

[15] *The Pursuit of Unhappiness*, 74–5.

to experience this positive hedonic state than unhappy people. That is why happiness matters, even if it is not an intrinsic value.

Haybron sees it as another advantage of his view of happiness that it explains why happiness is useful in practical deliberation. He points out that in choosing between possible vocations, we often ask whether we will be happier in one rather than the other, and suggests that this is a more sensible question to ask than whether one profession will bring us more pleasure than the other. This is because 'the better option with regard to the emotional state question will almost invariably be the better option with respect to the hedonic state question, and vice versa', so the real issue becomes '*Which question is easier to answer correctly?*' The breadth and diversity of the pleasures and pains likely to result from a choice between careers make them extremely difficult to tally, weigh up, and compare. It is likely to be easier, Haybron points out, to get a grip on the emotional states that are likely to go with each career. We can sensibly ask: will I be stressed, anxious, or will I have peace of mind? Will I often be in high spirits, or is this kind of work likely to make me irritable? In this sense, happiness, seen as an emotional state, is what Haybron calls 'a relatively *efficient* good' that 'packs a lot of value into a relatively compact, epistemically manageable package'.[16] The utilitarian can agree, while adding that this account is entirely consistent with—indeed is suggestive of—the view that happiness is an instrumental good, and the hedonic states to which it often leads are the intrinsic good that can be efficiently maximized if we choose a career on the basis of what will make us happy. Now we need to ask how plausible it is to hold that pleasure is the ultimate good.

4. Hedonism

i. *Internalist or Externalist?*

Hedonism is the view that what is ultimately good is pleasure, understood as desirable consciousness. In the previous chapter we saw that

---

[16] *The Pursuit of Unhappiness*, 75–6 (emphasis in original).

one question we can ask about a theory of what is good for someone is whether it accepts the resonance constraint. Internalist theories accept that what is good for someone must resonate with them
in some way, by being in accord with what they desire; externalist
theories reject this constraint. Because hedonism holds that what is
good for people is desirable consciousness, it straddles this divide.
For something to be pleasure for a person, it must be something
that the person apprehends as desirable, considered merely as a feeling. So the hedonist will not say that it is good for a person to be in
a conscious state that she does not take to be desirable, and to this
extent hedonism satisfies the resonance constraint and is internalist.
On the other hand, hedonism does insist that what is good or bad
for you is your states of consciousness, and nothing else, irrespective of whether what you desire is to have certain states of consciousness. Sidgwick, in arguing against psychological hedonism, gives an
example of the kind of desire that the ethical hedonist must think
mistaken: 'men have sacrificed all the enjoyments of life, and even
life itself, to obtain posthumous fame: not from any illusory belief
that they would be somehow capable of deriving pleasure from it, but
from a direct desire of the future admiration of others, and a preference of it to their own pleasure' (ME 51–2). The hedonist must say
that the fulfilment of your desire for posthumous fame is not good
for you, no matter how much you want it. To that extent hedonism is
externalist.

We can now see that, in this respect, what is true for hedonism also
holds for Heathwood's subjective desire satisfactionism, which we
encountered in the previous chapter. By stipulating that what counts
for a person's welfare is not whether her desires are in fact satisfied,
but whether she believes them to be satisfied, Heathwood avoids having to say that some state of the world makes a difference to someone's welfare even if she never knows about it and it has no impact
on her state of mind; but he loses the necessary connection between
what is good for someone and what that person wants or is concerned
about. The example we just used to show that this is true for hedonism applies directly to desire satisfactionism. What you want and are
concerned about is that you are famous after you die, not that you

believe that your desire to be famous after you die is satisfied (which is, in the nature of the situation, impossible). Desire satisfactionism, like hedonism, is intermediate between internalism and externalism, and does not fully embrace the resonance requirement.

ii. The Experience Machine

The best-known objection to mental state theories, including hedonism, is a thought experiment formulated by Robert Nozick:

> Suppose there were an experience machine that would give you any experience you desired. Superduper neuropsychologists could stimulate your brain so that you would think and feel you were writing a great novel, or making a friend, or reading an interesting book. All the time you would be floating in a tank, with electrodes attached to your brain. Should you plug into this machine for life, preprogramming your life's desires?...
>
> Of course, while in the tank you won't know that you're there; you'll think it's all actually happening. Others can also plug in to have the experiences they want, so there's no need to stay unplugged to serve them. (Ignore problems such as who will service the machines if everyone plugs in.) Would you plug in? What else can matter to us, other than how our lives feel from the inside?[17]

Nozick thinks that by imagining an experience machine, and realizing that we would not use it, we learn that our experiences are not all that matter to us. We want, he says, to *do* things and not just have *experiences*. We want to be a certain kind of person—loving, brave, intelligent, and so on, not just a body floating in a tank. We want, Nozick says, to live in contact with reality.

Many philosophers consider the experience machine thought experiment a knock-down objection to hedonism. (Dan Weijers gives 'just a sample' of authors who have stated or implied this, and then lists 28 references.[18]) If only states of consciousness have ultimate value, and an experience machine can provide us with much better—that is, more intrinsically desirable—states of consciousness than we could possibly get from an existence outside the experience machine, it seems to follow that a hedonist must say that we ought to plug into the machine.

Neither a desire-based theory of value nor an externalist theory has this implication. A standard desire theory of value holds that what

---

[17] Nozick, *Anarchy, State and Utopia*, 43.
[18] Weijers, 'Nozick's Experience Machine is Dead, Long Live the Experience Machine!', 18 n. 1.

is good for a person, or for any sentient being, is the satisfaction of his or her desires. Often, our desires will relate to mental states—for instance, we may desire not to be in pain. With such desires, the desire theory becomes equivalent to hedonism. But we can also have desires for things that are not mental states—for instance, I may desire that the people I consider to be my friends genuinely like and respect me. Suppose none of these people like or respect me at all; they think that I am a conceited fool. But they know about my desire to be liked and respected, and because they are kind, even to fools, they do not wish to cause me distress. So they pretend to like and respect me, and they do this so well that I never know the difference. All my life, I believe that these people like and respect me. My mental states, in fact, are *exactly* as they would have been if these people really liked and respected me. At a ripe old age, I die without ever knowing that I was mistaken about the opinions of the people I took to be my friends. Although I believed that my desire to be liked and respected was satisfied, there is clearly a sense in which it was not. As this example shows, the standard desire theory does not locate ultimate value in mental states alone. The desire theory therefore has an easy response to the experience machine thought experiment. If, as Nozick suggests, we would not want to plug into the machine, because we want to experience reality rather than an illusion, then the desire theory does not say that we should plug in. If our desire is to do things, and to be a certain kind of person—in short, to live in contact with reality— it follows from the desire theory that living in contact with reality is what has ultimate value for us.

Advocates of externalist theories need not be troubled by the experience machine either. If they value knowledge, or freedom, or courage, or autonomy, then they have grounds for not wishing to enter a state in which, whatever they might be imagining, they would not really have these goods.

Is the hypothetical possibility of an experience machine sufficient reason for rejecting hedonism? Sidgwick, as we have seen, considered the possibility of taking 'conscious life' in a wide sense that would include the 'objective relations' of the consciousness to reality, for example that the conscious subject lives virtuously, or knows the truth; but he concluded that when we distinguish these objective relations of the conscious subject from the consciousness that results from them, the objective relations themselves are not intrinsically desirable, any more than any material object is intrinsically desirable (*ME* 400–1). Does the experience machine refute Sidgwick's view?

What the hypothetical example of the experience machine achieves is to focus our attention on an imaginary choice between knowing the truth about our lives, and having the best possible experiences while being completely oblivious to our actual situation. With our attention thus focused, many people find the idea of entering the experience machine repugnant, and conclude that hedonism must be mistaken. In the remainder of this section, we suggest some possible explanations of this repugnance. These explanations are not intended to show that hedonism is right, but rather to suggest that we should not rely on our initial intuitive response to the experience machine to conclude that it is wrong.

Several writers have suggested that our intuitive judgment that we would not enter the experience machine could be influenced by the status quo bias.[19] Most people have a preference for something they already possess or a state they are in now, even when they are offered something better. For example, in one experiment some students were given a coffee mug, and then invited to sell it at a range of prices. Other students were not given a mug, but asked how much they would be willing to accept, in lieu of getting an identical mug. The students given the mug were unwilling to sell unless they received more than twice as much as the students not given the mug were willing to accept as an alternative to getting a mug.[20] Daniel Kahneman and Amos Tversky refer to this phenomenon as 'loss aversion' and write that: 'One implication of loss aversion is that individuals have a strong tendency to remain at the status quo, because the disadvantages of leaving it loom larger than advantages.'[21]

---

[19] The first to suggest this seems to have been Adam Kolber, 'Mental Statism and the Experience Machine'.

[20] Kahneman *et al.*, 'The Endowment Effect, Loss Aversion and Status Quo Bias', 193–206.

[21] Kahneman and Tversky, *Choices, Values, and Frames*, 163.

Both Adam Kolber and Joshua Greene have suggested we pose the question about the experience machine in a manner that reverses the impact of the status quo bias. Here is Greene's version:

you wake up in a plain white room. You are seated in a reclining chair with a steel contraption on your head. A woman in a white coat is standing over you. 'The year is 2659,' she explains, 'The life with which you are familiar is an experience machine program selected by you some forty years ago. We at IEM interrupt out client's programs at ten-year intervals to ensure client satisfaction. Our records indicate that at your three previous interruptions you deemed your program satisfactory and chose to continue. As before, if you choose to continue with your program you will return to your life as you know it with no recollection of this interruption. Your friends, loved ones, and projects will all be there. Of course, you may choose to terminate your program at this point if you are unsatisfied for any reason. Do you intend to continue with your program?'[22]

Felipe De Brigard decided to test whether the status quo bias does make a difference to our willingness to enter the experience machine. He asked people to imagine that they are already connected to an experience machine, and now face the choice of remaining connected, or going back to live in reality. Participants in the experiment were randomly offered one of three different vignettes: in the neutral vignette, you are simply told that you can go back to reality, but not given any information about what reality will be like for you. In the negative vignette, you are told that in reality you are a prisoner in a maximum-security prison, and in the positive vignette you are told that in reality you are a multi-millionaire artist living in Monaco. Of participants given the neutral vignette, almost half (46 per cent) said that they would prefer to stay plugged into the experience machine. Among those given the negative vignette, that figure rose to 87 per cent. Most remarkably, of those given the positive vignette, exactly half preferred to stay connected to the machine, rather than return to reality as a multi-millionaire artist living in Monaco.[23]

These results do not support Nozick's confident judgment that 'we' prefer to live in reality, rather than plugged into a machine.

---

[22] J. Greene, 'A Psychological Perspective on Nozick's Experience Machine and Parfit's Repugnant Conclusion'. We thank Theron Pummer for drawing our attention to this paper, and Joshua Greene for providing us with a copy.

[23] De Brigard, 'If you Like it, Does it Matter if it's Real?', 46–9.

Admittedly, they also do not support the view that people choose to maximize their pleasure—for if the latter were the case, surely the information that, in reality, you are a multi-millionaire artist in Monaco would have led many more to choose to detach from the machine. Surprisingly, it appears to have had no effect—fewer chose to detach when given that scenario than when given no information at all about their life in reality.

To test the hypothesis that status quo bias was affecting the answers he received, De Brigard presented another group of participants with a fourth vignette, which was identical to the neutral vignette, except that the participants were told that their life outside the machine would be 'not at all like the life you have experienced so far'. Given this information, only a minority, 41 per cent, wanted to disconnect, a finding that supports De Brigard's view that status quo bias is having an effect on people's choices.

De Brigard's findings are based on small samples, but his findings are supported by another study conducted by Dan Weijers with first-year New Zealand university students as his subjects. Weijers found that whereas only 16 per cent of students would connect to an experience machine after reading Nozick's original description of it, when the question was varied to eliminate status quo bias and to refer to what would be best for a stranger, rather than for oneself, 55 per cent of respondents thought the stranger should choose to live the rest of his life in the experience machine.[24] Taken together, the studies by De Brigard and Weijers provide strong evidence that Nozick's original thought experiment skews the answers people give towards remaining in contact with reality, rather than entering the machine.

Wayne Sumner has suggested a different reason why we may be reluctant to enter the experience machine: we may doubt that it will work as well as its manufacturers claim it will. Sumner asks:

How do we know that the technology is foolproof? What happens if there is a power failure?...In order to isolate the philosophical point which the experience

---

[24] Dan Weijers, 'Nozick's Experience Machine is Dead, Long Live the Experience Machine!' For discussion of the usefulness of this kind of research, see Smith, 'Can we Test the Experience Machine?'; Weijers, 'We Can Test the Experience Machine'; Smith, 'Affect, Rationality, and the Experience Machine'.

machine is meant to illustrate, we have to control for boundary conditions by supposing that all the risks have somehow been neutralized. But this is very difficult
to do, since we know that in real life we cannot eliminate all possible malfunc-
tions and screw-ups. For the thought experiment to yield any results at all we must
therefore imagine ourselves in a world quite alien to our own—and who knows
what we would choose in a world like that?[25]

Similarly, Adam Kolber suggests that some people might be repulsed
by Nozick's talk of a tank, and electrodes plugged into your brain,
because it reminds them of science fiction horror stories. That possibility can only have been made more likely by the popularity of
the film *The Matrix* which brought a scenario like the experience
machine to a wide audience.[26] The Matrix offers an image of being
immersed in fluids, cables attached to your body, and being made
use of by intelligent machines who need our body heat to generate
energy. Of course, in Nozick's experience machine, nothing of that
sort will happen. No one is going to suffer, nor will you be exploited
or used for any other purposes. Still, the suspicion that something
will go wrong is hard to avoid.[27]

Roger Crisp has shown that the experience machine objection to
hedonism can be restated in a way that eliminates both the status
quo bias and the worry that the technology may fail. He asks us to
compare the lives of two people, P and Q. P has lived a rich, full, and
autonomously chosen life, has written a great novel, made significant scientific discoveries, and has been courageous, witty, and loving. She has also greatly enjoyed her life. Q was connected at birth to
an experience machine that has given her exactly the same mental
states as P. Since the lives of P and Q are, from the inside, indistinguishable, the hedonist must say that P and Q have the same level of
well-being. That, Crisp writes, 'is surely a claim from which most of
us will recoil'.[28]

We are not sure that Crisp is right about this—Weijers's study gives
grounds for thinking that a majority of New Zealand students might
accept it, and more research would be needed to find out how widely

[25] Sumner, *Welfare, Happiness and Ethics*, 95.
[26] Kolber, 'Mental Statism and the Experience Machine', 14.
[27] See also Weijers, 'Intuitive Biases in Judgments about Thought Experiments'.
[28] Crisp, 'Hedonism Reconsidered', 635–6.

that view is shared. The available evidence suggests that opposition to the judgment that P and Q have the same level of well-being will be significantly lower than opposition to the idea of entering the experience machine.

Crisp—who is himself a defender of hedonism—suggests ways in which hedonists can respond to his own reformulation of the experience machine objection. One of these is an evolutionary debunking of values that might lead us to reject the idea that P and Q have equal well-being. We may reject this judgment because we have evolved as goal-seeking beings.[29] Our ancestors, over thousands of generations, were both competing and cooperating with other intelligent beings in order to improve their chances of surviving and of having offspring who in turn would survive and reproduce. To succeed, they had to have a strong tendency to override immediate pleasures and pains for the sake of some larger purpose. The 'paradox of hedonism' familiar to the ancients is based on the idea that we are most likely to find pleasure by setting ourselves some purpose or goal that stands apart from our own desire for pleasure. More recently, Mihaly Csikszentmihalyi has developed this idea into the theory that we are happiest when we experience the 'flow' of intense engagement in some activity.[30] Nozick's original experience machine objection asks us to imagine a world in which *everyone's* needs can be taken care of, completely, forever, and this includes not only their needs for food and shelter but also for having whatever experiences they want to have, and avoiding whatever experiences they wish to avoid. In such a radically different world, all of our usual purposes become otiose. There is no need for us to save for our old age, or ensure that our children and grandchildren will get a good education, or strive to end world poverty or protect human rights. All of those things have already been taken care of, or perhaps—like having an education—no longer matter. (Since we should, properly, be concerned about the welfare of all sentient beings, not only humans, let's make this already incredible thought experiment even more bizarre by imagining that animals get their

---

[29] Crisp, 'Hedonism Reconsidered', 638–9.
[30] Csikszentmihalyi, *Flow*.

own experience machines.) Yet if our need to live to some purpose is, as we have suggested, biological, it is no wonder that we feel that there is something wrong with the idea of entering the machine. So in contemplating life in the experience machine, we may be able to grasp intellectually that in such a world there are no longer any purposes worth pursuing, but our intuitions still tell us that it would be wrong to abandon all our purposes other than those directed towards our own experiences. Even when, in Crisp's reformulated version, we are not asked to enter the machine ourselves, but to compare the lives of P and Q, it is very difficult to prevent our judgments being affected by the idea that P is contributing to the world and Q is not. That would give us grounds for judging P's life as morally superior to Q's, but not for judging that P's welfare is higher than Q's.[31]

Our discussion of the experience machine objection is not intended to suggest that the way to discover what is really of intrinsic value is to find out what the majority of people think. Each of us needs to reflect further and do our best to put all biasing factors out of our minds. After doing so, you may still conclude that you would want neither to enter the experience machine, if you were living in reality, nor to stay in it, if you were already in it. You may also still think that, putting aside all other values, P's life was better for her than Q's life was for her. We do not claim to have shown that this would be an unreasonable judgment; our aim has only been to show that mental state theories of value are still viable, notwithstanding the initial reaction most people have to Nozick's thought experiment.

---

[31] This explanation of our reluctance to enter the experience machine can also be applied to Samuel Scheffler's discussion of the effect that knowledge of the coming end of the world (say, as a result of a collision with an asteroid) would have on us. Scheffler asserts that this would have immense significance for us, even we were certain that it was only going to happen after our own death, and he contends that this shows, not only that something other than our own experiences matters to us, but that it supports the conclusions Nozick draws from his discussion of the experience machine. (Scheffler, *Death and the Afterlife*, 19–20.) We agree that something other than our own experiences matters to us, because we think that the experiences of others matter; but we think that any residual sense that the end of life on Earth matters in a way that extends *beyond* its impact on the experiences of present and possible future beings may be accounted for by the importance to us of having purposes, which as we have argued can be explained in evolutionary terms. On the significance of the experiences of merely possible future beings, see also our discussion in Ch. 12.

iii. Can Hedonism Account for the Wrongness of Killing?

We saw in the previous chapter that a desire theorist can explain why we should respect the wishes of the dead. For a hedonist, or anyone who holds that a person's good consists of their mental states, nothing that happens after they die can make any difference to how well or badly their life went. The hedonist may respect the wishes of the dead so that when people are alive they will be able to feel confident that after they die their wishes will be carried out—and this confidence will increase their happiness. That may generally be the case, but it does suggest that whether you are under an obligation to carry out the wishes of the deceased depends on whether anyone else knows about those wishes. In the example we gave in the previous chapter, no one else knew of the existence of the novel given to you by your friend before she died, so this is not a reason against discarding it and this may make some uneasy. The desire theorist can justify this uneasiness; the hedonist cannot. But whereas the desire theorist must either hold that we should satisfy the desires of long-dead Romans, or else explain why we should satisfy some desires of the dead, but not others, hedonists can simply insist that once a person's life is over, we cannot change how well his or her life went.

Another, and more significant, area in which the desire theorist appears to have an advantage is in answering the question: 'Why is killing people wrong?' Both the hedonist and the desire theorist can appeal to weighty indirect reasons why killing is wrong, such as the grief it brings to those who love and care about the person killed, and the anxiety that knowledge of the killing will bring to others who fear that they could suffer the same fate. But the murder of a hermit seems to be wrong even if no one grieves for him or knows that he has died. The hedonist can say that, if the hermit is enjoying his life, to kill him would be wrong because of the loss of his future pleasure. If his future will be miserable, however, this reason against killing him becomes a reason *for* killing him, even if the hermit wants to go on living. For the desire theorist, this desire itself provides a reason against killing him. What can the hedonist say?

Hedonists may appeal to John Stuart Mill's arguments against paternalism, especially the claim that each is the best judge of his or her own interests, but this is a factual claim, and although it may be a good general rule, it will have exceptions. What if someone is a thoroughly bad judge of her own interests? Suppose we know that a friend has fallen into the hands of sadistic fiends who will torture her to death. We cannot rescue her, but we can kill her painlessly. She is, however, deluded about the nature of her captors, and does not consent to being killed. If there is no doubt at all about the awful fate awaiting her, killing her may be the right thing to do, notwithstanding her desire to go on living. To that extent hedonism gives us a plausible answer, and so does the version of desire-based theory that tells us to consider only fully informed desires, for if our friend were fully informed, she would not desire to live. A desire theorist who takes actual present desires into account would not permit us to kill her.

In more realistic situations, however, hedonism does clash starkly with our common moral intuitions. Suppose that a close friend is suffering from cancer and, even with the best available palliative care, is in some degree of pain or discomfort. He agrees that his life as it is now is not worth living, but wants to go on living because a friend has promised to bring him, next month, a special cactus juice that he is sure will cure him. We know that he has seen several medical specialists, all of whom agree that nothing can be done to prolong his life. The cactus juice will not help him—although we are unable to persuade him of this—and his condition will continue to deteriorate until he dies. He has at most a month or two to live. We enter his room. He is asleep, and we have the opportunity to give him an injection that will ensure he dies in his sleep. Because he is already so weak, no one will suspect that he died of anything other than his illness. Should we kill him? The hedonistic utilitarian must say that, despite his desire to go on living, it would be better for him if he died now, and so killing him would be justified. Again, the desire theorist who requires that desires must be based on accurate information can agree. But here many will think that the desire theorist who takes actual desires into account is on stronger ground, for it seems troubling to override someone's wishes on a matter of such significance as life and death.

We can modify the case again, to force a choice between hedonism and the full information desire theory. This time suppose that our friend is suffering as much as before, and the prognosis is as hopeless as before but also assume that this case takes place in the Netherlands, where a terminally ill patient can ask a doctor for euthanasia. We discuss with him the possibility of asking his doctor to do this, but he tells us that in a month he will be able to see Halley's comet. We ask him if he thinks that the pleasure he gets from seeing the comet will outweigh the suffering he will have to endure over the next month, and he says no, he does not expect that it will, but nevertheless he wants to see it. Once again, we have an opportunity to kill him, undetected, in his sleep. Here many people would say that it is wrong to do so, and all forms of desire theory would lead to that conclusion. What about hedonism? Can we conclude from the fact that he wants to see Halley's comet more than he wants to avoid the suffering that, despite what he says, he is judging that he will get more pleasure overall if he sees the comet? As we saw earlier in this chapter, Sidgwick accepts that someone might prefer one pleasure as 'higher' or 'nobler' than another, even though it is less pleasant (*ME* 128). Perhaps our friend believes that there is something 'higher' about seeing a comet that makes the experience worth having, even at the cost of greater overall pain. For Sidgwick, though, this is a mistake—the mistake that Mill committed in suggesting that some pleasures are higher in quality than others. If Sidgwick is right about that, as we think he is, and our terminally ill friend is making a mistaken judgment about the intrinsic worth of a certain kind of experience, then it is difficult to see how hedonism can avoid saying that it would be best if he died now, and killing him would, in the absence of indirect reasons against doing so, be justified.

These conclusions are somewhat shocking, and so they should be. We need to have strong prohibitions against killing people against their will, because we are very unlikely to ever find ourselves in circumstances in which it is right to do that. If these acts of killing can be justified, they provide no basis for public policy, because the justification depends on them remaining secret, so that others do not become fearful that they will also be killed. In the next chapter we will say more about whether, and under what conditions, it can be right to do in secret what it would not be right to do in the open.

A related question sharpens the issue: why is it normally worse to kill a human being than to kill a non-human animal? A desire theorist can reply that killing people who have sufficient self-awareness to understand that they exist over time and want to go on living is wrong because it thwarts these desires. Normal human beings are future-oriented to a higher degree than most non-human animals, and this provides a reason for thinking that it is worse to kill them. As Roger Scruton has put it:

There is a real distinction, for a human being, between timely and untimely death. To be 'cut short' before one's time is a waste—even a tragedy...No such thoughts apply to domestic cattle. To be killed at thirty months is not intrinsically more tragic than to be killed at forty, fifty, or sixty.[32]

Desire theorists cannot use this argument to defend the sharp distinction commonly drawn between killing *any* member of the species *Homo sapiens* and any non-human animal, for some humans—those with profound intellectual disabilities—are incapable of understanding that they exist over time, and some non-human animals—great apes, elephants, dolphins, and probably some others as well—do have this understanding. Still, the desire theorist can justify treating the killing of normal humans as more seriously wrong than killing non-human animals. For the hedonist, the distinction between beings with self-awareness and those without it is not intrinsically significant. Perhaps it can be argued that self-aware beings are capable of greater pleasure than beings lacking in self-awareness, but presumably they are also capable of greater misery. It isn't clear that the surplus of happiness over misery of self-aware beings is really greater than that of beings without self-awareness.

In explaining why killing humans is generally worse than killing animals (though not in all cases), the hedonist can once again appeal to indirect reasons: killing humans is likely to produce greater unhappiness among those close to the victim, and greater anxiety among others who fear being killed. But we might feel that this still leaves out something important about why killing human beings is normally worse than killing non-human animals. The problem becomes

---

[32] Scruton, 'The Conscientious Carnivore', 88.

more complicated still when we consider the possibility of replacing the being killed with another who will lead an equally enjoyable life. It has been urged, in defence of eating meat, that killing animals in order to eat them is justifiable when the animals live good lives and will be replaced by others living similarly good lives, so that the killing leads to no net loss of animal happiness. This argument strikes some people as absurd, because we cannot, in their view, put existing beings on the same footing as merely possible beings; but the issue is more complicated than that, and is best treated as part of a larger issue that Sidgwick was the first to raise: whether it is good to bring more people into existence if thereby we can increase the total amount of happiness. We consider this issue in Chapter 12.

iv. Hedonism and Debunking Arguments

In Chapter 7 we argued that Sidgwick's axiom of universal benevolence gains credibility from the fact that, unlike many other intuitively plausible moral principles, it can withstand evolutionary debunking arguments. In that chapter we sought to meet some difficulties that Guy Kahane has posed for evolutionary debunking arguments, but there is one we did not mention, because it is more relevant to the position we are seeking to defend in this chapter than it was to our argument in Chapter 7. In essence, Kahane's argument is that utilitarians who employ evolutionary debunking arguments are like people in glass houses who throw stones. He points out, correctly, that utilitarianism needs an account of value or well-being, and then adds: 'But many of our evaluative beliefs about well-being, including the beliefs that pleasure is good and pain is bad, are some of the most obvious candidates for evolutionary debunking.'[33]

Kahane's claim that utilitarians are in no position to use debunking arguments confuses two different kinds of claims. It is true, of course, that our nervous systems and the parts of our brain involved in our experiences of pleasure and pain have evolved because they

---

[33] Kahane, 'Evolutionary Debunking Arguments', 120; see also Kahane, 'Evolution and Impartiality'.

enhance our evolutionary fitness. They do this by creating in us feelings of pleasure at things that, for most of our evolutionary history, have enhanced our evolutionary fitness, like eating something sweet, or having sex; and unpleasant or painful feelings from things that threaten our evolutionary fitness, like being burned. So if we were to assert that sweet things are intrinsically good and fire is intrinsically bad, these claims would be subject to evolutionary debunking. Our beliefs in the goodness of pleasure and the badness of pain themselves, however, are grounded in a different way from our other moral beliefs. As Adam Lerner puts it, 'our belief in pain's badness seems to be justified by our immediate experience of how its object feels'.[34] Similarly, Neil Sinhababu argues that 'One can discover the badness of pain perfectly well just by experiencing it and knowing what it is like. There is something in pain, detectable through phenomenal introspection, which leads one to believe that it is a bad thing.'[35] Pain and pleasure are states of consciousness and we have direct knowledge of them. How could knowing something about the origins of these states undermine our judgment that, considered just as a state of consciousness, they are good or bad?

Lerner and Sinhababu turn around the debunking argument that Kahane tried to mount against hedonism, and instead use our uniquely direct acquaintance with pleasure and pain as an argument for hedonism. Lerner argues that all other claims about value, *except* those that hedonism makes about our conscious experiences, are subject to evolutionary debunking. Sinhababu briefly makes a similar claim, but places more weight on the breadth of moral disagreement, which he argues justifies scepticism about all moral judgments, except beliefs in the goodness of pleasure, and the badness of pain, which he thinks escape his sceptical argument because of the unique way in which these beliefs arise.

We can put the point in a different way. In an intriguing study, Thalia Wheatley and Jonathan Haidt hypnotized subjects to feel

---

[34] Lerner, 'Fine-Tuning Evolutionary Debunking Arguments', 14. See also Rachels and Alter, 'Nothing Matters in Survival'.

[35] Sinhababu, 'The Epistemic Argument for Hedonism', 28–9.

disgust when they read an arbitrarily chosen word—in this case, the word 'often'. The students then read the following:

Dan is a student council representative at his school. This semester he is in charge of scheduling discussions about academic issues. He *often* picks topics that appeal to both professors and students in order to stimulate discussion.

Students who had been primed under hypnosis to feel disgust at the word 'often' were then asked to judge whether Dan had done something wrong. A third of them said that he had.[36] The negative moral judgment was, of course, an illusion, created by hypnosis, and it gives us no reason at all to believe that Dan's conduct was wrong. Presumably once the experiment was over and the students had been debriefed, they would agree that Dan had done nothing wrong. Now suppose that the students had been hypnotized to believe that when they read the word 'often' they would develop a blinding headache. Soon after being given information containing the headache-triggering word, they held their heads, moaned, asked for analgesics, and tried to find somewhere quiet to rest. Asked to rate what they are now feeling, on a scale rating from 'very bad' to 'very good', they rated the experience as 'very bad'. After the experiment was over and they had been debriefed, would they change their judgment that they had had a very bad experience because the judgment was induced by hypnosis? Presumably not. Nothing they learned about the origins of the experience they had just had would be grounds for altering their judgment of how bad it felt at the time, because that is something of which they had direct acquaintance. Pain that is the result of an illusion is no less bad than pain that is the result of something real, and pain that is the result of evolutionary selection is no less bad than pain that has other origins, whatever they might be.

A further point can be made in defence of hedonism against evolutionary debunking arguments. To be motivated to seek pleasure and avoid pain it is not necessary that we have the normative belief that pleasure is good and pain is bad. The way pleasure and pain feel is already sufficiently motivating. Hence there is no reproductive

---

[36] Wheatley and Haidt, 'Hypnotic Disgust Makes Moral Judgments More Severe'; Haidt, *The Righteous Mind*, 53–4.

advantage in our holding that belief. In this respect, it contrasts with, for instance, the normative belief that incest is wrong, for some people are motivated towards having sex with members of their family and the belief, especially when socially reinforced, will help to combat that motivation.

5. The Indispensability of Psychology

Sidgwick was aware that for hedonistic utilitarianism to be useful as a guide to behaviour, we need to be able to form some estimates as to which actions bring about the greatest net surplus of pleasure over pain, and for that to be possible, we must be able to compare and in some way quantify pleasures and pains. He thought that this is something that we all do, to some extent, and so it cannot be a completely hopeless task, but at the same time he was very aware that our efforts in this area are highly fallible, and the results they yield are at best very rough.

During Sidgwick's lifetime, the Irish economist and philosopher F. Y. Edgeworth suggested how the science of measuring happiness, understood as the surplus of pleasure over pain, might, in theory, be developed. His major work, *Mathematical Psychics*, contains an appendix entitled 'Of Hedonimetry' in which he suggests that we take as our unit of utility, a 'just perceivable increment of pleasure', arguing that for any one individual, these units must be equal, for otherwise one could perceive a difference between them—and then they would not be a single 'just perceivable increment' but rather at least two such increments.[37] Edgeworth then imagines a 'hedonimeter' that could measure pleasure and pain by 'continually registering the height of pleasure experienced by an individual, exactly according to the verdict of consciousness, or rather diverging therefrom according to a law of errors'. The device would plot a graph, and the pleasure and pain of the individual subject would be represented by the areas above and below the zero-line—obviously the greater the net total area above the line after subtracting the area below the line,

---

[37] See Edgeworth, *Mathematical Psychics*, 98–102. We owe this reference to Colander, 'Edgeworth's Hedonimeter and the Quest to Measure Utility'.

the happier the individual would be. But Edgeworth did not stop at individual well-being. He proposes the postulate that 'any just perceivable pleasure-increment experienced by any sentient at any time has the same value'. This enables us to overcome the problem of interpersonal comparisons of utility, and we can then integrate data 'through all time and over all sentience' to measure the goal sought by utilitarianism.

Edgeworth's proposal made no headway. In economics, it was forcefully attacked by Irving Fisher, who wrote that it is not the province of economics to build a theory of psychology. Fisher was influenced by the belief noted in the previous chapter that economics needed to establish its standing as a science by ridding itself of all references to unobservable entities like pleasures and pains. So successful was this viewpoint that the period that followed *Mathematical Psychics* has been described as a 'century of separation' between economics and psychology.[38] Instead of Edgeworth's postulate of the equal value of just perceivable increments of pleasure, Fisher suggested 'a simple psychoeconomic postulate: '*Each individual acts as he desires.*'[39] Since Fisher's time, a desire-based view of utility has been dominant in economic thought, notwithstanding the obvious problems with such a view noted in the previous chapter. Fisher himself still believed in the importance of measuring utility, but he wanted to do it indirectly, by means of something observable, such as individual choices, rather than directly, as Edgeworth did. Economists subsequently abandoned the whole idea of interpersonal comparisons of utility, even if made indirectly. Instead, they used the much more restricted idea proposed by Vilfredo Pareto, of taking a change in utility distribution as an improvement only if it makes at least one individual better off and leaves no one worse off.

Then psychology struck back. Mainstream economic theory assumes that people are rational utility maximizers, and thus their choices, if adequately informed, maximize their utility. Daniel Kahneman and Amos Tversky showed that the economic model of

[38] The phrase is from Camerer *et al.*, 'Neuroeconomics'.
[39] Fisher, *Mathematical Investigations in the Theory of Value and Prices*, 11. We owe this reference to Colander, 'Edgeworth's Hedonimeter and the Quest to Measure Utility'.

rational choice does not correspond to psychological reality. People are more willing to take risks to avoid a loss than they are to make a greater gain, and so presenting options in a way that makes the risk of loss more salient leads to a different choice from that which is made when the options are presented in a way that focuses attention on the prospect of gain. In the best-known example of the effect of framing questions differently, one group of participants is told that the United States is preparing for an outbreak of disease that is expected to kill 600 people. They are then presented with the following options:

> If Program A is adopted, 200 people will be saved.
> If Program B is adopted, there is a one-third probability that 600 people will
> be saved and a two-thirds probability that no people will be saved.

Given these choices, a substantial majority favours the certainty of saving 200 lives over the risk of saving no one, and chooses Program A. Another group of participants is given the same information about the disease but presented with different options:

> If Program A' is adopted, 400 people will die.
> If Program B' is adopted, there is a one-third probability that nobody will die and
> a two-thirds probability that 600 people will die.

Although A and A', and B and B', are identical in their outcomes, a majority chooses Program B' in preference to A'. In the first set of options, the certainty of saving 200 people made option A attractive, although given the estimate that 600 would die, saving 200 still leaves 400 to die. In the second set of options, people were reluctant to accept the certainty of death, although if 400 die, 200 are saved.[40] Clearly, choices influenced by the way in which options are framed cannot be used as a basis for consistent evaluations of an individual's utility.

Moreover, consistently with what we saw earlier in this chapter about the status quo bias, people's initial endowments play an important role in how they judge the utilities of different outcomes. For

---

[40] See Tversky and Kahneman, 'The Framing of Decisions and the Psychology of Choice'. We have also drawn on Kahneman, 'Maps of Bounded Rationality: Psychology for Behavioral Economics' (this article is a revised version of the Nobel Prize Lecture).

example, if two people get their monthly report from their broker, and A is told that her wealth has fallen from $4 million to $3 million, while B is told that her wealth has risen from $1 million to $1.1 million, B is likely to be happier today, even though A is much wealthier. Standard models of economic rationality ignore the impact on utility that a change from the status quo often has.

For this work, Kahneman was honoured with the 2002 Nobel Prize in economics. He took the opportunity presented by his Nobel Prize Lecture to tell economists how badly they had got it wrong:

A theory of choice that completely ignores feelings such as the pain of losses and the regret of mistakes is not only descriptively unrealistic, it also leads to prescriptions that do not maximize the utility of outcomes as they are actually experienced—that is, utility as Bentham conceived it.[41]

Or, one might add, as Sidgwick conceived it.

6. Measuring Utility

Sidgwick struggled with the question of how to measure happiness. Economists, as we have seen, effectively gave up that effort and ended up measuring something quite different. Kahneman has put forward his own account of what happiness is, and how it may be possible to measure it. His account is really an updated version of Sidgwick's. The similarity is not coincidental: he frequently cites Edgeworth, on whom Sidgwick was a major influence.[42] Here is Kahneman's view of happiness:

as a first approximation, it makes sense to call Helen 'objectively happy' if she spent most of her time ... engaged in activities that she would rather have continued than stop, little time in situations she wished to escape, and—very important because life is short—not too much time in a neutral state in which she would not care either way.[43]

---

[41] Kahneman, 'Maps of Bounded Rationality: Psychology for Behavioral Economics' (the same sentence appears in the text of the lecture as given, 'Maps of Bounded Rationality: A Perspective on Intuitive Judgment and Choice').

[42] See Edgeworth, *Mathematical Psychics*. Kahneman refers to Edgeworth in several places, e.g. in Kahneman *et al.*, 'Back to Bentham: Explorations of Experienced Utility'; 'Experienced Utility and Objective Happiness'; 'Objective Happiness'.

[43] Kahneman, 'Objective Happiness', 7; see also *Thinking, Fast and Slow*, 391.

Although in this passage Kahneman refers to 'activities' rather than mental states, he also writes that 'being pleased or distressed is an attribute of experience at a particular moment' and he labels this attribute 'instant utility', adding that 'Instant utility is best understood as the strength of the disposition to continue or to interrupt the current experience.'[44] Elsewhere he uses the term 'experienced utility', which we prefer because 'instant' suggests the equivalent, for duration, of a mathematical point for space, and pleasure cannot be 'instant' in this sense.[45] To experience pleasure requires some period of time, even if it can be quite short. So Kahneman's concern is with mental states, and his first approximation at distinguishing the mental states that contribute to happiness from those that do not is by saying, just as Sidgwick initially does, that the former are those we desire to continue.

Feldman objects to Kahneman's account of happiness. He asks us to imagine a drag racer named Brett, who is competing in a race and enjoying the experience of accelerating rapidly. When Brett is one-tenth of the way down the track, he is happy to be going at 30 miles per hour; but he has no desire to continue to have the experiences associated with travelling at that speed, for he wants to be further down the track, and going faster, as soon as possible. Feldman also reminds us of his example of the woman giving birth. Although she is experiencing the happiest moment of her life, it is not a moment she wishes to prolong, for she is in great pain. Feldman concludes: 'These examples demonstrate that there is no close conceptual connection between a person's happiness during an interval and the strength of his desire for the continuation of the experiences he is having during that interval.'[46]

Feldman's examples make what is essentially the point Sidgwick made when he acknowledged that we can have pleasurable experiences that we do not try to sustain; for example, the pleasure of eating in a person who is in the habit of avoiding over-eating, and we

[44] Kahneman, 'Objective Happiness', 4.
[45] e.g. in Kahneman et al., 'Back to Bentham'. We thank Theron Pummer for the point about pleasure not occurring at an 'instant'.
[46] Feldman, What is This Thing Called Happiness? 50.

can have sensations that we try to avoid, though they are not painful, like the sensation of being tickled. Brett's happiness at reaching 30 miles per hour at an early point of the race is due to the fact that this is a point he must pass in order to go still faster later in the race. The woman's happiness at the moment of birth is due to the fact that this is the moment at which she becomes a mother. One's happiness at crossing a threshold cannot be increased by stopping indefinitely on the threshold, for then the threshold is never crossed. As Sidgwick noticed, such special situations mean that, strictly speaking, we cannot define pleasure or happiness as consisting of moments of consciousness that one wants to continue, and pain or unhappiness as moments of consciousness that one would like to end. He therefore amends his definition of pleasure, as we have seen, to 'a feeling which, when experienced by intelligent beings, is at least implicitly apprehended as desirable or—in cases of comparison—preferable'. Kahneman's first approximation also holds for most cases, but he too could no doubt move to a more exact definition of pleasure, akin to Sidgwick's.

Given such an account of happiness, can we measure it? It remains a subjective experience. Advances in neuroscience are making it possible for us to detect, in an objective manner, whether someone is having a pleasant or painful experience, but Edgeworth's 'hedonimeter' is still waiting to be invented—and when it is, we will have to tackle the problem of showing that similar brain states in different people are experienced as equally intense pleasures.[47] Nevertheless, Kahneman believes that experienced utility is measurable because we can ask people to report it. Following Edgeworth, we could graph the subject's reports of their pleasure or pain at a series of moments. In the absence of a hedonimeter, we can now use the ubiquitous mobile phone. Volunteers allow their phones to be programmed so that, as they go about their daily lives, the phone will interrupt them at random intervals and ask them questions.[48] It may, for example, ask

---

[47] For an overview of the state of brain science relative to pleasure and happiness, see Kringelbach and Berridge, 'The Neuroscience of Happiness and Pleasure'.

[48] You can volunteer to be part of this research at <www.trackyourhappiness.org> (last accessed 24 January 2014).

them to insert a number to indicate the quality of their experience at that particular moment. The data thus obtained for a given person over a given period—say, for Helen in the month of March—can be plotted on a graph in which zero marks a neutral state in which a person is indifferent to whether that state continue or not. If in March Helen's line is always above the zero level, that would mean that she always had positive utility; if the line is always below the zero level, she always had negative utility; and if the line is sometimes above and sometimes below the zero level, whether her utility is positive or negative would depend on whether the area above the line is greater than the area below the line.

These results we obtain from plotting graphs like the one just described will be different from the answers that we would obtain if we asked people, at the end of a day or a week, to evaluate their experiences over that time. Kahneman's research gives several vivid examples of this difference. Patients undergoing colonoscopies were asked to report, at 60-second intervals, the level of pain or discomfort they were feeling. Then, after the procedure was over, they were asked to assess how bad it was, and to make a hypothetical choice between having it repeated or having a different unpleasant medical investigation, a barium enema. The result was surprising. Two patients might have identically painful experiences for the first 10 minutes, but the experience of Patient A ends at that point, whereas Patient B's experience continues for another 5 minutes at a level that is still painful, but not as severely painful as the first 10 minutes. Who suffered the most pain, A or B? It seems obvious that Patient B did—for the first 10 minutes he had just as much pain as Patient A, and then he had an additional 5 minutes of pain, while during this period A was feeling no pain at all. Yet when the patients were asked, after the examinations were over, to rate the experience, typically A rated it worse than B, and when offered the hypothetical choice, was more likely to opt for the barium enema, rather than a repeated colonoscopy. This result was supported by a randomized experiment in which, for half the patients, after the examination was complete the physician did not immediately remove the instrument, but left it in place for a further minute. The experience during that minute was uncomfortable for the patient, but it ensured that the medical procedure never ended at a point at which the patient was in severe pain. These patients had significantly more favourable overall evaluations of the colonoscopy than the other patients. In other words, the patients' recollections of these experiences were significantly influenced by how painful the final moments were.

Similar results were obtained with other unpleasant experiences. For example, participants had one hand immersed in water at 14°C—which is cold enough to feel painful—for 1 minute and then had the other hand immersed in water at 14°C for the same period and then for an additional half minute during which the water was gradually warmed to 15°C, which is still painful, but slightly less so. They were more willing to repeat the latter experience than they were the former. Exposing participants to unpleasant sounds that in some cases became less unpleasant after a period produced the same preference.[49] These results illustrate what Kahneman calls a 'focusing illusion' that leads us to the phenomenon of 'duration neglect'—we give too much weight to the last moments of the experience, and neglect its duration.[50]

Kahneman has also put this in terms of saying that we all have 'two selves'—an experiencing self and a remembering self. This is relevant not only to many choices we make, which are based on our remembered experiences, but also to the answers people give to questions about life satisfaction which are, necessarily, addressed to the remembering self, not the experiencing self. For example, one study compared women in Columbus, Ohio, with those in Rennes, France, and found that although the American women reported higher levels of life satisfaction than the French women, the French women spent more time in positive moods, and in the kind of activities that, the French and American women agreed, tend to yield more pleasure.[51]

[49] Redelmeier and Kahneman, 'Patients' Memories of Painful Medical Treatments'; Redelmeier et al., 'Memories of Colonoscopy'; Kahneman et al., 'When More Pain is Preferred to Less'; Schreiber and Kahneman, 'Determinants of the Remembered Utility of Aversive Sounds'.

[50] See the discussion of focusing illusions in Kahneman, Thinking, Fast and Slow, 402–6.

[51] Krueger et al., 'Time Use and Subjective Well-Being in France and the US'.

Apart from this and other divergences between life satisfaction and mood or emotional well-being, Kahneman and his colleague Angus Deaton have demonstrated another important difference between asking people how satisfied they are with their life, and asking them questions about the emotional quality of their lives. The higher your income, the higher life satisfaction you are likely to report; but once your income reaches $75,000 per annum, higher income brings no further increase in emotional well-being.[52] If, as we shall argue shortly, emotional well-being is a better indication of happiness than life-satisfaction, we can conclude that while money can buy you satisfaction, it can't buy you happiness.

These empirical findings confront us with an important value question: what is of ultimate value? Is it the quality of life of the experiencing self, or of the remembering self? Kahneman leans towards the experiencing self, saying that 'the logic of duration weighting is compelling'—'duration weighting' being the idea that we should take account of how long an experience lasts. He has also written that 'the total utility of an episode is the product of average instant utility and duration' and that retrospective evaluation leads to 'erroneous estimates of the "true" total utility of past experiences.'[53] But Kahneman also says that duration weighting 'cannot be considered a complete theory of well-being because individuals identify with their remembering self and care about their story. A theory of well-being that ignores what people want cannot be sustained.' He concludes that 'The remembering and the experiencing self must both be considered because their interests do not coincide' and then adds: 'Philosophers could struggle with these questions for a long time.'[54]

Sidgwick did struggle with these questions, and concluded, as we saw in Chapter 5, that we should have 'impartial concern for all parts of our conscious life', while allowing us to discount future periods for uncertainty, and to adjust for possible changes in our capacity for happiness (*ME* 381). This is Kahneman's principle of duration

---

[52]   Kahneman and Deaton, 'High Income Improves Evaluation of Life But Not Emotional Well-Being'.

[53]   The quoted passages are from Kahneman, 'Objective Happiness', 15 and 20.

[54]   Kahneman, *Thinking, Fast and Slow*, 410.

weighting. We agree, and we question whether the remembering self does need to be considered, apart from its effect on the experiencing self. Kahneman himself has written that 'The time that people spend dwelling on a memorable moment should be included in its duration, adding to its weight.'[55] This isn't strictly accurate, because it isn't the duration of the memorable moment that is increased by the time spent dwelling on it—the moment of joy I experience when my child is born does not become longer because over the years I often remember it with pleasure. Instead, that moment makes possible many other pleasurable moments in which I remember that moment. So it would be more precise to say: the time that people spend dwelling on a memorable moment adds to the contribution that the memorable moment makes to a person's experiences over time. But this is already taken into account by duration weighting for the experiencing self, since the later moments of remembering it will count in the person's total utility over time. Similarly, while it is true that, as Kahneman writes, individuals identify with their remembering self and care about their story, presumably this also has some impact on their experiences—they have better experiences when they are remembering a positive story about their lives. To the extent that their caring about their story affects the quality of other experiences they have, of course it matters and is included in the total utility over time of the experiencing self, without giving special weight to the remembering self. To the extent that it does not affect the quality of their experiences, it does not matter.

Some additional support for Sidgwick's equal weighting position comes from studies in which the participants did not themselves undergo an unpleasant experience, but were given information about the experiences of another person, whom we shall call X. The participants were given information showing how X had, at regular intervals, rated on a numerical scale how unpleasant his or her experience was. If the information was presented numerically, the evaluators tended to average the numbers, a procedure that takes no account of duration, but if the information was presented graphically, as histograms,

---

[55] Kahneman, *Thinking, Fast and Slow*, 409.

each period of time was given equal weight and there was no duration neglect. This suggests that it is only when we are ourselves subject to the distorting effect of memory that we give disproportionate weight to how an experience ends; when we judge the experiences of others, if the information is presented to us in an easily graspable form, we give equal weight to all periods of time.[56]

What of Kahneman's assertion that 'a theory of well-being that ignores what people want cannot be sustained'? Perhaps the idea behind this remark is that ignoring what people want is paternalistic, but if so, the distinction we drew in the previous chapter applies here too: we are discussing what is intrinsically good, not what political action should be taken.[57] In any case, Kahneman has himself shown, in many different ways, that what people want is not a reliable indicator of what will maximize their well-being over time. So while we should not ignore what people want, we do not have to give it overriding weight in deciding what would be best for them.

Politically, of course, ignoring what people want is risky, and not only because in liberal democratic societies we tend to resist paternalism. If governments set out to measure happiness, and to promote it, they had better come up with an idea of happiness that people want and are prepared to support. It is the remembering self that votes, not the experiencing self. That poses an intriguing problem for democratic theory, but to explore it would take us too far from our topic. Here our interest is in what is of ultimate value, and for that enquiry, we conclude that people's memories of their experiences are not authoritative guides to the value of those experiences.

This leads to another question about the relationship between time and subjective experience. Sidgwick thinks it self-evident that we

---

[56] Liersch and McKenzie, 'Duration Neglect by Numbers—and its Elimination by Graphs'.

[57] Silverstein ('More Pain or Less?') points out that 'the preferences in question are the preferences of *ordinary, mentally undisturbed* people' and therefore 'to refuse to accede to their preferences seems straightforwardly, and offensively, paternalistic'. Silverstein is responding to Broome, 'More Pain or Less?' For further discussion see Beardman 'The Choice between Current and Retrospective Evaluations of Pain'; Gustafson, 'Our Choice between Actual and Remembered Pain'; and Beardman, 'Response to Gustafson's Comments'.

should have impartial concern for all parts of our conscious life and we have, in Chapter 5, defended that principle against criticisms from Williams and Slote. There is, however, a different way of questioning it. Suppose that in a week I will have the opportunity to take a drug that slows my perception of time, so that during the hour after I take the drug, it seems to me that two hours have passed. (There is some evidence that marijuana has this effect.[58]) I will also be able to arrange to have only pleasurable experiences for the entire duration of the hour. Am I justified in giving more weight to the hour when my sense of time's passing is influenced by the drug than I give to another hour when I have the same pleasurable experience, but it feels to me as if only one hour has passed?[59] The hedonist should answer in the affirmative and we do not see any contradiction between this answer and Sidgwick's principle of impartial concern for all parts of our existence, for Sidgwick allowed that 'a week ten years hence' could be more important to us than a week now because of 'an increase in our means or capacities of happiness' (ME 381). Taking the drug would be such an increase in our capacity to experience pleasure during that hour.[60]

7. Utility and Life Satisfaction

Before concluding this discussion of happiness and how we may be able to measure it, we should comment on one very popular method of attempting to do so. A great deal of social research on happiness is based on surveys that have asked millions of people how satisfied

[58] Atakan *et al.*, 'The Effect of Cannabis on Perception of Time'.

[59] Bradley raises this question, using the example of a special experience machine, in a comment posted on PEA Soup, <http://peasoup.typepad.com/peasoup/2008/02/objective-and-s.html#comment-101237434>; we owe this reference to Richard Chappell, who discusses the question in his unpublished paper, 'Value Holism'.

[60] Bastian Stern suggested, during a presentation of a version of this chapter at the University of Oxford in 2013, that there is a tension between choosing subjective rather than objective time in this case, and what we have said regarding duration neglect, where we disregard the subjective remembered experience in favour of the objectively measured one. We can understand why one might think this but we deny any contradiction, because in both cases we are upholding the judgment of the present experiencing self rather than something outside the present self (whether it is the remembering self, or the external measurement of the time that has passed).

they are with their life. For example, the World Values Survey asks people to give a number, between 1 and 10, indicating 'All things considered, how satisfied are you with your life as a whole these days?' Other surveys ask similar questions. Haybron argues convincingly that this is not the same as asking 'How happy are you now?' Part of his case draws on studies showing that there is surprisingly little correlation between how satisfied people say they are with their lives, and what their moods and emotions are like. One study has shown that 29 per cent of people who describe themselves as 'completely satisfied' with their life also report significant symptoms of anxiety and related forms of distress. More remarkable still, 6 per cent of the 'completely satisfied' report that they are 'usually unhappy or depressed'.[61]

How can a high degree of life satisfaction coexist with being usually unhappy or depressed? Perhaps some people are satisfied with their lives because they have low expectations. If someone has the attitude: 'How happy can a sinner like me expect to be?' that could explain the coexistence of a high life satisfaction rating and an unhappy life. In a repressive society we could get similar results from women, or members of ethnic minorities, or lower castes, who have internalized their society's negative attitude towards the group to which they belong. Another problem with reports of life satisfaction is that they are highly sensitive to what seem to be trivial incidents that occur shortly before the question is posed. Finding a coin, being given a candy bar, or sunshine instead of rain, can make a significant change in how positively people rate their lives. The order in which questions are asked can make a difference too. Gallup conducts a daily survey asking Americans a wide range of questions, including how satisfied they are with their lives. Angus Deaton, studying the results before and after the financial crisis of 2008–9, found a surprising rise in early 2009, to levels above those before the crisis hit. Eventually he concluded that the key factor in the reported rise was that, for several months beforehand, Gallup had been asking people questions related to the coming election, and the change of

---

[61] Haybron, *The Pursuit of Unhappiness*, 84–5, citing Glatzer, 'Quality of Life in Advanced Industrialized Countries'. Feldman also argues, on grounds that overlap with Haybron's, against life satisfaction views of happiness, in *What is This Thing Called Happiness*, 70–104.

government. After the election those questions were dropped. *Not asking Americans about politics caused a dramatic improvement in their reported life satisfaction.* In fact, Deaton found, 'Life evaluation questions are extremely sensitive to question order effects—asking political questions first reduces reported life evaluation by an amount that dwarfs the effects of even the worst of the crisis.'[62]

The fact that reported life satisfaction varies so greatly on the basis of trivial incidents or the order of questions asked suggests that most people do not have a settled evaluation of their life. If that is so, then when they are selected, at random, asked 'how satisfied are you with your life on the whole these days?', and presented with a numerical scale on which they are supposed to indicate the answer, they decide on an answer on the spot. But if life satisfaction is something that most people think about rarely, or not at all, is it really an important aspect of their lives? Perhaps, aggregated across different countries or very large samples, and taken over different time periods, the answers people give to this question tell us something about differences between populations and time-periods, but we doubt that it can be equated with well-being or happiness.

8. Conclusion

Each of the value theories that we presented in this and the previous chapter has its problems. A basic desire-based theory meets the resonance requirement, but holds that it is good for me to satisfy desires that I will later regret having satisfied. A switch to a different version of a desire-based theory will overcome this problem, but will open up another one. Restricting the desires that we take into account by requiring that they hold under conditions of full information, clear thinking, and so on, for example, fails to exclude some crazy desires that are not based on any false information, and can also involve so substantial a shift away from the actual desires people have that what it tells us to do for people may no longer resonate with them, thus giving up one of the major attractions of desire theory over an externalist

---

[62] Deaton, 'The Financial Crisis and the Well-Being of Americans'.

theory. If, however, we shift to an externalist theory, then the question becomes whether anything can really be good for me if it is not something I care about. Think again of the person who most desires to spend his life counting blades of grass, even though he could have a much more varied, fulfilling, and happier life by using his skills for other purposes. This example makes it hard to deny that a person's fully informed desires can lead him to adopt a life that is not the best life for him. In reaching this judgment, however, we are strongly influenced by the fact that the grass counter could have been happier if he had chosen a different life. If we remove that element, and replace it with other goods that he does not desire, *and* which will not give him more pleasure, or make him happier, it becomes more difficult to defend the view that he would then have had a life that was better for him. Would we, for example, want to say that his life was better for him because he gained knowledge, or freedom, or that his life met a higher aesthetic standard, even though he cared nothing about such matters, and they did not make him any happier? We do not think so. In the end, if there is no satisfactory form of desire theory, we find the most plausible alternative is to agree with Sidgwick that the only things that are intrinsically good for a sentient being are desirable states of consciousness, or pleasure.

The final step in this discussion of intrinsic value is to move from what is 'good for' a sentient being to what is 'good on the whole'. For a hedonist like Sidgwick, this move is straightforward, because if nothing is good apart from states of consciousness, and all states of consciousness are states of some sentient being, then what is good on the whole—or, good from 'the point of view of the universe'—is the sum total of what is good for all sentient beings.

Ross held that, even if pleasure is always 'good for' the being who experiences it, from the moral point of view, pleasure is only good when it is either the pleasure of a non-moral being, like an animal, or it is the pleasure of a moral being who deserves it. Ross supports this view by saying that if we compare two imaginary states of the universe with the same amount of pleasure and pain, but in one of which the virtuous are all happy and the vicious all miserable, while in the other the virtuous are miserable and the vicious happy, 'very few people would hesitate to say that the first was a much better state of the universe than the second.[63] That may be true, but it is readily explained by our evolved instinct to punish those who harm us or who harm others we care about, and to reward those who help us and cooperate with us, and with others we care about. An evolutionary debunking explanation of the type we discussed in Chapter 7 thus applies, and since evolution favours beliefs that enhance our fitness, rather than beliefs that are true, we have no reason to believe that the intuition to which Ross appeals is the kind of moral truth that he took it to be.

A hedonist will also resist the 'reverence for life' ethic advocated by Albert Schweitzer, for it fails to distinguish between sentient and non-sentient life.[64] The oft-cited 'land ethic' of the pioneering American naturalist and ecologist Aldo Leopold does no better, from a hedonist's perspective. Leopold wrote 'A thing is right when it tends to preserve the integrity, stability, and beauty of the biotic community; it is wrong when it tends otherwise.'[65] The hedonist can, while rejecting these claims about intrinsic value, grant that they may—like claims about the importance of preserving endangered plants—have instrumental value because they encourage a positive attitude to living things and to the ecological systems on which all sentient life depends.[66]

---

[63] Ross, *The Right and the Good*, 138.
[64] Schweitzer, *Civilization and Ethics*, 246.
[65] Leopold, 'The Land Ethic', 1949.
[66] For further discussion see Singer, *Practical Ethics,* 3rd edn, ch. 10.

10

Rules

1. Sidgwick on the Utilitarian Attitude to Moral Rules

The rules of common sense morality often do not bring about the best possible outcomes. At first glance, it seems that a utilitarian who sees that the rules of common sense morality are far from ideal should seek to persuade people to reject those rules and replace them with whatever rules will lead to the best consequences. But Sidgwick's cautious pragmatism emerges when he warns of 'that temper of rebellion against the established morality, as something purely external and conventional, into which the reflective mind is always apt to fall when it is first convinced that the established rules are not intrinsically reasonable' (*ME* 475). Utilitarians should discipline their rebellious instincts and instead compare 'the total amounts of pleasure and pain that may be expected to result respectively from maintaining any given rule as at present established, and from endeavouring to introduce that which is proposed in its stead' (*ME* 477).

Before openly supporting changes in a system of rules accepted by their society, utilitarians should take several factors into account. They must think about their own happiness as well as that of those close to them. It may be that 'social disapprobation' towards reformers and their families will diminish their powers of influence in the society. Of course, as Sidgwick notes, a utilitarian must be prepared to pay the price for the benefits of reform but the calculation of costs and benefits may still come down against attempting to change well-entrenched rules. (One cannot help wondering whether, in discussing the likely costs of social disapprobation for the utilitarian reformer, Sidgwick was thinking of the opprobrium that he and friends of his like John Addington Symonds could expect were they to seek to challenge the British law against male homosexual acts.)

The other more important question for the would-be utilitarian reformer is whether a new, more felicific rule, even if established and adopted, is likely to be obeyed. Perhaps, Sidgwick warns, the new rule will be too complex, or demand too much from citizens, including 'greater intellectual development, or a higher degree of self-control, than is to be found in an average member of the community, or an exceptional quality or balance of feelings' (*ME* 481).

In some cases, instead of changing an old rule by presenting a new one, it will be easier to change human habits by weakening the old rule and the habits that go with it. This strategy carries its own risks: just as breaking a positive law may encourage 'lawlessness', so too 'the forces that are always tending towards moral anarchy in any society' may be aided by a decline in obedience to a generally recognized moral rule (*ME* 482). It is not only the reaction of the whole society that a utilitarian needs to take into account but also the effect on his or her own will to obey the rules. Utilitarians might think that they should simply develop the habit of acting rationally, but habit and acceptance are strong forces leading to obedience to moral rules. Sidgwick reminds would-be reformers that 'the direct sympathetic echo in each man of the judgments and sentiments of others' is a powerful factor sustaining their own moral conduct. It is much easier to obey rules which are supported by people among whom you live than to obey a rule that you have yourself invented (*ME* 483).

What about rules that common sense morality treats as absolute and which on utilitarian grounds can generally be considered valid, but to which a utilitarian might permit exceptions under special circumstances? It may seem that, when disobeying the rule will produce better consequences than obeying it, a utilitarian could establish a new, more complicated rule that will tell us when we may break the old rule. But suppose that the new rule is so complicated that, if it should be generally accepted, people would often misapply it, with consequences that would be worse than if they accepted the old rule? In these circumstances, the utilitarian will not want the new rule to be generally adopted. Could the utilitarian nevertheless be justified in disregarding the old rule and doing what will lead to the best consequences, on the grounds that his or her action will not be widely imitated? Sidgwick believes that this could be justified in some circumstances. He begins by pointing out that the mere fact that bad consequences would result from a large number of people adopting a rule doesn't mean that it is wrong for an individual to act in accordance with that rule: 'no one (e.g.) would say that because an army walking over a bridge would break it down, therefore the crossing of a single traveller has a tendency to destroy it'. He then considers the objection that this violates Kant's fundamental principle that an act is right only if one can will it to be universal. His response is that we should understand the Kantian formula to mean only that 'an act, if right for any individual, must be right on general grounds, and therefore for some *class* of persons; it therefore cannot prevent us from defining this class by the abovementioned characteristic of believing that the act will remain an exceptional one' (*ME* 486–7).

When justifying a departure from the rule for a particular class of people, it is also important that we can be confident that the exception will not become widespread. Sidgwick offers celibacy as an example: from a utilitarian point of view (given the common assumption that human happiness is superior to that of animals) 'a universal refusal to propagate the human species would be the greatest of conceivable crimes'. But because we do not have to fear that many people will take up celibacy, or that too few people will be brought into existence, we can agree that some may live in celibacy, if that is their preference. One might think it is possible, in a similar manner, to justify departing from other well-established moral rules. For example, it could be argued that it can be justifiable for some to lie, in exceptional circumstances, because most people have firm attitudes against lying and so will continue to tell the truth. But, Sidgwick warns, it is one thing to rely on the persistence, in most people, of a non-moral desire (like the desire for sex), and another thing altogether to rely on the persistence of a moral attitude, like the view that it is wrong to lie. For while accepting the justifiability of celibacy for those who prefer it does nothing to weaken the sexual desires of the rest of us, to openly accept that some may justifiably lie seems bound, except in very rare cases, to weaken the general moral attitude that it is wrong to lie.

In a society of enlightened utilitarians, a utilitarian could provide grounds for permitting people to break moral rules in exceptional circumstances, and the community would accept these grounds as valid. As we have already noted, however, in society as it actually is, these more complicated rules may well do more harm than good. The other option, therefore, is for utilitarians not to advocate new rules at all, but to break the existing moral rules when the consequences of breaking the rule are, taken in themselves, better than the consequences of obeying it. Whether this can be justified, Sidgwick thinks, will largely depend on how much publicity the breach of the rule receives. This leads Sidgwick to what he calls 'esoteric morality', which he expresses in an oft-quoted sentence:

Thus, on Utilitarian principles, it may be right to do and privately recommend, under certain circumstances, what it would not be right to advocate openly; it may be right to teach openly to one set of persons what it would be wrong to teach to others; it may be conceivably right to do, if it can be done with comparative secrecy, what it would be wrong to do in the face of the world; and even, if perfect secrecy can be reasonably expected, what it would be wrong to recommend by private advice and example. (*ME* 489)

Sidgwick is well aware that the conclusions he is expressing here are 'of a paradoxical character'. He knows that 'the moral consciousness of a plain man broadly repudiates the general notion of an esoteric morality, differing from that popularly taught; and it would be commonly agreed that an action which would be bad if done openly is not rendered good by secrecy'. This common opinion itself has a utilitarian justification, for when people do something wrong, they have a natural tendency to conceal it, and we do not want to encourage this tendency. Therefore, Sidgwick suggests:

the Utilitarian conclusion, carefully stated, would seem to be this; that the opinion that secrecy may render an action right which would not otherwise be so should itself be kept comparatively secret; and similarly it seems expedient that the doctrine that esoteric morality is expedient should itself be kept esoteric. Or if this concealment be difficult to maintain, it may be desirable that Common Sense should repudiate the doctrines which it is expedient to confine to an enlightened few. (*ME* 490)

If we lived in a society consisting only of enlightened utilitarians, this 'swarm of perplexities and paradoxes' would vanish, and everyone could act on the moral principles he or she openly espouses. Sidgwick believes that every utilitarian should desire such a 'consummation' because conflicts of moral opinions are generally bad for morality, diminishing its force in resisting the 'seductive impulses' that lead us away from it; but in the actual world in which we live, in which there are 'so many different degrees of intellectual and moral development', these conflicts are a 'necessary evil'.

2. Moral Rules and Utilitarianism

Utilitarianism is generally understood as holding that we should do what will bring about the best consequences. At first glance, therefore, it would seem that moral rules have very little significance for utilitarians, but this is a mistake. The standard utilitarian position, held by Bentham, Mill, and, as we have just seen, Sidgwick, is that there are many good utilitarian reasons for observing and upholding accepted moral rules. A century after the publication of *The Methods*, R. M. Hare developed a 'two-level' account of utilitarianism that is in the spirit of Sidgwick's thinking on the role of rules in our moral thinking. Hare pointed out that it is extremely difficult, in everyday life, to calculate the consequences of each decision we make, and if we attempt to do so, we are likely to get it wrong. Sometimes we will be too rushed, or our thinking will be distorted by our emotions or our desire to do what is in our own interests. Hare suggested that society should promote a set of moral rules or principles that will, if used for moral decision-making in everyday life, lead to better consequences than any other set of rules. We should then seek to internalize these rules, so that our moral intuitions are in accordance with them, and educate our children so that they too have these intuitions. Hare called this the intuitive level of morality, and thought that it should be the basis for our everyday moral conduct. Occasionally, however, we will become aware that

acting in accordance with intuitive morality seems likely to produce an outcome that is clearly less good than the outcome we could
achieve by breaking the rule. Then, if we have the time to reflect crit-
ically on what we ought to do, and if we are confident that we are
not being swayed by our emotions or self-interest or other distorting
factors, we are justified in doing what will bring about the best consequences. When we act in this way, we are appealing to the critical
level of morality. It is also at the critical level that we may discuss
whether the intuitive moral principles that we have accepted are the
best ones for us to accept.[1]

One major reason for rejecting classical utilitarianism is reluctance
to accept that it can be right to break moral rules against lying, stealing, or killing, merely on the grounds that one can produce better
consequences by doing so. Brad Hooker invites us to consider 'an act
of murder that results in slightly more good than any other act would
have produced' and points out that utilitarians who judge every act
by its consequences have to admit that such an act is right.[2] Sidgwick
or Hare could reply that in real life we should not act on the belief that
committing murder will result in slightly more good than any other
act could have produced, because the odds are high that we have
underestimated the harm associated with breaking such an important rule and the costs of getting such a calculation wrong are great.
If, however, in a hypothetical example it is specified that we can be
completely sure that, after taking into account *all* the consequences,
the murder will produce more good than anything else we could have
done, then Hare would have said that it is right to commit the murder. He would have added, though, that it is still good to have intuitions that find the idea of murder abhorrent, because our intuitions
are formed for real-world cases, and not for fantastic examples.[3]

Many people are not satisfied with such an answer. They may be
broadly sympathetic to the idea that consequences matter, but they
want an ethical theory that provides a firmer guarantee that acts like

---

[1] Hare, *Moral Thinking*; for a more recent use of two-level utilitarianism, see Varner,
Personhood, Ethics, and Animal Cognition.

[2] Hooker, 'Rule Consequentialism'.

[3] Hare, *Moral Thinking*, 182.

murder are always wrong. This attitude led to the development of rule utilitarianism, a view generally dated from R. F. Harrod's influential 1936 essay, 'Utilitarianism Revised', although subsequently some of its defenders sought to improve its pedigree by suggesting that John Stuart Mill was a rule utilitarian before the term had been invented.[4] Rule utilitarians hold that we should take account of consequences only when deciding what rules to accept. Once we know which rules will have the best consequences, we ought to do what the rule prescribes, without regard for the consequences. Since a rule against murder will obviously have better consequences than a rule permitting murder, we should not murder, even if there could be occasions on which an individual murder will certainly have good consequences.

Once the term 'rule utilitarianism' came into use, another term was needed for what had been considered the standard form of utilitarianism. It became 'act utilitarianism' because it applied the consequentialist test not to rules, but to individual acts. At first, proponents of rule utilitarianism struggled to distinguish their position from act utilitarianism. Harrod, for example, suggested as the test for a right action: 'Would this action if done by all in similar relevant circumstances lead to the breakdown of some established method of society for securing its ends?'[5] But this leaves 'similar relevant circumstances' unspecified. Suppose, to illustrate the issue with a moral dilemma that Oxford academics confront on a daily basis, my college has a quadrangle surrounding a beautiful lawn. It would be convenient for me to take a shortcut across the lawn, but if everyone did that, the lawn would soon have an unsightly muddy path across it, thus lowering the utility of all college residents by more than it is raised by the convenience of taking the shortcut. So if I ask: 'would it be desirable if everyone takes a shortcut across the lawn whenever convenient?' the answer is no. But suppose that if only 10 people a day cross the lawn, there will be no damage. Suppose, too, that I know that fewer than

---

[4] Harrod, 'Utilitarianism Revised'; for the interpretation of Mill as a rule utilitarian, see Urmson, 'The Interpretation of the Moral Philosophy of J. S. Mill'.

[5] Harrod, 'Utilitarianism Revised', 149.

10 people a day are crossing the lawn. I now reformulate the rule so that the 'similar relevant circumstances' include these facts, and ask 'would it be desirable if, whenever so few people are crossing the lawn that one more will not result in any damage, another person crosses it?' Perhaps I have to add a further revision to the effect that no one else is around to see me walk across the lawn, so that I do not set a bad example to others. Whatever revisions need to be added, eventually the rule will no longer tell me not to cross the lawn. That outcome is consistent with act utilitarianism, so the distinction between act and rule utilitarianism collapses.[6]

This difficulty caused rule utilitarianism to suffer a near-death experience. It was resuscitated by the appreciation of a point of which Sidgwick was well aware, that if what we are interested in is a rule that can be accepted and acted upon by ordinary people, then there is a limit to how complicated that rule can be. Hooker, for example, used this insight to defend, in his book *Ideal Code, Real World,* a form of rule consequentialism suitable for the 'real world'. He argues that we should live by the moral rules, communal acceptance of which would have the best consequences. This version of rule consequentialism is clearly distinct from act consequentialism.[7] One way of seeing this difference is to note that, if we should follow the moral code that has the best consequences when the community accepts it, we cannot follow an esoteric morality. Sidgwick's defence of esoteric morality therefore illuminates the distinction between act consequentialism and rule consequentialism. It also casts light on other important differences

---

[6] This best-known formulation of this objection to rule utilitarianism was Lyons, *Forms and Limits of Utilitarianism.*

[7] It is also clearly distinct from global consequentialism, the idea that, as Pettit and Smith put it in an influential article, 'the right x, for any x in the category of evaluands—be the evaluands acts, motives, rules or whatever—is the best x, where the best x, in turn, is that which maximizes value' (Pettit and Smith, 'Global Consequentialism'). For the purposes of our discussion, the difference between act consequentialism and global consequentialism is not important, but Sidgwick would, we believe, have rejected global consequentialism on the ground that it wrongly assimilates all normative questions to the question about what is of ultimate value (*ME* 3–4). We also think, for reasons defended by Richard Chappell in 'Fittingness: The Sole Normative Primitive', that it is better not to ignore the fact that acts are subject to a distinctive form of normative judgment that does not apply to motives or rules, let alone eye colour or climate. For a contrary view, see Ord, 'Beyond Action'.

between Sidgwick's conception of ethics and other currently influential approaches. Hence it is to this topic that we now turn.

3. Defending Esoteric Morality

To begin this discussion, we set out some key tenets of what might be considered esoteric morality:

1. There are acts that are right only if no one—or virtually no one—will get to know about them. The rightness of an act, in other words, may depend on its secrecy. This can have implications for how often such an act may be done, if the chances of it remaining secret diminish with each repetition.
2. Some people know better, or can learn better, than others what it is right to do in certain circumstances.
3. There are at least two different sets of instruction, or moral codes, suitable for different categories of people. This raises the question whether there are also different standards by which we should judge what people do.
4. Though the consequentialist believes that acts are right only if they have consequences at least as good as anything else the agent could have done, the consequentialist may need to discourage others from embracing consequentialism.
5. Paradoxically, it may be the case that philosophers who support esoteric morality should not do so openly, and so should not even discuss—as we are about to do—possible justifications for esoteric morality.

As these points show, the notion of esoteric morality has two distinct though related elements. The first is indicated by the first tenet and relates to individual acts being done in secret—as Sidgwick puts it, to the rejection of the commonly accepted view that 'an action which would be bad if done openly is not rendered good by secrecy'. There is nothing esoteric about the idea that it is sometimes justifiable to act in secret—that view is widely known. The distinctive element here is that of secrecy making good an act that would normally be bad. The second element is constituted by the other tenets we have just given, which all relate to knowledge of what it is right to do in certain circumstances. That this knowledge should itself remain secret is the most distinctive element of esoteric morality.

The idea that it is better if some moral views are not widely known was not invented by Sidgwick. In Plato's *Republic*, Socrates proposes that ordinary people be brought up to believe that everyone is born 'from the earth' into one of three classes, gold, silver, or bronze, and living justly consists in doing what is in their nature. Only the philosopher-rulers will know that this is really a myth, a 'noble lie'.[8]

More surprisingly, perhaps, Catholic moral theology has also found that it cannot avoid the need for a doctrine that is plainly not intended to be widely known. This applies, for example, to the doctrine of 'mental reservation', which holds that it is permissible to say something that misleads, and yet avoid the sin of lying by mentally adding information that would, if spoken, make the response truthful. In Charles McFadden's *Medical Ethics*, a text written from a Roman Catholic perspective, doctors and nurses are advised that if a feverish patient asks what his temperature is, and the truth would alarm him and make his condition worse, it is justifiable to reply 'Your temperature is normal today', while making the mental reservation that it is 'normal' for someone in the patient's precise physical condition.[9]

It is, however, in the context of utilitarianism that most recent discussion of esoteric morality has taken place. In order to better understand the case for it, let us return to the key passage from Sidgwick that we have already quoted. We will break it up into its distinct elements, and supply examples that help us to see what he means and why he says it.

1. *'It may be right to do and privately recommend, under certain circumstances, what it would not be right to advocate openly'*

On consequentialist grounds, it is plausible to believe that people who have more than they require to meet their basic needs ought to

[8] Plato, *Republic*, 414b–415d.
[9] We owe this reference to Bok, *Lying*, 31. For more on the doctrine of mental reservation, see also *Catholic Encyclopedia*, <http://www.catholic.org/encyclopedia/view.php?id=7895>.

give everything they can spare to effective organizations that work to improve the lives of people living in extreme poverty in developing nations.[10] For present purposes, we can leave the notion of 'everything we can spare' undefined; what is important is that it is a highly demanding level of giving. But it is also plausible to believe that, given the way human beings are, very few of them will respond to an appeal to give away everything they can spare to help the poor. In that case, such an appeal will do little to help the poor. Perhaps advocating so demanding a standard will just make people cynical about morality as a whole: 'If *that* is what it takes to live ethically', they may say, 'let's forget about ethics, and just have fun'. If, however, we were to promote the idea that living ethically involves donating, say, 10 per cent of your income to the poor, we may get better results: many would give, and none would become moral cynics. Let's assume that this is the case, and the total amount raised to help the poor by advocating that morality requires every comfortably off person to give 10 per cent of their income will be much greater than would be raised by advocating that we should give everything we can spare. After we have done what we can to spread the message that every ethical person should give a tenth of their income to the poor, however, there remain many people in great need. Although I have myself given a tenth of my income to Oxfam, I still have enough left to dine out, go to movies, and take vacations abroad. I know that the consequences would be better if I were to stop doing this and give everything I can spare to Oxfam. Since I am a consequentialist, I know that that is what I ought to do.

Now Sidgwick's first element of esoteric morality applies. It would not be right to advocate openly that people ought to give everything they can spare to the poor, because that would be counterproductive. The right level of giving to advocate openly is 10 per cent. On the other hand, assuming that I have no other relevant obligations that constrain me from giving more than 10 per cent, I ought to give more, and in not giving more, I am doing something wrong. What if Helen, an old friend, asks me, privately, how much she should give? If I know that she is one of those rare people who would respond positively to

---

[10] Singer, 'Famine, Affluence and Morality'; Singer, *The Life you Can Save.*

a highly demanding standard, I should privately tell her what, as a consequentialist, I believe: that she ought to give substantially more than 10 per cent.

2. *'It may be right to teach openly to one set of persons what it would be wrong to teach to others'...*

An anti-terrorist officer teaches a carefully selected elite how to break down terrorists psychologically, so as to get significant information that will make it possible to prevent further terrorist attacks. At the same time he teaches others, who cannot be trusted to use such methods only when necessary, that they must always treat prisoners humanely and that humane treatment rules out the very methods that he is instructing the elite to use.

Can such a distinction be defended? It is difficult for a consequentialist to defend the view that torture is always wrong—consider the famous 'ticking bomb' scenario in which torturing a terrorist, or even the terrorist's child, is the only way to prevent a nuclear bomb exploding in a city that will kill millions and maim or sicken millions more. But it is also plausible that, without a general prohibition on torture, military and police personal will frequently torture people in a far wider range of situations, and that all of these instances of torture will be unjustifiable. Whether it is possible to find a few people who will, after the appropriate training, be able to restrict the use of torture or other inhumane techniques to the very rare occasions when it is clearly justified is an empirical question on which we do not need to offer an opinion. It is enough if we can show that, on the basis of facts that are not obviously false, it could be right to teach one group something that it would be wrong to teach another group.

3. *'[I]t may be conceivably right to do, if it can be done with comparative secrecy, what it would be wrong to do in the face of the world'*

A soldier is brought before a general, charged with desertion in battle, for which the mandatory penalty is a long term of imprisonment. The soldier admits that he did desert, but begs for pardon, saying that he does not want his two small children to grow up without a father. Only one or two other people, whom the general feels he can trust, know that the soldier deserted. The general assigns the soldier to duties behind the front line, telling him he must never say a word to anyone about deserting, or being charged with desertion. He tells his administrative officers to destroy all records of the charge and forget all about it.

Assume that the army is fighting a just war and if it were to become generally known that the fathers of small children may desert with impunity, this would materially hinder the ability of the army to fight, and that this would have bad consequences. Therefore it would have been wrong for the general to allow everyone to know of his decision regarding the deserter. It may still have been right for him to make that decision. Two children will have their father at home, the soldier and his wife will have a much better life, and the army's fighting ability is not materially impaired.

4. *'And even, if perfect secrecy can be reasonably expected, [it may conceivably be right to do] what it would be wrong to recommend by private advice and example'*

This is the most puzzling of Sidgwick's categories of esoteric morality. How is it possible that an act might be right to do, but not right even to recommend, in private, by advice or example? In critical discussions of utilitarianism the following case is sometimes raised: a surgeon has to do a delicate brain operation on a patient who happens to be the ideal organ donor for four other patients in the hospital, each of whom will die shortly unless they receive, respectively, a heart, a liver, and—for two of them—a kidney. The doctor is highly skilled, and is confident of her ability to carry out the brain surgery successfully. If she does, her patient will lead a more or less normal life. But because the operation is a delicate one, no one could blame her, or have any reason to suspect anything, if the patient were to die on the operating table. Moreover, the hospital is experienced in organ transplantation, and the surgeon knows that if the patient were to die, the recipients of the patient's organs would soon be able to go home and lead a more or less normal life. The surgeon knows no other details about her patient or the other patients, such as whether they are married, have children, or are about to discover a cure for cancer. In these circumstances, critics of utilitarianism say, the utilitarian must think that the doctor ought to kill her patient, since in that way four lives will be saved, and only one lost, and this must be better than four dying and only one being saved. But, so the objection runs, it is obviously morally wrong for the surgeon to kill her patient, and any moral theory that says the contrary must be rejected.

We agree that the utilitarian must accept that, in these circumstances, the right thing for the surgeon to do would be to kill the one to save the four, but we do not agree that this means that utilitarianism should be rejected. We think, on the contrary, that the appearance of unacceptability here comes from the fact that this is one of those rare cases in which the action is right only if perfect secrecy can be expected. Moreover, it is not an action that should be recommended to others. We realize that there is a paradox in saying both that the action is right, and that it should not be recommended, since to say that it is right *is,* in a sense, to recommend it. We shall come back to this point shortly.

It is easy to see why in the transplant case, like the deserter case, it would be disastrous for it to become generally known that doing what the doctor did was regarded as right. The doctor's act violates some core principles of medical ethics. It is contrary to the ancient rule *primum, non nocere* ('first, do not harm') which tells doctors to give priority to not harming patients. That rule is said to encourage humility in doctors, reminding them of their fallibility and the power they have to cause harm. In contrast, encouraging doctors to believe that they are justified in killing one patient to save others will only reinforce their occupational tendency to arrogance and may lead them to do what is wrong more often than it leads them to do what is right. Moreover, killing a patient is the most flagrant breach imaginable of the ethics of the doctor–patient relationship, which is founded on the patient's trust in the doctor to put the interests of the patient first, and the necessity for the doctor to live up to that trust. If patients believed that doctors might kill them in order to help other patients, they would be unable to have confidence in their doctors, they would become fearful about going to hospital, and their health would suffer.

Given the widespread damage that would flow from general acceptance of a doctor killing a patient to benefit others, and the extreme rarity of the circumstances in which killing one patient could benefit several others, we think it obvious that a rule absolutely prohibiting such acts by doctors is justified. In this respect this case is like the ticking bomb justification for torture. Both are hypothetical cases that are unlikely to arise. But would the transplant case also be one in which it is wrong to recommend, even privately, that someone should act in that way? One factor here is the damage that would be done if the act were to become public. Of our four examples, it seems likely that this would be greatest in the transplant case, whereas the benefit in that case would be much less than in the ticking bomb scenario. And of course, whatever one may say about hypothetical cases, in reality the more often a doctor kills one patient to save several others, the more likely it is that eventually this will become known. When considering the transplant case as a hypothetical case in which we can know that perfect secrecy will be preserved and the doctor is so self-disciplined that she will not be led by her success in this instance to continue the practice of killing patients in other, more risky, situations, the utilitarian can hardly deny that what the doctor did was right. In the real world, however, we do not have such perfect foreknowledge, doctors may have flaws in their character, and it is likely to be better to say, not only in public, but also as a matter of private advice, that no doctor should ever contemplate killing a patient who wants to live. One way to put that would be to say that patients have rights that doctors must always respect. Although such statements are often cast in the form of absolute moral rules, utilitarians can support it for the reasons just given. This adds a further response utilitarians can make to the objection we considered in Chapter 5, that they fail to take seriously the separateness of persons.

As Sidgwick's examples show, esoteric morality takes distinct forms, requiring varying degrees of secrecy in different circumstances. Sidgwick is correct to maintain that utilitarians must accept some examples of esoteric morality as justified in each of the categories that he describes, and we have sought to provide suitable examples. But is the fact that utilitarianism implies esoteric morality a damaging objection to utilitarianism, or simply an implication that utilitarians can and should embrace?

4. The Publicity Condition

Some people think that the fact that something *would* be wrong if it were done openly shows that it *is* wrong, even if done in secret. Rawls endorses something like this view, as does Bernard Gert, for they both make it a condition of something being a normative theory that it be public. Rawls asserts that, from a contractarian standpoint, it is natural to see the choice of ethical principles as incorporating a 'publicity condition'. In choosing principles of justice, for instance, 'The parties assume that they are choosing principles for a public conception of justice.' Although Rawls here refers to principles of justice, he also says that the condition applies 'for the choice of all ethical principles and not only for those of justice'. This is, for Rawls, linked to the fact that the moral principles that apply to institutions are more basic than those that apply to the actions of individuals.[11] Bernard Gert is another advocate of a publicity condition. As we saw in Chapter 3, he defines morality as 'an informal public system that applies to all rational persons'. By 'public system' he means that 'all those whose behavior is to be judged by the system, understand it, and know what kind of behavior the system prohibits, requires, discourages, encourages and allows'. Gert holds that: 'Hardly anyone denies that morality must be such that a person who adopts it must also propose its adoption by everyone.'[12]

Sidgwick denied it, and we deny it, for the simple reason that such a definition of ethics, or morality, unduly narrows the most important practical question it is possible to ask. As we saw in Chapter 1, in the first sentence of *The Methods of Ethics* Sidgwick defines a 'method of ethics' as 'any rational procedure by which we determine what individual human beings "ought"—or what it is "right" for them—to do, or to seek to realise by voluntary action' (*ME* 1). Note here the reference to 'individual human beings'. It seems that Rawls and Gert want to define ethics as 'any rational procedure by which we determine what a community of human beings ought to take as a standard of right or wrong for the voluntary actions of its members'. That simply

---

[11] Rawls, *A Theory of Justice*, 112.
[12] Gert, *Morality*, 8–11.

rules out of court what is surely a proper normative question: whether it is sometimes ethically justifiable to do what will, if and only if it remains secret, have best consequences. To answer that question we need substantive moral argument, not a definitional *fiat*.

A defender of the Rawls-Gert definition might claim that we can't define concepts in whatever manner we like. Isn't it just *true* that every society has its own morality, and as any anthropologist will tell us, morality is a social institution, not a matter of individual judgment? Here we have to be careful to distinguish descriptive claims from normative ones. Descriptively, it may be true that the morality of any society is its collective, shared code of behaviour. That's the kind of thing an anthropologist may say, and in that sense we have no objection to it. But if we are asking what we ought to do, we are asking a normative question that no anthropologist's account of the nature of morality can answer. At most it can give us what R. M. Hare called an 'inverted commas' sense of what we 'ought' to do.[13] This no more determines what we ought to do—in the full-blooded, normative sense of the term—than rules of etiquette determine to whom we ought to speak without an introduction. We still need to decide whether we should act in accordance with that shared code.

To avoid misunderstanding, we will add that to reject the view that we ought always to act on a rule that can be part of a public system of morality is not to reject Sidgwick's axiom of justice, that 'it cannot be right for A to treat B in a manner in which it would be wrong for B to treat A, merely on the ground that they are two different individuals, and without there being any difference between the natures or circumstances of the two which can be stated as a reasonable ground for difference of treatment' (*ME* 380). People who want to practise esoteric morality should ask themselves if they are willing to agree that anyone else should do the same when in relevantly similar circumstances. But one relevantly similar circumstance is the fact that the act is very likely to remain secret.

Like Rawls, Thomas Scanlon is a contractarian; but unlike Rawls, he does not endorse the publicity condition, as such. Instead, in *What*

---

[13]   Hare, *The Language of Morals*, 124–6, 163–5.

we Owe to Each Other, he asserts that 'thinking about right and wrong is, at the most basic level, thinking about what could be justified to others on grounds that they, if appropriately motivated, could not reasonably reject'.[14] Scanlon's emphasis on 'justification *to others*' is the distinctive element of his approach to morality. He tells us that thinking about what could be justified to others goes beyond a mere concern that one's actions should be morally justifiable and it does so in a way that appears to exclude the possibility of esoteric morality. In *On What Matters,* Parfit draws on this aspect of Scanlon's theory in arguing that Scanlonian contractualism provides us with grounds for rejecting act utilitarianism (although he is careful not to say that these grounds are conclusive). Parfit discusses a case we have also used in this chapter as an example of an act that may be right to do in secret, but not right to recommend, even in private: that of the doctor who, by secretly killing one of his patients, can use that patient's organs to save the lives of five other patients. Assuming that the consequences of the act becoming known would be so bad as to outweigh the net saving of four lives, Parfit argues:

But when we apply some Contractualist formula, such as the Kantian or Scanlonian Formulas, we don't consider particular acts on their own. We ask which are the principles that everyone could rationally choose, or that no one could reasonably reject, if we were choosing the principles that everyone would accept. In answering *this* question, we must take into account the effects of everyone's accepting, and being known to accept, these principles.[15]

What needs to be demonstrated, however, is that what Parfit describes as '*this* question' is indeed the question that the doctor ought to be asking. Many philosophers have been interested in the question how we should determine the public standards of right or wrong on which a community should agree. That is a legitimate and interesting question to ask, but it is not the only question that ethics can investigate, and it is not the question with which Sidgwick began *The Methods.* 'What ought I to do?' is a distinct question from: 'What are the principles that it would be reasonable to accept, if everyone were to accept, and be known to accept, these principles?' At the very least,

---

[14] Scanlon, *What we Owe to Each Other,* 5.
[15] Parfit, *On What Matters,* Volume One,. 363–4; italics in original.

an argument is needed to show that the former question does lead to the latter.

5. Should we Follow the Best Moral Code for the Real World?

The opening sentence of Brad Hooker's *Ideal Code, Real World* sets up a challenge to esoteric morality: 'Shouldn't we try to live by the moral code whose communal acceptance would, as far as we can tell, have the best consequences?' Hooker apparently sees this as an open question, for here at least he eschews the easy answer 'Yes, because that is what it means to act morally'. Later in the book, when explicitly considering the challenge that Sidgwick's account of esoteric morality presents to his moral theory, Hooker gives a moral, not a conceptual, response, saying 'Such paternalistic duplicity would be morally wrong, even if it would maximize the aggregate good.'[16]

In maintaining that elitism of the kind endorsed by Sidgwick is objectionable, Hooker goes so far as to say that he would stand by this view, even if the world consisted of a million imbeciles who could understand only ultra-simple rules, and one genius who could grasp much more complex rules, and better consequences would result from the genius following the more complex rules. Nevertheless, says Hooker, the genius should follow the same rules as the rest.[17] Exemption is only granted to the genius if following the simple rules would result in disaster. We'll return to this exemption shortly. Meanwhile, why does Hooker think that the genius should follow the simple rules, although she could do more good by following the complex ones? He mentions the convenience of having just one code for internalization by everyone, but that can't be the major reason, for we can suppose that the good the genius could do by acting on the more complex reasons would outweigh the inconvenience she would suffer by having her own set of rules. At this point Hooker swings towards a conceptual answer to the question, referring to 'the idea that morality

---

[16] Hooker, *Ideal Code, Real World*, 85.
[17] Hooker, *Ideal Code, Real World*, 86. Hooker attributes the objection to an unpublished comment made by Margaret Little.

should be thought of as a *collective, shared* code'. He acknowledges that this thought is not a 'peculiarly consequentialist one'—indeed, we would say that it is not a consequentialist one at all—but he adds that 'we may favour one version of rule consequentialism over any other because this version coheres best both with our *general* beliefs about morality and with our beliefs about what morality requires *in particular cases*'.[18]

Hooker is here referring to his endorsement of reflective equilibrium. In the introduction to *Ideal Code, Real World* he lists it among the methodological criteria on which he will base his argument, and states it as follows: 'Moral theories must cohere with (i.e. economically systematize, or, if no system is available, at least endorse) the moral convictions we have after careful reflection.'[19] A few pages later he restates this as 'We should evaluate rival moral theories in terms of their ability to cohere with the convictions in which we have the most confidence after due reflection.'[20]

Who are the 'we' to whom Hooker is referring? There are two possibilities. One is that it refers to the general public—in other words, that we should evaluate rival moral theories in terms of their abilities to match what Sidgwick called 'commonsense morality' or what philosophers nowadays sometimes call 'folk morality'. The other possibility is that 'we' refers to those of us who are evaluating various moral theories in order to decide which one to accept.

If Hooker is referring to the general public, we reject the idea that the test of a sound moral theory should be how well it coheres with the moral convictions of the general public, even after 'careful reflection'. For reasons that we discussed earlier, in Chapters 4 and 7, encouraging members of the general public to reflect carefully on their moral convictions is all very well, but it is unlikely to diminish to any significant extent the influence of a variety of factors that are irrelevant to the soundness of a moral theory, including false religious beliefs, cultural and ethnic prejudices, and the innate predispositions that are a legacy of the process of millions of years of evolutionary selection.

[18] Hooker, *Ideal Code, Real World*, 88.
[19] Hooker, *Ideal Code, Real World*, 4.
[20] Hooker, *Ideal Code, Real World*, 12.

If, on the other hand, Hooker is referring to those of us who are evaluating the various moral theories—in other words, people who read and discuss *Ideal Code, Real World*—then the appeal to reflective equilibrium is otiose. Of course we should evaluate rival moral theories in terms of their ability to cohere with the convictions in which we have the most confidence after due reflection. The due reflection is what we are doing right now, and for philosophers and anyone else capable of considering the arguments we are presenting, to say that we accept a moral theory just *is* to say that it is the one that, after going through this process, coheres with the convictions in which we have most confidence. Because we are philosophers discussing what fundamental normative theory we should accept, everything is at least open to discussion. If our firmest conviction is that we should do whatever will have the best consequences, and after due reflection this conviction remains firmer than the idea that we should always avoid paternalism and duplicity; and if in particular cases where duplicity has better consequences than honesty, we still think we should do what has the best consequences, then Hooker's appeal to reflective equilibrium gives us no reason to accept his version of rule consequentialism nor to reject esoteric morality. We are not trying to match our theory with common moral judgments: it's only our own convictions that have to be coherent. Hooker may, of course, have different convictions. To the extent that he does, he is not a consequentialist and that is a fundamental point of difference between us.

We want to forestall one possible response. In saying that the best normative theory does not have to match the moral convictions of the general public, we are not saying that these convictions are irrelevant to moral decisions, or can generally be ignored. As we have seen earlier in this chapter, Sidgwick warned utilitarians that they cannot ignore anything that may have an impact on the consequences of their actions, and the moral convictions of ordinary people will have an impact on the consequences of our actions in a wide variety of fields, including the extent to which useful moral rules are observed. We entirely agree with Hooker that in proposing or promoting a moral rule for general acceptance in a society, it is vital to know whether it coheres with the prior moral convictions of most people, and hence has good prospects of easy acceptance, or clashes with these prior moral convictions, and so runs a high risk of rejection. In that sense, these moral convictions are data that we must take into account in deciding what we ought to do. But that is a very different thing from giving them probative force in deciding which normative theory we should accept.

As we already noted, Hooker's version of rule consequentialism allows us to breach rules when doing so is the only way to avoid disaster.[21] Indeed, Hooker believes that one of the most important rules that should be in a moral code is a rule telling people to prevent disasters. We need to know, of course, what is to count as a 'disaster'. In order to keep rule consequentialism distinct from act consequentialism, Hooker needs to maintain some conceptual space between his 'avoid disaster' rule, and the act consequentialist rule that we should break other rules any time doing so would maximize the good. In responding to an objection from Richard Arneson, Hooker shows that he is prepared to shrink this space significantly. Here is Arneson's objection:

In war, soldiers fighting for a just cause ought to stand by their post when attacked, unless outnumbered by attacking enemy so that even stout defence would be futile. Suppose this rule, followed by nearly everybody, would produce ideal results. But the rule in fact is not internalized by the military forces fighting for a just cause in a particular war. The enemy have attacked and most of your fellow troops have run away. You can stand and fight, in conformity with the ideal rule, or you can run and live to fight another day. The consequences of conformity to the rule would not be disastrous, but would be decidedly negative. You will die and gain very little if anything for your side... Common sense morality, which holds that the obligation to obey hypothetically useful rules is sensitive to the actual degree to which others are complying here and now, surely says one should run and live to fight another day. Act consequentialism to its credit says the same. Rule consequentialism, even sophisticated rule consequentialism with the disaster avoidance proviso added, would have to hold that one ought to stand and fight and die. So much the worse for sophisticated rule consequentialism.[22]

In his reply, Hooker admits that his account of what is a disaster is vague, but suggests that 'Perhaps... you are not required to stand by your post when this would do your side no good but would be

---

[21] See Hooker, *Ideal Code, Real World*, 86, 98–9.

[22] Cited by Hooker, 'Reply to Arneson and McIntyre', 270–1. Arneson, 'Sophisticated Rule Consequentionalism', 239.

disastrous for you'.[23] That seems reasonable, in itself, but what does it do to Hooker's objection to esoteric morality? Let's combine Arneson's example with the case of the million imbeciles and the one genius. Regrettably the imbeciles are too stupid to decide when stoutly defending their posts has some chance of producing good results, and when it is futile. Attempts to get them to internalize a 'prevent disaster' rule have proven unsuccessful, because if they are given permission to use their own judgment about when a rule needs to be broken in order to prevent a disaster, the slightest danger leads them to sense that disaster is imminent, and they abandon their posts. The only way in which the nation can defend itself against unjust aggression from a tyrannical neighbour is to get its overwhelmingly imbecilic army to internalize the rule: 'Stand by your post at all times, unless you are ordered to retreat'.

Serving among these imbeciles, however, is the genius, who can be highly confident of her judgment about the utility, or futility, of standing by one's post when under attack. One day the platoon of imbeciles with which she serves comes under attack. Correctly judging resistance futile, she runs away, thus saving her life. When she reaches safety, she happens to encounter a television crew and the journalist asks her what happened to her comrades. She says that they bravely followed the rule 'Stand by your post at all times, unless you are ordered to retreat' and since no retreat was ordered, presumably have all been killed. The journalist then asks her why she did not follow the same rule. What would Hooker have her say? That she followed the disaster avoidance rule? But for her to say this on television would fatally weaken the internalization by 90 per cent of the population of the 'Stand by your post' rule and this would itself have disastrous consequences. So perhaps, in order to prevent disaster, the genius should lie, and invent some plausible story about her escape? While doing so she can tell herself that she is only doing this because the audience will not be able to understand the more complex moral rule on which she rightly acted. But now she is practising esoteric morality.

---

[23] See Hooker, *Ideal Code, Real World*, 133–4; Hooker, 'Reply to Arneson and McIntyre', 273.

Although the example of the single genius and the million imbeciles is far-fetched, the point is a general one: in order to prevent a disaster, we may have to do something that, if it were to become known, would itself bring about a disaster of a different kind. So the 'avoid disaster' rule may *require* us to practise 'paternalistic duplicity'. Hooker could stand by his original claim that the esoteric morality Sidgwick supports 'would be morally wrong, even if it would maximize the aggregate good', but he needs to add 'unless it is necessary to prevent disaster'. He will, however, have to withdraw his claim that his form of rule consequentialism 'rules out the objectionable elitism and duplicity from the start' because that implies that elitism and duplicity can never be right, even when it would prevent disaster.

So Hooker's approach can justify esoteric morality, but only to prevent disaster, not simply to promote the good. How big a difference does this leave between his rule consequentialism and act consequentialism? Remember that on Hooker's view the death of a single innocent person may be a disaster, so there are many acts that can be construed as necessary to avoid disaster. Moreover, as we shall see in more detail shortly, act consequentialists have many good reasons for favouring transparency in most situations, and hence for not accepting esoteric morality when—apart from the risks of not acting and living in a transparent manner—it produces a modest net benefit. In practice the difference between the circumstances in which the two theories permit esoteric morality will be quite narrow.

Hooker, in defending the publicity condition against our critique, points to two features of morality that he believes support his position. The first draws on Mill's statement that 'We do not call anything wrong, unless we mean to imply that a person ought to be punished in some way for doing it; if not by law, by the opinion of his fellow creatures; if not by opinion, by the reproaches of his own conscience.'[24] Hooker sets out his argument as follows:

> 1st premise: Moral wrongness ought to be identified with what agents ought to encounter hostile reactive attitudes for doing without excuse.

---

[24] Hooker, 'Publicity in Morality'. The quotation is from Mill's *Utilitarianism,* ch. 5.

2nd premise: What agents ought to encounter hostile reactive attitudes for doing without excuse ought to be determined (insofar as it can be determined) by public, rather than secret, moral rules.

Conclusion: Moral wrongness ought to be determined (insofar as it can be determined) by public, rather than secret, moral rules.

Mill's statement appears, on its face, to be a description of common usage of the word 'wrong'. We saw in Chapter 2 that Sidgwick argues that it is not an adequate account of what we mean by the term.[25] Putting that problem aside, however, if Hooker were to read Mill's statement as a description of common usage, his argument would commit the fallacy of moving from 'is' to 'ought'. Instead he goes beyond Mill's words and reads it normatively, as a statement about how moral wrongness ought to be identified. In addition, Hooker ignores the final clause of Mill's statement, 'if not by opinion, by the reproaches of his own conscience'. This truncated 'Millian' claim should be rejected. Sidgwick's argument, and ours, is that there are situations in which the right thing to do is to breach a widely held moral rule, but to do it in secret. If, as a result of unforeseeable bad luck, the breach of the rule becomes known, then, at least in some of these cases, the agent ought to encounter a hostile public reaction to the breach, for in the absence of such a reaction, people will come to believe that the rule does not hold at all, which will have bad consequences. (One way of thinking about this is to say that, although the agent is not blameworthy, in the sense of deserving blame, he ought to be blamed, in the sense that blaming him will have good consequences.) But the fact that the agent ought to be blamed does not mean that the action was wrong. So we cannot identify 'wrong' with 'ought to encounter hostile reactive attitudes'. It is more plausible to believe that we can identify wrong with 'ought to encounter hostile reactive attitudes or the reproaches of his own conscience' but now we can see that reading the statement normatively with its final clause risks making it trivial—for we can then ask 'for what ought we to be reproached by our own conscience?' and the obvious answer is: 'when we have done something wrong'.

[25] See p. 36–7.

The second feature of morality to which Hooker points, in defending the publicity condition, is that of impartial and interpersonal justifiability. 'If moral rules must be suitable for justifying our behaviour to one another,' he writes, 'then they must be suitable for public acceptance.'[26] But there is a difference between a rule being impartially and interpersonally justifiable, and it being publicly justifiable. In the case of the genius serving with the platoon of imbeciles, the genius would be able to justify her action impartially and interpersonally, as long as she was speaking to people who were sufficiently intelligent to apply successfully the disaster avoidance rule on which she acted. She is prevented from doing that only by the low intelligence of the population in which she lives. We do not think it essential to a moral rule that it must be possible to justify it to everyone in the population, irrespective of his or her level of intelligence.

6. A Consequentialist Approach to Publicity

We have rejected the idea that ethics is necessarily public, and we have shown that Hooker's defence of rule consequentialism does not provide a sound basis for rejecting esoteric morality. We have offered examples of where we believe esoteric morality is justifiable. Nevertheless there are good reasons why consequentialists should share in the broad support for transparency in ethics, and hence should avoid esoteric morality in most circumstances.

i. The Benefits of a Shared Code

It is plausible to hold that, if a society is to work well, it needs to have a shared moral code that its members can internalize, follow, and expect others to follow. Many studies indicate that trust is an important factor in assuring social welfare.[27]

ii. The Benefits of Open Discussion

Transparency permits open discussion and criticism of rules and policies that are being considered for implementation. To accept a morality

---

[26] Hooker, 'Publicity in Morality', 117.
[27] See e.g. Fukuyama, Trust.

that is only for the elite implies that we are permitted to manipulate those who are not part of the elite, in order to produce the best consequences. When we do so, we are unable to seek the opinions of those who we are manipulating on the policies we are actually implementing. This is the essence of Bernard Williams's scathing description of esoteric morality as 'Government House utilitarianism'.[28] We imagine the white colonial administrators sitting around in their cane armchairs under the ceiling fans, discussing how best to rule the 'natives'. They may discuss their policies among themselves, and with the imperial government back home, but not with those who are most directly affected by them, the local people themselves. Under these circumstances they will have a tendency to convince themselves that what is in the best interests of the imperial power is the right thing to do. The danger is great that it will all go wrong because of the absence of exchange of ideas that could have happened if the policies had been transparent.

iii. The Dangers of Elitism

Even if the lack of transparency does not lead to evils in any way comparable to those of oppressive colonial regimes, there are good grounds for objecting to dividing society into an elite and the masses. Whether it is nobles over peasants, whites over blacks, capitalists over workers, Bolsheviks over the masses, or men over women, we know that those who are part of the elite will feel superior and have no difficulty in justifying, in their own terms, granting themselves privileges that in no way benefit—and often grievously harm—those they consider beneath them.

iv. The Public Nature of Moral Education

We must also remember that morality is, at least in part, a social institution that exists only because each generation of children is educated to accept it. Since education is a public process, this cannot be education in an esoteric morality, at least not unless the children of a special elite were to be educated in secret, which would have the undesirable implications just mentioned. So a large part of morality must consist

---

[28] Williams, 'A Critique of Utilitarianism', 139.

of rules or principles that are known by everyone, including teachers and children.

When we deceive people about the reasons why they should act in a certain way, we make it impossible for them to develop their critical capacities, at least in respect of those reasons for action about which they are being deceived. The ideal kind of political entity, we may well think, is one in which all citizens are capable of deliberating on the reasons for acting and for adopting particular policies. If they are unaware of the true reasons for the principles and policies they are following, they will not learn these habits of deliberating, or will not learn them well.

Consequentialism generally accepts that it is desirable for a society to have a publicly accepted set of rules or principles that people internalize and generally follow. Both act and rule consequentialists can agree that it is important for people to be able to rely on the moral rules and to know that others will follow them—society will function better if there is a generally accepted set of rules than if there is not. The two forms of consequentialism differ on when exceptions from these rules can be allowed, and whether such exceptions should be made public or not.

7. Consequentialism as a Criterion of Right Action versus Consequentialism as a Guide to Action

As we have acknowledged at the outset, consequentialists may, to bring about the best consequences, need to discourage others from embracing consequentialism. Though they are ready to justify their criterion of moral rightness—the best possible consequence—and the correctness of consequentialism as a criterion of right action, they may state that people should adopt other criteria (or *also* other criteria) as a guide to action as that will produce the best consequences.

Though we do believe that act consequentialism is the right moral theory, we agree with Hooker that 'Maximize the good' is not the best decision procedure.[29] For the reasons that Sidgwick and Hare gave,

---

[29] Hooker writes: 'if we had just the one rule "Maximize the good" sooner or later awareness of this would be become widespread. And becoming aware of this would undermine

we should encourage people to keep to a publicly known set of rules, to be truthful, to improve their character, and not to focus on maximizing the good all the time. But it may not be enough to say: 'What you should aim at is to maximize the good, but in order to achieve it do not think about that all the time, try to follow the rules, work on your character, etc.' It is at least *possible* that in order to achieve better results we have to keep the consequentialist aim itself secret.

To this line of thought, Bernard Williams objects:

> If utilitarianism...determines nothing of how thought in the world is conducted, demanding merely that the way in which it is conducted must be for the best, then I hold that utilitarianism has disappeared, and that the residual position is not worth calling utilitarianism. If utility could be globally put together at all...then there might be maximal total utility from the transcendental standpoint, even though nobody in the world accepted utilitarianism at all.[30]

There are three main reasons why Williams's critique misses the mark. First, as Parfit observes, even if a theory is self-effacing (that is, it tells us 'that we should try to believe, not itself, but some other theory'[31]), this does not make it self-defeating, because:

> It is not the aim of a theory to be believed. If we personify theories, and pretend that they have aims, the aim of a theory is not to be believed, but to be true, or to be the best theory. That a theory is self-effacing does not show that it is not the best theory.[32]

A second objection to Williams's critique is that, as Toby Ord has argued, even if utilitarianism does dictate that everyone should publicly follow non-utilitarian principles, this would not mean that utilitarianism 'determines nothing of how thought in the world is conducted'. The requirement that 'thought in the world' is conducted

---

people's ability to rely confidently on others to behave in agreed-upon ways. Trust would break down. In short, terrible consequences would result from the public expectation that this rule would prescribe killing, stealing, and so on when such acts would maximize the good.' *Ideal Code, Real World*, 94.

[30] Williams, 'A Critique of Utilitarianism', 135. See also Scheffler: 'There is a persistent feeling of discomfort generated by the idea of a moral theory which is willing to require widespread ignorance of its own principles': *The Rejection of Consequentialism*, 48–9.

[31] Parfit, *Reasons and Persons*, 40.

[32] Parfit, *Reasons and Persons*, 24.

in such a way as to lead to the best outcome *is* a way of determining how it is conducted.[33]

Our third reason for rejecting Williams's critique is that it is, in any case, unrealistic to think that it would follow from a consequentialist theory that no one should try to act in accordance with its criterion of rightness. With Parfit, we believe that a consequentialist theory is likely to be only partially self-effacing (and also partly esoteric).[34] There are, and will be, people who believe in the principle of consequentialism and its rightness and who try to act to maximize general good. We doubt that the world would be a better place if no one were a consequentialist. Utilitarians have made the world a better place: Bentham, Mill, and Sidgwick are among these, along with many other utilitarian reformers. In addition, as Peter Railton argues, consequentialism is more flexible than many deontological theories. It allows us to avoid any sort of 'self-defeating decision procedure worship' by taking into account the consequences of using particular decision procedures.[35] Finally, Parfit has suggested another, and especially powerful, reason why we should not adopt a moral outlook that entirely rejects consequentialism. Even if in our present circumstances we could bring about better consequences by wholly rejecting consequentialism and taking up some other moral view that does not have as its goal bringing about the best possible state of affairs, circumstances may change in future in such a way that following the morality we have adopted will lead to catastrophe; perhaps, for example, to a nuclear war. If we had succeeded in making consequentialism totally self-effacing, so that we were no longer even aware of the fact that we had adopted the other morality in order to bring about the best consequences, we would not be able to avoid this disaster, because we would think it wrong to do what it is necessary for us to do.[36]

[33] Ord, 'Beyond Action', 101–2.

[34] According to Parfit, consequentialism could be a partially self-effacing theory, if it prescribes that some people reject it, and it could also be esoteric, if it tells those who still believe in it that they should not 'enlighten the ignorant majority'. See *Reasons and Persons*, 41–2.

[35] Railton, 'Alienation, Consequentialism, and the Demands of Morality', 156.

[36] Parfit, *Reasons and Persons*, 41–2.

8. Different Codes, Different Moral Judgments

Suppose that we believe that generally people will produce better outcomes if they act according to the rule 'Do not lie' and so we encourage
someone to follow this rule. We fear that if we tell him to break the rule
when by doing so he can bring about better consequences, he will make
too many mistakes in his judgments, so we tell him to follow the rule
under all circumstances. As a result he doesn't lie even when by doing so
he could have saved an innocent person's life. How should we judge his
action? Did he do wrong, because he failed to do the act that would have
had the best consequences? Or did he do what he ought to have done,
because he obeyed the principle that he was, rightly, advised to follow?

Hooker regards the issue these questions raise as an objection to
global consequentialism; that is, to the view that everything, including acts, is to be judged right or wrong by whether it leads to the best
consequences.[37] As he puts it:

> Suppose, on the whole and in the long run, the best decision procedure for you to
> accept is one that leads you to do act x now. But suppose also that in fact the act
> with the best consequences in this situation is not x but y. So global consequential-
> ism tells you to use the best possible decision procedure but also not to do the act
> picked out by this decision procedure. That seems paradoxical.[38]

Is this really so paradoxical? Global consequentialism, like act consequentialism, makes separate judgments about decision procedures
and about acts. It may be that, over a lifetime, we will bring about
better consequences by adopting a decision procedure that will,
occasionally, lead us to do something that is not the optimal thing
to do. As far as the choice of decision procedure is concerned, that is
an unavoidable cost. It would not have been possible for us to adopt
a decision procedure that brought about better results. Of course,
if in some way we could know that it would be best to change our
decision procedure just for this occasion, we ought to do that. But
assuming we do not know that on this occasion our wisely chosen

---

[37] On global consequentialism, see Hooker, *Ideal Code, Real World*, 237 n. 306.

[38] Hooker, 'Rule Consequentialism'; different versions of this objection are made by
Streumer, 'Can Consequentialism Cover Everything?'; Crisp, 'Utilitarianism and the Life
of Virtue'; and Lang, 'A Dilemma for Objective Act-Utilitarianism'. For discussion, see Ord,
'Beyond Action'.

decision procedure is not going to lead us to do the act that will have the best consequences, or that even if we do know it, for some reason we are now locked into that decision procedure, then the situation is just what it is, and we have to accept it. Even if what we then do is, when viewed from an objective perspective, wrong, there is no blame attached to doing what does not bring about the best outcome, for we made the right decision regarding the choice of decision procedure, and given that decision, we may now be unable to do what will have the best consequences. For example, having been brought up to love our children, we now cannot give as much consideration to the children of strangers as we give to our own children. Sidgwick held, as we shall see in the next chapter, that whether someone should be praised or blamed depends on the consequences, in the circumstances in which we find ourselves, of praising and blaming. If that is right, then it is hard to see how it could have good consequences to blame someone for acting in accordance with the best decision procedure.

9. The Paradoxical Nature of Esoteric Morality

Sidgwick was aware that his conclusions are paradoxical. In public, he says, esoteric morality should be disavowed. Yet he has published a book in which he says that it is justified. So, now, have we. Admittedly, Sidgwick buried his doctrine near the back of a long work of philosophy, and our book is not likely to become a best-seller either. Most of you reading this will be philosophers, or students of philosophy, but you are also members of the public, and your resistance to esoteric morality is therefore the 'right' response, in the sense that it is good that you should have that response. We should be reluctant to embrace esoteric morality, and you should feel that there is something wrong with our conclusion. Arguably, we should not even have written this chapter; yet in a book on Sidgwick, to fail to discuss the topic of esoteric morality would be to leave the impression that on this issue Sidgwick's stance—and therefore utilitarianism in general—is indefensible. That impression could also have bad consequences. In the end, we have chosen to defend, in this relatively public manner, both utilitarianism and the view that sometimes we are right to do in secret what it would be wrong to do, or to advocate, in public.

11

Demandingness

1. Sidgwick on the Demands of Morality

That morality demands something from us is obvious. The very notion of 'moral obligation' or 'ought', Sidgwick notes, implies that we may do otherwise than the 'ought' prescribes (*ME* 217). This, in turn, means that morality asks us to do something that we may not want to do, or that may give rise to a conflict of motives. In this respect we are different from a god who always wills what is good or right, and to whom the concept of duty or obligation would not apply.

The question that is really of philosophical significance, therefore, is not whether morality demands something from us, but how demanding morality can be. Here the comparison between the demands of common sense morality and utilitarianism becomes a central issue. Sidgwick is aware of the fact that utilitarianism is sometimes charged with 'making exaggerated demands on human nature' (*ME* 87). The conflict is obvious when we realize that impartiality is the basis of utilitarianism and that the principle of benevolence tells us to seek the greatest possible goodness impartially. Common sense morality, on the other hand, stresses the special set of obligations that we have towards those close to us. It supports us in having feelings such as love and affection and even self-love, thus making morality relatively undemanding. Sidgwick faces this and similar problems in book IV of *The Methods,* in which he aims to defend utilitarianism from a variety of criticisms. With regard to the objection that it is too demanding, he seeks to show that, although in theory utilitarianism demands a lot from us, in practice its demands will differ little, if at all, from those of common sense.

The key to resolving the problem of the potentially excessive demands of utilitarianism lies in its own axiom. If our obligation is to maximize the general good, we should be interested in how best to do it in practice. When we ask that question we find, Sidgwick says, that 'the practical application of this theoretical impartiality of Utilitarianism is limited by several important considerations' (*ME* 431). First, each of us is likely to do better in obtaining his own happiness than in bringing about the happiness of strangers. We know what we need and want much better than we know what others need and want, so we maximize good on the whole by giving priority to our own happiness. Further, when we are happy ourselves, we are better able to increase the happiness of others. Sidgwick writes: 'it is under the stimulus of self-interest that the active energies of most men are most easily and thoroughly drawn out: and if this were removed, general happiness would be diminished by a serious loss of those means of happiness which are obtained by labour' (*ME* 431). Second, similar practical reasons apply when we look beyond our own interests. It is conducive to the utilitarian end that we first and foremost work for the happiness of those close to us, our family and friends. Close relations bring people pleasures, Sidgwick tell us, of the most 'intense and highly valued' kind. Moreover, people who are happy and satisfied with those relations are better able to be involved in activities that benefit strangers.

Utilitarianism thus supports the 'cultivation of affection' for special individuals. But how about encouraging a feeling 'more universal in its scope—charity, philanthropy, or (as it has been called) the "Enthusiasm of Humanity"'? (*ME* 434). Should not a utilitarian encourage others to cultivate such feelings? To this Sidgwick answers that most people can have strong feelings only towards a few people and 'if these were suppressed, what they would feel towards their fellow-creatures generally would be, as Aristotle says, "but a watery kindness" and a very feeble counterpoise to self-love: so that such specialised affections as the present organisation of society normally produces afford the best means of developing in most persons a more extended benevolence, to the degree to which they are capable of feeling it' (*ME* 434). Further, Sidgwick adds, the limits to our power or our knowledge mean that each of us, for the most part, is 'not in a position to do much good to more than a very small number of persons' and this is a sufficient reason for limiting our 'chief benevolent impulses'.

Sidgwick observes that we have developed certain ways of attaining general happiness by focusing on attaining the happiness of a small unit. So the whole society is better off if children are brought up and cared for in a small unit such as a family. On the other hand, we have special obligations to strangers under certain circumstances. Sidgwick takes the issue of helping the poor:

the main utilitarian reason why it is not right for every rich man to distribute his superfluous wealth among the poor, is that the happiness of all is on the whole most promoted by maintaining in adults generally (except married women), the expectation that each will be thrown on his own resources for the supply of his own wants. But if I am made aware that, owing to a sudden calamity that could not have been foreseen, another's resources are manifestly inadequate to protect him from pain or serious discomfort, the case is altered; my theoretical obligation to consider his happiness as much as my own becomes at once practical; and I am bound to make as much effort to relieve him as will not entail a greater loss of happiness to myself or others. If, however, the calamity is one which might have been foreseen and averted by proper care, my duty becomes more doubtful: for then by relieving him I seem to be in danger of encouraging improvidence in others. In such a case a Utilitarian has to weigh this indirect evil against the direct good of removing pain and distress... (ME 436)

If we follow this line of thought, how demanding the obligations of the rich to the poor are will depend on whether or not we find ourselves in a situation in which a calamity that could not have been foreseen or averted leaves others without the means to live without 'pain or serious discomfort'.

Sidgwick also seeks to narrow the differences between the utilitarian principle of benevolence and the morality of common sense by indicating that the latter can also be demanding. In the chapter on 'Philosophical Intuitionism' he acknowledges that the common sense reading of the virtue of benevolence does not meet the standard of impartiality implied by his axiom of rational benevolence. But, as we saw in Chapter 5, he argues that 'a "plain man", in a modern civilised society, if his conscience were fairly brought to consider the hypothetical question, whether it would be morally right for him to seek his own happiness on any occasion if it involved a certain sacrifice of the greater happiness of some other human being,—without any counterbalancing gain to any one else,—would answer unhesitatingly in the negative' (*ME* 382). As we noted in Chapter 5, in saying this, Sidgwick may have displayed his optimistic view of the average person's willingness to make impartial moral judgments.

When our moral obligations are highly demanding, utilitarian calculations can lead to paradoxical implications. Usually, we encourage people to do what is right and obligatory and blame those who fail to meet their obligations. Sidgwick points out this paradox when he discusses the relation between obligation and virtue and notices that there are virtuous acts that we do not regard as obligatory. Sidgwick notes, for example, that 'a Utilitarian must hold that it is always wrong for a man knowingly to do anything other than what he believes to be most conducive to Universal Happiness' (*ME* 492). In contrast, common sense morality might say that people who act in this way display excellence of character, but they are going beyond their duty, and we have no obligation to emulate them. For instance, Sidgwick says, in describing common sense morality: 'Certainly we should agree that a truly moral man cannot say to himself, "This is the best thing on the whole for me to do, but yet it is not my duty to do it though it is in my power": this would certainly seem to common sense an immoral paradox.' But at the same time 'there seem to be acts and abstinences which we praise as virtuous, without imposing them as duties upon all who are able to do them; as for a rich man to live very plainly and devote his income to works of public beneficence' (*ME* 220).

Utilitarianism, strictly speaking, lacks this distinction between doing what is our duty or obligation, and what is virtuous, or displays excellence of character. The distinction may, however, be useful and so a utilitarian can retain it for practical reasons. It seems 'natural' for us to compare our character or what we do to a certain 'average standard' and if anyone does more than this average standard we praise them, and refrain from blaming them even if they are doing less than they ought to be doing.

Sidgwick believes that there are two different questions to ask: 'what a man ought to do or forbear' and 'what other men ought to blame him for not doing or forbearing' (*ME* 221). The difference between these

questions can be explained in a number of ways. First of all, sometimes we cannot say whether a particular person has an obligation to
do something as we do not have sufficient knowledge of all the circumstances in which he is to act. 'Thus I may easily assure myself that
I ought to subscribe to a given hospital: but I cannot judge whether
my neighbour ought to subscribe, as I do not know the details of his
income and the claims which he is bound to satisfy' (*ME* 221). But a
more important explanation is that there are situations in which we
do not blame others because the practical outcome of our approbation
and disapprobation is important. Sidgwick suggests that we can best
promote moral progress by 'praising acts that are above the level of
ordinary practice, and confining our censure—at least if precise and
particular—to acts that fall clearly below this standard'. He adds that
the standard is inevitably vague, and will be different in different com-
munities with different average levels of morality. Teachers of morality
should seek to raise it continually (*ME* 221). Sidgwick returns to this
line of thinking later in *The Methods* when he is talking about dispositions and which ones we should support. Then he says that we should
distribute our praise of human qualities by considering primarily 'not
the usefulness of the quality, but the usefulness of the praise' (*ME* 428).

Sidgwick again comes back to this question much later in *The
Methods*, when considering it explicitly from a utilitarian standpoint.
Here he notes that 'human nature seems to require the double stimulus of praise and blame from others, in order to [achieve] the best
performance of duty that it can at present attain'[1] (*ME* 493). He then
points out that, 'since the pains of remorse and disapprobation are in
themselves to be avoided', utilitarianism will itself point against using
them, unless it is clear that using them will bring about a significant
addition to happiness. His conclusion is that:

it is reasonable for a Utilitarian to praise any conduct more felicific in its tendency
than what an average man would do under the given circumstances:—being aware
of course that the limit down to which praiseworthiness extends must be relative
to the particular state of moral progress reached by mankind generally in his age
and country; and that it is desirable to make continual efforts to elevate this standard. (*ME* 493)

---

[1] The sentence appears to lack a word, which we have suggested might be 'achieve'.

2. Is Demandingness a Decisive Objection to Utilitarianism?

Utilitarianism is widely regarded as demanding much more of us than other theories, and this has been pressed as an objection, sometimes even a decisive objection, to utilitarianism, or at least to act utilitarianism.[2] This charge against act utilitarianism comes both from other utilitarians, like Brandt or Hooker,[3] and from philosophers who are not utilitarians in their normative thinking, such as Williams, Scheffler, and Miller.[4] Brandt writes: 'Act-utilitarianism makes extreme and oppressive demands on the individual, so much so that it can hardly be taken seriously; like the Sermon on the Mount, it is a morality only for saints.'[5] He also quotes M. G. Singer who says that act utilitarianism leads to 'moral fanaticism, to the idea that no action is indifferent or trivial, that every occasion is momentous'. Some utilitarians have suggested that we should lower the standard, so that we are required to 'satisfice' rather than do what is best. We examined, and rejected, this option in Chapter 5 when we discussed the maximizing implications of Sidgwick's axiom of rational benevolence.

Utilitarianism's high demands are a result of its fundamental principle or axiom. The theory states that an act is right if and only if it impartially maximizes utility. Out of many possible actions only the one that has the best consequences is right; no 'good enough' action will do. Even if an agent has to sacrifice a lot, as long as his action will bring the best possible result overall, this is what he should do. We will explore two ways of defending utilitarianism against this objection. One follows Sidgwick's argument that, though in principle utilitarianism could be very demanding, in practice the requirements of utilitarianism may not be so different from those of common sense

---

[2] The demandingness objection is connected with two other issues that we have looked at closely in Ch. 5, i.e. the Integrity Objection, presented by Williams, and the Separateness of Persons objection.

[3] Hooker, *Ideal Code, Real World*, 149–58.

[4] Scheffler, *The Rejection of Consequentialism*; Miller, 'Beneficence, Duty, and Distance'; Cullitty, *The Moral Demands of Affluence*; Murphy, *Moral Demands in Nonideal Theory*.

[5] Brandt, *A Theory of the Good and the Right*, 276–7. For a similar view, with some qualifications, see Wolf, 'Moral Saints', 428.

morality. This is in part the case because utilitarians must, if they are to succeed in maximizing good on the whole, take into account the natural dispositions and capacities that people have. Pressing the ultimate utilitarian standard in too direct a form may be counterproductive. This argument may have been sound in Sidgwick's time, but as we shall discuss in more detail shortly, the world has changed since then, in ways that are relevant to his argument.

The other way of defending utilitarianism is to show that the fact that it is highly demanding cannot be an argument against the theory. First, it can be demonstrated that many other normative theories are also highly demanding—Kantian theory or contractualism, for example—and so a high degree of demandingness is not unique to utilitarianism.[6] But this argument goes further than that. Even if it were true that utilitarianism demands greater sacrifices from us than any other moral theory, this would not refute it. After all, demands arise from facts about the world, such as the fact that millions of people die each year from hunger and easily treatable diseases.[7] That a moral theory has highly demanding implications may be a result of a clash between the morally undesirable state of the world and our own evolved human nature. On the one hand, we have a very imperfect world, in which billions of people live under conditions far more difficult than those faced by most of those who discuss whether moral theories are too demanding. On the other hand, it is natural, even if not rational, for us to think mostly of ourselves and of those with whom we have close personal relationships. As we saw in Chapter 7, however, what is natural is not necessarily right or even rational. We should reject what is partial in us and accept that, in the world in which we live, people who are comfortably off ought to be doing a lot to improve the world, whether they like it or not.

Finally, if the demandingness of utilitarianism follows from its fundamental principle or axiom, and if the case we have made in this book for that principle is sound, then it is a mistake to think

---

[6]   See Ashford and Mulgan, 'Contractualism'.

[7]   For this argument see Ashford, 'Utilitarianism, Integrity and Partiality', and the same author's 'The Demandingness of Scanlon's Contractualism'.

that because the theory has implications that only saints will be able to meet, it should not be taken seriously. The sentence from Parfit that we quoted in the previous chapter can be adapted to make this point: 'If we personify theories, and pretend that they have aims, the aim of a theory is not to be easy to follow, but to be true, or to be the best theory.'[8]

3. Demandingness and the Facts of the World

We have seen how Sidgwick argued that in practice utilitarianism is not much more demanding than common sense morality. One issue he considered was that of special obligations towards those close to us. In a fundamental sense, utilitarianism requires us to be impartially concerned with the good of everyone, but in our everyday lives, Sidgwick argued, taking care of our children and caring for those close to us will lead to better outcomes than being completely impartial in all our thoughts and actions. First of all, we are better aware of the needs of those close to us than we are to those whom we do not know, who are far from us, and who differ significantly from us in their customs, culture, and religion, and therefore we can more easily increase the utility of those close to us than we can of those far away. Second, we are beings with a strong need for love and with special feelings towards our children, which for most people are a great source of happiness and fulfilment. This aspect of our psychological nature is not likely to change anytime soon, and most of us would not like it to change anyway. Those loving feelings can persist only if we treat those to whom we are close in a way that is different to how we treat others. To this extent we agree with Sidgwick's argument.

As we have seen, for Sidgwick one important reason why utilitarianism is in practice less demanding than its impartiality might lead one to expect is that the limits to our knowledge and power mean that we are 'for the most part…not in a position to do much good to more than a very small number of persons'. One might wonder why Sidgwick should have thought this, given that there were many poor people in England

---

[8] For the original quote, see p. 313.

in his own time; the answer is that he considered that the solution to this problem was more likely to come from improvements to the public system of relief for the poor than from private charity, which, as we saw, he thought runs the risk of 'encouraging improvidence' and reducing the incentive to find employment.[9] He must have been aware of the existence of famines in other parts of the world, including parts of the British Empire. Although by the time *The Methods of Ethics* was published, the telegraph was beginning to spread, news of famine in remote regions of the world could still take a long time to reach London, and it might take months for any substantial amounts of grain to be gathered and transported to those in need. Now we can receive news instantly, and transport food and medical supplies within days. It is true that sometimes knowing how best to help people in need is not as straightforward as it might appear, but in that area we have made considerable progress since Sidgwick's time, and we are continuing to improve our knowledge and abilities today.

When it comes to our power to help, the improvements in communications and transport are obviously relevant. Also highly significant, however, is the fact that the gap between per capita income in the richest nations and the poorest nations—and thus the power of the rich to help the poor—has greatly increased, roughly by a factor of five between Sidgwick's time and our own.[10] Our vastly greater wealth increases our power to do much more for others without putting our own welfare at risk.

These changed circumstances mean that the reasons Sidgwick gave for limiting our 'benevolent impulses' are no longer as generally applicable as they were in his day. Recall the point Sidgwick made, in the long passage we quoted earlier, with regard to circumstances in which 'I am made aware that, owing to a sudden calamity that could not have been foreseen, another's resources are manifestly inadequate to protect him from pain or serious discomfort'. He appears to have

---

[9] In the interests of promoting further discussion of how the English system of poverty relief could be improved, Sidgwick encouraged the publication of, and wrote a preface to, an English translation of P. F. Aschrott's *Das Englische Armen-Wesen,* which was published as *The English Poor Law System* in 1888.

[10] Pritchett, 'Divergence, Big-Time'.

thought that such circumstances are rare, and his use of the singular suggests that he had in mind calamities that befall individuals, rather than large numbers of people; but in our own time, only a determination to remain ignorant about the world in which we live can prevent us being aware of a never-ending series of such calamities, each affecting thousands or sometimes millions of people. Moreover, it seems true that these disasters either could not have been foreseen, or the victims did not have the resources to take the steps necessary to avert a foreseen disaster or its consequences. If, as Sidgwick writes, my awareness of the needs of a victim of such disasters means that 'I am bound to make as much effort to relieve him as will not entail a greater loss of happiness to myself or others', then it seems that everyone living in comfort and security with money to spare is so bound, and hence utilitarianism has become much more demanding.

Frank Jackson has defended a view somewhat like Sidgwick's by arguing that the question is not whether we can do good to strangers in need far away, but rather how the expected utility of such actions compares with the expected utility of helping our 'nearest and dearest'. After considering the probabilities, Jackson concludes that 'the good consequentialist should focus her attentions on securing the well-being of a relatively small number of people, herself included, not because she rates their welfare more highly than the welfare of others but because she is in a better position to secure their welfare'.[11] On the other hand he acknowledges that it is plausible to hold that 'many of us in advanced Western societies could achieve a great deal more good if we devoted our energies to a systematic, informed program of transferring any excess wealth toward the Third World'.[12] On Jackson's view, then, we may be justified in giving some priority to our 'nearest and dearest' because when we do so the better odds of achieving our aims will tilt the balance against the risk that, when we attempt to assist people we do not know, something will go wrong and we will fail to benefit anyone. Such calculations must be highly sensitive to the facts about these probabilities and the different

---

[11] Jackson, 'Decision-Theoretic Consequentialism', 481.
[12] Jackson, 'Decision-Theoretic Consequentialism', 477.

utilities to be achieved, and it is possible that the priority we are justified in giving to those close to us will be quite small, leaving utilitarianism much more demanding than the moral standards most people
accept today.

4. Contractualism and Demandingness

The claim that utilitarianism is absurdly demanding is usually put
forward by someone who, according to utilitarianism, ought to fulfil those demands. The demands of utilitarianism may seem much
less absurd, however, when considered from the perspective of a
person who needs help. To judge those demands properly we need
to take a point of view that is impartial between these different perspectives. One way of satisfying this requirement of impartiality is to
ask, as Scanlon does in developing his form of contractualism, what
'could be justified to others on grounds that they could not reasonably reject'.[13] Scanlon developed his theory in the hope that it would
avoid the most significant objections to utilitarianism. Surprisingly,
Scanlon's account may be even more demanding than utilitarianism.
Scanlon—in keeping with the contractualist understanding of the
significance of the 'separateness of persons'—rejects the aggregation
of benefits and burdens across individuals. Accordingly, every person, separately, has to agree on the burdens he has to face. What a
person can reasonably reject depends on the strength of the reasons
that a person has to reject the various options. As Elizabeth Ashford
has argued, this means that, for Scanlon: 'The essentially comparative nature of reasonable rejection, combined with the restriction to
individuals' reasons, together entail that any individual can reasonably reject a principle when she can propose an alternative principle
to which no other single individual has an equally strong objection.'[14]
Whether Alice, who earns a good income as a lawyer in California,
can reject a principle because it is very demanding for her, therefore
depends on whether Fatim, a peasant farmer in Mali who cannot
earn enough to afford health care for her child, has an even stronger

---

[13] Scanlon, *What we Owe to Each Other*, 5.
[14] Ashford, 'The Demandingness of Scanlon's Contractualism', 276.

reason to reject all alternatives to it, on the grounds that these alternatives, precisely because they are less demanding for Alice and those similarly situated to Alice, will all result in Fatim and those similarly situated to her not receiving the health care their children need. If Alice argues that, because of the amount of help she is required to give, she will lack the means to send her child to an elite private school, Fatim can say that, without help, her child may not survive at all. Therefore, Ashford concludes, '[c]onsideration of the comparative strengths of the burdens faced by various individuals...will lead to nonrejectable principles of aid that will impose demands on the agent which could be and are likely to be just as extensive as those imposed by utilitarianism'.[15]

This argument shows that act utilitarianism may not be a more demanding theory than contractualism, which is often viewed as utilitarianism's major rival. Some will no doubt see this as sufficient grounds to reject both these theories. We shall therefore argue that a highly demanding morality is reasonable, given the world in which we are living. In this we follow Shelly Kagan and Elizabeth Ashford, who argue that the state of the world is such that it is hard not to think that those who can make a positive difference to it face demanding obligations to do so.[16]

5. Objections to a Demanding Morality

There are those who say that we have obligations to help others only when we have harmed them, or violated their rights, or accepted a role, such as that of a nurse, that requires us to help.[17] To this we respond, first, that we are doing more harm to others than we care to think about. Those of us living in affluent countries affect those who are poor

---

[15] Ashford, 'The Demandingness of Scanlon's Contractualism', 288.

[16] Kagan writes: 'Given the parameters of the actual world, there is no question that promoting the good would require a life of hardship, self-denial, and austerity' (*The Limits of Morality*, 360); and Ashford puts it this way: 'in the current state of the world it may not be possible to defend less demanding obligations to those in need within an impartial moral framework' ('The Demandingness of Scanlon's Contractualism', 274).

[17] Gert, *Morality*, 210; Schmidtz, 'Islands in a Sea of Obligation'; Narveson, 'We Don't Owe Them a Thing!'

and live far from us by our high levels of greenhouse gas emissions that are changing the climate of our planet, and by purchasing oil and minerals from corporations that do deals with dictators, which means that in effect we are receiving stolen goods that should benefit all the country's people, but instead enrich only the despots.[18] Secondly, however, we hold that, even if we did not cause the global poor to suffer in these ways, it does not follow that we would be justified in not doing anything to help them. An overwhelming majority of people accept the rule of 'easy rescue'. They agree that, for example, to allow a child to drown in a shallow pond merely because one did not want to ruin an expensive pair of shoes would be wrong.[19]

Liam Murphy and Anthony Appiah have argued, separately, that morality cannot demand that I do more than my 'fair share' of resolving the world's problems.[20] Suppose, for instance, that there are a billion people who are as comfortably off as we are, and if all of them would give 2 per cent of their income to effective anti-poverty organizations, that would generate sufficient resources to eliminate most of the extreme poverty in the world.[21] In that case, Murphy and Appiah argue, my obligation in respect of global poverty would be limited to giving 2 per cent of my income to an effective anti-poverty organization. Even if giving 10 per cent would save many more lives, and would not involve any great hardship for me, they hold that I have no obligation to do it. But imagine that there are ten people standing by a shallow pond in which ten children are drowning. I do my share and save one but as I emerge from the pond I see that the other nine adults, instead of jumping into the cold water and saving a child, are walking away. Is it really all right for me to walk on, saying that I have

---

[18] See Pogge, *World Hunger and Human Rights*; Wenar, 'Clean Trade in Natural Resources'.

[19] See Singer, 'Famine, Affluence and Morality'; and Singer *The Life you Can Save*. One of us (PS) has often asked audiences, some drawn from students and others from the general public, and in several different countries, for a show of hands on whether it would be wrong to allow the child to drown. They agree—usually unanimously, and never with more than one or two dissenters—that it would be wrong.

[20] Murphy, *Moral Demands in Nonideal Theory*, esp. ch. 6; Appiah, *Cosmopolitanism*, ch. 10.

[21] Although we offer this only as a hypothetical example, for a discussion of whether it is realistic see Singer, *The Life you Can Save*, 141–4.

done my share and so have no obligation to save another child? We cannot accept that view. Whether I am the only adult near the pond, or there are others who could help but do not, I cannot leave other children to die when the only cost to me is getting cold and wet, or causing some additional damage to my clothing.

This is a point on which Brad Hooker would, to an extent, agree with act utilitarians. He is well aware that our obligations cannot be limited *only* to those that are in accordance with the rule that would have best consequences, if the vast majority of the society were to act upon it. That might result in an undemanding rule, because if *everyone* were giving aid, a relatively modest donation from each person could provide enough aid to relieve the needs of those living in extreme poverty. If, however, very few people are acting in accordance with the rule, our obligation is to give more because Hooker thinks (as we will remember from the previous chapter) that there is an overriding rule to 'prevent disaster'. And the death of a child is surely a disaster. On the other hand, Hooker still maintains that his view is distinct from act utilitarianism. He would agree with the act utilitarians that I have an obligation to save the other nine children in the pond after the other adults failed to help. But I do not, on his view, have an obligation when there is 'an *unlimited* requirement to prevent disaster'.[22] The internalization of a rule that would demand so much from us would have, he maintains, very high psychological costs, and hence no rule that imposes such demandingness is acceptable. We can praise those who live according to a highly demanding standard, but we should not require it.

It is one thing to say that our psychological nature is such that it would be difficult for us to fulfil the demands of morality, and quite a different thing to say that morality does not make such demands on us. The utilitarianism we accept has the advantage of taking both sides into account. We accept that our natural capacities must play a role in deciding what people ought to do in a given situation, but at the same time we do not want to surrender ethics to the limits on

---

[22] Hooker, *Ideal Code, Real World*, 165.

those capacities. In the following section, we will show how this can be done.

6. Demandingness and Blame

One reason why many people—philosophers included—are likely to reject the idea that our obligations can be as demanding as utilitarianism suggests is that they assume that, if we fail to act in accordance with our obligations, we deserve to be blamed for that failure. This is a mistake. To see why, suppose that Sidgwick is right when he says that our psychological nature is such that in order to live well we need to have close and loving ties with a few people. Suppose that cultivation of these loving relationships tends to make people happier and more satisfied with their lives, and more likely to help others, including strangers. We can add that children are most likely to thrive, and become well-balanced, productive, and ethical people if brought up in a loving family. We will then be justified in forming these close loving relationships, and in loving our children. To do so is to choose the path that is most likely to lead, not only to our own happiness and that of our children, but to the greatest good for all. But the existence of these loving relationships may mean that, in some circumstances, we do not do what we ought to do.

In *Reasons and Persons,* Derek Parfit considers the example of Clare, who has to choose between giving a small benefit to her child or a much greater benefit to an unfortunate stranger. Taking this situation in isolation, Clare ought to give the much greater benefit to the stranger, but because she loves her child, she gives the benefit to her child. Her love for her child led her to do what is wrong, but it does not follow that she should not have this motive. On the contrary, for the reasons we have given, she should have it, and given the benefits that her love brings to her child, we cannot say that she should have tried to love her child less. This, Parfit suggests, could be regarded as 'blameless wrongdoing'.[23] Clare's act may be wrong, but there are good

---

[23] Parfit, *Reasons and Persons,* 32.

reasons not to blame her for doing it, because on the whole it will be best if we encourage parents to love their children.

This is consistent with the distinction that, as we noted earlier in this chapter, Sidgwick drew between what we ought to do and what people ought to blame us for not doing. To praise or blame someone is an act that has consequences, and hence for a utilitarian, something that should be done when those consequences will, all things considered, be good.[24] If unusual circumstances force a mother to choose between the life of her own child and the lives of several strangers, we should not blame her if, because of her love for her child, she allows the strangers to die, because we do not want to discourage parents from loving their children and we recognize that loving them will mean saving them rather than strangers. If, on the other hand, again because of her love for her child, the mother buys him yet another expensive toy, instead of sharing the money with someone desperately in need of food or medicine, even the fact that she acted from a motive as strong and as generally desirable as love for her child is not sufficient reason to refrain from blaming her. Sidgwick makes this point when he asks us to suppose that I land upon a desert island with my family and find an abandoned orphan there. 'Is it evident', he asks, 'that I am less bound to provide this child, as far as lies in my power, with the means of subsistence, than I am to provide for my own children?' (*ME* 346–7). Apparently, Sidgwick thought that this was not evident at all.[25]

As we have already noted, the way in which the world has changed makes utilitarianism more demanding because it increases the tension between, on the one hand, our self-interested desires and the feelings that we have towards those close to us, and on the other hand, the utilitarian requirement that we make the world better from an impartial point of view. At the same time, what the moral standards of our society should openly demand from us, and what we ought to praise and

---

[24] Does this mean abandoning the notion of 'blameworthiness' as something distinct from 'ought to be blamed because it will have good consequences to do so'? Richard Chappell argues that it does not, while acknowledging that the question of whether any acts are blameworthy, in the sense of warranting certain negative responses, lies outside consequentialism. See his 'Satisficing by Effort'.

[25] For discussion, see Kolodny, 'Which Relationships Justify Partiality', 37–75, esp. at 56 n. 24.

blame people for, will still depend largely on the productiveness of those demands. As we suggested in our discussion of esoteric morality in the previous chapter, it may well be that advocating too high a standard is less effective in motivating people to give than advocating a lower standard.[26] In that case, a utilitarian ought to advocate the lower standard, and we should praise those who meet this standard, rather than blame them for failing to meet a higher standard.

7. A Matter of Degree?

If we accept Sidgwick's view that we should praise people who give more than most but less than they ought to give, a further question arises: what else should we say to those who do enough to merit praise, but no more than that? In the previous chapter we discussed a related case of esoteric morality. If Helen, an old friend who had given as much as it was desirable to advocate as a public standard, should ask us privately whether she had really done all that she ought to do, we said that, assuming we knew this would not discourage her from giving at all, we would tell her that she ought to give more.[27] Richard Arneson makes the following comment on such situations:

the act consequentialist should downplay the distinction between acts that are right and wrong. Her more important task is to grade acts as 'righter' and 'wronger' depending on the extent of the shortfall between the act being evaluated and the best that could have been done in the circumstances... We can think of the acts an agent could do on some occasion as ordered in an array of groups of acts that have consequences that range from very close to the consequences of the best act to very close to the very worst one could have done. With this picture in view, we can see that options of a sort have an important role in moral life and moral assessment. Far more important than determining whether one's act on an occasion was right or wrong would be fixing the degree of wrongness if it is not the very best one could have done.[28]

---

[26] We pick this simple standard for simplicity of exposition. In fact, we think people should give in accordance with a progressive scale, so that the percentage they give increases with their income. For an example, see Singer, *The Life you Can Save*, 164, and <www.thelifeyoucansave.org>.

[27] See p. 295-6.

[28] Arneson, 'What do we Owe to Needy Distant Strangers', 288, 292.

The position that Arneson sketches here has been more fully developed by Alastair Norcross under the name 'scalar utilitarianism'. As Norcross puts it:

Goodness and badness, especially in the utilitarian value theory, are clearly matters of degree. So the property of an act that makes it right or wrong—how much good it produces relative to available alternatives—*is* naturally thought of as a matter of degree. Why, then, is rightness and wrongness not a matter of degree?[29]

This view does seem, at first glance, to be a good fit for consequentialists, especially when we consider issues like our obligation to give aid, where the amount we can give is on a scale that changes by tiny increments from nothing to all we have. But Norcross goes too far when he writes:

Utilitarianism should not be seen as giving an account of right action, in the sense of an action *demanded* by morality, but only as giving an account of what states of affairs are good and which actions are better than which other possible alternatives and by how much. The fundamental moral fact about an action is how good it is relative to other available alternatives. Once a range of options has been evaluated in terms of goodness, all the morally relevant facts about those options have been discovered. There is no further fact of the form '*x* is right,' '*x* is to-be-done,' or '*x* is demanded by morality.'[30]

For Sidgwick, as we have seen in various places in this book, it is precisely the other way round: the concept of 'what ought I to do?' or its equivalent, 'What do I have most reason to do?', is fundamental.[31] Sidgwick suggests we should understand what is good for a person in terms of what she has most reason to desire. Granted, utilitarianism tells us that we ought to do what will have the best consequences, and in that sense, what we ought to do is derived from what is good, but we must distinguish normative priority from conceptual priority. As utilitarians, we cannot decide what we ought to do until we know what will produce the most good, but that does not mean that

[29] Norcross, 'The Scalar Approach to Utilitarianism', 217. Slote discussed the idea earlier, in *Common-sense Morality and Consequentialism*, ch. 5. For critical discussion see Hooker, 'Right, Wrong and Rule-Consequentialism', 239–41; Lawlor 'The Rejection of Scalar Consequentialism'; Lang, 'Should Utilitarianism be Scalar?'

[30] Norcross, 'The Scalar Approach to Utilitarianism', 228.

[31] Lang, 'Should Utilitarianism be Scalar?' has a helpful discussion of the role of normative reasons in scalar utilitarianism.

the concept of 'good' is prior to the concept of 'ought'. Once we accept the indispensability, for ethics, of the concept of what we ought to do, or what we have most reason to do, ideas of 'right' or 'demanded by morality' come trailing close behind, and it doesn't really make sense to try to separate them. If there is something we ought to do, it is demanded by morality, and right to do it.

Norcross does consider this view, asking: 'But doesn't (morally) right simply mean "supported by the strongest (moral) reasons" or "what we have most (moral) reason to do"?'[32] He answers this objection by saying that it is 'highly implausible that there is such a simple conceptual connection between rightness and maximal reason', offering as grounds for rejecting this connection the concept of supererogation, which we looked at in Chapter 5. That concept is at home in deontological conceptions of morality, but for utilitarians it is a concept that confuses what we ought to do with what it is appropriate to praise or blame people for doing. To abandon core moral concepts like 'right' and 'wrong' in order to avoid having to reject supererogation is truly to strain at a gnat and swallow a camel. Norcross, in the very article in which he argues that we should abandon these moral concepts, is unable to avoid using them himself. He discusses, for example, the various options that we have when confronted with an old lady who needs help to cross the road. We could, he says, help her, or we could mug her, or we could kidnap her, or we could kill her and eat her. In this situation, he says, 'there is no question as to what to do'—which seems indistinguishable from saying that it is clear that some of these options are wrong, and that morality demands that we not do them.[33]

Our moral concepts do not need the drastic surgery that scalar utilitarianism envisages. The judicious consequentialist use of praise and blame suffices to enable us to respond appropriately to the wide-ranging differences between the differing amounts of good that people do, and the extent to which their efforts go beyond what we expect most people to do.

---

[32] Norcross, 'The Scalar Approach to Utilitarianism', 227.
[33] Norcross, 'The Scalar Approach to Utilitarianism', 228. We owe this point to Lawlor, 'The Rejection of Scalar Consequentialism', 109.

8. Conclusion

It may seem that act utilitarianism tries to have things both ways, demanding 'everything' and 'nothing' at the same time. On the one hand a utilitarian morality places almost limitless demands on us, making us feel that we will never be able to be fully moral. Yet because this may discourage people from even trying to get anywhere near to living ethically, utilitarianism does not blame you if you do not do your very best. In fact, it may even praise you for doing rather little, if this praise will provide the necessary motivation for you to do something rather than nothing. But then, what is the point of telling you that something is your obligation if no one will express disapproval of your failure to do it? In this situation, how can morality encourage us to make moral progress, and do more to further the good of all?

Sidgwick's idea was that we should encourage people to do better by praising 'any conduct more felicific in its tendency than what an average man would do under the given circumstances' (*ME* 493). To move people in a positive direction, we can praise those who do better than others, even if what they do still falls short of what they ought to do, by utilitarian standards. We should also, of course, seek to raise the standard that the average person follows, and we can hope to do so by the judicious use of praise and blame. In concluding this book we will mention some of the areas of ethics in which this has happened, and is continuing to happen.

12

Distribution

1. Sidgwick on Distributing Happiness

Book IV of *The Methods* is on utilitarianism. In the opening chapter Sidgwick defines utilitarianism as the ethical theory according to which the objectively right conduct is 'that which will produce the greatest amount of happiness on the whole; that is, taking into account all whose happiness is affected by the conduct' (*ME* 411). That definition leaves unspecified the 'all' whose happiness we are to take into account. First, is utilitarianism concerned only with the happiness of human beings, or with that of animals as well? Second, should we include in our calculations also the pleasures and pains of those who do not yet exist, but will live in future? If we do take future people into account then a third question arises, for we need to consider the fact that we can affect the number of people who will come into existence. The choice we make will have consequences both for the amount of happiness there will be in the universe, and for the average level of happiness among future people. Finally, if we can answer these questions, and know who the 'all' are, how ought we to distribute happiness among them?

On the question of the moral status of animals, Sidgwick agreed with his great utilitarian predecessors. Jeremy Bentham had suggested that 'The day may come when the rest of the animal creation may acquire those rights which never could have been withholden from them but by the hand of tyranny.' Anticipating the objection that animals do not have rights because they are less intelligent than we are, he urged: 'The question is not, Can they reason? nor, Can they talk? but, Can they suffer?'[1] Mill took a similar stance. When the intuitionist William Whewell used as a damning objection to utilitarianism the fact that it disregards the moral significance of 'the universal tie of humanity' and of the absence of any such tie between us and animals, Mill responded emphatically:

We are perfectly willing to stake the whole question on this one issue. Granted that any practice causes more pain to animals than it gives pleasure to man; is that practice moral or immoral? And if, exactly in proportion as human beings raise their heads out of the slough of selfishness, they do not with one voice answer 'immoral,' let the morality of the principle of utility be for ever condemned.[2]

Sidgwick, in his usual more measured tone, thought it obviously most in accordance with the universality characteristic of the utilitarian principle that we should extend moral consideration to 'all the beings capable of pleasure and pain whose feelings are affected by our conduct'. If our duty is to aim at 'the Good Universal' then, he wrote, it is 'arbitrary and unreasonable to exclude from the end . . . any pleasure of any sentient being' (*ME* 414).

In another essay, on 'The Establishment of Ethical First Principles', Sidgwick discusses how one might accept a limited and qualified principle as self-evident, without seeing that this principle is part of a wider and simpler principle, 'of which the limitations and qualifications may then appear as accidental and arbitrary'. The example he gives illuminates his thinking on the moral status of animals:

I may begin by laying down as a principle that 'all pain of human or rational beings is to be avoided'; and then afterwards may be led to enunciate the wider rule that 'all pain is to be avoided'; it being made evident to me that the difference of rationality between two species of sentient beings is no ground for establishing a fundamental ethical distinction between their respective pains.[3]

Some may object that expanding the circle of our concern to non-human animals will greatly increase the difficulty of calculating and comparing the pleasures and pains that result from different

---

[1] Bentham, *Introduction to the Principles of Morals and Legislation,* ch. 17, s. 1, and repr. in Regan and Singer (eds), *Animal Rights and Human Obligations,* 130.

[2] Mill, 'Dr Whewell on Moral Philosophy', 185–7.

[3] Sidgwick, 'The Establishment of Ethical First Principles', 106–7. We owe this reference to Shaver, *Rational Egoism,* 90–1.

possible actions. It is difficult enough, these critics will say, to compare the pleasures and pains of other human beings, let alone of members of other species. But, Sidgwick points out, this problem holds
for 'any other moralists who recoil from the paradox of disregarding
altogether the pleasures and pains of brutes'. In other words, if we give
any weight at all to the suffering of non-human animals—even if we
heavily discount animal suffering when we face a choice between it
and human suffering—we will have to calculate how great that suffering is, and compare it with human suffering.

Moreover, Sidgwick continues, even if we limit our calculations
only to other human beings, it is not at all clear who exactly we should
take into account. Do we have obligations towards future generations? Do we have those obligations if the happiness of future people
conflicts with the happiness of people who are living now? Sidgwick
again repeats that 'the time at which a man exists cannot affect the
value of his happiness from a universal point of view' (*ME* 414).
Hence 'the interests of posterity must concern a Utilitarian as much
as those of his contemporaries, except in so far as the effect of his
actions on posterity—and even the existence of human beings to be
affected—must necessarily be more uncertain'.

Sidgwick notices that our choices may affect not only the amount
of happiness future people experience, but also the number of those
future people. Is it good to increase the size of the future population?
Sidgwick begins his discussion of this question by assuming that 'for
human beings generally, life on the average yields a positive balance of
pleasure over pain'. He recognizes that 'thoughtful persons' have denied
this, but finds the denial contrary to 'the common experience of mankind', pointing out that 'The great majority of men, in the great majority
of conditions under which human life is lived, certainly act as if death
were one of the worst of evils, for themselves and for those whom they
love'. Therefore, Sidgwick says, 'it seems clear that, supposing the average happiness enjoyed remains undiminished, Utilitarianism directs
us to make the number enjoying it as great as possible'.

At this point Sidgwick notices a further ethical issue that 'has not
only never been formally noticed, but which seems to have been
substantially overlooked by many Utilitarians'. The issue arises if 'we

foresee as possible that an increase in numbers will be accompanied by a decrease in average happiness'. To make this more concrete, imagine we face a choice between:

Option 1: We maintain the present population size, so that the average happiness of those who will exist in future remains as high as possible.

Option 2: We increase the future population, with the result that the average level of happiness falls, but since the average remains positive, the much larger number of people at this lower average results in a greater total amount of happiness than results from the first option.

What should we do? As Sidgwick himself noted, no one had considered this problem before. Here, in full, is what he wrote about how a utilitarian should respond to it:

if we take Utilitarianism to prescribe, as the ultimate end of action, happiness on the whole, and not any individual's happiness, unless considered as an element of the whole, it would follow that, if the additional population enjoy on the whole positive happiness, we ought to weigh the amount of happiness gained by the extra number against the amount lost by the remainder. So that, strictly conceived, the point up to which, on Utilitarian principles, population ought to be encouraged to increase, is not that at which average happiness is the greatest possible, as appears to be often assumed by political economists of the school of Malthus—but that at which the product formed by multiplying the number of persons living into the amount of average happiness reaches its maximum.

Having reached this conclusion, Sidgwick concedes that it 'wears a certain air of absurdity to the view of Common Sense; because its show of exactness is grotesquely incongruous with our consciousness of the inevitable inexactness of all such calculations in actual practice'. But he points out that, although in practice our calculations are inevitably rough, this

is no reason for not making them as accurate as the case admits; and we shall be more likely to succeed in this if we keep before our mind as distinctly as possible the strict type of the calculation that we should have to make, if all the relevant considerations could be estimated with mathematical precision. (*ME* 414–16)[4]

---

[4] Bentham it seems, would have agreed. In a note that remained unpublished during Sidgwick's lifetime, Bentham considers the 'The Calculation of Pleasures and Pains' and

After presenting these perplexing issues, Sidgwick asks about the best way of distributing 'the same quantum of happiness among the same number of persons'. He acknowledges that, if we could calculate precisely the amount of pleasure and pain that two different alternatives would bring about, we would be unlikely ever to find them exactly equal, and if they are not exactly equal, then it is, he says, 'an obvious and incontrovertible deduction from the Utilitarian principle' that we ought to distribute happiness so as to produce more of it, 'whatever inequality in the distribution of the means of happiness this may involve' (*ME* 417 n. 5). But in practice, we lack such precision and therefore two alternative distributions of the means of happiness will quite often appear to be equally balanced, in terms of how much pleasure and pain they produce, even if in reality there is a small difference between them. Therefore there is some practical importance to the question of whether any given form of distribution is any better than any other. On this issue Sidgwick accepts that the utilitarian principle itself does not provide any answer to this question. It seems that we have to 'supplement' the utilitarian principle by a principle of 'Just or Right distribution'. Sidgwick observes that most utilitarians have agreed that the best solution would be to adopt some kind of 'pure equality' rule. Bentham famously formulated it as: 'everybody to count for one, and nobody for more than one'. According to Sidgwick the advantage of this rule is that 'this principle seems the only one which does not need a special justification; for, as we saw, it must be reasonable to treat any one man in the same way as any other, if there be no reason apparent for treating him differently' (*ME* 417).

In less than seven pages of *The Methods*, Sidgwick raised four major ethical issues, about each of which there is now an extensive literature. Our discussion of each issue will necessarily be brief, and we will, for reasons of continuity, vary the order in which we discuss them.

---

after discussing how to calculate the value of an individual's pleasure, adds: 'when a whole community, that is a multitude of individuals, is considered as being concerned in it, the value of it is to be multiplied by the number of such individuals. The total value of the stock of pleasure belonging to the whole community is to be obtained by multiplying the number expressing the value of it as respecting any one person, by the number expressing the multitude of such individuals.' Bentham, 'Le Calcul des plaisirs et des peines', 402.

2. Animals

If, as Sidgwick thought, it is arbitrary and unreasonable to exclude the pleasures or pains of any sentient being from the 'all' with whose happiness we should be concerned, it would be no less arbitrary to include those pleasures and pains, but at a discount to the similar pleasures and pains of human beings. Animals no doubt have different interests from humans, and may experience different pleasures and pains, but the principle of equal consideration for similar interests still holds, and pleasures and pains of similar intensity and duration should be given equal weight, whether they are experienced by humans or by animals.

The failure to give proper weight to the suffering of animals is, as Robert Shaver notes, 'one of the very few places where [Sidgwick] explicitly corrects, on utilitarian grounds, what some take to be common sense'.[5] In this Sidgwick was, with Bentham and Mill, ahead of public opinion in his own time, and ahead of philosophers like Whewell, and Kant too, for Kant thought that animals are not ends in themselves, and we have no direct duties to them.[6] Whewell's idea, that our greater ties to humans mean that we have duties to other human beings that we do not have to animals, finds an echo in the claims of—to take just one of several possible examples—the American evolutionary psychologist Lewis Petrinovich, who argues that some biological boundaries have moral significance. Petrinovich thinks that we have special obligations to 'children, kin, neighbors, and species'.[7] In this we can see echoes of Sidgwick's account, more than a century earlier, of those to whom his contemporaries thought that we owe duties of benevolence. In a passage we have already quoted in our account of Sidgwick's view of common sense morality's understanding of the duty of benevolence, Sidgwick described different levels of concern that included children, kin, and neighbours, but also two categories that are conspicuously absent from Petrinovitch's list: 'fellow countrymen' and 'those of our own race'

[5] Shaver, *Rational Egoism*, 92.
[6] Kant, 'Duties to Animals and Spirits', 239, and repr. in Regan and Singer (eds), *Animal Rights and Human Obligations*, 122.
[7] Petrinovich, *Darwinian Dominion*, 29.

rather than 'black or yellow men' (*ME* 246). The omission of these categories from Petrinovich's list should make us suspicious of the claim that the broader biological distinction of species gives us moral reasons for discounting the interests of those sentient beings who lie on the other side of that boundary. If such biological distinctions do give rise to stronger moral obligations to those to whom we are closer, how can we reject the nationalist and racist arguments that we are also justified in discounting the interests of those to whom we have no national or racial affinity? Conversely, if we reject other 'isms' like racism and sexism, why should we defend speciesism?

Thirty years ago, Robert Nozick argued that we can't infer much from the fact that we do not yet have a theory of the moral importance of species membership, because 'the issue hasn't seemed pressing' and so no one has spent much time trying to formulate such a theory.[8] But the rise of the animal rights movement in the 1970s made the issue very pressing indeed and many philosophers and other thinkers have spent a lot of time asking whether we are entitled to continue to eat animals and use them for research and for our entertainment. Thus Nozick's comment now takes on a different significance: the fact that no one has come up with a really convincing reason for giving greater moral weight to members of our own species, simply because they are members of our species, strongly suggests that there is no such reason. Like racism and sexism, speciesism is wrong.

Although species is not morally important in itself, there could be some other morally significant characteristic that happens to coincide with the species boundary, and justifies the inferior consideration we give to non-human animals. One difference between humans and animals that is frequently said to be morally significant is the capacity to reciprocate. On this view ethics arises out of a mutual agreement: if I do not harm you, you will not harm me. As we saw in Chapter 6, David Gauthier takes this position, and we gave there grounds for rejecting it.[9]

---

[8] Nozick, 'About Mammals and People', 11.
[9] See pp. 171–2; for another example, see Carruthers, *The Animals Issue*.

Some philosphers, seeking a clear line between humans and other animals, have referred to the ability to reason or to use language in order to justify the superior moral status of human beings. Bentham indicated why it is difficult to use such characteristics to attribute superior moral status to humans, pointing out that 'a full-grown horse or dog is beyond comparison a more rational, as well as a more conversable animal, than an infant of a day, or a week, or even a month, old'.[10] That argument has since become known as 'the argument from marginal cases'—that is, the argument from the moral status we accord to those who are in some sense at the margins of humanity.[11] The label is unfortunate, but the point made by the argument remains sound. If we want to use higher cognitive abilities, or capacities like autonomy that require a certain level of cognitive capacity, as the basis for drawing a line between human beings and other animals, we cannot overlook the fact that some animals have higher cognitive abilities than some humans. If we draw the line low enough to include all human beings, we will include many non-human animals; if we draw it high enough to exclude all non-human animals, we will also exclude many human beings.

Sidgwick, as we have seen, considered the objection that including the pleasures and pains of animals in our calculations of the consequences of our actions will add to the challenge of an already difficult task, responding that even if we discount the interests of animals, as compared with humans, we will still need to do the calculation, presumably before applying the discount. The only way of avoiding the need to include the pleasures and pains of animals in our calculations is to disregard them entirely, which Sidgwick thought to be a 'paradox' from which we should recoil. But while most people today would agree that the pains of animals do matter, and so should not be disregarded, many think quite differently of the painless killing of animals. Neither in *The Methods* nor in any of his other writings does Sidgwick discuss whether, or under what circumstances, the killing

---

[10] Bentham, *Introduction to the Principles of Morals and Legislation*, ch. 17, s. 1, and repr. in Regan and Singer (eds), *Animal Rights and Human Obligations*, 130.

[11] See Dombrowski, *Babies and Beasts*.

of animals is justifiable. Perhaps he agreed with Bentham, who justified killing animals for food on the grounds that animals

have none of those long-protracted anticipations of future misery which we have. The death they suffer in our hands commonly is, and always may be, a speedier, and by that means a less painful one, than that which would await them in the inevitable course of nature. If the being killed were all, there is very good reason why we should be suffered to kill such as molest us: we should be the worse for their living, and they are never the worse for being dead.[12]

Paola Cavalieri has suggested that in this passage Bentham falls below his normal standard of argument. She begins by pointing out that the slaughter of animals is not painless (and was even more painful in Bentham's day than it is in our own); she then notes that Bentham applies the argument in an arbitrary fashion, because it is not only non-human animals, but also some intellectually disabled human beings, who are unable to anticipate future misery; and finally she asks why Bentham fails to consider that killing involves the loss of the possible future happiness of those being killed.[13]

The first point is not entirely fair to Bentham, for he makes no claim that animals killed for food die painlessly, but only that their deaths are less painful than the deaths that they would otherwise have had. Many of the animals we eat would—if they had existed at all—otherwise have been killed by predators, or in the absence of predators, have succumbed to disease or lack of food in winter or during droughts. Death at the hands of a predator may or may not be quicker than death in a slaughterhouse. It does at least have the advantage of avoiding the horrors of long-distance transport suffered by many animals killed for food today. But death from starvation is probably significantly worse than death in a modern slaughterhouse, and may be worse even than death in a slaughterhouse in Bentham's time.

Cavalieri is right to point out that Bentham's justification of killing animals on the grounds that they do not anticipate their deaths applies also to some human beings. Cavalieri is here invoking the argument from marginal cases that Bentham himself used. Bentham might have been so bold as to accept this implication for those marginal

[12]   Bentham, *An Introduction to the Principles of Morals and Legislation*, ch. 17, s. 1 n. 2.
[13]   Cavalieri, *The Animal Question*, 65.

cases, for in protesting against the cruelty of inflicting the death penalty on mothers who kill their newborn infants, he described infanticide as 'of a nature not to give the slightest inquietude to the most
timid imagination', for all those who come to learn of an act of infanticide are themselves too old to be threatened by it. He might, perhaps, have added that in most cases of killing infants or humans with
intellectual disabilities so severe as to prevent them fearing their own
death, the suffering is experienced not by those who anticipate being
killed, but by those who love and care for these human beings. Still,
there will be cases in which humans lacking the powers of anticipating their own death will not be missed by anyone, and then Bentham
would have no alternative but to accept that his argument applies to
them as it does to non-human animals.

Cavalieri's third point raises the central issue for utilitarians: in
considering the justifiability of killing an animal, the utilitarian must
take into account the loss of whatever surplus of pleasure over pain
it would otherwise have experienced. The significance of this will
depend, of course, on whether the animal would have experienced
more pleasure than pain. In the case of wild animals, the difficulty lies
in understanding what the conscious experiences of the various kinds
of animals, under varying conditions, are like.[14] That is by no means
easy to do. With animals raised for food, however, there is a more
difficult philosophical issue to consider. As the British essayist Leslie
Stephen, a contemporary of Sidgwick, wrote: 'Of all the arguments for
Vegetarianism none is so weak as the argument from humanity. The
pig has a stronger interest than anyone in the demand for bacon. If all
the world were Jewish, there would be no pigs at all.'[15] In other words,
it is not only the loss of pleasure experienced by the animal killed
that the utilitarian should consider, but also whether the death of that
animal will make possible (for example, by the income it provides
for the farmer) the existence of another animal who will also, before

[14] See Horta, 'Debunking the Idyllic View of Natural Processes' and several essays by
Brian Tomasik available at <http://www.utilitarian-essays.com>. For evidence of animal
enjoyment, often neglected in the focus on animal suffering, see Balcombe, *Pleasurable
Kingdom*.

[15] Stephen, *Social Rights and Duties*.

being killed in turn, experience more pleasure than pain. If it does, then the practice of raising and killing animals for food may, overall, bring about more pleasure than pain. This argument is not limited to the arcane writings of philosophers: Michael Pollan invokes it in his best-selling *The Omnivore's Dilemma*.[16]

Henry Salt, an early advocate of animal rights, brusquely dismissed Stephen's argument: 'A person who is already in existence', Salt writes, 'may feel that he would rather have lived than not, but he must first have the *terra firma* of existence to argue from; the moment he begins to argue as if from the abyss of the non-existent, he talks nonsense, by predicating good or evil, happiness or unhappiness, of that of which we can predicate nothing.'[17] Sidgwick took a contrary view, as we saw at the beginning of this chapter, holding that it is good to make the number of beings enjoying happiness as great as possible, as long as bringing more beings into existence does not reduce the happiness of others. To decide whether this claim is indeed nonsense, as Salt believed—and therefore whether Stephen's argument can be used to defend killing animals for food—we need to discuss the difficult question of whether, when utilitarians calculate the amount of happiness produced by their actions, they should also include the happiness of beings who, but for the action in question, would not even have existed. For that reason we will postpone the remainder of this discussion until we come to that topic later in this chapter.

There is, however, one final point to be made about how we should respond to arguments about whether it is right to treat animals in certain ways; for example, to raise them for food, kill them, and eat them. In general, when we face an ethical choice between doing X or Y, there can be reasonable arguments, supported by competent judges, favouring each option. Suppose we examine the arguments and decide that the arguments for doing X are stronger than the arguments for doing Y. One might think that there is nothing more to be said about what you ought to do. Dan Moller has pointed out,

---

[16] Pollan, *The Omnivore's Dilemma*, 310.

[17] Salt, 'The Logic of the Larder', repr. in Regan and Singer, *Animal Rights and Human Obligations*, 186.

however, that in these situations of moral uncertainty we should also consider the risk of being wrong, and this risk may weigh more heavily against one choice than against the other. Suppose that I conclude that, with regard to animals, the stronger arguments are those that deny animals the kind of moral status that would make it wrong to kill and eat them, but I admit that I might be mistaken about this. If I act on my assessment of the arguments, and I do turn out to be mistaken, I will be contributing to a huge amount of unjustifiable suffering and death, and therefore doing something seriously morally wrong. Eating meat in a situation of moral uncertainty is therefore a high-risk option. On the other hand, there are no strong moral arguments that would make it morally wrong for me to become a vegetarian, so that is a risk-free option. In these circumstances, I ought to act to reduce my moral risk.[18]

This argument applies wherever there is moral uncertainty and asymmetry of moral risk. Moller applies it to abortion as well as vegetarianism and, as we shall see shortly, it can also be applied to questions of distribution of resources.

3. Equality and Priority for Those Who are Worse Off

We have seen that some regard it as an objection to utilitarianism that when it comes to human and non-human animals, it is too egalitarian. At the same time, utilitarianism is often thought to be insufficiently egalitarian, or insufficiently concerned about those who are worse off, because it gives no intrinsic weight to human equality, and no intrinsic priority to improving the position of those who are worse off. It is true that utilitarians do not give any independent weight to equality, beyond the kind of equality that is, as we shall explain in a moment, built into the idea of utility itself. Nor do they give any intrinsic weight to improving the position of those who are worse off, beyond what they give to improving anyone's position. But we

---

[18] Moller, 'Abortion and Moral Risk'. We have also benefited from MacAskill's discussion in 'Moral Caution and Moral Compromise'.

think it is a mistake to see this as an objection to the utilitarian view. Utilitarianism supports those forms of equality (or of priority for the worse off) that should be supported, and does not support those that should not be supported.

Utilitarianism has, from its inception, offered a radical critique of prevailing inequalities, not only between humans and other animals, but also between humans. The kind of equality utilitarianism supports is given by Bentham's formula, to which Sidgwick refers: 'everybody to count for one, and nobody for more than one'.[19] This is really a constitutive element of utilitarianism, a rule requiring honest counting of utility, rather than an independent principle. Utilitarianism seeks to maximize happiness, and in deciding how to calculate whether happiness is being maximized, no one's pleasures or pains should count for less because they are peasants rather than aristocrats, slaves rather than slave-owners, Africans rather than Europeans, poor rather than rich, illiterates rather than doctors of philosophy, children rather than adults, females rather than males, or even, as we have seen, non-human animals rather than human beings. That is all that the formula means. Nevertheless, against the background of how the world has long been, and still remains, its implications are often radically egalitarian. This is *instrumental* egalitarianism—aiming for equality in order to achieve more happiness.

There is, however, a further question that can be asked about the formula. Utilitarians should always be open to the facts, whatever they may prove to be. The idea that each counts for one and none for more than one must therefore be compatible with the possibility of individual variations in capacities for happiness. Nozick imagined

[19] Although everyone, including Sidgwick, follows John Stuart Mill in attributing this 'dictum' to Bentham, it is a misquotation. The closest variant to be found in his works is: 'Every individual in the country tells for one; no individual for more than one', which occurs in Bentham's *Rationale of Judicial Evidence, specially applied to English practice*, ed. J. S. Mill, London, 1827, IV, (book 8, ch. 29), 475. The inclusion of the words 'in the country' appear to reflect the focus of the work in which the passage appears, which is how to make a country's legal system work for the benefit of all who come under it, rather than of judges and lawyers. It is clearly not Bentham's view that utilitarians in general should only count the well-being of their compatriots. (We are grateful to Philip Schofield, Director of the Bentham Project at University College London, for this reference. Mill's version is to be found in ch. 5 of his *Utilitarianism*.)

that there might be 'utility monsters' who get so much more utility from eating people than the people would have experienced had they not been eaten that utility is maximized by sacrificing everyone else to them.[20] There are no such utility monsters, but there could well be lesser differences between individuals. Sidgwick comes close to acknowledging this when, in discussing hedonism, he criticizes Plato's argument that the life of the philosopher has more pleasure than the life of the sensualist. As Sidgwick describes Plato's argument, it rests on the claim (subsequently also made by Mill in a similar context) that the philosopher has experience of both sensual and intellectual pleasures, and prefers the latter, so the sensualist should follow his example. Sidgwick comments: 'But who can tell that the philosopher's constitution is not such as to render the enjoyments of the senses, in his case, comparatively feeble? while on the other hand the sensualist's mind may not be able to attain more than a thin shadow of the philosopher's delight' (ME 148). In envisaging these possibilities, Sidgwick must surely also have recognized another: some people might have 'comparatively feeble' capacities for enjoying both intellectual and sensual pleasures. If so, the idea that each should count for one and nobody for more than one will conflict with the idea that we should maximize happiness. We should, of course, give equal weight to equal amounts of pleasure, whoever gets the pleasure, but nevertheless the interests of the person with comparatively feeble capacities for pleasures or pains will not, taken as a whole, count as much as the interests of those with much greater capacities, because the amount of pleasure the former are capable of attaining is smaller.

This is not as strange as it may at first seem. Many people think that non-human animals have less capacity for pleasure and pain than normal humans. They may be wrong about that, in many cases, but it is surely true that there are *some* non-human animals—snails, for instance?—with less capacity for pleasure and pain than normal humans. It is then reasonable—and compatible with the principle of equal consideration for similar interests—to give less consideration to the interests of those animals than we give to the interests of

---

[20] Nozick, *Anarchy, State and Utopia*, 41.

normal humans. The same holds within our own species. If someone is so brain-damaged as to have only a minimal capacity for conscious experiences—perhaps the best he can do is respond to being
stroked with noises that seem to express contentment—we would not
be justified in devoting as many resources to maximizing that human
being's happiness as we would to maximizing the happiness of someone with normal capacities.

Sidgwick does not explicitly address the problem of possible differences in human capacities for happiness, but Bentham does:

> Lacking the power to determine the relative degree of happiness that different
> individuals are susceptible of, it is necessary to start with the assumption that the
> degree is the same for all. This assumption, if it is not exactly true, will more nearly
> approach the truth than any other general supposition which can be put in its
> place.[21]

Granting this working assumption of equal capacities for happiness
meets one way in which egalitarians might object to utilitarianism,
but does not meet the basic objection that utilitarianism could accept
a very unequal distribution of happiness. So, for example, we can
imagine that there are only three individuals in the world, and only
two possible distributions of happiness, which are indicated here.
(The numbers give an artificial precision to this discussion, but we will
return to that issue shortly. We should think of each unit indicating
an equal benefit, so that for any individual it is as much of a benefit to
move from 1 unit to 2 units as it is to move from 14 units to 15 units.)

Distribution 1: A: 5 units; B: 5 units; C: 5 units
Distribution 2: A: 15 units; B: 1 unit; C: 0 units.

Utilitarianism will tell us to prefer Distribution 2. Some
non-utilitarians will think this is the wrong answer. This may be
because they regard equality as an important intrinsic value, or
because they are prioritarians, thinking that benefiting people matters more the worse off those who are benefited are.[22] In defence of

---

[21] Bentham, 'Essai sur la représentation', 427. The translation is from Mack, *Jeremy Bentham*, 449. We owe this reference to Guidi, 'Everybody to Count for One, Nobody for More than One', 43 n. 153.

[22] Parfit, 'Equality and Priority', 213.

Distribution 2, utilitarians can remind us that the figures refer to distributions of *happiness,* not of income or resources or any other means to happiness. If we think of the units as indications of the relative incomes or wealth of the individuals, or of some other assets that friends or a voluntary organization or a government might distribute to them, we can easily imagine that Distribution 1 would lead to more happiness overall. If we choose Distribution 2, won't B and C resent the fact that A has so much more than they have? And if the figures stand for money—each unit, let's say, for $1000—then it is difficult to believe that taking $5000 from A, who has $15000 and giving it to C, who has nothing, would not increase overall happiness. We are all familiar with the idea that, as income rises, the utility of each additional dollar added diminishes. (This is the 'law of diminishing marginal utility'.) But because the figures in the distributions represent happiness, rather than income or other material means to happiness, the law of diminishing marginal utility must have already been taken into account in reaching these figures. Similarly, the figures must have taken into account any negative impact on the welfare of B and C that their envy or resentment of A's position may have caused, as well as any other consequences for their happiness that may come from the inequality of their situation. To judge the two possible distributions fairly, we have to keep in mind that, despite A's higher level of happiness, any redistribution of happiness from A to B or C will cost A *more* than it benefits B and C combined. If that were not the case—and putting aside the case of a tie, which we will come to shortly—utilitarians would favour the redistribution. It is, however, very difficult for people to keep this distinction in mind. Joshua Greene and Jonathan Baron have shown experimentally that people asked to judge how good it would be to live in different countries are apt to confuse information about income with information about utility levels. Greene calls this the 'wealthitarian fallacy'.[23]

Let's now move to the real world. As we saw in Chapter 11, we live in a world with an extremely unequal distribution of income. The law of

---

[23] Greene and Baron, 'Intuitions about declining marginal utility'; for discussion of the 'wealthitarian fallacy' see Greene, *Moral Tribes*, 279–84.

diminishing marginal utility therefore favours very extensive income redistribution. Utilitarians must, of course, also take into account any negative aspects of adding to the income of the poor—for example, the disincentive effects on the rich of having money taken from them, presumably by means of a tax, and the disincentive effects on the poor of receiving money they have not earned. Nevertheless it is hard to imagine that anything remotely like the present unequal global distribution of income could be defensible on utilitarian grounds.

Utilitarians can also argue that, because few things cause more avoidable human suffering than being unable to meet one's basic needs, a society governed in accordance with the principle of utility will, to the extent that its resources permit, provide a social welfare net that gives everyone sufficient income (or in-kind distribution) to enable them to obtain adequate food, housing, education, safe drinking water, sanitation, and health care. If a society lacks the resources to do this, then utilitarians can argue that richer nations should do their best to provide the resources that can ensure that this happens.

Curiously, the objection that utilitarianism is insufficiently egalitarian is often made by adherents of positions that are in this important respect significantly *less* egalitarian than utilitarianism. Those who defend John Rawls's theory of justice, for instance, may suggest that it shows more concern for those who are worst off, because it insists that any departures from equality can only be justified if they will benefit the worst off. Utilitarianism, on the other hand, as we have just seen, allows, or indeed requires, departures from equality whenever such departures will maximize overall happiness. But what this comparison overlooks is that, when in *A Theory of Justice* Rawls sets up his 'original position' from which people will choose principles of justice, he assumes that the people making the choice all belong to the same society. They are to choose principles that they can all accept as forming just principles for their political institutions. Therefore when Rawls argues that they would choose principles that would benefit the worst off, he has in mind the worst off within their society—which for Rawls's own society, the United States, and the rich societies in which most of his readers live, means people who, though poor relative to others in their society, are in absolute terms *much* better off than the world's worst-off people. If Rawls had argued that the veil of ignorance behind which people choose the basic principles of justice covers not only one's level of income, but also the country in which one lives, his theory would have had much more radically egalitarian implications.[24] In this, Rawls's discussion is typical of much of the philosophical debate about equality, which is frequently focused on achieving greater equality within a society and ignores the much greater inequality that exists between societies.

To the utilitarian there is little merit in Rawls's idea of lexical, or absolute, priority for the worst-off members of society, whether applied to a single society or globally. To see why, consider the following possible distributions. (This time we can, to accommodate Rawlsians, interpret the figures *either* as referring to levels of welfare, or to the Rawlsian primary goods by which political institutions should evaluate how well citizens are doing. These primary goods include such things as basic rights and liberties, freedom of movement and of occupation, powers of office and responsibilities, income and wealth, and the social bases of self-respect.[25])

Present Distribution

Best off	(10% of society)	80
Middle	(80%)	20
Worst off	(10%)	19

Our choices are limited. We can either leave things as they are, or move to:

Future Distribution 1

Best off	(10% of society)	85
Middle	(80%)	80
Worst off	(10%)	19

---

[24] This objection to the approach taken in *A Theory of Justice* has previously been made by Barry in *The Liberal Theory of Justice*; Beitz, *Political Theory and International Relations*, and 'Social and Cosmopolitan Liberalism'; and Pogge, *Realizing Rawls*. Rawls's late work, *The Law of Peoples,* still assumes that the basic principles of justice apply internally, rather than between societies, although it does accept that wealthier societies have some duties— not specified in any detail—to help other societies.

[25] John Rawls, *Justice as Fairness: A Restatement,* 58–9.

To the utilitarian, it is obvious that we should move to *Future Distribution 1* because it greatly improves the lives of 80 per cent of the society (who previously were barely above the level of the worst off) and makes a modest improvement for 10 per cent of the society who are already well off. It also leaves no one worse off (and remember, again, this is after taking into account any envy or powerlessness that they might feel because they are now much worse off than the overwhelming majority of their fellow-citizens). Because Rawlsian justice allows deviations from equality only if they benefit the worst off, however, Rawlsians reject this move.[26]

There are more plausible ways of giving weight to our intuitive sense that it is unfair to benefit those who are already better off, rather than those who are worse off. We might be pluralist egalitarians, giving some weight to utility, and some weight to equality. Giving weight to equality, however, suggests that there is some value in levelling down, and if the weight given is great enough, it could lead to choosing, instead of *Future Distribution 1*:

Future Distribution 2

Best off	(10% of society)	20
Middle	(80%)	20
Worst off	(10%)	20

Utilitarians would of course reject such a move, and so could pluralist egalitarians, if they give sufficient weight to utility. But egalitarians of any kind have difficulty in denying that there is some value in achieving greater equality by reducing the welfare of those at the top, even if this makes no one better off. In this respect prioritarianism seems a better view, for prioritarians want to make everyone better off, while giving some degree of priority to benefiting those who are worse off.[27] Neither pluralist egalitarians nor prioritarians, however,

---

[26] This seems to us the position that Rawls most commonly embraces. As Parfit has pointed out, however, he also makes other, incompatible claims that would rank Future Distribution 1 above the Present Distribution. For references to these passages, see Parfit, *Equality or Priority,* appendix.

[27] The standard reference for prioritarianism is Parfit, *Equality or Priority?* Other influential articles include: Arneson, 'Luck Egalitarianism and Prioritarianism'; Crisp, 'Equality,

have any agreed way of weighing up the importance of the different things they value; that is, for the pluralist egalitarians, how we should trade off utility and equality, and for the prioritarians, how much bigger the benefit going to those who are better off has to be in order to outweigh a smaller benefit going to those who are worse off. In practice, those who hold these views will have to rely on their intuitions, which will vary from person to person.[28]

Despite these weaknesses in the pluralist egalitarian and prioritarian positions, there is one argument that points to a conclusion rather like prioritarianism, and yet is compatible with believing that utilitarianism is likely to be the correct normative theory. It is a variant of the argument from moral risk that we applied to vegetarianism in the previous section of this chapter, here applied by Will MacAskill to the case of benefiting the worse off:

> one should treat benefits to the badly off as being more important than providing the same benefits to the well off, even if one is fairly confident that they should be treated in the same way. It's at least plausible that they are more important, but very implausible that they are less important.[29]

MacAskill calls this a 'moral compromise' argument, distinguishing it from a moral risk argument (or in his terminology, a 'moral caution' argument) because the essential feature of moral risk arguments is that the stakes are asymmetrical. Killing and eating a being with the moral status that makes that seriously wrong is much worse than not eating meat when you had the opportunity to do so. A moral compromise argument requires, not asymmetry of what is at stake, but uncertainty in only one direction. Utilitarians think that we should give equal weight to benefits to the well off and the badly off. Prioritarians think we should give more weight to benefits to the badly off. No one thinks we should give more weight to benefits to the better off. Therefore if we are utilitarian, we are taking a position

---

Priority and Compassion'; Temkin, 'Equality, Priority, and the Levelling Down Objection' and Temkin, 'Equality, Priority, or What?.'

[28] Theron Pummer has argued that prioritarianism is vulnerable to an objection that parallels Nozick's 'utility monster' objection to utilitarianism. See Pummer, 'The Priority Monster'.

[29] MacAskill, 'Moral Caution and Moral Compromise'.

that is on one end of the spectrum. We could be wrong, so we should compromise, and move somewhat closer to the middle of the spectrum. We should aim somewhere between the measures implied by utilitarianism and those implied by prioritarianism. This means, in effect, that we should act as if we were prioritarians, for we should give some extra weight to benefits that go to the worse off—but not as much extra weight as we would give if we accepted the most plausible form of prioritarianism. This task would be much easier if we knew how much extra weight the most plausible form of prioritarianism would give to the worse off, but since prioritarians themselves tend to be vague about that, this vagueness is transferred to, and further increased by, the risk-reducing compromise between that view and utilitarianism.

The only circumstances in which Sidgwick thinks we should appeal to what might be generally considered to be an egalitarian principle is when different distributions will lead to the same total amount of happiness and we need somehow to break the tie. If we had perfect knowledge, such circumstances would be extremely rare, but because there are many cases in which we can only roughly forecast how our actions will affect the utility of those affected by them, in practice we may quite often need to break such ties. For example, in the standard type of example used to show the inegalitarian implications of the principle of utility, it is assumed that we can know that the less egalitarian distribution will lead to a greater quantity of happiness; but unless the difference is very large, we may not be able to distinguish the two outcomes. In that case the principle of utility does not tell us what to do, and needs to be supplemented by some other principle of 'Just or Right distribution'. In this context Sidgwick mentions, as the principle that most utilitarians have adopted, 'pure equality—as given in Bentham's formula, "everybody to count for one, and nobody for more than one."' That formula, however, will have already been used in calculating how much happiness results from the different distributions. So it must really be a different principle of equality—one that treats people equally in some other sense—that serves as a tie-breaker in these situations. Sidgwick does not really say what form of equality he has in mind, though the words he uses—'it must be reasonable to treat any one man in the same way as any other, if there be no reason apparent for treating him differently'—suggests a principle of similar treatment, rather than the desirability of achieving equal outcomes or an equal level of happiness.

4. Not Discounting the Future

When we consider how we should treat the interests of future generations, utilitarians are more egalitarian than a significant section of contemporary thinking. Sidgwick's treatment of this issue parallels his account of the weight a person should give to different periods of his own life. As we saw in Chapter 5, he holds that 'Hereafter *as such* is to be regarded neither less nor more than Now' and the same applies to his view of the weight we should give to the interests of posterity.

Economists typically apply a discount rate to future costs and benefits. Some of the justifications for this do not violate Sidgwick's principle that 'the time at which a man exists cannot affect the value of his happiness'. For example, Sidgwick would accept discounting future costs and benefits on the grounds that we can invest money now and earn interest on it, so that in future we will have more than we have now. He also agrees with discounting for uncertainty—perhaps some calamity will cause the extinction of our species, or perhaps actions that now seem likely to benefit future generations will have unforeseen consequences that will instead harm them. Nor would he reject discounting the importance of a benefit conferred on future generations if we have reason to believe that future generations will be wealthier than ours, and so a given amount of money or quantity of resources will make less difference to them than it makes to us. None of these reasons discounts the future, as such, and so none of them is contrary to Sidgwick's principle. But some economists also apply 'pure time discounting' which means that they give less weight to the future simply because it is still to come. The arguments by which they defend pure time discounting, however, often confuse it with one of the other reasons for discounting. For example, the Austrian economist Ludwig von Mises defended 'the universal validity of time preference' by arguing that, if we did not prefer the near future to the more distant future, we would invest everything we have, never consuming anything now. He claims: 'Every penny spent today is, precisely under the conditions of a capitalist economy in which institutions make it possible to invest even the smallest sums, a proof of the higher valuation of present satisfaction as compared with later satisfaction.'[30] It is, however, not a proof of that at all. If we did not consume anything now, we would be as poor as we could possibly be—in fact we would starve and have no future at all—and so the fact that we do spend something on consumption can be explained by our desire to gain maximum benefit from each dollar we spend, without any preference for the present. Admittedly, we do consume more now than we need for our bare survival, but that can also easily be explained: it would be crazy to think that we would maximize our lifetime utility by investing everything we have, beyond what we need to survive, for the future and spending it all near the end of our life. Von Mises seems to assume that greater wealth means greater happiness, but that is plainly false.

Economists sometimes argue that we should accept pure time discounting because the actions of ordinary people in the marketplace indicate that they do discount the future, and it is not the task of the economist to impose his or her ethical views on what people prefer. One problem with this approach is that it is difficult to interpret the behaviour of ordinary people in the marketplace as expressing their pure time-preferences, because we do not know what they are assuming about the probabilities of their own survival or of their future wealth. More significantly, however, we should question the idea that, when economists draw their discount rate from the market behaviour of ordinary people, they are taking a democratic, ethically neutral approach, rather than imposing their own values on others. Consider the positions of A. C. Pigou, who held the chair of political economy at Cambridge University from 1908 to 1943, and had been a student of Sidgwick's, and the contemporary economist Stephen Marglin, who holds a chair at Harvard University. Pigou, consistently with the views of his teacher, considered that governments

---

[30] Von Mises, *Human Action*, 483.

should act as 'the trustee for unborn generations' and should 'protect the interests of the future…against the effects of our irrational discounting and of our preference for ourselves over our descendants'.[31] Marglin, on the other hand, has written: 'I consider it axiomatic that a democratic government reflects only the preferences of the individuals who are presently members of the body politic.'[32] This claim is either false or settles nothing. It is false if the preferences in question are those that the individuals express in the marketplace, rather than in the ballot box. The question of what weight is to be given to the interests of future generations is one for democratic politics, and no matter how people behave when buying or selling products, it would be wrong to seek to exclude from that debate the view that we should give equal weight to the interests of future generations. Such a stance, far from being ethically neutral, would itself be the imposition of a specific ethical view. If, on the other hand, the claim is that a democratic government reflects the preferences of those who elect it, the claim settles nothing, for both voters and politicians ought to consider what weight to give to the interests of future generations. We would hope that such questions would be discussed before elections, and that informed and rational voters would see the merits of Sidgwick's and Pigou's view. In any case, there is no way in which democratic principles alone can tell us whether we ought to discount the future. A substantive ethical decision is inescapable.

Whether or not we accept pure time discounting makes a critical difference to the economics of climate change, where the extent to which we discount the future is a key determinant of the amount we should be prepared to spend to avoid disasters that will otherwise occur many decades, and even centuries, from now. For example, at the discount rate of 5.5 per cent used by William Nordhaus, one of the leading economists writing in this area, it would not be worth spending more than \$1 today to prevent \$240 worth of harm a century from now.[33]

---

[31] Pigou, *The Economics of Welfare*. We owe this reference to Broome, *Climate Matters*, 142–3.

[32] Marglin, 'The Social Rate of Discount and the Optimal Rate of Investment', 97. This reference too is from Broome's *Climate Matters*, 142.

[33] Nordhaus, *A Question of Balance*. Nordhaus derives from his economic model an annual discount rate for the next 50 years of 5.5%. He uses a lower rate, 4%, for the next

The same would apply to saving lives—if we have a choice between increasing the health care budget by $100 million to save one life now, or to use the same sum to reduce greenhouse emissions in a manner that would, with complete certainty, save 239 lives in a century, a discount rate of 5.5 per cent implies that we should save the one life now.

Sidgwick would have sided with Nicholas Stern, who in a major review of the economics of climate change written for the United Kingdom government says that he treats 'the *welfare* of future generations on a par with our own'.[34] Stern discounts only for uncertainty about the future (he takes into account the small probability that, for example, a meterorite might wipe us all out) and for the likelihood that we may be wealthier in future. As Stern notes, economists with a strong interest in philosophy tend to reject pure time discounting. He quotes F. P. Ramsey as attributing it to 'weakness of the imagination', and R. F. Harrod who viewed it as a 'human infirmity' and 'a polite expression for rapacity and the conquest of reason by passion'.[35] Harrod's suggestion that it is a human infirmity has been echoed by Dean Buonomano who, as we saw in Chapter 5, calls it a 'brain bug'.[36] In this debate we think that the philosophers, and the economists who are most influenced by them, get it right.

5. How Many People Should There Be?

We can affect not only the quality of life of future generations, but also the number of people that there will be in future. As we saw at the beginning of this chapter, Sidgwick begins his discussion of this issue with the assumption that the average human life contains more pleasure than pain. In a footnote, he comments that those who take the

century as a whole, although it is not clear why. Even at 4%, the well-being of a person in the middle of the next century is worth only one-fortieth of the well-being of a person today. See John Broome, *Climate Matters*, 139, and Dimitri Zenghelis, 'The Question of Global Warming: An Exchange'.

[34] Nicholas Stern, *Stern Review on the Economics of Climate Change*, ch. 2, s. 4, p. 31.

[35] F. P. Ramsey, 'A Mathematical Theory of Saving', 543, and R. F. Harrod, *Towards a Dynamic Economics*, 37–40; both quoted by Stern, *Stern Review on the Economics of Climate Change*, 31.

[36] Buonomano, *Brain Bugs*; see p. 129, above.

opposite view generally assume that 'the appetites and desires which are the mainspring of ordinary human action are in themselves painful: a view entirely contrary to my own experience, and, I believe, to the common experience of mankind'. David Benatar has revived this pessimistic view of human life, and he does so in the way that Sidgwick anticipates, arguing that to have a desire for something is to be in a negative state. Like Schopenhauer, he holds that when we do get what we desire, we have a fleeting moment of satisfaction, but it is not long before we are again dissatisfied, so that the brief satisfactions of our lives do not outweigh the much longer periods of dissatisfaction or striving for things we want but do not have. He adds that the fact that, once we are alive, we do not wish to die does not show that this view is false, because once we are alive we may have reasons for continuing to live—for example, the grief that our death would cause others. This does not show that it is good to bring children into existence, and the view that in doing so we confer something good on them is, Benatar believes, an illusion, perhaps one that is common because taking a rosy view of life helped our ancestors survive.[37]

We agree with Benatar that the fact that we want to go on living does not settle the question of whether it is good to bring a being into existence, and we also accept that the widely held—but by no means universal—view that life is good does not prove that it really is good. But we also agree with Sidgwick that to have an unsatisfied desire is not in itself to suffer or to be in a negative state. To be moderately hungry is not unpleasant, at least when one knows that food will be available before the hunger gets really serious. Desires give us purposes and goals and so add interest and stimulation to our lives. We often cultivate them just for that reason, as we do when we get involved in competitive sports, whether as a participant or a spectator. The desire to win—or that our team should win—makes the activity more enjoyable. If it also makes us suffer when we (or our team) lose, we take that as an unavoidable part of a package that we judge to be, on the whole, good. A similar verdict about life as a whole is not unreasonable: for people who are able to satisfy the basic necessities of life

[37] Benatar, *Better Never to Have Been.*

and who are not suffering from depression or chronic pain, life can reasonably be judged positively.

From this positive view of life it follows, Sidgwick believes, that it is good to bring more beings into existence, other things being equal. Even if other things are *not* equal—that is, if bringing more beings into existence will cause the average level of happiness to fall—he thinks it will still be good to bring more beings into existence as long as the happiness of the additional beings is greater than the loss of happiness to others. In deciding how many beings should exist, we should be guided by the total amount of happiness that will result, and not by the average level of happiness.

Sidgwick's discussion of the choice between a higher average or greater total amount of happiness received very little attention until the late 1960s. One of the very few exceptions is C. D. Broad, who accepted that utilitarianism has the implication that we should increase the total happiness even if this means reducing the average level of happiness, but added that it is 'perfectly plain' that this is the wrong thing to do.[38] When Jan Narveson wrote about 'Utilitarianism and New Generations' in 1967, he denied that the classical utilitarian view implied that we have a duty to produce children if they would be happy, and showed no awareness of Sidgwick's contrary opinion.[39] The following year Timothy Sprigge responded to Narveson, and did refer to Sidgwick's distinction between the total and average views.[40] Around that time Derek Parfit began discussing the question in seminars at Oxford University, although he did not publish on the topic until 1976, and it took a further 8 years for a full account of his arguments to appear as Part IV of *Reasons and Persons*.[41] Meanwhile, many other articles stimulated by his approach to the problem began to appear. Inevitably, our own account of the issue is heavily indebted to Parfit.

We note, first, that this problem is not specific to utilitarianism. Any ethical theory that is able to offer guidance on decisions affecting

---

[38] Broad, *Five Types of Ethical Theory*, 249–50.
[39] Narveson, 'Utility and New Generations', 62–72.
[40] Sprigge, 'Professor Narveson's Utilitarianism', 339–40.
[41] Parfit, 'On Doing the Best for our Children' and 'Rights, Interests, and Possible People', 369–75.

the size of future generations must in some way deal with these issues, and it is a weakness if it is unable to do so. This is the case with contractualist views that base moral principles on the choices made by people in some 'original position'. In Rawls's version, for instance, people choose the basic principles of justice behind a veil of ignorance that prevents them from knowing their sex, race, talents, and so on. The idea is that they will then choose principles that treat these different groups fairly. But everyone in the original position does know that he or she *exists*. If the question of changing the size of the population is raised, the theory is therefore open to the accusation that it is biased in favour of those whose existence is a given, and has no way of fairly judging whether it is desirable to bring more people into existence, not for the sake of those who already exist or will exist anyway, but for the sake of the people who will exist only if the decision is taken to increase the size of the population.

Second, although the population problem Sidgwick poses does have some applications in the world in which we now live, to grasp the fundamental issues we must disregard environmental or other constraints on the population that our planet can support. It is arguable that we already have too many people, in both the average *and* the total sense—that is, that any further growth in the world's population will reduce both the average and the total happiness in the world. Nevertheless, to consider the principles we should adopt, we must imagine situations in which it is possible to add to the world's population in ways that increase the total amount of happiness in the world.

Imagine that you are a member of a government advisory committee that has been asked to make recommendations on population policy in a world like ours, but with only one million people in it, all of whom have a very high level of welfare. You could recommend that the government seek to maintain the population as it is at present, or you could recommend offering people an incentive to have larger families. For simplicity, we will assume that no non-human animals will be affected by this choice. We can diagram the options as in Figure 12.1, using the vertical axis to indicate the average level of happiness, and the horizontal axis to indicate the number of people in the world.

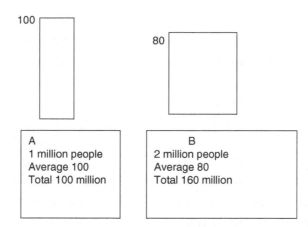

Figure 12.1: Average v. Total

Assume that people at level 100 are extremely happy, and that people at 80 are slightly less happy but still very happy. Given this choice, Sidgwick believes that we should choose B, since that has the higher total quantity of happiness. The only alternative principle he mentions, which he thinks is assumed by followers of Malthus, is to seek the highest possible average level of happiness, which in this case would mean choosing A. But the average view has implausible implications, as we can see by considering a different choice (Figure 12.2).

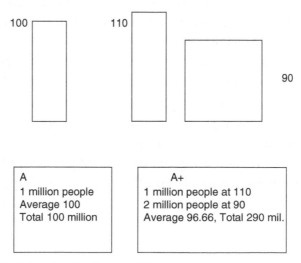

Figure 12.2: A Problem for the Average View

Assume that the people in the left-hand column of A+ are the same people as the entire population of A and that though the additional two million people in A+ are less happy than the other one million, this is not because of any injustice, but because of natural phenomena that cannot be changed and for which compensation is impossible. The average level of happiness is higher in A than in A+, so the average view tells us to choose A. But this seems very odd, because A+ contains as many people as are in A, all at a higher level than anyone in A, and the additional people who exist only in A+ are leading very good lives and are pleased that they exist. We can see no good reason for preferring A to A+, and therefore we reject the average view.

If this example is not enough to persuade you that the average view should be rejected, consider a world we can call Mini Hell, in which there are only ten people, but all of them suffer agony for their entire lives. We have the option of changing this world to Maxi Almost-Hell in which there are ten billion people all suffering the same kind of agony as the people in Mini Hell, except that in each person's life there is 1 minute which, though still painful, is slightly less agonizing. So the average life in Maxi Almost-Hell is a tiny bit better than the average life in Mini Hell, but the total amount of suffering is vastly greater. It is hard to believe that we ought to bring about the change from Mini Hell to Maxi Almost-Hell.

Was Sidgwick right, then, to say that we should increase population up to the point at which we have maximized the total amount of utility? The problem with this view is that it leads to what Parfit has called 'the Repugnant Conclusion'.[42] For any population of very happy people it is possible to imagine a world in which everyone is living a life that is only barely worth living, but because there are so many people, the total amount of happiness is greater. The total view would then tell us to choose this much larger population. Most people refuse to accept that simply increasing the number of people leading lives just barely worth living would eventually bring about a better world than one containing a large number of people leading very good lives.

[42] Parfit, *Reasons and Persons,* ch. 17.

Because both the average view and the total view lead to conclusions that are difficult to accept, many people have looked for a different view. It is intuitively plausible to believe that the mistake lies in the assumption that utilitarianism is concerned with making happy people, rather than with making people happy.[43] Certainly there seems to be a big difference between improving the life of an existing person, and bringing into the world a new person who would not otherwise exist. To many people it is obvious that we have obligations to improve the lives of existing people, but not at all obvious that we ought to bring people into existence because they would be happy. Parents, for instance, are commonly seen as having obligations to promote the welfare of their children, but couples are not seen as having an obligation to reproduce merely because their children are likely to be happy.

Sidgwick seems to have been aware of this distinction, for the sentences in which he appears to advocate the total view begin with the conditional: 'For if we take Utilitarianism to prescribe, as the ultimate end of action, happiness on the whole, and not any individual's happiness, unless considered as an element of the whole' (*ME* 415). Presumably Sidgwick does think utilitarianism should prescribe 'happiness on the whole' as the ultimate end, for otherwise he would surely discuss what it would mean for utilitarianism to prescribe, as the ultimate end of action, the happiness of individuals rather than happiness on the whole. One way of understanding the difference would be the one we have just outlined: we should promote the welfare of existing beings, rather than of beings we could bring into existence. But that is insufficient, because we also have obligations to beings who do not yet exist, but will exist, or are very likely to exist—for example, if our nuclear power plants produce waste that will be radioactive for thousands of years, it would be wrong for us to put it in containers that will only last 200 years, and dump them in a lake. We might therefore reformulate 'utilitarianism that aims at the happiness of individuals' as holding that we should promote

---

[43] Narveson, 'Moral Problems of Population'; see also Roberts, 'A New Way of Doing the Best that we Can'.

the welfare of existing beings and those who will exist, independently of our decisions. We will call this the 'prior existence' version
of utilitarianism, with the understanding that 'prior' is used, not in
a chronological sense, but rather in the sense that the existence of
the being is already determined, prior to the choice we are about to
make.[44]

Although at first glance the prior existence view offers an intuitively appealing alternative to the total view, it struggles to deal with
several situations. First, there seems to be an asymmetry in our
intuitions about bringing a happy child into existence and bringing a miserable child into existence. The fact that the prior existence
view does not imply that couples have an obligation to bring a happy
child into existence seems to be a clear advantage over the total view,
but this brings with it a difficulty in explaining what is wrong with
a decision to bring into existence a child who—perhaps because
the parents know that they carry the gene that causes Tay-Sachs
disease—would have a miserable life before dying at an early age.
Once the child exists, and is suffering, then the prior existence view
implies that we have an obligation to reduce its suffering, perhaps
even by killing it, if that is the only possible way to do so. The child's
existence is not a given, though, prior to the decision to conceive
it, and therefore the prior existence view provides no grounds for
objecting to that decision.

The prior existence view also needs to give a plausible answer to
situations in which the identity of the person who will be born varies
according to what we choose to do. Parfit's example of two women fac-
ing the possibility of having children with disabilities illustrates the
problem.[45] The first woman is pregnant when her doctor tells her that
her child will have a disability, unless she takes a certain drug, which
he offers to prescribe for her. The drug is free and has no side-effects.
The second woman is planning to stop using contraception, as she

[44] Parfit uses the term 'person-affecting principle' to describe something that could be
equivalent to the prior existence view, but can also have different implications, depending
on whether we consider that causing a person to exist is a way of affecting her. See *Reasons
and Persons*, 393ff.

[45] This is a variant on an example originally given by Parfit in *Reasons and Persons*, 366–7.

wishes to have a child, when her doctor tells her that she has a temporary medical condition as a result of which she will have a child with a disability, unless she waits 3 months before conceiving her child. The disability the child will have is the same in both cases. It significantly affects the child's life, but the child's life will still be worth living. The first woman does not take the drug, and the second woman does not wait before conceiving. They both have a child with the predicted disability. The first mother has harmed her child, who already existed at the time of the decision. The second mother's child, however, only came into existence because she chose not to wait before conceiving. If she had waited, she would have had a different child—conceived from a different sperm and a different egg, perhaps a girl instead of a boy, and in any case no more like the child she did have than two non-identical twins. On the prior existence view, only the first mother has done something wrong, for only the first child existed independently of his mother's decision.

Some people have a 'who can complain?' view of morality. They think that if no one has a ground for a complaint against what you have done, you cannot have done anything wrong. On this basis, they argue that it is wrong to conceive a child who will have a miserable life because that child can complain that you should not have conceived her. If, on the other hand, you refrain from having a happy child, there is no child who can complain, because there is no child waiting around in limbo who would have had a happy life, if you had conceived that child. Similarly, in the two-women example, only the first woman's child can justly complain to his mother. He can say: 'You should have done as the doctor advised. Then I would have had a better life.' If the second woman's child makes the same complaint, his mother can say: 'No you wouldn't. I would have had a different child and you would not have existed. Since your life is worth living, despite your disability, I did not harm you by conceiving you.'

We should reject the 'who can complain?' view of morality. If you have a child who has a happy life, that child can thank you for bringing her into existence. We think that it is good to increase someone's happiness, as well as to reduce someone's suffering, so we should take into account, when it applies, the fact that there will be someone to thank us, as well as the fact that there will be someone to reproach us. In the case of the two women, even though only one child can reproach his mother, we think both women did something wrong—indeed, we would say that what they did was equally wrong. The problem is that, while a form of utilitarianism that seeks to maximize the total net surplus of happiness over misery can easily explain why the two women did something equally wrong—for they both reduced the quantity of happiness in the world by the same amount—the prior existence view does not allow us to reach this judgment.

We might instead say: 'Both women have decided to have a child. In both cases, therefore, the existence of their child is prior to their decision not to do what would prevent their child having a disability. The women have not done the best for their child, and consistently with the prior existence view, their actions can be judged to be wrong.' This response, with its use of the term 'their child' to range over more than one possible individual, resembles the actress Zsa Zsa Gabor's method of keeping her husband young: when he approached middle age, she got a new one.[46] But we could reformulate the prior existence view so that, instead of referring to 'the welfare of existing beings and those who will exist, independently of our decisions', it refers to 'the welfare of that number of beings who exist, and will exist, independently of our decisions'. This formulation solves the problem of the two women, and other problems in which we are choosing *who* will exist, but not *how many* people will exist. But this approach stumbles over cases in which our decisions also affect the number of people who will exist. Such situations can give rise to what Parfit calls the 'mere addition paradox'.[47] Consider the choice we discussed between A and A+, in which the extra people in A+ were a 'mere addition' to those in A, and now add a third possibility we can call C (see Figure 12.3).

---

[46] Caspar Hare, 'Voices from Another World', 514.
[47] Parfit, *Reasons and Persons*, ch. 19.

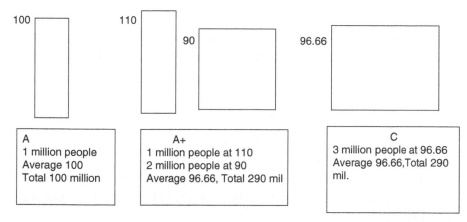

Figure 12.3: The Mere Addition Paradox

C contains the same number of people as A+, and at the same average level of happiness, so on the interpretation of the prior existence view that we are now considering, C is not worse than A+. If as we saw earlier, however, A+ is not worse than A, it seems that C cannot be worse than A either. Yet on the prior existence view, if we were choosing between A and C then C *would* be worse than A because the number of people who will exist independently of our decision is only one million, so we count only the welfare of one million people and they are less happy in C than in A.

That is not all. We can now make a new comparison with C as the baseline (Figure 12.4).

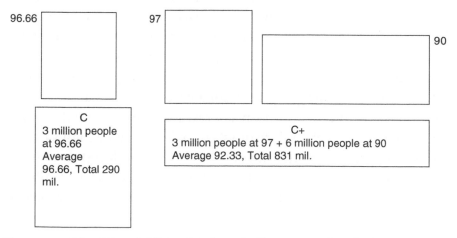

Figure 12.4: How Mere Addition Leads to the Repugnant Conclusion

Once again, C+ contains the same number of people as in C at a higher average level of welfare than anyone in C and also contains additional people at a lower, but still good, level, who are happy that they are alive. Just as we argued that A+ is not worse than A, we can argue that C+ is not worse than C. Next, we can imagine a new D that is not worse than C+. The process can be repeated indefinitely with the average level of happiness dropping and the population increasing. Eventually we will get to Z, a very large population at a level of happiness that is only just positive, and yet this world seems to be not worse than A—in other words, another version of the repugnant conclusion.

The problems we have here outlined have baffled many philosophers, spawned a large and complicated literature, and led to proposals that in other contexts would not be given serious consideration. Larry Temkin thinks that we must abandon transitivity in our judgments that one state of affairs is, all things considered, better than another. In other words, he thinks that we might agree A is, all things considered, better than B, and B is, all things considered, better than C, but *not* accept that A is, all things considered, better than C.[48]

Parfit, in his most recent work on this topic, appeals to the idea of a fundamental imprecision in comparisons involving different values. To illustrate, he points out that Einstein and Beethoven were both geniuses, but claims that it is implausible to maintain that the greatness of their genius could be precisely equal. Yet we can say that Einstein was a greater genius than a lesser composer than Beethoven, and that Beethoven was a greater genius than a lesser scientist than Einstein. To take a more practical example, imagine that you are offered a position working in a corporate law office at a salary of $200,000, and another position as a researcher observing the behaviour of forest birds at a salary of $50,000. You prefer a high salary to a lower one and a job that involves working in a forest to one that is entirely indoors. You might conclude, not just that it is difficult to decide which job is better for you, but that the two positions are

[48] Temkin, 'Intransitivity and the Mere Addition Paradox'.

imprecisely equally good. If you are then offered a third position in a corporate law office at a salary of $250,000, you may judge that job to be better than the lower-paid law position, but still only imprecisely equally as good as the position of bird researcher. Here the relationship of 'imprecisely as good' does not allow for the usual transitive judgments that we would have to accept if we agreed that the bird researcher position was precisely as good as the less well-paid law position. Similarly, Parfit argues, we may hold that different worlds with different numbers of people in them at different levels of happiness are imprecisely equally as good as each other. If we apply this to the different populations we used in illustrating the mere addition paradox, then because the relationship 'not imprecisely better than' is not transitive, it may be true that, although A is not better than B, and B is not better than C, and so on, all the way down to Z, A *is* better than Z.[49]

In contrast to such novel proposals, Sidgwick's suggestion that we should maximize total utility remains a straightforward and consistent way of handling these questions, even if it has a deeply counter-intuitive consequence. Sidgwick did not consider the repugnant conclusion, so we do not know what he would have said about it. Perhaps he would not have been troubled by counter-intuitive conclusions that have little application to the real world. That is a reasonable position to take, because, as Joshua Greene has suggested, it may simply be too hard for our intuitions to grapple with the numbers involved in the comparison we are being asked to make. Our intuitions don't really respond to the difference between 100 million and 10 billion.[50]

The deep difficulties standing in the way of a defensible solution to ethical problems involving bringing more people into the world also apply to questions about bringing non-human animals into the world, and therefore to the issue we postponed earlier in this chapter: Stephen's argument that killing some animals is justifiable when it makes it possible for others to exist, if those animals have

[49] Parfit, 'How We Can Avoid the Repugnant Conclusion'.
[50] Greene makes this point in *Moral Tribes*, 380.

good lives and everything else is equal. We can now see that Salt, who rejected this view as 'nonsense' because it takes into account the interests of beings who may never exist, assumes the prior existence view, whereas Stephen takes the total view. Our inability to resolve the issue between these two views means that we are also unable to reach a decision on the defence of eating meat in the circumstances described, in which animals lead good lives and would not exist if it were not for the practice of killing them for meat. Here arguments from moral uncertainty do not help us either, because there are risks on both sides. If we eat meat from animals who have led good lives, we are risking killing a sentient animal and depriving it of further life. Some philosophers have advanced strong arguments for thinking that this is wrong. On the other hand we will be supporting a system that gives good lives to many animals, as well as to humans who want to combine farming with concern for animal welfare. Some philosophers and other thinkers have argued that such a system of farming benefits animals and humans, and that without it, important values will be lost.[51] If we cannot be completely confident about the choice between these two views, that uncertainty does not point us in one direction rather than the other.

To conclude this section, we ask a supremely important question: how should we respond to the risk of a catastrophe that would bring about the extinction of our species? If, with Sidgwick, we agree that 'life on the average yields a positive balance of pleasure over pain'—or if we are not hedonists, but agree that on average it has more positive than negative value of some other kind—we are likely to think that human extinction would be a very bad thing. One reason for not drawing this conclusion would be that the suffering humans cause, and will continue to cause, animals outweighs the value of human existence. But animals also suffer greatly when they

---

[51] For the arguments against eating meat from happy animals, see e.g. Visak, *Killing Happy Animals,* and McMahan, 'Eating Animals the Nice Way'. For the arguments on the other side, see Scruton, 'The Conscientious Carnivore', and Pollan, 'An Animal's Place'. For the views of one of us on this question as a practical issue in the world in which we are living, see Singer and Mason, *The Ethics of What we Eat,* ch. 17.

live naturally, without human interference, and if humans become extinct, there is no hope of that situation changing, whereas the continued existence of human beings does offer the hope that eventually we will be both intelligent enough and compassionate enough to reduce that suffering.

How bad, though, would human extinction be? That question is not merely theoretical, because there are things that we can do to reduce the risk of human extinction. There is, for example, a small chance that our planet will be hit by an asteroid large enough to wipe us out. We are already tracking such objects in space and seeing if they pose a risk to us. It is probably within our capabilities, if we were willing to devote enough resources to it, to build a rocket that would intercept any asteroid that is on a collision course with us and deflect it from that course. If the chances of a doomsday asteroid hitting Earth during the next century are around one in a million, how much should we be prepared to spend on such a project?[52] To reach a sound answer to that question we would need answers to many relevant factual questions, including whether we could spend the resources better combating other risks of extinction (nuclear war, a pandemic, global warming speeding up to the point at which it makes our planet uninhabitable, and so on). But the philosophical issue we have been discussing is also relevant. Parfit shows this by asking his readers to imagine three possible scenarios for the future of our planet:

(1) Peace.
(2) A nuclear war that kills 99 per cent of the world's existing population.
(3) A nuclear war that kills 100 per cent.

Any sane person will agree that (2) would be worse than (1) and (3) would be worse than (2). But which is the greater of those differences? Parfit's judgment is that the difference between (3) and (2) is '*very much* greater' and he justifies this by pointing out that the Earth will remain habitable for at least a billion years, and if we do not

---

[52] Matheny, 'Reducing the Risk of Human Extinction'.

destroy ourselves, the entire history of civilization will be just a tiny fraction of human existence.[53]

Those who accept the prior existence view will not share Parfit's judgment. They will focus on the loss of life of those who exist now, or will exist in future, irrespective of what we do. On the prior existence view, the difference between (3) and (2) is relatively small, whereas the difference between (2) and (1) is very large. Parfit's answer presupposes that there is some value in the existence of beings who would not otherwise exist, as long as they live good lives. Because there are so many people who will exist, if our species survives for a billion years, Parfit would not have to hold that their lives have the same value as the lives of presently existing people, but he must hold that they have some value.

We can now return to the question of how much we should be prepared to spend to prevent threats of extinction. The debate over the value of bringing into existence beings who will have good lives, but whose existence is contingent on our making certain choices, is lively, complicated, and raises deep philosophical questions. The widespread belief that couples are under no obligation to have children, even when those children will have good lives, provides some intuitive support for denying that there is value in bringing new beings into existence. This position also has the merit of avoiding the repugnant conclusion. On the other hand it makes sense to hold—as Sidgwick seems to have held—that in contemplating bringing them into existence, we should give the lives they will lead as much value as the equally pleasant lives of anyone else. No one, on the other hand, thinks that the lives of future possible beings should count for more than the similarly good lives of presently existing beings. This situation again seems one in which we ought to compromise, and in our practice, give some positive value to the lives of future beings. Even if we think the prior existence view is more plausible than the total view, we should recognize that we could be mistaken about this and therefore give some value to the

---

[53] Parfit, *Reasons and Persons*, 453–4.

life of a possible future—let's say, for example, 10 per cent of the value we give to the similar life of a presently existing being. The number of human beings who will come into existence only if we can avoid extinction is so huge that even with that relatively low value, reducing the risk of human extinction will often be a highly cost-effective strategy for maximizing utility, as long as we have some understanding of what will reduce that risk.[54]

[54] The use of moral compromise in regard to existential risk is discussed by MacAskill, 'Moral Caution and Moral Compromise'. On the importance of avoiding the risk of extinction, see Bostrom, 'Astronomical Waste'; Bostrom and Cirkovic (eds), *Global Catastrophic Risk*.

Conclusion

In this book we have followed the main lines of Sidgwick's thinking about ethics, and tested his views both against our own reasoning and against the best of the vast body of recent and current philosophical writing on the topics he addresses. The overarching question we have sought to answer is whether Sidgwick's form of utilitarianism can be defended. In most respects we believe it can be. Parfit's claim that, in the long tradition of ethics, 'Sidgwick's book contains the largest number of true and important claims' stands up well.[1]

Greatly as we admire *The Methods of Ethics,* no work of philosophy should be seen as immune to revision. Our most significant revision is our attempt to strengthen the foundations of Sidgwick's idea of taking 'the Point of View of the Universe'. We have argued, as he hesitated to do, that the 'the Point of View of the Universe' is the perspective of a rational being, in a way that alternative perspectives, such as that of egoism, are not.

Though we hope to have established some important points, we know, as Sidgwick did, that we are dealing with questions on which there are different views, and when writers in ethics invoke the term 'proof', what follows usually turns out to be something much weaker than a proof. Sometimes the best we can do is follow Sidgwick in appealing to 'the sober judgment of reflective persons' and hope that they will find themselves in agreement with us. At the same time, like Sidgwick, we believe that ethics is based on reason, and this makes it possible to expect that, as our reasoning develops and builds on the work of those who have thought about ethics before us, we will improve our understanding of ethics and get closer to the truth about what we ought to do.

[1] Parfit, *On What Matters,* i, p. xxxiii.

For much of the 20th century, Sidgwick's belief that ethics has a rational basis was decidedly unfashionable. In some circles it still is. There are signs, however, that on this issue opinion is swinging back in Sidgwick's direction, and not only among philosophers, but among scientists too. The role of reason in leading us to act more ethically is a major theme of Steven Pinker's *The Better Angels of our Nature*, a study of the factors that have, over the course of human history, reduced violence and cruelty.[2] Pinker assembles an impressive body of evidence to show that, although the 20th century saw two terrible world wars and the atrocities committed by Hitler, Stalin, Pol Pot, and others, anyone born in that century had a lower chance of meeting a violent death at the hands of another human being than people born in any previous century. Pinker regards our ability to reason as one of the key factors in this ethical improvement, which has been taking place over many centuries and even millennia.

In support of his argument that reason leads to moral improvement, Pinker refers to the 'Flynn effect'—the remarkable finding by the philosopher James Flynn that, ever since IQ tests were first administered, the scores achieved by those taking the test have been rising. The average IQ is, by definition, 100; but to achieve that result, raw test scores have to be standardized. If the average teenager today could go back in time and take an IQ test from 1910, he or she would have an IQ of 130, which would be better than 98 per cent of those taking the test then. This change cannot be attributed solely to improved education, because the aspects of the tests on which scores have risen most do not test vocabulary or mathematical skills, but powers of abstract reasoning. Flynn himself thinks that the scientific mode of reasoning has spread through the population, and that this has played a role in the improvement in reasoning.

Pinker argues that enhanced powers of reasoning give us the ability to detach ourselves from our immediate experience and from our personal or parochial perspective, and frame our ideas in more abstract, universal terms. If he had read Sidgwick, he might have written that our enhanced reasoning abilities make it more

---

[2] Pinker, *The Better Angels of our Nature*.

likely that we will take the point of view of the universe, and begin to see that the good of any one individual is of no more importance than the good of any other. It is just this kind of reasoning ability that has improved during the 20th century. Pinker therefore suggests that the 20th century has seen a '*moral* Flynn effect'.

The results of this change are impressive. It takes something of an effort to read an enlightened thinker like Sidgwick and realize that, in England in his day, women could not attend university. Changing that was a cause to which he was deeply committed, and except in some isolated parts of the world in which traditionalists or religious fundamentalists still hold sway, it is a cause that has triumphed. Not only that: over the past century, hundreds of millions of men have accepted that women are their equals, even though this new view commits them to abandoning the idea that they are entitled to be head of the household, simply because they are men.

Something similar has happened to the kind of racism that is evident in Sidgwick's description of the view of beneficence held by common sense morality in his day: that we owe kindness 'to those of our own race more than to black or yellow men'. Like men in regard to women, white racists have, by and large, ceased to defend the idea that they have inherently superior status over those outside their group. This has meant a reduction in their political power, for example in accepting that colonialism is not justified—a point on which contemporary moral thinking has advanced beyond the views that Sidgwick himself expressed.

Another cause that we have reason to believe Sidgwick would have supported, were it not that he considered the personal costs of doing so too great, and the prospect of achieving any desirable reform too small, is the rights of people with sexual orientations that are not heterosexual. Sidgwick might have privately looked forward to the day when homosexual acts between consenting adults would cease to be a crime, but he surely could not have foreseen that in many countries, including his own, it would be possible for people of the same sex to marry.

The ethical gulf between humans and animals remains wide, but many of us now acknowledge that we should not inflict suffering on animals without an overriding reason for doing so. Sidgwick, like his utilitarian predecessors, was a firm supporter of the view that the pains and pleasures of animals are not to be excluded from our moral calculations, nor are they to be discounted merely because they are not the pains and pleasures of members of our own species. Here too Sidgwick would have been encouraged by the progress made since his time, admittedly not so much in the treatment of animals—for the spread of industrialized animal production has greatly increased the suffering we inflict on them—but in the increasing recognition in many countries that animal suffering matters, and that what we are doing to them is ethically indefensible.

Ethics is a unique subject. As an area of philosophy, it challenges us to develop theories, construct arguments, weigh objections, and above all, to reason clearly; but ethics is also the point at which philosophy engages with our everyday lives, and can have an impact on the way we live and on the world as a whole. Sidgwick was well aware of these two faces of ethics. In the preface to the first edition of *The Methods of Ethics* he wrote that he saw his work as a contribution to knowledge, seeking to show 'what conclusions will be rationally reached if we start with certain ethical premises, and with what degree of certainty and precision'. But this quest was not for knowledge for the sake of knowledge; rather it was a necessary element of a proper response to 'the urgent need which we all feel of finding and adopting the true method of determining what we ought to do'. Our aim in this book has been the same as Sidgwick's, to make progress in philosophy in order to make progress in practice. Ultimately, we hope that our work will be seen as part of a long line of thought that has helped many generations to live in ways that are happier, more fulfilling, less prone to inflict cruelty or to suffer it, and committed to improving the well-being of other conscious beings. In a word, lives that are more ethical.

Bibliography

Aknin, L. B., Barrington-Leigh, C. P., Dunn, E. W., Helliwell, J. F., Burns, J., Biswas-Diener, R., Kemeza, I., Nyende, P., Ashton-James, C. E., and Norton, M. I., *Prosocial Spending and Well-Being: Cross-Cultural Evidence for a Psychological Universal*, National Bureau of Economic Research Working Paper, 16415 (2010), available at <http://www.nber.org/papers/w16415>.

Alexander, R., *The Biology of Moral Systems* (New York: Aldine de Gruyter, 1987).

Alfano, M., 'Some Normative Implications of Indeterminate and Unstable Preferences', a paper delivered to the Fellows Seminar of the University Center for Human Values, Princeton University, 13 Nov. 2012.

Alfano, M., 'Wilde Heuristics and Rum Tum Tuggers: Preference Indeterminacy and Instability', *Synthese*, 189 (2012), 5–15.

Anik, L., Aknin, L., Norton, M., and Dunn, E., *Feeling Good about Giving: The Benefits (and Costs) of Self-Interested Charitable Behavior*, Harvard Business School Working Paper, 10-012 (Cambridge, Mass.: Harvard Business School, 2009).

Anscombe, G. E. M., 'Modern Moral Philosophy', *Philosophy*, 33/124 (Jan. 1958), 1–19.

Appiah, K. W., *Cosmopolitanism: Ethics in a World of Strangers* (New York: Norton, 2006).

Aristotle, *Nicomachean Ethics*, ed. and tr. R. Crisp (Cambridge: Cambridge University Press, 2000).

Arneson, R., 'Luck Egalitarianism and Prioritarianism', *Ethics*, 110 (2000), 339–49.

Arneson, R., 'Sophisticated Rule Consequentionalism: Some Simple Objections', *Philosophical Issues*, 15 (2005), 235–51.

Arneson, R., 'What do we Owe to Distant Needy Strangers', in J. Schaler (ed.), *Peter Singer Under Fire* (Chicago, IL: Open Court, 2009), 267–93.

Aschrott, P. F., *Das Englische Armen-Wesen*, publ. as *The English Poor Law System, Past and Present*, tr. Herbert Preston-Thomas with a preface by Henry Sidgwick (London: Knight, 1888).

Ashford, E., 'The Demandingness of Scanlon's Contractualism', *Ethics*, 113/2 (Jan. 2003), 273–302.

Ashford, E., 'Utilitarianism, Integrity, and Partiality', *Journal of Philosophy*, 97 (2000), 421–39.

Ashford, E., and Mulgan, T., 'Contractualism', in Edward N. Zalta (ed.), *The Stanford Encyclopedia of Philosophy* (Fall 2012 edn), <http://plato.stanford.edu/archives/fall2012/entries/contractualism/>.

Atakan, Z., Morrison, P., Bossong, M. G., Martin-Santos, R., and Crippa, J. A., 'The Effect of Cannabis on Perception of Time: A Critical Review', *Current Pharmaceutical Design*, 18 (2012), 4915–22.

Audi, R., 'Foundationalism, Coherentism and Epistemological Dogmatism', *Philosophical Perspectives*, 2 (1988), 407–42.

Baier, A., 'What do Women Want in a Moral Theory?', *Nous*, 19 (1985), 53–63.

Balcombe, J., *Pleasurable Kingdom: Animals and the Nature of Feeling Good* (London: Palgrave Macmillan, 2007).

Baron-Cohen, S., 'Does Autism Need a Cure?', *The Lancet*, 373/9675 (9 May 2009), 1595–6.

Baron-Cohen, S., *The Science of Evil: On Empathy and the Origins of Cruelty* (New York: Basic Books, 2012).

Barry, B., *The Liberal Theory of Justice* (Oxford: Oxford University Press, 1973).

Batson, C. D., *Altruism in Humans* (New York: Oxford University Press, 2011).

Batson, C. D., Klein, T., Highberger, L., and Shaw, L., 'Immorality from Empathy-Induced Altruism: When Compassion and Justice Conflict', *Journal of Personality and Social Psychology*, 68/6 (June 1995), 1042–54.

Beardman, S., 'Response to Gustafson's Comments', *Philosophical Psychology*, 13 (2000), 121–2.

Beardman, S., 'The Choice between Current and Retrospective Evaluations of Pain', *Philosophical Psychology*, 13 (2000), 97–110.

Beitz, C., *Political Theory and International Relations* (Princeton, NJ: Princeton University Press, 1979).

Beitz, C., 'Social and Cosmopolitan Liberalism', *International Affairs*, 75/3 (1999), 515–29.

Benatar, D., *Better Never to Have Been: The Harm of Coming into Existence* (Oxford: Oxford University Press, 2006).

Bentham, J., 'Le Calcul des plaisirs et des peines', in E. Halévy, *La Formation du radicalisme philosophique, i. La Jeunesse de Bentham* (Paris: F. Alcan, 1901), 398–415.

Bentham, J., 'Essai sur la représentation', in E. Halévy, *La Formation du radicalisme philosophique, i. La Jeunesse de Bentham* (Paris: F. Alcan 1901), 424–39.

Bentham, J., *Introduction to the Principles of Morals and Legislation* (Oxford: Clarendon Press, 1907; first publ. 1789).

Bentham, J., *Rationale of Judicial Evidence, Specially Applied to English Practice*, ed. J. S. Mill (London: Hunt & Clarke, 1827).

Berker, S., 'Particular Reasons', *Ethics*, 118/1 (2007), 109–39.

Berridge, K., and Kringelbach, M., 'Affective Neuroscience of Pleasure: Reward in Humans and Animals', *Psychopharmacology*, 199 (2008), 457–80.

Blackburn, S., *Ruling Passions* (Oxford: Clarendon Press, 1998).

Blair, J., Mitchell, D., and Blair, K., *The Psychopath* (Oxford: Blackwell, 2005).

Bok, S., *Lying* (New York: Pantheon, 1978).

Borg, J. S., and Sinnott-Armstrong, W., 'Do Psychopaths Make Moral Judgments?', in K. Kiehl and W. Sinnott-Armstrong (eds), *Handbook on Psychopathy and Law* (New York: Oxford University Press, 2013), 107–29.

Bostrom, N., 'Astronomical Waste: The Opportunity Cost of Delayed Technological Development', *Utilitas*, 15 (2003), 308–14.

Bostrom, N., and Cirkovic, M. (eds), *Global Catastrophic Risk* (Oxford: Oxford University Press, 2008).

Bowles, S., 'Group Competition, Reproductive Leveling and the Evolution of Human Altruism', *Science*, 314 (2006), 1569–71.

Bradley, F. H., *Mr. Sidgwick's Hedonism: An Examination of the Main Argument of "The Methods of Ethics"* (London: Henry S. King & Co., 1877).

Brandt, R., *A Theory of the Good and the Right* (Oxford: Clarendon Press, 1979).

Brandt, R., *Morality, Utilitarianism, and Rights* (Cambridge: Cambridge University Press, 1992).

Brandt, R., 'Two Concepts of Utility', in H. Miller and W. Williams (eds), *The Limits of Utilitarianism* (Minneapolis, MN: University of Minnesota Press, 1982), 169–85.

Brentano, F., *The Foundation and Construction of Ethics*, tr. E. Schneewind (New York: Humanities Press, 1973).

Brink, D., 'Objectivity and Dialectical Methods in Ethics', *Inquiry*, 42 (1999), 200–10.

Brink, D., 'Self-Love and Altruism', *Social Philosophy and Policy*, 14/1 (Winter 1997), 122–57.

Broad, C. D., *Five Types of Ethical Theory* (London: Kegan Paul, Trench, & Trubner, 1930).

Broome, J., *Climate Matters* (New York: Norton, 2012).

Broome, J., 'More Pain or Less?', *Analysis*, 56 (1996), 116–18.

Buonomano, D., *Brain Bugs: How the Brain's Flaws Shape our Lives* (New York: Norton, 2011).

Camerer, C., Loewenstein, G., and Prelec, D., 'Neuroeconomics: How Neuroscience Can Inform Economics', *Journal of Economic Literature*, 53 (2005), 9–64.

Carruthers, P., *The Animals Issue: Moral Theory in Practice* (Cambridge: Cambridge University Press, 1992).

Cavalieri, P., *The Animal Question: Why Non-Hman Animals Deserve Human Rights*, tr. C. Woollard (New York: Oxford University Press, 2001).

Chappell, R., 'Fittingness: The Sole Normative Primitive', *Philosophical Quarterly*, 62/249 (Oct. 2012), 684–704.

Chappell, R., 'Natural Arbitrariness', a blog posted at <http://www.philosophyetc.net/2010/09/natural-arbitrariness.html>.

Chappell, R., 'Sacrifice and Separate Persons', a blog posted at <http://www.philosophyetc.net/2005/06/sacrifice-and-separate-persons.html>.

Chappell, R., 'Satisficing by Effort: From Scalar to Satisficing Consequentialism', a paper read to the Rocky Mountains Ethics Congress, Aug. 2013.

Chappell, R., 'Value Holism', unpublished.

Chappell, T., 'Bernard Williams', in Edward Zalta (ed.), *The Stanford Encyclopedia of Philosophy* (Winter 2013 edn), <http://plato.stanford.edu/archives/win2013/entries/williams-bernard/>.

Colander, D., 'Edgeworth's Hedonimeter and the Quest to Measure Utility', *Journal of Economic Perspectives*, 21/2 (2007), 215–25.

Confucius, *The Analects of Confucius*: written *c*.500 BCE; available at <http://classics.mit.edu/Confucius/analects.html>.

Crisp, R., 'Equality, Priority and Compassion', *Ethics*, 113 (2003), 745–63.

Crisp, R., 'Hedonism Reconsidered', *Philosophy and Phenomenological Research*, 73 (2006), 619–45.

Crisp, R., *Reasons and the Good* (Oxford: Clarendon Press, 2006).

Crisp, R., 'Sidgwick and the Boundaries of Intuitionism', in P. Stratton-Lake (ed.), *Ethical Intuitionism: Re-evaluations* (New York: Oxford University Press, 2002), 56–75.

Crisp, R., 'Utilitarianism and the Life of Virtue', *Philosophical Quarterly*, 42 (1992), 139–60.

Crisp, R., critical précis for *Ethics* Discussions at PEA Soup: Katarzyna de Lazari-Radek and Peter Singer, 'The Objectivity of Ethics and the Unity of Practical Reason' (3 Dec. 2012), <http://peasoup.typepad.com/peasoup/2012/12/ethics-discussions-at-pea-soup-katarzyna-de-lazari-radek-and-peter-singer-the-objectivity-of-ethics-1.html>.

Csikszentmihalyi, M., *Flow* (New York: Harper, 1991).

Cullity, G., *The Moral Demands of Affluence* (Oxford: Oxford University Press, 2005).

Dancy, J., *Ethics without Principles* (Oxford: Clarendon Press, 2004).

Dancy, J., 'Moral Particularism', in Edward N. Zalta (ed.), *The Stanford Encyclopedia of Philosophy* (Fall 2013 edn), <http://plato.stanford.edu/archives/fall2013/entries/moral-particularism/>.

Dancy, J., *Moral Reasons* (Oxford: Blackwell, 1993).

Daniels, N., *Justice and Justification* (Cambridge: Cambridge University Press, 1996).

Darwin, C., *The Descent of Man* (London: John Murray, 1901).

Dawkins, R., *The Selfish Gene* (Oxford: Oxford University Press, 1976).

Deaton, A., 'The Financial Crisis and the Well-Being of Americans', *Oxford Economic Papers*, 64/1 (2012), 1–26.

De Brigard, F., 'If you Like it, Does it Matter if it's Real?', *Philosophical Psychology*, 23/1 (Feb. 2010), 43–57.

Deigh, J., 'Sidgwick's Epistemology', *Utilitas*, 19 (2007), 435–46.

Deigh, J., 'Some Further Thoughts on Sidgwick's Epistemology', *Utilitas*, 22 (2010), 78–89.

Dombrowski, D., *Babies and Beasts: The Argument from Marginal Cases* (Chicago, IL: University of Illinois Press, 1997).

Donagan, A., 'Sidgwick and Whewellian Intuitionism: Some Enigmas', *Canadian Journal of Philosophy*, 7 (1977), 447–65.

Dunn, E., Aknin, L., and Norton, M., 'Spending Money on Others Promotes Happiness', *Science*, 319 (2008), 1687–8.

Ebertz, R., 'Is Reflective Equilibrium a Coherentist Model?', *Canadian Journal of Philosophy*, 23 (1993), 193–214.

Edgeworth, F. Y., *Mathematical Psychics: An Essay on the Application of Mathematics to the Moral Sciences* (London: Kegan Paul, 1881).

Edgeworth, F. Y., *New and Old Methods of Ethics* (Oxford: Parker & Co., 1877).

Edmonds, D., *Would you Kill the Fat Man? The Trolley Problem and What your Answer Tells us about Right and Wrong* (Princeton, NJ: Princeton University Press, 2014).

Ewing, A. C., *Second Thoughts in Moral Philosophy* (London: Routledge and Kegan Paul, 1959).

Fehr, E., and Fischbacher, U., 'The Nature of Human Altruism', *Nature*, 425 (2003), 785–91.

Feldman, F., *What is This Thing Called Happiness* (Oxford: Oxford University Press, 2012).

Finnis, J., *Natural Law and Natural Rights* (Oxford: Clarendon Press, 1980).

Fisher, I., *Mathematical Investigations in the Theory of Value and Prices* (New Haven, CT: Yale University Press, 1925).

Frye, M., 'A Response to *Lesbian Ethics*', *Hypatia*, 5 (1990), 32–7.

Fukuyama, F., *Trust: The Social Virtues and the Creation of Prosperity* (New York: Free Press, 1995).

Garrett, A., 'Joseph Butler's Moral Philosophy', in Edward N. Zalta (ed.), *The Stanford Encyclopedia of Philosophy* (Winter 2013 edn), <http://plato.stanford.edu/archives/win2013/entries/butler-moral/>.

Gauthier, D., 'Morality and Advantage', *Philosophical Review*, 76/4 (1967), 460–75.

Gauthier, D., *Morals by Agreement* (Oxford: Clarendon Press, 1986).

Gauthier, D., *Practical Reasoning* (Oxford: Clarendon Press, 1963).

Gert, B., *Morality* (Oxford: Oxford University Press, Rev edn, 2005).

Gilligan, C., *In a Different Voice* (Cambridge, Mass.: Harvard University Press, 1982).

Glatzer, W., 'Quality of Life in Advanced Industrialized Countries. The Case of West Germany', in F. Strack, M. Argyle, and N. Schwarz (eds), *Subjective Well-Being* (New York: Pergamon Press, 1991), 261–79.

Grandin, T., *Thinking in Pictures: And Other Reports from my Life with Autism* (New York: Doubleday, 1995).

Greene, J., 'A Psychological Perspective on Nozick's Experience Machine and Parfit's Repugnant Conclusion', a paper presented at the Society for Philosophy and Psychology, Annual Meeting, Cincinnati, Ohio, 2001.

Greene, J., *Moral Tribes: Emotion, Reason, and the Gap between Us and Them* (New York: Penguin, 2013).

Greene, J., 'The Secret Joke of Kant's Soul', in W. Sinnott-Armstrong (ed.), *Moral Psychology*, iii. *The Neuroscience of Morality: Emotion, Disease, and Development* (Cambridge, Mass.: MIT Press, 2007), 35–79.

Greene, J., and Baron, J., 'Intuitions about Declining Marginal Utility', *Journal of Behavioral Decision Making*, 14 (2001), 243–55.

Grisez, G., *The Way of the Lord Jesus*, i. *Christian Moral Principles* (Chicago, IL: Franciscan Herald Press, 1983).

Guidi, M., '"Everybody to Count for One, Nobody for More than One": The Principle of Equal Consideration of Interests from Bentham to Pigou', *Revue d'études Benthamiennes*, 4 (2008), 40–69, available at <http://etudes-benthamiennes.revues.org/182#ftn12>.

Gustafson, D., 'Our Choice between Actual and Remembered Pain and our Flawed Preferences', *Philosophical Psychology*, 13 (2000), 111–19.

Haack, S., *Evidence and Inquiry* (Oxford: Blackwell, 1993).

Haidt, J., 'The Emotional Dog and its Rational Tail: A Social Intuitionist Approach to Moral Judgment', *Psychological Review*, 108 (2001), 814–34.

Haidt, J., *The Righteous Mind* (New York: Pantheon, 2012).

Haidt, J., Björklund, F., and Murphy, S., 'Moral Dumbfounding: When Intuition Finds No Reason', unpublished.

Hamilton, W. D., 'The Genetical Evolution of Social Behaviour. I', *Journal of Theoretical Biology*, 7/1 (1964), 1–16.

Hamilton, W. D., 'The Genetical Evolution of Social Behaviour. II', *Journal of Theoretical Biology*, 7/1 (1964), 17–52.

Harbaugh, W. T., Myer, U., and Burghart, D. R., 'Neural Responses to Taxation and Voluntary Giving Reveal Motives for Charitable Donations', *Science*, 316 (2007), 1622–5.

Hare, C., 'Voices from Another World: Must we Respect the Interests of People Who Do Not, and Will Never, Exist?', *Ethics*, 117/3 (2007), 498–523.

Hare, R. D., *PCL-R: Hare's Psychopathy Checklist*, rev. 2nd edn (North Tonawanda, NY: Multi-Health Systems, 1991).

Hare, R. M., 'Abortion and the Golden Rule', *Philosophy and Public Affairs*, 4/3 (Spring 1975), 201–22.

Hare, R. M., 'Ethical Theory and Utilitarianism', in H. D. Lewis (ed.), *Contemporary British Philosophy 4* (London: Allen & Unwin, 1976), 113–31.

Hare, R. M., *Freedom and Reason* (Oxford: Clarendon Press, 1963).

Hare, R. M., *Moral Thinking* (Oxford: Clarendon Press, 1981).

Hare, R. M., 'Rawls' Theory of Justice—I', *Philosophical Quarterly*, 23/91 (1973), 144–55.

Hare, R. M., 'Rights, Utility, and Universalization: Reply to J. L. Mackie', in R. G. Frey (ed.), *Utility and Rights* (Minneapolis, MN: University of Minnesota Press, 1984), 106–20.

Hare, R. M., *The Language of Morals* (Oxford: Clarendon Press, 1952).

Hare, R. M., 'Universal Prescriptivism', in P. Singer (ed.), *A Companion to Ethics* (Oxford: Blackwell, 1991), 451–63.

Harman, G., 'Moral Relativism Defended', *Philosophical Review*, 84/1 (Jan. 1975), 3–22.

Harrod, R., *The Life of John Maynard Keynes* (London: Macmillan, 1951).

Harrod, R., *Towards a Dynamic Economics* (London: Macmillan, 1948).

Harrod, R., 'Utilitarianism Revised', *Mind*, 45 (1936), 137–56.

Harsanyi, J., 'Morality and the Theory of Rational Behaviour', in A. Sen and B. Williams (eds), *Utilitarianism and Beyond* (Cambridge: Cambridge University Press, 1982), 39–62.

Hastings, R., *The Theory of Good and Evil* (Oxford: Clarendon Press, 1907).

Haybron, D., *The Pursuit of Unhappiness* (Oxford: Oxford University Press, 2008).

Heathwood, C., 'Desire Satisfactionism and Hedonism', *Philosophical Studies*, 128 (2006), 539–63.

Heathwood, C., 'Subjective Desire Satisfactionism', unpublished.

Heathwood, C., 'Subjective Theories of Wellbeing', in B. Eggleston and D. Miller (eds), *The Cambridge Companion to Utilitarianism* (Cambridge: Cambridge University Press, 2014), 199–219.

Heyd, D., 'Supererogation', in Edward N. Zalta (ed.), *The Stanford Encyclopedia of Philosophy* (Winter 2012 edn), <http://plato.stanford.edu/archives/win2012/entries/supererogation/>.

Hooker, B., 'Rule Consequentialism', in Edward N. Zalta (ed.), *The Stanford Encyclopedia of Philosophy* (Spring 2011 edn), <http://plato.stanford.edu/archives/spr2011/entries/consequentialism-rule/>.

Hooker, B., 'Publicity in Morality: A Reply to Katarzyna de Lazari-Radek and Peter Singer', *Ratio*, 23 (2010), 111–17.

Hooker, B., 'Reply to Arneson and McIntyre', *Philosophical Issues*, 15 (2005), 270–1.

Hooker, B., 'Right, Wrong and Rule-Consequentialism', in Henry West (ed.), *Blackwell Guide to Mill's Utilitarianism* (Oxford: Blackwell, 2006), 233–48.

Hooker, B., *Ideal Code, Real World* (Oxford: Oxford University Press, 2002).

Horta, O., 'Debunking the Idyllic View of Natural Processes', *Telos: Revista iberoamericana de estudios utilitaristas*, 17/1 (2010), 73–88.

Hume, D., *A Treatise of Human Nature*, ed. D. F. Norton and M. F. Norton (Oxford: Oxford University Press, 2000).

Hurka, T., *Virtue, Vice, and Value* (Oxford: Oxford University Press, 2001).

Jackson, F., 'Decision-Theoretic Consequentialism and the Nearest and Dearest Objection', *Ethics*, 101 (Apr. 1991), 461–82.

Kagan, S., *Normative Ethics* (Boulder, CO: Westview Press, 1997).

Kahane, G., 'Evolution and Impartiality' *Ethics*, 124 (2014), 327–341.

Kahane, G., 'Evolutionary Debunking Arguments', *Nous*, 45/1 (2011), 103–25.

Kahneman, D., 'Maps of Bounded Rationality: A Perspective on Intuitive Judgment and Choice', Nobel Prize Lecture, Dec. 2002, <http://www.nobelprize.org/nobel_prizes/economics/laureates/2002/ kahnemann-lecture.pdf>.

Kahneman, D., 'Maps of Bounded Rationality: Psychology for Behavioral Economics', *American Economic Review*, 93/5 (Dec. 2003), 1449–75.

Kahneman, D., 'Objective Happiness', in D. Kahneman, E. Diener, and N. Schwarz (eds), *Well-Being: The Foundations of Hedonic Psychology* (New York: Russell Sage Foundation, 1999), 3–25.

Kahneman, D., *Thinking Fast and Slow* (New York: Farrar, Straus & Giroux, 2011).

Kahneman, D., and Deaton, A., 'High Income Improves Evaluation of Life But Not Emotional Well-Being', *Proceedings of the National Academy of Sciences of the United States of America*, 107/38 (2010), 16489–93.

Kahneman, D., and Tversky A., *Choices, Values, and Frames* (Cambridge: Cambridge University Press, 2000).

Kahneman, D., and Tversky, A., 'Experienced Utility and Objective Happiness: A Moment-Based Approach', in D. Kahneman and A. Tversky (eds), *Choices, Values and Frames* (New York: Cambridge University Press and the Russell Sage Foundation, 2000), 673–92.

Kahneman, D., Fredrickson, B. L., Schreiber, C. A., and Redelmeier, D. A., 'When More Pain is Preferred to Less: Adding a Better End', *Psychological Science*, 4/6 (Nov. 1993), 401–5.

Kahneman, D., Knetsch, J., and Thaler, R., 'The Endowment Effect, Loss Aversion and Status Quo Bias', *Journal of Economic Perspectives*, 5/1 (Winter 1991), 193–206.

Kahneman, D., Wakker, P., and Sarin, R., 'Back to Bentham: Explorations of Experienced Utility', *Quarterly Journal of Economics*, 112/2 (May 1997), 375–405.

Kant, I., *Critique of Practical Reason*, tr. T. K. Abbott, http://www.philosophy-index.com/kant/critique-practical-reason.

Kant, I., *Groundwork for the Metaphysics of Morals*, tr. Allen W. Wood (New Haven, CT: Yale University Press, 2002).

Kant, I., 'Duties to Animals and Spirits', repr. in *Lectures on Ethics*, tr. L. Infield (New York: Harper & Row, 1963).

Kennett, J., 'Autism, Empathy and Moral Agency', *Philosophical Quarterly*, 52/208 (2002), 340–57.

Kennett, J., 'Reasons, Emotion and the Psychopath', in Luca Malatesti and John McMillan (eds), *Responsibility and Psychopathy: Interfacing Law, Psychiatry and Philosophy* (International Perspectives in Philosophy and Psychiatry; Oxford: Oxford University Press, 2010), 243–59.

Kennett, J., 'Reasons, Reverence and Value', in W. Sinnot-Armstrong (ed.), *Moral Psychology*, iii. *The Neuroscience of Morality: Emotion, Brain Disorders, and Development* (Cambridge, Mass.: MIT Press, 2008), 259–64.

Kennett, J., and Fine, C., 'Internalism and the Evidence from Psychopathy and Acquired Sociopathy', in W. Sinnot-Armstrong (ed.), *Moral Psychology*, iii. *The Neuroscience of Morality: Emotion, Brain Disorders, and Development* (Cambridge, Mass.: MIT Press, 2008), 173–90.

Keshen, R., *Reasonable Self-Esteem* (Montreal and Kingston: McGill-Queens University Press, 1996).

Keynes, J. N., 'Obituary', *Economic Journal*, 10/40 (Dec. 1900), 585–91.

Kolber, A., 'Mental Statism and the Experience Machine', *Bard Journal of Social Sciences*, 3 (1994), 10–17.

Kolodny, N., 'Which Relationships Justify Partiality: The Case of Parents and Children', *Philosophy and Public Affairs*, 38/1 (2010), 37–75.

Kringelbach, M., and Berridge, K., 'The Neuroscience of Happiness and Pleasure', *Social Research*, 77/2 (2010), 659–78.

Kroger, J. K., Nystrom, L. E., Cohen, J. D., and Johnson-Laird, P. N., 'Distinct Neural Substrates for Deductive and Mathematical Processing', *Brain Research*, 1243 (2008), 86–103.

Krueger, A. B., Kahneman, D., Fischler, C., *et al.*, 'Time Use and Subjective Well-Being in France and the US', *Social Indicators Research*, 93/1 (2009), 7–18.

Lang, G., 'A Dilemma for Objective Act-Utilitarianism', *Politics, Philosophy and Economics*, 3 (2004), 221–39.

Lang, G., 'Should Utilitarianism be Scalar?', *Utilitas*, 25 (2013), 80–95.

Lawlor, R., 'The Rejection of Scalar Consequentialism', *Utilitas*, 21 (2009), 100–16.

Lazari-Radek, K. de, and Singer, P., 'The Objectivity of Ethics and the Unity of Practical Reason', *Ethics*, 123/1 (2012), 9–31.

Lazari-Radek, K. de, and Singer, P., 'Secrecy in Consequentialism: A Defence of Esoteric Morality', *Ratio*, 23 (2010), 34–58.

Lechler, A., 'Do Particularists have a Coherent Notion of a Reason for Action?', *Ethics*, 122 (2012), 763–72.

Leopold, A., 'The Land Ethic', repr. in his *A Sand County Almanac* (Oxford: Oxford University Press, 1949).

Lerner, A., 'Fine-Tuning Evolutionary Debunking Arguments', unpublished.

Lewis, C. I., *An Analysis of Knowledge and Valuation* (La Salle, IL: Open Court Publishing, 1946).

Liersch, M., and McKenzie, C., 'Duration Neglect by Numbers—and its Elimination by Graphs', *Organizational Behavior and Human Decision Processes*, 108 (2009), 303–14.

Lillehammer, H., 'Methods of Ethics and the Descent of Man: Darwin and Sidgwick on Ethics and Evolution', *Biology and Philosophy*, 25 (2010), 361–78.

Loftus, E. F., Schooler, J. W., Boone, S. M., and Kline, D., 'Time Went by So Slowly: Overestimation of Event Duration by Males and Females', *Applied Cognitive Psychology*, 1 (1987), 3–13.

Lyons, D., *Forms and Limits of Utilitarianism* (Oxford: Oxford University Press, 1965).

MacAskill, W., 'Moral Caution and Moral Compromise', unpublished.

McGeer, V., 'Varieties of Moral Agency: Lessons from Autism (and Psychopathy)', in W. Sinnot-Armstrong (ed.), *Moral Psychology*, iii. *The Neuroscience of Morality: Emotion, Brain Disorders, and Development* (Cambridge, Mass.: MIT Press, 2008), 227-257.

McGinn, C., 'Evolution, Animals and the Basis of Morality', *Inquiry*, 22 (1979), 81–99.

MacIntyre, A., *After Virtue*, 2nd edn (Notre Dame, IN: University of Notre Dame Press, 1984), ch. 1.

Mack, M. P., *Jeremy Bentham: An Odyssey of Ideas, 1748–92* (New York: Columbia University Press, 1963).

Mackie, J. L., *Ethics: Inventing Right and Wrong* (Penguin: Harmondsworth, 1977).

McMahan, J., 'Eating Animals the Nice Way', *Daedalus*, 137 (2008), 66–76.

Mahabharata ed. and tr. Ramesh Menon (New Delhi: Rupa & Co, 2009).

Maibom, H., 'Moral Unreason', *Mind and Language*, 20/2 (Apr. 2005), 237–57.

Maibom, H., 'The Mad, the Bad, and the Psychopath', *Neuroethics*, 1 (2008), 167–84.

Marglin, S. A., 'The Social Rate of Discount and the Optimal Rate of Investment', *Quarterly Journal of Economics*, 77 (1963), 95–111.

Matheny, J., 'Reducing the Risk of Human Extinction', *Risk Analysis*, 27 (2007), 1335–44.

Mikhail, J., *Elements of Moral Cognition* (Cambridge: Cambridge University Press, 2011).

Mill, J. S., 'Dr Whewell on Moral Philosophy', in J. S. Mill, *Collected Works* (Toronto: University of Toronto Press; London: Routledge & Kegan Paul, 1985).

Mill, J. S., Letters to Sidgwick, 3 Aug. 1867 and 26 Nov. 1867; in J. B. Schneewind, 'Two Unpublished Letters of of John Stuart Mill to Henry Sidgwick', *The Mill Newsletter*, 9/2 (Summer 1974); available at <http://www.ucl.ac.uk/Bentham-Project/journals/Mill009-2>.

Mill, J. S., 'On Nature', repr. in J. S. Mill, *Three Essays on Religion: Nature, the Utility of Religion, Theism* (London: Watts & Co., 1904).

Miller, R., 'Beneficence, Duty, and Distance', *Philosophy and Public Affairs*, 32 (2004), 357–83.

Moller, D., 'Abortion and Moral Risk', *Philosophy*, 86 (2011), 425–43.

Moore, G., *Ethics* (London: Williams & Norgate, 1912).

Moore, G., *Principia Ethica* (Cambridge: Cambridge University Press, 1903); rev. edn with 'Preface to the second edition' and other papers, ed. T. Baldwin (Cambridge: Cambridge University Press, 1993).

Murphy, L., *Moral Demands in Nonideal Theory* (Oxford: Oxford University Press, 2000).

Nagel, T., *The Possibility of Altruism* (Princeton, NJ: Princeton University Press, 1978).

Nagel, T., *The View from Nowhere* (New York: Oxford University Press, 1986).

Nakano-Okuno, M., *Sidgwick and Contemporary Utilitarianism* (Basingstoke: Palgrave Macmillan, 2011).

Narveson, J., 'Moral Problems of Population', in M. Bayles (ed.), *Ethics and Population* (New York: Shenkman, 1976).

Narveson, J., 'Utility and New Generations', *Mind*, NS 76/301 (Jan. 1967), 62–72.

Narveson, J., 'We Don't Owe Them a Thing! A Tough-Minded But Soft-Hearted View of Aid', *The Monist*, 86 (2003), 419–34.

Neumann, C. S., and Hare, R. D., 'Psychopathic Traits in a Large Community Sample: Links to Violence, Alcohol Use, and Intelligence', *Journal of Consulting and Clinical Psychology*, 76 (2008), 893–9.

Ng, Y-K., 'Utility, Informed Preference, or Happiness: Following Harsanyi's Argument to its Logical Conclusion', *Social Choice and Welfare*, 16 (1999), 197–216.

Nichols, S., 'How Psychopaths Threaten Moral Rationalism, or is it Irrational to be Amoral?', *The Monist*, 85 (2002), 285–304.

Noddings, N., *Caring* (Berkeley-Los Angeles, CA: University of California Press, 1984).

Norcross, A., 'The Scalar Approach to Utilitarianism', in H. West (ed.), *Blackwell Guide to Mill's Utilitarianism* (Oxford: Blackwell, 2006), 217–32.

Nordhaus, W., *A Question of Balance* (New Haven, CT: Yale University Press, 2008).

Nowell-Smith, P. H., *Ethics* (Harmondsworth: Penguin, 1954).

Nozick, R., 'About Mammals and People', *New York Times Book Review* (27 Nov. 1983).

Nozick, R., *Anarchy, State, and Utopia* (New York; Basic Books, 1974).

Okasha, S., 'Biological Altruism', in Edward N. Zalta (ed.), *The Stanford Encyclopedia of Philosophy* (Fall 2013 edn), <http://plato.stanford.edu/archives/fall2013/entries/altruism-biological/>.

Olds, J., and Milner, P., 'Positive Reinforcement Produced by Electrical Stimulation of Septal Area and Other Regions of Rat Brain', *Journal of Comparative and Physiological Psychology*, 47 (1954), 419–27.

Oppenheim, J., 'A Mother's Role, a Daughter's Duty: Lady Blanche Balfour, Eleanor Sidgwick, and Feminist Perspectives', *Journal of British Studies*, 34 (Apr. 1985), 196–232.

Ord, T., 'Beyond Action: Applying Consequentialism to Decision-Making and Motivation' (Ph.D. thesis, University of Oxford, 2009).

Parfit, D., 'Equality and Priority', *Ratio*, 10 (1997), 202–23.

Parfit, D., *Equality or Priority (The Lindley Lecture, 1991)* (Lawrence, KS: University of Kansas, 1995).

Parfit, D., 'How We Can Avoid the Repugnant Conclusion', Mala Kamm Memorial Lecture in Value Theory, New York University, 2012 (unpublished).

Parfit, D., 'Innumerate Ethics', *Philosophy and Public Affairs*, 7 (1978), 285–301.

Parfit, D., 'On Doing the Best for our Children', in Michael D. Bayles (ed.), *Ethics and Population* (Cambridge, Mass.: Schenkman Pub. Co., 1976), 100–15.

Parfit, D., *On What Matters* (Oxford: Oxford University Press, 2011).

Parfit, D., *Reasons and Persons* (Oxford: Clarendon Press, 1984).

Parfit, D., 'Rights, Interests, and Possible People', in S. Gorovitz, A. L. Jameton, R. Macklin, J. M. Beverly Page St. Clair, and S. Sherwin (eds), *Moral Problems in Medicine* (Englewood Cliffs, NJ: Prentice-Hall, 1976), 369–75.

Petrinovich, L., *Darwinian Dominion: Animal Welfare and Human Interests* (Cambridge, Mass.: MIT Press, 1999).

Pettit, P., 'Satisficing Consequentialism', *Proceedings of the Aristotelian Society*, supplementary volumes, 58 (1984), 165–76.

Pettit, P., and Smith, M., 'Global Consequentialism', in B. Hooker, E. Mason, and D. E. Miller (eds), *Morality, Rules and Consequences: A Critical Reader* (Edinburgh: Edinburgh University Press, 2000), 121–33.

Phillips, D., *Sidgwickian Ethics* (Oxford: Oxford University Press, 2011).

Pickard-Cambridge, W. A., 'Two Problems about Duty (II)', *Mind*, 141 (1932), 145–72.

Pigou, A. C., *The Economics of Welfare*, 4th edn (London: Macmillan, 1932).

Pinker, S., *The Better Angels of our Nature* (New York: Viking, 2011).

Pogge, T., *Realizing Rawls* (Ithaca, NY: Cornell University Press NY, 1990).

Pogge, T., *World Hunger and Human Rights* (Cambridge: Polity Press, 2nd edn 2008).

Pollan, M., 'An Animal's Place', *New York Times Sunday Magazine* (10 Nov. 2002).

Pollan, M., *The Omnivore's Dilemma* (London: Bloomsbury, 2007).

Post, S. (ed.), *Altruism and Health* (New York: Oxford University Press, 2007).

Prior, A. N., *Logic and the Basis of Ethics* (Oxford: Clarendon Press, 1949).

Pritchett, L., 'Divergence, Big-Time', *Journal of Economic Perspectives*, 11/3 (1997), 3–17.

Pummer, T., 'The Priority Monster', unpublished, available at <https://sites.google.com/site/tgpummer>.

Pummer, T., 'The Problem of Joyless Life', unpublished.

Rachels, S., and Alter T., 'Nothing Matters in Survival', *Journal of Ethics*, 9 (2005), 311–30.

Railton, P., 'Alienation, Consequentialism, and the Demands of Morality', *Philosophy and Public Affairs*, 13 (1984), 134–71.

Railton, P., *Facts and Values* (Cambridge: Cambridge University Press, 2003).

Railton, P., 'Reply to John Skorupski', *Utilitas*, 20 (2008), 230–42.

Ramsey, F. P., 'A Mathematical Theory of Saving', *Economics Journal*, 38 (1928), 543–59.

Rashdall, H., 'Professor Sidgwick's Utilitarianism', *Mind*, 10 (1885), 200–26.

Rashdall, H., *The Theory of Good and Evil* (Oxford: Clarendon Press, 1907).

Rawls, J., *A Theory of Justice* (Cambridge, Mass.: Belknap Press of Harvard University Press, rev edn 1999).

Rawls, J., *Justice as Fairness: A Restatement* (Cambridge, Mass.: Belknap Press of Harvard University Press, 2001).

Rawls, J., 'Justice as Fairness: Political, Not Metaphysical', *Philosophy and Public Affairs*, 14/3 (Summer 1985), 223–51.

Rawls, J., 'Kantian Constructivism in Moral Theory', *Journal of Philosophy* 77 (Sept. 1980), 515–72.

Rawls, J., 'The Independence of Moral Theory', *Proceedings and Addresses of the American Philosophical Association*, 48 (1974–5), 5–22.

Rawls, J., *The Law of Peoples* (Cambridge, Mass.: Harvard University Press, 2001).

Redelmeier, D. A., Katz, J., and Kahneman, D., 'Memories of Colonoscopy: A Randomized Trial', *Pain*, 104 (2003), 187–94.

Redelmeier, D. A., and Kahneman, D., 'Patients' Memories of Painful Medical Treatments: Real-Time and Retrospective Evaluations of Two Minimally Invasive Procedures', *Pain*, 66 (July 1996), 3–8.

Regan, T., and Singer, P. (eds), *Animal Rights and Human Obligations* (Englewood Cliffs, NJ: Prentice-Hall, 1976).

Rice, M. E., and Harris, G. T., 'Psychopathy and Violent Recidivism', in K. Kiehl and W. Sinnott-Armstrong (eds), *Oxford Handbook of Psychopathy and Law* (New York: Oxford University Press, 2013).

Ridley, M., *The Origins of Virtue* (London: Viking, 1996).

Roberts, M. A., 'A New Way of Doing the Best that we Can: Person-Based Consequentialism and the Equality Problem', *Ethics*, 112/2 (Jan. 2002), 315–50.

Ross, W. D., *Foundations of Ethics* (Oxford: Clarendon Press, 1939).

Ross, W. D., *The Right and the Good*, ed. P. Stratton-Lake (Oxford: Clarendon Press, 2002).

Salt, H., 'The Logic of the Larder', in H. Salt, *The Humanities of Diet* (Manchester: Vegetarian Society, 1914).

Samyutta Nikaya, tr. Bhikkhu Bodhi (Somerville, Mass.: Wisdom Publications, 2003).

Sarkissian, H., Park, J., Tien, D., Wright, J. C., and Knobe, J., 'Folk Moral Relativism', *Mind and Language*, 26 (2011), 482–505.

Scanlon, T. M., *Being Realistic about Reasons* (The Locke Lectures at the University of Oxford): <http://www.philosophy.ox.ac.uk/lectures/john_locke_lectures/past_lectures>.

Scanlon, T. M., 'Rawls on Justification', in S. Freeman (ed.), *The Cambridge Companion to Rawls* (Cambridge: Cambridge University Press, 2003), 139–67.

Scanlon, T. M., *What we Owe to Each Other* (Cambridge, Mass.: Harvard University Press, 1998).

Scheffler, S., *Death and the Afterlife* (New York: Oxford University Press, 2013).

Scheffler, S., *The Rejection of Consequentialism* (Oxford: Clarendon Press, 1994).

Schmidtz, D., 'Islands in a Sea of Obligation: Limits of the Duty to Rescue', *Law and Philosophy*, 19 (2000), 683–705.

Schneewind, J. B., *Sidgwick's Ethics and Victorian Moral Philosophy* (Oxford: Clarendon, 1977).

Schreiber, C. A., and Kahneman, D., 'Determinants of the Remembered Utility of Aversive Sounds', *Journal of Experimental Psychology, General*, 129/1 (Mar. 2000), 27–42.

Schultz, B., 'Mill and Sidgwick, Imperialism and Racism', *Utilitas*, 19 (Mar. 2007), 104–30.

Schultz, B., *Henry Sidgwick: Eye of the Universe* (Cambridge: Cambridge University Press, 2004).

Schweitzer, A., *Civilization and Ethics* (London: Adam & Charles Black, 1946).

Scruton, R., 'The Conscientious Carnivore', in S. Sapontzis (ed.), *Food for Thought: The Debate over Eating Meat* (Amherst, NY: Prometheus, 2004), 81–91.

Shaver, R., 'Sidgwick on Moral Motivation', *Philosophers' Imprint*, 6/1 (Feb. 2006), 1–14.

Shaver, R., *Rational Egoism* (Cambridge: Cambridge University Press, 1998).

Shaver, R., 'Sidgwick's Axioms and Consequentialism', *Philosophical Review*, forthcoming.

Sidgwick, A., and Sidgwick, E., *Henry Sidgwick. A Memoir* (London and New York: Macmillan, 1906).

Sidgwick, H., 'Professor Calderwood on Intuitionism in Morals', *Mind*, 1 (1876), 563–6, repr. in H. Sidgwick, *Essays on Ethics and Method*, ed. M. G. Singer (Oxford: Oxford University Press, 2000).

Sidgwick, H., 'Review of Cobbe's Darwinism in Morals', *The Academy*, 3/50 (15 June 1872), 230–1.

Sidgwick, H., 'The Theory of Evolution in its Application to Practice', *Mind*, 1 (1876), 52–67, reprinted in H. Sidgwick, *Essays on Ethics and Method*, ed. M. G. Singer (Oxford: Oxford University Press, 2000).

Sidgwick, H., 'The Establishment of Ethical First Principles', *Mind*, 4 (1879), 106–11, repr. in H. Sidgwick, *Essays on Ethics and Method*, ed. M. G. Singer (Oxford: Oxford University Press, 2000).

Sidgwick, H., Letter to Mill, 28 July 1867, in *The Complete Works and Select Correspondence of Henry Sidgwick*, ed. Bart Schultz (Charlottesville, VA: InteLex, 1999).

Sidgwick, H., *The Methods of Ethics*, 7th edn (London: Macmillan, 1907).

Silverstein, H., 'More Pain or Less? Comments on Broome', *Analysis*, 58 (1998), 149.

Simon, H., 'A Behavioral Model of Rational Choice', *Quarterly Journal of Economics*, 69 (1955), 99–118.

Singer, M. G., 'The Many Methods of Sidgwick's Ethics', *The Monist*, 58/3 (July 1974), 420–48.

Singer, P. (ed.), *Does Anything Really Matter? Parfit on Objectivity in Ethics* (Oxford: Oxford University Press, forthcoming).

Singer, P., 'Ethics and Intuitions', *Journal of Ethics*, 9/3–4 (2005), 331–52.

Singer, P., 'Famine, Affluence and Morality', *Philosophy and Public Affairs*, 1 (1972), 229–43.

Singer, P., *Practical Ethics*, 1st edn (Cambridge: Cambridge University Press, 1979); 2nd edn (1993); 3rd edn (2011).

Singer, P., 'Reasoning towards Utilitarianism', in D. Seanor and N. Fotion (eds), *Hare and Critics: Essays on Moral Thinking* (Oxford: Clarendon Press, 1988), 147–60.

Singer, P., 'Sidgwick and Reflective Equilibrium', *The Monist*, 58/3 (1974), 490–517.

Singer, P., *The Expanding Circle* (Princeton, NJ: Princeton University Press, 2011; 1st publ. 1981).

Singer, P., *The Life you Can Save* (New York: Random House, 2009).

Singer, P., and Mason, J., *The Ethics of What we Eat* (New York: Rodale, 2007).

Sinhababu, N., 'The Epistemic Argument for Hedonism', unpublished.

Skelton, A., 'Henry Sidgwick's Moral Epistemology', *Journal of the History of Philosophy*, 48/4 (Oct. 2010), 491–519.

Skelton, A., 'On Sidgwick's Demise: A Reply to Professor Deigh', *Utilitas*, 22 (2010), 70–7.

Skelton, A., 'Sidgwick's Philosophical Intuitions', *Etica e Politica/Ethics and Politics*, 10 (2008), 185–209.

Skelton, A., 'William David Ross', in Edward N. Zalta (ed.), *The Stanford Encyclopedia of Philosophy* (Summer 2012 edn), <http://plato.stanford.edu/archives/sum2012/entries/william-david-ross/>.

Skorupski, J., 'Three Methods and a Dualism', in R. Harrison (ed.), *Henry Sidgwick* (New York: Oxford University Press, 2001), 61–81.

Slote, M., *Beyond Optimizing* (Cambridge, Mass.: Harvard University Press, 1989).

Slote, M., *Common-Sense Morality and Consequentialism* (London: Routledge & Kegan Paul, 1985).

Slote, M., *Goods and Virtues* (Oxford: Oxford University Press, 1983).

Slote, M., 'Satisficing Consequentialism', *Proceedings of the Aristotelian Society*, supplementary volumes, 58 (1984), 139–63.

Smart, J., and Williams, B., *Utilitarianism: For and Against* (Cambridge: Cambridge University Press, 1973).

Smith, B., 'Affect, Rationality, and the Experience Machine', *Ethical Perspectives*, 19/2 (2012), 268–76.

Smith, B., 'Can We Test the Experience Machine?', *Ethical Perspectives*, 18/1 (2011), 29–51.

Smith, M., 'Desires, Values, Reasons, and the Dualism of Practical Reason', in J. Suikkanen and J. Cottingham (eds), *Essays on Derek Parfit's On What Matters* (Oxford: Wiley-Blackwell, 2009), 116–43.

Smith, M., *The Moral Problem* (Malden, Mass.: Blackwell, 1994).

Sober, E., and Wilson, D. S., *Unto Others* (Cambridge, Mass.: Harvard University Press, 1998).

Sprigge, T., 'Professor Narveson's Utilitarianism', *Inquiry*, 11 (1968), 332–46.

Stern, N., *Stern Review on the Economics of Climate Change* (London: UK Government Economic Service, 2006), <http://www.webcitation.org/5nCeyEYJr>.

Stephen, L., *Social Rights and Duties* (London: Swan Sonneschein & Co., 1896).

Stocker, M., *Plural and Conflicting Values* (Oxford: Clarendon Press, 1990).

Stocker, M., 'The Schizophrenia of Modern Ethical Theories', *Journal of Philosophy*, 73 (1976), 453–66.

Street, S., 'A Darwinian Dilemma for Realist Theories of Value', *Philosophical Studies*, 127/1 (Jan. 2006), 109–66.

Streumer, B., 'Can Consequentialism Cover Everything?', *Utilitas*, 15 (2003), 237–47.

Sumner, L. W., *Welfare, Happiness and Ethics* (Oxford: Oxford University Press, 1996).

Sverdlik, S., 'Sidgwick's Methodology', *Journal of the History of Philosophy*, 23/4 (1985), 537–53.

Taurek, J., 'Should the Numbers Count?', *Philosophy and Public Affairs*, 6 (1977), 293–316.

Temkin, L. 'Equality, Priority, or What?', *Economics and Philosophy*, 19 (2003), 61–87.

Temkin, L., 'Equality, Priority, and the Levelling Down Objection', in M. Clayton and A. Williams (eds), *The Ideal of Equality* (London: Macmillan, 2000), 121–61.

Temkin, L., 'Intransitivity and the Mere Addition Paradox', *Philosophy and Public Affairs*, 16 (1987), 138–87.

Temkin, L., *Rethinking the Good* (Oxford: Oxford University Press, 2012).

Terence, I., *The Development of Ethics: From Kant to Rawls*, iii (Oxford: Oxford University Press, 2009).

Terry, H., *Golden and Silver Rules of Humanity*, 5th edn (West Conshohoken, PA: Infinity Publishing, 2011).

Tersman, F., 'The Reliability of Moral Intuitions: A Challenge from Neuroscience', *Australasian Journal of Philosophy*, 86/3 (2008), 389–405.

Thaler, R., 'Some Empirical Evidence on Dynamic Inconsistency', *Economic Letters*, 8 (1981), 201–7.

Trivers, R. L., 'The Evolution of Reciprocal Altruism', *Quarterly Review of Biology*, 46/1 (Mar. 1971), 35–57.

Tversky, A., and Kahneman, D., 'The Framing of Decisions and the Psychology of Choice', *Science*, 211 (Jan. 1981), 453–8.

Twain, M., 'The Lowest Animal', in J. Smith (ed.), *Mark Twain on Man and Beast*, (Westport, CT: Lawrence Hill, 1972), 152–61.

Urmson, J. O., 'Saints and Heroes', in A. Melden (ed.), *Essays in Moral Philosophy* (Seattle, WA: University of Washington Press, 1958), 198–216.

Urmson, J. O., 'The Interpretation of the Moral Philosophy of J. S. Mill', *Philosophical Quarterly*, 10 (1953), 33–9.

van den Berghe, P. L., 'Bridging the Paradigms: Biology and the Social Sciences', in M. S. Gregory, A. Silvers, and D. Sutch (eds), *Sociobiology and Human Nature* (San Francisco, CA: Jossey-Bass, 1978), 33–52.

Varner, G., *Personhood, Ethics, and Animal Cognition: Situating Animals in Hare's Two Level Utilitarianism* (New York: Oxford University Press, 2012).

Velleman, D., 'Well-Being and Time', *Pacific Philosophical Quarterly*, 72 (1991), 42–77.

Visak, T., *Killing Happy Animals: Explorations in Utilitarian Ethics* (London: Palgrave Macmillan, 2013).

Von Gizycki, G., 'Review of *The Methods of Ethics*', *Ethics*, 1 (1890), 120–1.

von Mises, L., *Human Action* (Auburn, AL: Ludwig von Mises Institute, 1998).

Voorhoeve, A., 'Discussion of "A Defense of Hedonism" by Katarzyna de Lazari-Radek and Peter Singer' (Fellows' Seminar, University Center for Human Values, Princeton University, Dec. 2013), unpublished.

Walker, M., 'Feminism, Ethics, and the Question of Theory', *Hypatia*, 7 (1992), 23–38.

Weijers, D., 'Intuitive Biases in Judgments about Thought Experiments: The Experience Machine Revisited', *Philosophical Writings*, 41 (2013), 17–31.

Weijers, D., 'Nozick's Experience Machine is Dead, Long Live the Experience Machine!', *Philosophical Psychology* (print version forthcoming, published online 2013, DOI: 10.1080/09515089.2012.757889).

Weijers, D., 'We Can Test the Experience Machine', *Ethical Perspectives*, 19/2 (2012), 261–8.

Wenar, L., 'Clean Trade in Natural Resources', *Ethics and International Affairs*, 25 (2011), 27–39.

Wheatley, T., and Haidt, J., 'Hypnotic Disgust Makes Moral Judgments More Severe', *Psychological Science*, 16 (2005) 780–4.

White, N., *Individual and Conflict in Greek Ethics* (Oxford: Oxford University Press, 2002).

Williams, B., 'A Critique of Utilitarianism', in J. J. C. Smart and B. Williams, *Utilitarianism For and Against* (Cambridge: Cambridge University Press, 1973), 75–155.

Williams, B., *Ethics and the Limits of Philosophy* (Cambridge, Mass.: Harvard University Press, 1986).

Williams, B., 'Internal and External Reasons', repr. in *Moral Luck* (Cambridge: Cambridge University Press, 1981), 101–13.

Williams, B., *Moral Luck* (Cambridge: Cambridge University Press, 1981).

Williams, B., 'Persons, Character and Morality', in A. Rorty (ed.), *The Identities of Persons*, (Berkeley-Los Angeles, CA: University of California Press, 1976), 197–216.

Williams, B., 'The Point of View of the Universe: Sidgwick and the Ambitions of Ethics', *Cambridge Review* (May 1982), 183–91.

Wilson, J. Q., *The Moral Sense* (New York: Free Press, 1993).

Wolf, S., 'Moral Saints', *Journal of Philosophy*, 79 (1982), 419–39.

Woodard, C., 'Classifying Theories of Welfare', *Philosophical Studies*, 165 (2013), 787–803.

Wright, R., *The Moral Animal* (New York: Pantheon, 1994).

Zenghelis, D., 'The Question of Global Warming: An Exchange', *New York Review of Books* (25 Sept. 2008).

Index

(Note: Footnotes are indexed only if they include a substantial discussion of the indexed item.)